Roundball at PHS

Coach "B"

PublishAmerica
Baltimore

First printing

ISBN: 1-4241-8006-6
PUBLISHED BY PUBLISHAMERICA, LLLP
www.publishamerica.com
Baltimore

Printed in the United States of America

John

Thank you for

being such a

loyal fan to

Pella High

Mike Baldwin

Pella High B-Ball 2006/2007

The Players:

Kyle Kramer
Brandon Esterbrook
Kaleb Korver
Tyler Linn
Justin Pothoven
Jesse Wineland
Brock Pope
Klarc Korver
Zachary Morgan
Andrew Ter Louw
Colin Boswell
Clayton Boeyink
Brandon Caldwell
Nathan Klyn
Craig Newendorp
Kirk Korver
Tyler Terlouw
Student Coaches:
Will Lubberden
Andrew Barber
High School Coaches:
Mark Core
Mike Ballenger

Chapter 1—The Beginning

November 13, 2006 Practice #1
Healthy Players, Slow Feet, Coaches, NC Drill, Aggressiveness, and ESPN Moments

Three starters are back from last year, and a total five seniors that have played a lot of ball return for this year's squad. If everybody stays healthy we should have a chance to have a good season.

Unfortunately, our all-state player, Kaleb Korver, and his brother Kirk, who also has a chance to play this year as a sophomore, are both absent from practice, as they couldn't catch a flight out of Philadelphia. They have been visiting their brother Kyle, who is a player for the 76ers, an unusual occurrence at PHS basketball, to say the least.

When I took the court myself it was about 3:18. Kids were going through their own warm-up procedures and using all six baskets. While I had eagerly awaited the start of this season there is also a part of me that knows how long this season is and says, *Hold on pal, this really gets to be a grind.* Besides the kids that are warming up I see Andrew Barber. Andrew is our manager/ statistician for this year's team. He held the position last year as well. Does a returning stat man increase your chances for success?

We do lay-ups to start practice. As in every other year the players are so worried about their footwork going to the basket that they forget to go game speed. I have always been a believer in getting the kids to go as hard as they can, and let the footwork catch up with them. When kids do too much thinking, as their brain works harder (as in their footwork situation) their feet literally get slower. Free the mind, and free the player.

Two other coaches beside me and Coach Core (the head coach) that are present are the sophomore coach, Mike Van Wyk, and Adam Miller, a young man that helped us last year and will help the sophomore team this year. He will also fill a kind of consultant role for us this year as well. Adam would have made a good head coach some day. He really loves the game and has good instincts for coaching. I say, "would have" rather than "will" because I'm afraid we will lose him to the administrative side of education some day. I can't blame him; you can work for about $1.00 an hour in coaching or support your family with real money as an administrator. I'm prejudiced, I know, because I coach, but I think coaches are way underpaid. Coaches and leaders of extracurricular activities set the tone for school systems. They are the extra voices that support the proper attitude and effort things that go on in good school systems.

Our second drill is the NC drill, named after North Carolina the team that I stole the drill from. It is a drill that, if done right, requires the coaches to suck on their whistles. Coaches want to coach, and there is a great temptation to blow the whistle and correct every single mistake. But when you do that it destroys the atmosphere of the practice. It grinds down the attention of the kids. Our point of emphasis for this practice was to make every mistake that we make an aggressive one. I can't tell you how important that is! An aggressive mistake is one that a kid's psyche can live with. However a coach cannot say, "Be aggressive with your mistakes," and then chew them out for doing just that. There is no quicker way than that to ruin that aggression. In my opinion the teams that are most aggressive are the teams that are going to win games. This is especially true if you have equal or more talent, and oftentimes true even if you don't have the talent level that the other team has. There are very few things as important as aggression in this or in any other sport.

Anyway, the NC drill is a fast-break, full-court drill that is a make-it-take-it drill (if you make the basket you get the ball back) that oftentimes looks out of control. But again, besides the aggression it teaches it also teaches the players to play and make decisions at a high rate of speed. I like to think of it as an offensive rebounding drill as well. I would rather have the kids shoot it from half-court and rebound it than throw it away trying to run the perfect play. For the first night I thought it went really well.

We did a lot of up and down the court in this first practice; I love that. People like to watch it, and kids like to play it. But it's not as easy as just running. You must have kids that want to work. They have to work on both ends of the court. One of the things we talk about a lot we call "ESPN moments," named after the sports show of the same name. These moments are the ones that make everyone go, "Wow!" the dunk, the amazing pass, the dunk, the unbelievable three-pointer, and oh, yeah, did I mention the dunk? Kids see this stuff, fans (parents) see this stuff, and they think that this is what wins games. It ain't! Let me give you an example that comes from the NC drill. It's called running the floor. The fast-break doesn't work unless the guys without the ball get in front of the guy with the ball; now you will never see that on ESPN, commentators, but if you don't do that NON—ESPN thing—you don't win games. People tend to be *me first,* but the most successful teams are *team first.* Really, the thing that comes out of that is a lot of individual recognition. The most selfish (in a good way) thing a kid can do for himself is to be unselfish!

So about half way through practice Clayton Boeyink starts to complain about his injured groin. Poor old Clayton has fought this injury since he was a freshman at Pella High. He is such a good athlete, the kind of kid that can really get out and run with great quickness, but this type of injury can really ruin that whole athletic type of ability. Then with about one-third of the practice left B-Mo, our nickname for Brandon Caldwell, who is one of our returning starters, comes over complaining about his injured shoulder. He says that he can't feel his hand; I'm not real sharp, but that is always a bad sign. So he sits out with an ice bag on his shoulder. We are now down to two seniors that have played a lot of ball. I hope this is not an omen; again, I said at the beginning, if we don't have injuries we should be pretty good.

Tuesday, November 14 Practice #2
Coach and I, Injuries, Chiropractors, Three-on-Two, Balls in the Lane, Score, One-on-one, Short Practices and Kaleb O Rebounding

I got to school early today to listen to my Dictaphone about yesterday's practice. I found carrying one of those around is a lot easier and quicker than writing myself notes. Mark came in to talk about practice. I've had more than one staff member ask about how we can talk so much about that sport. We talk a lot of round ball! We both love it, and we talk a lot about how we can get better. I gave Mark my thoughts. My two main ones were to do a better job of playing to win when we do drills so the kids learn to compete. Then I encouraged him to have a very small consequence such as a jog to the other end of the floor, just to remind them that they lost. I want kids who, above all else (I mean basketball-wise above all else), want to win. And my second thought was a very small change in the way we run one of the drills; it's the small things that make the difference. We also discussed our injury situation, something bothering both of us.

Our opening practices are open to any player in the system who wants to play varsity basketball. That way the freshman and sophomores can compete with the upper-class men to see if they might be varsity-level players; it also gives the coaches a chance to look at all players for their own information. The player must attend his own grade-level practice as well. Currently the sophomores are practicing with us, so that is not a problem. The gym is full, but the sophomore coaches also hear what the varsity coaches are doing and pick up drills as well as theory during this time. The freshmen, however, practice at 6:00 A.M. Little Matt Dowey, a freshman, has shown up to both of our practices. I call him little because I think he might be the smallest player in our program right now. And I bring him up specifically because of the fact he is attending two practices a day and also (in spite of his size) must seriously be looking at himself as a varsity-level player.

They are gone, at least for a while. B-Mo is out for sure for about two weeks. His shoulder is called a grade-two separation. He re-injured it in practice yesterday, and Coach Core and I talked it over and decided it is best to hold him out. We would rather be good at the end of the season than at the beginning. Obviously we want to win every game that we go into, and oftentimes it is so hard to think long term, but I really think this is a strength of Mark Core that he really does think long term. Clayton's situation is dicey. The groin is such a weird animal. You just never know what is going to happen. Clayton has fought this injury for so long, but now he seems to be changing his approach to the healing of it. We talked the other day, and I suggested to him that if he continues to treat this injury the same way he has always treated it he would probably get the same results. Thus, to get different results, try something new. My son, Luke, is going to be a chiropractor, and I'm a believer in that type of healing. My best friend and his brother, whom I have known for years, are also chiropractors—I suggested that he see Dr. Russ. Russ had helped him get ready for the season. Clayton thought he was better, but obviously he regressed again. His next step is an MRI. We are waiting on that.

Clayton is such an X factor for us. As I've mentioned, he can run and is ultra quick. As a coach, having Clayton available at full speed would really allow us to do some things that we won't be able to do without him.

We did power lay-ups today. That is probably my favorite lay-up drill. In essence it amounts to shooting a lay-up with a defender coming at you full speed, trying to block your shot. When coaches talk about going game speed that is what they are talking about; going as fast as you would if there were an offensive or defensive player playing against you. This drill incorporates that situation.

We ran the three-on-two, full-court drills today. I love the drill; I hate it when we don't attack it correctly. Many coaches instruct their players to pull up at the free-throw line; I disagree. I think if you talked to any coach in the country that they would expect a lay-up in a two-on-one situation. But for some reason many are happy with a 15-foot jumper from the free-throw line when it is three on two. That makes no sense to me. Okay, so you're coming down, three on two, and IF you attack the front defender, what's he going to do? He's going to defend, right? If he doesn't, now you are three on one. Is that a bad thing? Let's assume he defends the dribbler at the free-throw line so the ball handler has to give up the ball to the wing. Now we've got two wings attacking the back defender; in other words we have a two-on-one if the dribbler attacks the front defender rather than pulling up at the free-throw line. I WANT A lay-up in the three-on-two drill just like I do in the two-on-one drill. Enough with this rant, but this is just one of many things that the talking heads on TV drive me crazy with their expert commentary.

One of my points of emphasis with the kids this year is to keep the ball out of the lane. I thought we did a really poor job of that last year. There are just too many bad things that can happen to our defense when the ball gets in there. Some of the bad things are: a lay-up, a foul, a defensive rotation on our part, takes away our weak-side defenders, and a basket and foul is one of the worst combinations for us defensively. That last thing: the hoop and the foul get them three points. It makes them more assertive (us less), and it puts another foul on not only our team but also our individual team player. The rotation thing and the weak-side defensive thing basically mean that each defender tries to cover for his teammate. When the ball goes into the middle of the lane—there is no weak or help side; we don't know how to help or where to come from. I love it offensively for us; I hate it defensively against us.

It's really ironic, isn't it, when we have to tell the kids to catch ready to shoot. What we mean with this basically is that when you catch you should always look at the basket and be ready to shoot it. Don't get me started on these

11

little-kids' coaches that over-coach those poor little people. But let me ask you this; when you were a kid and you got a ball with a hoop out in the driveway did anybody have to tell you to look at the basket? I'm guessing not! Why do we now? Once again I have a theory. Kids have been told to run the play so often by coaches that wanted to hear themselves talk that the kids have forgotten the most important elements: one being, "Shoot the ball!" When I was coaching my son's little guys' group I told them I'd rather have them shoot and miss so we can go rebound it than throw it away or run a play just so I can say to myself, *What a beautiful play.* Here is the offense—SCORE! Here is the defense—DON'T LET THEM SCORE. It goes back to that aggressive attitude; if you are filling up the player's minds, you are slowing down their feet. Keep it simple and attack.

Here is another thing about looking to score—it makes passing and dribbling easier. If you are looking to pass the defense will play you for a pass. If you are looking to shoot the defense will play you for a shot and open up your ability to pass, because they are no longer playing you to pass. The same is also true with dribbling. If you want to be a better dribbler or passer—look at the basket more!

We ran a one -on-one, full-court drill today. It's another one of my favorite drills. It's also one of the few drills that I like that the players don't; usually we are pretty close in this regard. I like it probably for some of the same reasons the kids don't. My main reason is that it makes them tougher mentally. Yes, it adds to ball handling and defensive shuffle and all of that stuff, but you've got to be tough mentally to guard a guy full-court on the dribble when he is trying to blow by you, and you are getting no help, and that, my friend, is why I like it. Sometimes you aren't going to have the talent other people have; when you don't, you'd better be tougher; if you aren't you've got no chance.

Our legs are tired today. The kids put out lots of energy. We trade off long practices for tremendous effort. While many programs may open the season with two-or-more-hour practices, we are done by approximately 5:00 or after about an hour and a half. It's my opinion that much longer than that and you are literally teaching kids not to pay attention. (The average attention span is about twenty minutes) In exchange, and probably because of this fact, the kids know that they are done in an hour and a half, and they work extremely hard. If kids know when they are done they don't save up that little something in case the coach comes up with one of those crazy drills that we can sometimes come up with.

Kaleb Korver, our all-state player, has so much more than he has given. He is a great kid; I don't mean this is intentional; I just mean that he could be even better than he is, and he is pretty darn good right now. I'm trying to get him to rebound more on the offensive end. Offensive rebounding is something that is extremely valuable to a team, but again most of the time goes unnoticed by the media. I reminded Kaleb four times (in a row) today to rebound; he forgot each time. Does that mean he doesn't want to? No, it means he hasn't gotten in the habit yet. That is a coach's job, to get players in appropriate habits. But hey, it's just like you and me: our own habits are hard enough to break. They've got the same problem; only they are trying to break them in the middle of high-speed and pressure-filled situations.

We continue to evaluate players. That is one of our many jobs this week; we are trying to figure out who our varsity-level players are. Today I was pleased with many kids, but in particular I liked Brandon Esterbrook and C.J. Newendorp's play.

Wednesday, November 15, Practice #3
Three-Man Passing, Kaleb's O Rebounding, Shell Drill Fakes, Pressing, Dribbling, Zach and Brock

This is three for three for Matt Dowie, our little freshman. He is up and going in basketball by six in the morning and now again at 3:30.

B-Mo is able to workout a little bit with non-contact drills. We don't have many of those, so he isn't out here very much. I've glimpsed him riding the stationary bike, trying to keep shape, but it is not the same as running the court. Clayton is not working out at all. Both come to practice to watch and try to stay up on what we are doing. When you are a senior this is pretty tough.

We are running a three-man passing drill for the first time today. It is a drill that puts one man in the middle without a ball and two players on the wings, each with a ball. The drill has the players at the wings alternately passing the ball to the middleman and then he returns that ball back to that same wing prior to receiving the next pass. Seems simple enough, right? It always amazes me to see how much traveling goes on during this drill. In a ball game, a high school player trying to advance the ball up court would know to dribble until his teammate opens up; in this drill for some reason we can't figure out when to dribble and when to pass. Question, why would you practice something that

13

you would never do in a game? Obviously you wouldn't. We, as coaches, need to help our players understand this.

I am so proud of Kaleb. I mentioned yesterday that he just couldn't get himself going to the offensive boards. Today every time I watched him he was going! After practice I brought this up to him in front of the rest of the team. We catch kids being bad so often; I want to do a better job of catching them being good. I asked Kaleb how many rebounds he actually got. He got a total of one. Now, I am about to find out how mentally tough Kaleb has become. Normally if a player were to attempt rebounding ten times and only got one offensive rebound he would quit making the attempt. It would be easy to continue if he were to have gotten five or six rebounds. But good teams, good players are willing to try ten times and only be successful one time because it is that one time that may make the difference in winning and losing. The media picks up on the one great play that a player may make; they don't realize that so often they have tried nine other times that didn't work out. This separates the kids that say they want to be successful from the ones who are successful. They talk a good game, but they are not willing to pay the price. To be great is hard—it should be, or everybody would do it!

Brother Kirk Korver (sophomore) has thrown two very passive passes, and both have been picked off. Kirk, as we all do, needs to get more aggressive. One of his passes was actually backward; going away from his scoring end, and the other was sideways. We need him throwing attacking passes, going forward.

We work hard on our defense. We do a lot of shell drill. In a shell drill we pick out specific defensive concepts and drill them, usually in a four-man set up. We work constantly on helping each other out on the defensive end. Funny, the best thing we can do is not help. This is a contingency plan that we are practicing. One of the things that we need to really improve upon is our help and recover. We are helping and staying. The best form of help we can do is for the guys away from the ball to help really early towards the ball and then get right back to their man. In some ways this is really like a fake. The best teams we've ever had here have been great fakers. They were great at a one-step fake. This seems so simple, but it is extremely hard to get the kids to do. The one-step fake is exactly what it sounds like. A player away from the ball takes one sudden step towards the ball like he's coming at the player with the ball, and then quickly recovers back to his man. This creates an illusion to the offensive player that more than one man is guarding him. It also helps to set

14

up our trapping defenses that we put in at a later date. Eventually we want our opponents to not know if this is just a fake or if we are really coming to trap them. A moment's hesitation by the opposing team is what we are shooting for.

Actually, as I think about it, we already have started setting up our press defense. We number our presses with two-digit numbers. The first digit tells the players what kind of press we are in; the second the pick up point or the place on the floor where we want our players to start pressing their players. We have started the 44 press. It is a press designed to go from a man press into a zone press and then back to man-to-man. It is not as complicated as it sounds. I've had groups of kids doing this as young as sixth grade.

This is the type of team that needs to be able to press and run. They are not big and strong players more suited to a power game but quicker, faster players that can slash and dribble the ball. A coach at the high-school level needs to play to the player's strengths.

Speaking of dribbling, believe it or not, we need to do more of it, especially in the quarter-court offense. The modern game is less about running plays and more about penetrating with the dribble to create a help situation for the defense (the very thing we don't want our own defense to do unless absolutely necessary) and then pass the ball out to the open man. It seems like kids nowadays don't have the ability to dribble as well as yesteryear. They seem to spend all of their time on shooting the three or going all the way to the hoop. That also tends to eliminate the mid-range game or the pull-up jump shot. We are no exception. When we don't dribble-penetrate once in while when we run our offense, the defense really pressures our passers. We've got to dribble more. If nothing else, driving a gap makes the next pass easier.

I've been pleased with players Zach Morgan (nicknamed "Z-Mo") and Brock Pope. There are certainly other players I've been pleased with. I don't mean that these are the only two. Maybe what I mean is that I didn't expect some things out of them, and at least for today they have proven me wrong.

Thursday, November 16, Practice #4
Transfer, Stance, Block Outs, O Boards, Close Outs, the Box-and-One, and 34

Matt Dowie makes practice number 3.

Transfer, to convey, to carry over; it's the main purpose of a drill. We run drills (which are really small parts of the game, isolated). The purpose of the drill then is, carry over into the big picture or the game itself. The best teams can do it; the teams that struggle toil with the ability to transfer.

We ran the three-on-two, full-court drill today, and at times it looked pretty good. (Remember, we want a lay-up). Unfortunately, the first time we got into a game situation we had a three-on-two break, and we didn't come close to handling it correctly—it didn't transfer; that's the bad news. The good news was that the player that didn't handle it correctly was young Mr. C.J. Newendorp, knew before I got to him that was the reason that I wanted to talk with him. C.J. is a sharp kid and a really good kid; it was truly a good moment. Before a player will change they have to know that they made a mistake; he is on his way to change.

I was talking with my son Luke, and he told me that the human head weighs about 12 lbs. So when we want our kids in a stance we want them with their heads over their shoulders, not ahead of them. The latter stance seems to be the easier one, however. (Have you ever noticed that most of us take the easiest path?) This head-out stance is easier because it allows you to straighten your legs and still gives the athlete the appearance of being down and low as if they are ready to move. This is not true; with 12 lbs. in front of your shoulders, and your legs straight, the last thing you are ready for is movement. Another problem occurs when the players get tired, because then they come up even more out of that ever-important stance. If you want to play defense, you must get in a stance. We want to play defense.

Part of playing defense is blocking out when the shot goes up. I can't tell you how important this is. This doesn't take great skill, but there is an art to it. One of the most important parts of the technique is for the defender to take his eyes off the ball when the shot goes up. Man, that is a difficult habit to break! Think about it. When the shot goes up, where is it going? Unless it's a really bad shot it is going to the rim area. You don't need to watch that. What the defender needs to watch is the hips of the guy he is trying to block out. We don't know where he is going; we need to watch, and he is definitely not going anywhere without his hips. He may fake with his head or his feet, but he is not going to fake with his hips.

Once the defender knows where he is going he simply needs to impede his progress to the basket then rebound the ball. We impede with an arm bar. An arm bar has the arm bent at the elbow with the forearm facing the offensive player. We don't want our players to turn back to the ball until they have made contact with this arm bar. Then we want them to turn back to the ball, keeping their bodies between their man and the ball and then go board the thing. We don't want them doing a lot of shuffling right and left, maybe only a step or two.

When we fail to block out there are many bad things that could happen to our team. When our opponent gets the rebound, oftentimes that means they have the inside position at their own offensive board—I know that cannot be good. It probably means they will score. Oftentimes it means we will foul them, giving them more points and adding to our own personal and team fouls. Conversely, we love it when our kids can get offensive rebounds.

So who are the guys that can help us get to the offensive boards? Good question. I don't know, but I do know that it doesn't require a certain position or size or quickness or bulk or any of those things. I would say that tremendous effort is huge and so is anticipating your teammate's shot. That is a skill. Some kids seem to have it, and others struggle to find it.

Today we worked on closing out on an offensive player. Coach Miller is teaching the kids the appropriate method. Adam has done it before. His days at Wartburg College, where he played ball, have been beneficial to our players and to us as coaches. This is one of the most difficult things that a defender has to do. They are in a recovery mode. The defender has helped a teammate, and now he has to get back to his man after his man has received the ball. Adam teaches them to sprint towards their men but then to break down into short choppy steps as they approach the offensive player. Here is the why— because the offensive player might drive by them, and as such, the defender must have his feet on the floor to react rather than feet up in the air that occurs during longer steps. But, the offensive player may also take an outside shot so the defender must get out there in a hurry, and he has to get out there with his hand up to contest the outside shot. So the defender must sprint, break down, and still and stop both the drive and the outside shot, and oh, yeah, just to make it more difficult, the offensive player may fake before his choice of attack. We don't want to help because we don't want our defenders in a recovery mode— this is why.

Tyler Linn is a senior, and is also a good athlete. I think he and we as a team are both better when he drives to the basket more often. I am trying to convince him of this. He is getting better. I guess that is what we are all trying to do, get better.

We've started now with the 34 press. The 34 is a run-and-switch press designed to surprise the dribbler and create a turnover caused by a bad pass or a mistake in the dribble. It works because although it is not a trap but a switch, the offensive player (if we do it right) can't tell the difference and assumes he is about to be trapped, therefore picking up the ball and getting rid of it before the trap gets there. But instead, if we switch (unlike the trap where one man is always open) all of the receivers get covered up again by defenders. I refer to the 44 as our run-and-stay press and the 34 as our run-and-switch press. We didn't do badly, but once again we need to be more aggressive.

We are anticipating box-and-one defenses against us this year. The defense is designed to go man-to-man with one guy, probably against Kaleb, and set in a zone with the other four defenders in the form of a box around the basket. We need to attack with two main thoughts: 1) Fast-break the ball to the other end before the defense, and 2.) Rebound the heck out of the ball because the middle of the lane (or of the box) is not covered, and since it is a zone there are no specific assignments for the defenders to follow. Other thoughts in attacking a gimmick defense would be to post up Kaleb (a good-sized wing) or use lots of screens in combination with Kaleb, with him both setting and receiving screens from teammates.

Friday, November 17, 2006, Practice #5
Old Gym Fast-breaks and Webster, Adding a Fake to Shell, Defending Down-Screens, Flair Cuts, Zone Offenses, Head (Non Coaching) Duties and Vince

Started with dribble tag today and followed that with a three-point-shooting contest with each grade level competing against the other grade level; by the way, surprisingly the juniors won that contest. Also, Klarc Korver, our starting big man won the dribbling twice; figure that out. It was a light beginning to practice; one I'm sure designed to add enjoyment to the work. There is a danger in starting practice this way in that players may read this to be all fun and games with no work involved. Thank goodness that didn't happen. When we went to work, once again we worked hard.

Klarc Korver came to see me about adding power lay-ups to practices. He must have spoken with Coach Core about adding them to today's practice because even though they weren't listed on the practice schedule this was our next drill. I'm glad for this; I believe this to be one of our best lay-up drills; evidently so does Klarc.

We've spent a lot of time in our three-on-two drills. We run this drill at both the quarter-court and the full-court. The quarter-court rule limits the players to two dribbles and one pass before a shot goes up. Once again, I don't think we've got the right attitude about this drill. We are coming in looking to pass. I want us coming in looking to shoot and then adjust to the pass. So often we have come in, gotten deep to the basket, then tried to throw a pass that turns into a turnover. If we get deep, I want us to put it up. We've got a great chance to make it when we are deep, and if we don't we can go get the rebound; it's impossible to rebound a turnover.

We have two gyms at PHS. We have worked out in the newer, larger gym since the beginning of practice. I can't wait until we get into the small, old gym to run our fast-break stuff. We actually run our fast-break drills the width of the court to the sideline baskets.

I found out a long time ago when I was coaching little kids that too much time is spent in the middle of the court dribbling the ball towards the basket for my liking. I coached my boys' teams when they were young, and we used to workout in Webster School, which had a tiny gym. That, I found out, was a blessing. I found out because those kids talked me into taking them up to the high school to work out one day. The difference was amazing. We spent way too much time dribbling the ball up the floor with no action. At Webster, in a very few dribbles we were at the opposite basket, and we were either shooting or rebounding the ball with very little wasted time in between. I want to shoot it and rebound it a lot. And you know my passion for aggressive play; it was like play-station basketball in that old gym. The walls were close (shoot, sometimes we played passes off the walls), and so were the baskets. We were doing a lot of practicing of things that occurred a lot in ball games—shooting and rebounding. That cannot be bad!

We continue to work one-on-one, full-court. I have noticed a lack of ability by our varsity players to blow by with the dribble very effectively. We don't seem as though we explode out with the dribble; I am hoping this is just tired legs: either that or great defense.

We have added a fake-to-shell drill. We have taken the first shell that we do every year, in which we try to jump to the ball quickly with every pass and added a fake to it. Now the defender must jump to the ball (we call this getting on line and up line) and then fake like he is coming to double-team the ball handler. We've added to the effort that the defender must expend. Everyone thinks that defense is just a matter of stopping your guy; that would be great if every one of our players were better than every one of the other teams' players, but it doesn't work out that way very often. Our defensive system is much more complicated than our offensive system.

Man, did the kids get after it in the NC drill today! Green got down four to two and then went ahead 12 to four. We finally called it off after a 16-15 green team lead. Normally we play to 21, but today it was just too competitive to keep going because it was taking so much time. The NC drill is non-stop. Tons of running, scoring on the run, attacking the basket, rebounding, and trying to get back on stops categorize this game. It's fun for the kids, but it is really hard work. During this drill I noticed Tyler Linn giving the ball up to a post man when it was he and the post in a two-on-one situation. This normally is okay but not when the post is catching the ball 20 yards from the hoop. I spoke with Tyler. He complained of his legs hurting.

I said, "You mean you are out of shape?"

He replied, "It's just different from football; you get to rest."

I interrupted him. "So you mean you are out of shape?"

He looked at me, smiled, and said, "Yeah, I guess so. This is a fun but tough drill; it separates those who are in shape from those who aren't."

Tyler isn't yet.

Shell drill today has us working on defending the down-screen. Again, coaching defense is not as easy as the average fan would assume. Our approach to defending the down-screen is to not get screened. Sounds easy, but it is hard. But it does convey the message to our defender not to rely so much on help from a teammate. If the man getting screened can, he comes up the middle of the lane so he can be positioned in an on-line up-line stance. This does leave our defense vulnerable to a flair screen, where the offensive player fakes as though he is going up, encouraging our defender to beat him up to the spot, and then the offensive player actually goes out sideways, putting his offensive partner and screener between him and the defender. In other words, the defender tries to beat the offensive player to the ball by beating the screen. When the offensive player realizes that the defender has over committed himself to beat him up through the screen, he flairs back to the corner area again using the his same partner for the screen, just a different angle. The man with the ball now just throws a pass over the top, and the defender cannot get back to cover his man.

We try to counter this and all down-screen moves by getting help from the defender whose man set the screen. We don't want to switch, but we will. A switch in this case would simply mean that the screener's defender would cover for the man being screened and vice versa. Sounds simple; in reality it is another thing that we must work on. We will talk more about switching later.

When we work on defense we also work on offense. It would be crazy to let our offensive players get sloppy and develop bad habits just because we are working on our defense. One of our points of emphasis on the offensive end is to get your butt to the ball when you screen the defender. I know it is a small point, but all of these small details add up to big results.

We tried a new offensive set today against a zone offense. We are trying a one-four set that has the point guard at the top, the two posts at the elbows of the lane, and the two wings at (where else?) the wings. Once the ball is entered to one of the four players across the free-throw line, the next move for the offense is dictated by where the ball was entered into, whether it goes to the post or to the wing. Hey, I thought I told you the defense was more complicated! I could be wrong. At any rate, I liked the way the offense looked. Now we just need to practice it to get some chemistry as to where and when to pass the ball to create open looks. Then it is simple; we just need to make the open shots! Nothing to this: do everything right, get a great shot, then just ask a 17-year-old kid in front of 1,000 people to make it. Piece of cake. More people should coach. It's easy.

We run more set plays against a zone defense than we do against man-to-man defense. It's easier because against a zone, if you throw the ball down to the corner of the floor to a shooter, you will force the defense into a two-three zone with three players along the baseline and two up in the guard area. It doesn't matter that the zone may have started in a one-two-two or one-three-one; when the ball goes to the baseline corner the zone forms into a two-three. But with the knowledge of exactly where all the defenders will be at a given moment, it is easy to come up with ways to hurt the defense. I repeat, it is easy to come up with ways to hurt the defense. I did not say we always perform those things the way they are supposed to be done, but we certainly have offensive sets we can run. One of our set plays that we have run for a number of years is called "Open." We call it that because it eventually turns into somewhat of an overload (where we outnumber the defenders with the number of offensive players in one area of the floor) and we almost always end up with somebody open. Funny, though, it seems as though every team we've coached has their own idea of which option to employ the most or which one they have the most success with, even though in my mind there are certain options within each play that seem the best to me. For instance, last year's team may have run an option out of this play and done it over and over again with great success, and this year's team (running the same play) may never run that option, or if they do have limited success with it. We did okay with Open for the first time running it.

We continue to run our zone offense out of a box set as well. This is a very simple offense—(I know this because I can understand it) that surrounds one post player in the middle by four players set in a box formation. We don't have a lot of player movement, with the exception of our post man, but we do have the ability to move the ball quickly, and we are facing the basket in good balance when we make the catch of the ball. Oftentimes if you aren't shooting the ball well from the outside it may come from too much movement! Sounds strange to say that. If players are moving and cutting too much and too quickly, often they catch the ball off balance and shoot hurried and off-balance shots. I am a much bigger fan of spacing the floor out, with the floor balanced, meaning that we have approximately the same number of players on the ball side of the floor as we do the weak side and with the players themselves balanced up, ready to catch and drive or shoot, hopefully against recovering defenders. Again, recovering defenders are ones that have helped and now must get back to their offensive men because they are about to get or have already received the ball.

One of the reasons I don't want to be head coach is all the stuff that comes with the position that doesn't include coaching. After practice today Coach Core had to deal with some of those things.

We have more players than we have uniforms. We also have players that are hurt. So who should get the uniforms and how should we handle this situation with players that are hurt? Mark did a great job with his talk to the players after the practice. He explained that we will be rotating uniforms and explained the fact that even in practice, the players that play a lot will need the most repetitions in the five-on-five settings, and that meant that there would be quite a bit of standing around if you were not in the top twelve or so players. He also made it available to those players not in the top twelve the possibility of practicing with our junior varsity team. He also indicated to the kids that if they choose not continue to play because of these things that he would understand and hold no ill will towards them.

After the meeting two kids immediately came up and wanted to work out with the JV squad. Peter Naschke and Nathan Klyn volunteered. They are both good kids that work hard in practice and have great attitude. Nathan's dad, Vince, is my best friend and was my best man at my wedding. I want Nathan to do well, if for no other reason than for his dad. This is kind of a touchy thing for both me and Mark Core, who also knows and respects Vince highly. If Nathan were 6 foot 3" he would be a solid post for us. But he is five foot nine and plays the post position. His fundamentals on defense and on offense are pretty darn good, although not perfect enough to get away with his lack of height; in particular he can't quite do it because his quickness is not as good, either. But again, he is a good person from a good family with a good attitude; this is hard for both of us coaches. The good news is that Nathan appears fine with it. I think he knows his limitations and is okay with this decision—that's what I mean: great attitude and good kid.

Saturday, November 18, 2006, Practice #6
Pre-practice, Spin Lay-Ups and Footwork, Balance of Team Scoring and Kaleb's Scoring

It's a Saturday morning, and I would guess by the looks of them that some of the boys had some late nights last night.

When I first get to the gym Mark is getting uniforms ready to hand out after practice is over. I can't help him so I run up to the gym and sweep the floors. Our custodians do a very good job of keeping the floors clean, but once in a while it still falls to the coach. It reminds me of when I first started coaching. Not only did I do the floors, but also I drove the bus to practice and taped every injury we had. So this doesn't seem bad to me; it just brings me back to reconsider how good we have it now.

While the players are coming out slowly from the locker room I spy Jesse Wineland warming up. He is not attacking the basket like I would like him to; he is too tentative, and I would like to help set the tone for him today by getting into a more aggressive mind set. I ask Andrew Barber (manger, stat man par excellence) to hold a football-blocking dummy that I want Jesse to create contact with as he goes to the hoop for a lay-up. I toss the ball to Jesse, and play some fake defense that gives him the idea of beating a man to the basket. I want him to take a really quick look at the hoop first, then go hard for the lay-up while protecting the ball from the defender (the blocking dummy) by leaning in to create contact and keeping the ball out to the opposite side with his other hand. We work on all angles, he gets better; but can he transfer this into a game-like situation?

I don't want to wear out Jesse before practice officially starts, so I let him go and then walk over to work with Kirk Korver on post moves. I told Kirk the other day that he is better by accident than most people are on purpose. He just looked at me and smiled. When a coach believes in a player I think that the player can sense that, and when they know you believe in them it gives them confidence, and they play better. I had a discussion the other day with a coach at the high school and I indicated that I thought one of our past players could have and still could play Division One football. He didn't; he thought that the athlete didn't have enough size and speed. I argued that while those two things are important (he is no bum, but maybe not quite as fast or big) I felt that he made up for it with his never-say-die attitude. The coach (I won't name him) then accused me of believing in this athlete too much. I'm guilty. I do, and that may have been one of the best backhanded compliments I have ever received.

Be that as it may, I asked Kirk to work with me on drop steps and short hooks and then combined them to do the up-and-under move. Coach Core saw us working and sent our other big guy, Andrew Ter Louw, to do the same workout. Again, I thought both got better at what we were doing, but in order to carry it over during the heat of the game they will need more repetitions to ingrain the habit. We don't have the time nor the coaching staff to give them those reps. If they are going to improve they will need to work on this on their own. Isn't that true of most things? When we as people want to get better at something we have to be willing to work at it, oftentimes alone.

We opened practice with two-ball and tennis-ball dribbling. One would assume if a player can learn to dribble two balls at one time and do a variety of moves with them, then when they have only one ball it should be easy. The dribbling of a tennis ball is a drill that we stole from current NBA star Steve Nash. That guy is truly amazing the way he can control the ball. Coach Core announced to the kids that from now on during pre-practice he would like the kids to work on their ball-handling skills.

Our next drill was a lay-up drill. We added the Magic Move named after Ervin Magic Johnson, which is a spin move coming down the lane from the guard position in which the player spins to the inside for a short hook, and the Brunner Move named after Gregg Brunner, the former University of Iowa player. This is also a spin-dribble move, but it starts in the wing or baseline area and spins back towards the baseline for a lay-up. The latter move is one I have encouraged B-Mo to develop. He really likes the corner three-point shot, and eventually the defenders really come out hard to play that shot. This then would give a perfect opportunity to drive the ball. Since that is not his strength but something that he can do if he must, the Brunner move would be a more controlled drive to the basket that would just add to the defenders' worries.

As we are practicing these moves you can see the kids trying to get the footwork down and without great results. Again, like everything else, when your mind gets too involved your feet get slower. I want the athletes to go as hard as they can and spin as fast as they can without worries about footwork; they just need to attack the basket, and let their footwork catch up with them—it works.

We did partner shooting today. The drill is simple: one rebounder and one shooter, the shooter shoots continually for one minute, and then they switch positions. I believe that early in the season we need to do this drill more often. A player can go through an entire practice, and unless the player is a guy that is expected to score and shoot a lot in practice, he may not get up many shots. Shoot, even our shooters don't do a lot of shooting unless we are very intentional about getting up shots in practice.

We attempted a drill today that neither Mark nor I had run before. The drill was a three-on-three, full-court drill that was designed to advance the ball down court without the dribble. It wasn't long before Coach Core called it off. We had a lot of backward and sideways passing, something neither of us like; we like the ball going ahead. Hey, sometimes what you think is going to work doesn't; you can get stubborn and try to make it work, or you can get out of it if it feels like you're fighting a losing battle.

C. J. Newendorp's brother, Brett, played for us last year and was a great hustle player that got a lot of offensive rebounds. I know after talking with C.J. that he really liked the way big brother played and wanted to emulate his play. That is music to my ears. But I think C.J. is maybe fouling a little too much while he is attempting to play aggressively. But honestly, right now I'm okay with that. I've found that as a coach you can always pull an athlete back from being too aggressive, but you really struggle to increase aggression if you teach controlled play first. We will let him go for now.

It's almost a given that we will be doing shell drill. Today's pattern again calls for down-screens. As a coach I am looking for a balance of aggression, good offensive play, running the pattern enough to get an opportunity for the defense to practice against down-screens but continued play from an offensive standpoint. What I mean by that is that the kids must catch and shoot sometimes or drive the ball sometimes so the defense doesn't play the pattern and so the offense doesn't get sloppy. The group that I supervised did some transfer stuff that really was pleasing to see. Most of our screens were butt to the ball, and we actually had some defensive fakes at the ball. We still didn't rebound offensively very well—as a coach you'd better be hard to please; you'll get what you put up with.

Next came four-on-four live. Our best shooter, Kaleb Korver, didn't even take a shot. I don't think. C.J. and Klarc Korver were appropriately aggressive. Nate Klyn looked at the basket only once during this entire time, and Kirk Korver again did a nice job. I'm not sure what is up with Kaleb, did he stay up too late last night?

All of our press work has been either with the 44 press or 34 press. We've spent time on each individually; today we are putting them together. We have a quick huddle after every full-court possession to make a call as to which press we are running for the next possession. This requires the players to do a little more thinking and know which press they are in and respond accordingly. Our little huddle is something that we will not be able to do when the games start; it's illegal. What we'd like to do is be able to call our defense immediately after a basket (that we make) and before our opponent in-bounds the ball with hand signals. All this will take place in seconds, and our players will need to be able to think and react very quickly. And if one player out of the five isn't on the same page as the others our presses will not only not work but also will oftentimes cost us a basket.

As with any good defense, players must be aware of where their opponents are as well as where the ball is. Most kids get ball bound; in other words they focus on the ball and forget where their man is. We have a lot of that during our press work. Right now we are not ready to press anybody.

On Thursday we worked on attacking the box-and-one defense. There is very little question that we will see that this year. Today we try putting Kaleb in the post and surrounding him with the other offensive players. I liked it. I would assume that Kaleb would be fronted in the post, which puts him inside for offensive rebounds. It also may confuse the defense as to their jobs; should they stay in and help on Kaleb or should they go out to cover? This way we will get some perimeter shots.

At the end of practice I talked with the players. Kaleb went through almost the entire practice without shooting the ball. In fact, I even privately called Kaleb over and asked him to be a little more selfish on the offensive end. My message was a little bit mixed. I told K (my nickname for Kaleb) that he needed to be more assertive. I felt like our other players were taking good aggressive shots but that I would like to see one of our best shooters take more shots. It just makes sense. But I also tried to give the other end of my thinking to the players, especially our guards. If I were a guard on this team, and I had a guy on my team that could shoot, and he hadn't shot in a while, I'd make darn sure he got the next shot. I think I'm right in both ways; Kaleb has to be more assertive and his teammates, while I want them thinking about attacking and scoring, once in a while somebody has to be smart enough to get our scorer involved. If I had to pick one thought over another, I would have said Kaleb must get more aggressive.

Monday, November 21, 2006, Practice #7
Green Team, Intangibles, Floaters, Lane D, Back Screens, Kyle, Press Attack, Stop-Score-Stop, and Three Perfect Possessions

Coach Core alters the green team make-up almost on a daily basis. We are still searching for the right combination of players to make up the starting line-up as well as determining who plays the most minutes in a ball game. Today's green team is made up of the players that over the first six practices have been our best rebounders. This includes Kaleb, Klarc, Kirk (all of the Korver fame), Jesse, and Brock.

Also one of the players for the green team is C.J. Newendorp, who in a poll of players is one of the top three vote getters in performing the intangibles consistently in practice. Ah, the intangibles, those are the things that set the good teams apart from the average ones. Teams that perform the intangibles usually are very successful. What are the intangibles? Good question. Sometimes they are hard to explain and oftentimes they occur in practices or games without the total awareness of coaches or fans. Intangibles are most often the things that can't be measured, things like: diving on the floor for loose balls, throwing the extra pass on offense, helping on defense, or running the floor; I guess the intangibles are almost the opposite of the ESPN moments that I talked about earlier.

At any rate, before I got distracted with the intangibles I was talking about the make-up of the green team. In my mind it has really been a tight race for our open spots. The wing/guard positions are really close. Brock Pope has done a nice job of handling the ball and continuing to attack on offense. His athleticism has improved dramatically since last year. I would guess he is probably four or five inches taller. Tyler Linn has an ability to get to the basket; that's a good thing. I can't get him to attack like I'd like him to, which is the downside. He is a guy that might make a really good play one time and then make a really bonehead play the next. C.J. Newendorp (intangibles) is not the smoothest player but a great hustler. Jesse has skills but doesn't believe in himself as much as I'd like him to; that's part of our job: to help him to believe. I've spoken with a variety of players as well about who they are most comfortable playing with. They seem about as undecided as I am. It seems as though all of the afore mentioned players are listed in every conceivable order in order of preference. All of this, and I haven't even mentioned Colin Boswell, one of the returning seniors. Now, when you add to the mix Clayton Boeyink (injury), there is really a lot of competition for those outside positions.

Clayton's next appointment with a specialist is the 5th of December. I hope for his sake and ours that something good comes out of that. B-Mo seems certain that he will get clearance soon so he can begin to practice and play with us; I hope so.

We worked today on floaters, so named because it is a lay-up that we want shot over a big guy on the run; it should arch up high and float down into the basket. Pros and good college players master this shot and can shoot over big men trying to block their shots.

Our effort to keep the ball out of the paint (the lane) when we are on defense is still a work in progress. In basketball, as in life, there is usually a balance. Last year we worked pretty hard at contesting shots and taking away the offense's ability to pass the ball around from side to side of the court (what we would call swinging the ball). When you do that the defensive players are out on the perimeter contesting passes as well as shots. This tends to leave gaps in the defense, and these are gaps where dribble drives occur. Our ability right now to defend these drives is not very good. We must improve if we are to be successful. Again, our shell drills are designed to practice help, but help should only occur in an emergency. The best defense is one that doesn't require a lot of help.

We are working today on denying the ball from coming into the post. There are three passers, one offensive post player, and one defensive post player. It's a tough drill that requires tremendous effort; I wonder if parents know just how hard their kids work at this game. They'd be shocked to see the kids that they can't convince to put out the garbage are now sprinting, sweating, and defending for almost an hour and a half, straight.

Back screens are some of the toughest screens for our or any defense to defend—that's our shell today. Kyle Korver (Philadelphia 76ers and past Pella High Player) used to make a living on the basketball court with this screen. He'd set the back screen; this is a screen set from behind a defender, and then open up to the ball after screening. The reason this worked was that the defender guarding Kyle would often help his teammate being screened, if he didn't the offensive player was headed to the basket with nobody guarding him. This moment of help by Kyle's man gave Kyle, or for that matter any offensive player, an opportunity to catch and shoot the ball. I've tried to get more players to set back screens for just this reason. I haven't been as successful with this as I'd like, and I'm not sure why. Tomorrow when we go into our five-on-five work we should emphasize this as an offensive move.

One of the best ways that we have found to defend a back screen is to switch it. In other words, defenders trade offensive players rather than stay with the same one when they screen. We aren't allowing that yet; it brings up an entirely new set of circumstances that we don't have time to cover yet. Besides switching easier. We always try to make stuff harder now than what they will see in a game. Part of the problem with a shell drill is finding that right balance between running the pattern to get enough reps on the skill we are trying to defend and actually playing realistic offense. Today we were a bad offensive team running through the shell.

Coach Core has stayed true to his word as we work on the NC drill every day. The green team won 24 to 0. Wow!

Our press offense is actually quite simple, as most of our other offenses are. Once the ball comes in we want receivers available on the same sideline as the ball, the middle of the floor, and one available as a reversal man. The reversal man should actually be somewhat behind the ball to make the pass easier. If the ball does get reversed we want receivers stationed in the same areas. We combine that with the dribble, and that is our offensive attack. Simple, but very effective for us, and once again the more aggressively we attack the press the better we attack it. Some presses try to prevent the initial inbounds pass; if that happens we add some initial receivers by putting more players up front, but after the ball comes in the attack remains the same. There are some differences when attacking different presses in terms of when to make what pass, and we try to give the kids tendencies of the various presses, and then once again we encourage them to play the game.

It's amazing to me how little Kirk Korver, our sophomore post man does glaringly wrong. For a young player he is a fast learner. He is also our biggest player. I'm anxious to see him in action against another team with a bigger player to see how he handles that. My guess is that he will do just fine.

Our Stop-Score-Stop drill originated from the game itself. Teams that win games do this all the time. They make a stop on the defensive end, then they score, and then they make another stop. At this point they are up two points. If they do this often enough the lead grows accordingly. So we made this scenario into a drill. To win, a team has to get a stop score, and then get another stop. When there are only three possessions involved, both the offense and defense are pretty tuned in.

I've been pleased with Kaleb. He took my little talk to heart and became more aggressive without taking away from the other players. In fact, he is the only player that I've noticed that has carried over a defensive fake at the ball during our five-on-five segment.

Another great drill that we run is called three perfect possessions. This is another drill that where the defense must make three stops in a row. In addition the stops must be perfect. Not only must they stop the offense from scoring they cannot allow the following: a loss of vision, the ball in the lane, an uncontested outside shot, or lack of a block out. Should the defense allow one of these things to happen, regardless of the ball going in or not, the possession is not perfect, and therefore the stop is not made. It's a tough, time-consuming drill but one that creates a competitive, game-like atmosphere.

Tuesday, November 22, 2006, Practice #8
Charges, Legs and Shooting, Impressing the Coaches, Staying, Safety, Z-Word, and Good Offense or Bad Defense

One of the reasons we work on lay-ups, especially the more difficult ones, is for emergency situations. Players won't be shooting any lay-up other than straight in unless they are under duress. Our kids must do a better job of going game speed when we do these because that is absolutely the only speed that they will ever shoot them in a game—if they have time they will shoot the regular lay-up. I can see improvement in our power lay-ups. I encourage our offensive players to protect the ball from the defender by using their bodies to shield it. If there is contact from the side (which there will be if done right) there will be a foul. When is the last time you saw an official call a foul on the offensive player? I want them to not only get fouled but score as well; this is an opportunity to practice concentration and focus.

During the three-on-two, quarter-court drill today again I think we improved. There is some definite carry over from the power lay-up drill. Colin Boswell is a slim player that doesn't have a whole lot of body, but I was really pleased to see him using what he has to protect the ball today. That is a step for him. Since we only allow two dribbles and one pass before shooting, the offensive player ends up needing to shield quite often. One of the things that our underclassmen want to do during this drill is to take their time getting the ball back out to the lines so they can get their defense set before the offensive attack begins. I don't. I want that ball back to the next person in line immediately so the offense can attack, and the defense has to react, just like a game situation when the defense is out numbered.

One of the best things a defense can do is draw a charge. Klarc today drew at least two of them. I've failed as a coach to note this to the other players enough. Last year B-Mo was far and away our best at drawing a charge. I also think C.J. has drawing a charge high on his list of things to do; shoot, he was even trying to do that in summer games when nobody calls them. Intangibles: this is one of them, and I like players who do them.

I noticed in partner shooting today that almost everything Tyler Linn shoots is short. To me that is a function of his legs. It's not that I want him to jump as high as he can to shoot not at all, but I do believe that it is easier to control consistent distance with the larger muscles of the legs than the arm muscles. I'm just convinced he needs a little more leg, but this means he has to catch the ball with his legs in position and down. This is a little harder, and therefore, most players resist this stance. But with a little success with the shot that resistance goes away.

Our shell drills are tough. Today Klarc did two different sets because we were short of players. That is really tough. Now Klarc, barring injury or fouls or something unforeseen, is going to play and play a lot. It says something about his level of character that he would be the one to go the extra time. But the other end of this is that it also means that the guys that are not assured of playing time did not jump in there. In the coaches' minds we want effort guys; that would have been a great opportunity to impress us. Klarc didn't need to but he did; many others need to and they didn't. Hmm.

All of our faking at the offensive player when we are defense is designed to give the illusion to the offensive player of taking away gaps and double-teaming him. This creates a moment of indecision in the offensive player's mind, which gives the defense an advantage. But there is a fine line between faking and staying. We want a fake at the ball and then recover quickly back to the man that you are guarding. If you go to the ball and stay, your man is going to be open and then we are going to need to cover for the man that stayed which gets us into a defensive rotation. Our defensive rotations are for emergencies only, we certainly don't want to create this emergency situation with our own mistakes; rather, this situation should come from an opponent's great offensive play. C. J. is one of those guys staying too long. He's a junior; he will get better as the season goes on. Our seniors have been through this; we expect more from them.

We've added a new shell drill today, another facet of the game that the offense can attack us with. We've added dribble penetration. The drill consists of a down-screen on one side of the floor with dribble penetration on the other side. The help-side defenders (the defenders on the opposite side of the floor from the ball) must handle the screen and at the same time be there to support against dribble penetration coming from the other side of the floor. We call the man under the hoop on the weak side of the floor our safety. The safety can change within an instant; he can go from safety to the guard position as his man screens down. But while he plays safety (whoever that ever-changing player is) he must: be a weak-side rebounder if the shot goes up, he must be open up so that he can see both sides of the floor to stop a dribble drive, he must help with the screen situation by talking, and he must fight through the screen to the top of the floor. And oh yeah, if the ball does get driven along the baseline when he is in the safety spot we want him to stop the dribbler outside of the lane.

We don't want to err, but if we do, if we absolutely have to choose between one thing or another we want to err on the side of helping against the dribble drive from the other side of the floor and give up our recovery to the outside man.

Today I've noticed that one of our sophomore big guys, Andrew Ter Louw, is struggling in the shell. I'm about to say something to Andrew, and then I realize he is guarding Kaleb. Now it's not like I'm making excuses for Andrew; again we want every player we have becoming good enough to guard any player. But I'm in hopes that Kaleb is going to be a hard guard for a bunch of players this year. I decided to give Andrew a break, but it won't be long, and my expectations for him will go up, and I will expect a better effort, even against Kaleb.

We are throwing a lot of long passes in the NC drill, but I guarantee you that we are getting more aggressive every day. Mark has done a great job of letting them play and not blowing the whistle. We are definitely a little wild with our shots and passes; now we are trying to find that line between dumb and aggressive. I'm convinced we are getting closer.

Our straight z, zo, zon, zone press is named with a series of numbers that are labeled in the 50s. Sorry, for the longest time I viewed the Z-word as a naughty word to say. I'm still working at getting over the hump. In any case, we worked on our 53 press today for the first time. We are putting our bigger guys up front in this press; again something new but it allows our faster guys to be the intercept positions at the back of the press. I don't know if we are out-thinking ourselves or if this is a good move. We will find out soon.

Our one-four zone offense has been really effective. Is this great offense or bad defense? I'm starting to think the latter; we need to do a better job on our zone defenses to make our zone offenses better.

We really struggled with our out-of-bounds plays under the basket today. We couldn't even get the ball in, let alone score. That must improve.

I asked Andrew Barber to chart Tyler Linn's catches of the ball and the times he attacked the basket with the dribble when he was in a five-on-five situation. The day before I had talked with him about attacking more with the dribble and wanted to see if it had taken, it had. Eleven catches and five attacks with the dribble...cool! I asked Tyler if he was intentional with this or if it was just luck (he didn't know we were charting him). He said he was intentional. Wow, way to go, Ty.

At the end of practice today we talked a little bit about this weekend. We are off on Thursday for Thanksgiving and then on Friday we scrimmage at Urbandale, and then play in the Turkey Shootout for a half at Knoxville. Mark talked of the need to play a physical brand of ball, especially against Urbandale, a 4A school from Des Moines. I talked of the ability to be mentally tough. We are allowed three scrimmages. We almost never scrimmage at home, and we almost always scrimmage against larger schools. Why do we do that? Because we want to put the kids in the toughest setting we can; we want to find out how they respond and who it is that responds best to adversity. This is especially true with our younger kids. Sometimes just walking into a different gym scares the pants off of the young ones. The shootout will be against Melcher Dallas, a small school and probably one with less talent. But it will be the first time we actually wear our uniforms and play in front of a crowd. It will also be our second scrimmage in the same day. Again we will face some new situations and find out who can handle them.

Wednesday, November 23, Practice #9
Mental Toughness, Thanks, Rebounding, Two New Shells, Penetrating and Non-Penetrating Dribbles, Talking Too Much, and Time for a Break

We opened practice with the Magic Move and the Brunner move for layups; everybody is getting better at these moves. Next we work on the fast-break by working on a two-on-one with a chaser. We still need to develop the right attitude; we need to think, *Score first, and pass second,* as we attack the basket. It sounds selfish, but the defense must first be extremely concerned about stopping the man with the ball; if they are they will more likely leave open the men without the ball, and thus make the pass more available to our offense. The man with the ball can go in thinking shot and then adjust to the pass. It is much tougher, almost impossible to go in thinking, *Pass and adjust to the shot.*

The John Wooden teams at UCLA that won something like nine NCAA championships in row had an offensive rule that called for the man receiving a scoring pass from one of his teammates to acknowledge that teammate with some type of thank you. Normally it would occur as a point at the passer by the receiver. Mark wants our kids thanking the passer as well. I think it is an excellent idea. Actually, I think it might begin with us coaches. We need to do a better job of jumping up and down about the guy who throws the pass, ourselves. We need to set the tone and let the kids see our own positive reaction to the passer. The guy that scores—he really doesn't need the acknowledgment; he receives that from the response that he gets from the crowd and the way he feels inside. By us recognizing the passer it encourages more passes from that player. The players need to understand that the guys who make the passer feel good, will get more passes sent their way.

Our best defensive teams have given up more outside and three-point shots than our other teams. Why? I think it's because the offenses against tried to get the ball inside; we were determined not to let that happen, so they settled for the perimeter shot. Again, I think this is an attitude presented by the good defender who is very determined not to let the ball inside, and if the offense does get by the defense we rotate off of outside men with our help defenders to stop penetration and thus give up the outside shot. But it all starts with the first line of defense: me stopping you from penetrating. I'd do that by practically giving up the outside shot (at least appearing to give it up) by my body position against the offensive man. I would play back off him far enough that he would feel pretty comfortable about shooting it. Then I would react up to contest the shot. We play too close right now. By backing off a little bit it not only gives the appearance of being open; it gives the defender a little bit more time to react to the drive to the basket.

Coach Core is relentless about working on rebounds. That is a good thing. We are relatively small, especially right now without B-Mo. Rebounding is positioning and effort; it is not so much about size. We can do it, but we need to make it a high priority, that is what drilling it on a daily basis does.

Today's shell drill is a give-and-go cut on the ball side and a down-screen on the weak side. As we go on, each shell drill adds more movement and more difficult situations to defend, especially for the help-side defenders. This whole defensive concept of the guys on one side of the floor helping the guys on the other side would be a simple recipe for success if the offensive players just wouldn't move or screen for each other or dribble penetrate. Unfortunately, we can't get other teams to cooperate with us in that regard very often, at least not willingly. Sometimes unwittingly they will (if we get good enough at individual defense and mix in good help defense) stop doing some of these things because they get frustrated and just settle for bombing up shots.

Jesse and C.J. both lose their men quite a bit when we go shell. They both have a habit of getting ball bound. They see the ball and forget to look where their men are, which again is okay if their men never move, but moving seems to be something that most offensive players do. Jesse and C.J. are doing this because they are anxious to be in the right spot to help and in order for them to recognize these situations they know that they need to see where the ball is. They can do a better job of keeping an eye on their men by moving their head, by pointing with one hand at the ball and the other at their men, and finally by physically touching their men as often as they can. They can't hold, but they certainly can touch, in particular when they turn to look for the ball.

Our next shell involved on-ball screens. In other words the man that has the ball gets a screen from one of his fellow offensive players. To counter this we want the man being screened to go over the top of the screener and follow his man (the dribbler) so he doesn't go baseline (if the screen is from guard to wing). The man that is guarding the screener must momentarily hedge at the man with the dribble, so it is an instant switch and then immediately recover back to his man. The hedger should have his shoulders square to the dribbler so that his numbers look him right in the eye. We do this to try to force the dribbler to charge, or if not that, widen his dribble out around the hedger so the man that got screened can catch up. Once again our weak-side guys need to be there if the dribbler beats the help or the man setting the screen rolls to the basket. By the way, we were terrible in this shell; I shouldn't say that. Our veterans weren't too bad; the rookies, they were.

Clayton Boeyink just came over to me in practice and whispered to me that he thought we were blowing the whistle too much! I love that. I think the worst style of leadership is top down. We want our kids (the guys in the trenches) to talk to us about what we are doing and chiefly about what we are doing wrong. Everybody's ego loves to hear the good things, but you learn more from the bad, and you can make corrections if you know about these things. But it's hard to correct things if you don't know they are occurring. Coaches have a fine line to walk; they must correct and teach (that is why they get the big bucks—now there is a topic for another day) but if they talk too much in practice; even if it's good stuff, the kids stop listening. The trick is to coach on the run and not stop things too much; you want to stop talking before they stop listening and not vice versa. I will talk with Coach Core about this tomorrow sometime; he will be pleased with the input from Clayton, even if he disagrees, which I don't think he will.

Offensively today we seem to be doing a lot of non-penetrating dribbles. That is fine if they are dribbling to improve a passing angle into a post; in my mind everything else should at least start at the basket. Even one dribble, that brings a help defender (who leaves his man open to receive a pass), and all of a sudden the offense has the defense in a recovery mode. This mode is the easiest one to score against, much easier than a set defense that isn't forced to help. Justin, Tyler Terlouw, and Jesse are the main offenders right now. Ironically the guy on the white team that attacks pretty well with dribble is Zach Morgan, our six foot one, super-strong post player. You'd think that the post would be the last one to do this; not so.

Old C.J. has put up two air balls today in practice. The kid is such a hustler, you can put up with that type of thing because he gives you so many of the other things. I know that he is frustrated with this, however. Sometimes you don't shoot well; sometimes you do. That is why we want defenders that play hard. Defense can be pretty consistent; offense oftentimes isn't. Defense keeps you around so you usually have a chance at the end.

We run a four across against a really tough press that is trying to sell out by denying the inbounds pass. We worked on that today really quickly in preparation for the weekend, just in case.

We also put in a set play against a man-to-man offense. It is the first one of the year. We don't use many, but the ones we do use we try to take advantage of the offensive skills that the players have. I'd tell you what it was and how it plays out, but then I'd have to kill you so other teams won't know our play. We also made some adjustments to our out-of-bounds plays.

After practice I gave Nate Klyn and Andrew some stats that I would like them to take at the scrimmages. Nate is a sharp young man who wants to help out; he doesn't have to do this. He wants to.

Now it's off to Thanksgiving break, a day, one of very few, that we will not practice on. The boys really commit a lot when they decide to play basketball. I wish people would understand how much this is and how hard they work.

Chapter 2—The Preseason

Friday, November 24, 9:30 A.M., Scrimmage at Urbandale
Game Stats, Turnovers, Keeping the Ball out of Post, Individual
Defense, Staying Too Long, Helping Too Late, Slowing the Swing,
Creating Motion, and Louisville

The rule at scrimmages is that it is illegal to keep score. We didn't. It is not illegal to keep stats. We did. The stats should be at least somewhat accurate, although I doubt that they are perfect. Urbandale's strength was their size and players inside. Not that their guards were bad, they weren't; they were just more skilled inside. We shot the ball 60 times; they shot it 59. That's a good thing. We made 27 shots and they made 33. They also made one more free throw than we did. I don't know how many of the made shots were three-point shots but assuming that it was about even, give or take a shot or two, we would have gotten beat by about 12 to 15 points. We shot 45% and they shot about 55% against us. Our ability to shoot 45% is probably good enough for us to win some ball games. Our defense giving up 55% is really bad. If we give up 55% shooting we are going to need to limit the number of shots our opponents take. In other words, if Urbandale shoots 11 shots and makes five while we force them into 40 turnovers, we'd win the game easily because they couldn't get up enough shots. That didn't happen; we actually had 24 turnovers while they had just seven! And here I thought our ball handling would be our strength. We must, and I do emphasize *must*, stop turning the ball over so much if we are to be a good team.

Last year when we went to this scrimmage Carroll was there as well. Both teams last year creamed us. Actually, this year we did better. When you factor in that we were missing two starters and will get one of those guys back Monday, I'm starting to feel better about this whole thing. If we could get Clayton back as well I'd really almost be feeling good right now.

The challenge from the moment we walked into the gym was to see which players would succumb to the pressure of playing in a hostile environment against good players. I'm not talking about shots not falling; I'm talking about the fear factor. Who would be playing afraid?

It didn't take long to see the difference between the juniors and the seniors. Our two senior captains, Kaleb and Klarc, while a long ways from perfect played aggressively. Kirk, while not playing extremely aggressively played pretty solidly. From that point out it depended on the moment as to how people were playing.

Offensively Klarc was 3-9 from the field; Brock 0-1, Kaleb 4-12, all four made were three-point shots. Tyler Linn was 1-3, Brandon Esterbrook was 2-4, Kirk 2-4 and Jesse was 4 for 5. The rest of the shooting went like this; Tyler 0-3, Colin 3-8, Zach 1-3, Justin 1-3, C.J. 2-4, Andrew Ter Louw 0-3 Nate 0-1, and Peter 2-4.

One thing we must do defensively is to learn how to do a better job of keeping the ball out of the post. We trailed cuts, which means that the offensive player got to the ball ahead of our defender and then was able to catch the ball in an area that made him an offensive threat. As I mentioned earlier the Urbandale big kids were good; Kirk and Andrew must learn that it is easier to defend a man by not allowing him to catch the ball rather than letting him catch and then defending. When the ball goes into the post it is like a dribble penetration into the lane; regardless of how the ball enters the lane it creates havoc to our defense.

We have worked very hard on situations that call for help, this is where our weak-side defender help against the man with the ball if he gets past the first defender. This is supposed to be a last-measure defense. We are supposed to handle our men individually first. I wonder if the message we are unintentionally sending to the individual is not to worry if you get beat; somebody will pick your man up. That allows the individual to shirk responsibility and makes us weak. Another thing we are doing is helping and staying rather than momentary help and immediate recovery. We are also helping too late. If we help early the offense hesitates, the initial defender recovers, and the helper is already back to his man. When our defender stays too long without recovering or goes too late his man will be open, and when the ball comes back to his man he is in a recapture mode, trying to get back to his man who has gained the upper hand on him.

An extremely pleasing thing for us was the block outs. Urbandale only had nine offensive rebounds, part of that was the fact that they shot 55% and didn't have as many rebounds available to get.

Our one set play that we just put in yesterday Cyclone, got a wide-open look for Kirk. Now we need a more subtle way to call it and a second play that is a counter to it so that our opponents can't see it coming.

One of the most obvious signs of our lack of aggression to me was the way we didn't even look to fast-break. We had that deer-in-the-headlights look. We have worked every day for ten minutes a day getting the ball up the court, and today it took us until the third fifteen-minute session to really look for our break. I spoke with a couple of players about this later on, and they indicated that the NC drill has become a place to look to throw the ball like a deep touchdown pass over the top rather than an outlet and fast-break. Based on that we don't want to stop our offense from looking deep, so we don't want to limit the offense, but we do need to get our defenses to recognize defensive floor balance and make sure we are getting someone back. That will improve our outlets, make it more of a true fast-break, and improve our sense of defense as well.

Another area that we struggled with defensively was jumping to the ball when the offense was setting a screen that hindered our defender from getting from the side of the floor to the other. Urbandale was running a flex cut where the wing would pass, receive a screen from the post, and cut to the other side of the floor where the opposite offensive wing received the swing pass and now could enter the ball into the post. We actually have a shell drill for this; looks like it's time to break it out. Slowing the swing and preventing perfect timing by the offense would have been helpful.

I learned something today myself. We, as coaches, have worked hard at keeping the ball out of the paint with the dribble. We haven't worked hard enough to prevent the post pass. Furthermore, we don't do a lot of screening in our offense; therefore other than the shell we don't defend a lot of offenses that screen. We may need to add a simple screen offense or do more of it in shell. And finally I was reminded of something that I just didn't think of until today at the scrimmage. A team that wants to run their offense (this is what Urbandale does) is a team you must slow the ball swings and get more in the passing lanes. While a team such as ours, where we are looking to attack more with the dribble, you may not need to get in the lanes so much as keep it out of the lane with the dribble. Either way I'm convinced that both keeping the ball out of the lane is something we must stop defensively and improve upon offensively.

Some individual things that happened today were also quite obvious. Colin lost his man in transition quite often; he also got back cut at least three times. That tells me he is watching the ball too much and doesn't have a sense for where his man is, again, maybe a sign that because of our own offensive structure that requires more spacing and less movement we need special emphasis on movement in our shell. Brandon Esterbrook tended to dribble once and pick the ball up or hold it too long on offense; he also got lost a couple of times on defense with the offensive movement. It's a given, once the ball is dribbled it should finish with a shot or a pass immediately! Both Brandon and Colin shot the ball pretty well. Zach Morgan, who didn't play much, did play pretty well. So did Justin Pothoven; he just didn't get in very much. Coach Core is setting playing time by practice stats. He is playing the guys that rebound and get defenses touches in practice. If you want to play, this is what you have to do. I think we found a post player in Kirk. He is pretty solid for a kid who played in his first varsity scrimmage. Andrew is a worker and hustler; he doesn't finish as well as Kirk or have quite the floor awareness, but it's hard not to like a guy that works and hustles.

I still don't see as much aggression out of Jesse as I'd like, especially when we get the ball to him on the break (he did get better as the scrimmage went on). He, Colin, and Brock have been our point guards, and if they aren't aggressive with the ball, we as a whole aren't aggressive. Brock was definitely not the same player that we have been seeing in practice. He shot only once and didn't play very assertive basketball. In their defense I will say that our wings are not looking back for the ball very well either; it makes it tough to kick it ahead if the wings aren't running to get in front of the ball (instead jogging along beside it) or if they don't look back when they are ahead.

Our 20 (even) out-of-bounds play underneath is an adventure. We almost never set up our man to really come off the double screen to get open. We are running past the screen as though it isn't there. By mistake today our post man that pops out high set a screen for the guard coming around and got him open; maybe this is an adjustment to put in.

As I mentioned, we must stop turning the ball over. We also must make a decision faster with the ball in the quarter-court. We must either catch and shoot it, penetrate the defense with the dribble or the pass, and we must do it within two seconds. We are hanging onto the ball too long and allowing the defense to recover. The only place we want to keep the ball for longer than two seconds is in the post; there they can keep it as long as they want. Additionally, our floor balance must get better. At the end of our scrimmage I saw four guys running to the ball with no one staying opposite the ball for a ball reversal. I think we will put in a very simple Louisville offense tomorrow to give us some work on balance and just little more structure. This will still allow the kids to play rather than being bound by a pattern.

It's off to the Knoxville Shootout, more later tonight.

Friday, November 24 (7:00 P.M.)
The Turkey Shootout, Twin Cedar, Guarding Your Man, and Four Out One In

We played Twin Cedars. I think the final score was something like 40-12. We won. We had them out-gunned to say the least. We shot 65% from the field (seven lay-ups) had nine offensive rebounds and gave up zero. We turned the ball over four times while turning them over 15 times, all of this in one half of "basketball" (using the term loosely). It was men against boys. We had bigger, faster, stronger athletes that had played much more basketball.

Individually Klarc was 5-9, Kaleb 0-2, Kirk 2-4 Colin 7-8, Jesse 1-1, Brock 0-1, Tyler Terlouw 0-1, Tyler Linn 0-2, Andrew didn't shoot, Justin 0-1, C.J. 1-1, Brandon E. 0-1, Zach 1-2, Nate 0-1 and Peter 0-3.

I definitely feel that Brock was better tonight than this morning. He was my most-improved player from then until now. He was also the best at getting the ball up the court in hurry, as the point guard. I'd like to get the ball up as fast as we can even after a made shot.

The stats that I have the kids keep are just team turnovers, free throws, shots, and offensive rebounds. I also have them keep individual shooting for both teams. Coach Core keeps the other stats and reviews the tape when he gets home to be as accurate as he can be.

Our fast-break is still not top notch. It's hard to run when our fastest man down the court is our ball handler. Either the ball handler is complaining about the wings not being open, or the wings are saying the ball handler isn't passing when they're open.

There is not much to tell. We started slowly, but once we figured out we were better we got more aggressive. We got out in the passing lanes this time because TC was not attacking with the dribble but trying to swing the ball from side to side with the pass. We need to find a balance between pressuring the passing lanes and keeping the ball out of the paint with the dribble. This is where our kids need to make individual adjustments as to whether they are guarding a driver or a shooter. Make the driver shoot and the shooter drive.

We talked prior to the game about the importance of guarding your own man and not getting help. Initially Jesse lost his man two or three times, Brock allowed a straight line to the basket, as did Tyler Linn, Brandon stayed too long in help, but it's pretty hard to be really critical when your team gives up only 12 points in a half.

We also made a small adjustment by going with a four-out-and-one-inside set. Kirk stayed closer to the lane while the other players played the perimeter area. I thought we did okay with this, too.

I had an "I wonder moment" tonight. It went like this: sometimes I wonder if the kids know that we are all on the same side, and it's not the coaches vs. the players.

Saturday, November 25, Practice #10
Saturday Meetings, Handle Your Man, B-Mo, Who Are Our Players, Justin, Kaleb, and Colin Give It Up and Don't Forget the Presses

I asked them that very question the next day. I didn't wait for an answer but instead tried to help them understand that while it may seem that we want different things because we don't always agree with the method to make things happen, ultimately we want the same team goal—get to the state tournament.

Notice I said the same team goal. As a coach and a father of a player I found out that in order for me to be happy, our team and my son had to play pretty well for me to be happy. So if a *coach* feels that way, I know that *parents*, regardless of winning or losing, will almost always think of their son before the team.

After every game or scrimmage that we have we have a sit-down meeting with the players. Mark talked about effort and attitude and the opportunity to do other things in life if you don't have the correct attitude about playing for this team. We are looking for people that put out tremendous effort and have a team attitude. I almost always talk to kids about worst-case scenario. I know that if they are first team all state and average 30 points per game they are probably going to have a pretty good attitude. On the other hand, if they sit on the bench, never play, and rarely spend much time on the court during practice there is a very good chance they might struggle with their attitude. And therein lies the question: if it is worst-case scenario for you, then what? What can you get out of this season? And, if the player's answer is, "Nothing," or something similar to that, he should probably consider doing something else.

I talked more about defending your own man. To me that is just a by-product of playing aggressively. Unselfish defense is caring enough about your teammates that when your man gets the ball you don't want to put your teammates in the kind of spot that they must help and possibly lose their own man. Aggressive defense is a mind set that comes to a young man that is driven (not frightened) by a challenge, and that challenge is: stop your man. I just feel as though we are actually helping too much.

We then did a little warming up and then proceeded with practice by running a couple of set plays, one against a zone called Open (explained earlier) and the other against a man-to-man called Cyclones, also mentioned earlier. After that we reviewed our out-of-bounds plays underneath the basket. We really like our out-of-bounds plays to be the same play against a man or a zone. We ask the boys to adjust their cuts according to the gaps in the zone.

The practice started pretty poorly. I think we have a number of players that spent a late night out. Their legs also have to be a little bit shot because they have played a 90 minute scrimmage and a half a game Friday.

B-Mo (Brandon Caldwell) comes back Monday! I am pumped about that. I know that B-Mo is pretty pumped too. B-Mo gives us not only another big man but he also gives us a senior with experience and a winning attitude.

Tyler Linn is really having a hard time this morning. This is the type of practice that could take him out of contention for playing time. Right now we are looking for anything to separate our pack of wings. Soon we must know who are going to be the players that should have playing time in games. We need to get this done soon so we can give them the most repetitions. Right now the reps are pretty even; we just can't afford to do that much longer. Jesse showed up today with a hip flexor injury. He had the same injury to the other hip last year. That, too hurts his chances just because it allows other players an opportunity to get better while he sits. And as he sits, there is really no standing still; you are either getting better or getting worse. He is probably losing ground.

Our driving line drill is a one-on-one drill from about nineteen feet from the hoop. The offense is limited to two dribbles. Coach Core runs this drill by lining up four or five players, and they just alternate attacking each other. I would prefer to have the kids pair up and keep score so it becomes a win-loss situation. I just think we would get better effort. Besides I want to see who wants to compete regardless of who wins. I've told him this before, but we are somewhat limited by space. But I will tell him again. Don't get me wrong; he is the one that gets the big $$$ (yeah right). He is actually the one who takes all the heat if things don't go right and he needs to do and does what he thinks is best. But I made a decision a long time ago that when I first became an assistant coach that I was not going to be a yes man. When I was the head man I really wanted opinions. I really wanted honest opinions regardless of whether they agreed with my opinion. Besides, if I just agreed with everything Mark does, what good would I be? I feel it's my job to give the head coach honest feedback. And depending how strongly I feel about it tells me how many times I should suggest it to Mark. There also comes a point when the head coach is going to get tired of hearing something, especially when it's obvious he has made a decision. The assistant also has to understand that just because he suggests it doesn't mean the head man has got to do it. It also doesn't mean that the assistant is correct.

Wow, do we a do a great job in a drill that was designed to keep the ball out of the post! Kaleb, our Creighton recruit and all-state player was diving on the ground to keep the ball out of there. He knows he is going to not only start but also play heavy minutes, he really doesn't have to do it, but he does. I think maybe he knows this is his senior year. By the way, Colin did the same. Neither Colin nor Kaleb are what you would call, "beefy" players, but they were giving up their bodies; I like that kind of guy.

Something as small as learning how to screen out in a free throw situation might win a game so we work on it. All of this small stuff takes time. When you work on one thing you are taking time away from working on something else. That's why the players have to be able to transfer from a drill into a game skill, the sooner the better and that is also why coaches must determine the more pressing needs to work on after reviewing games and practices.

After getting screened on our coverage to the ball (against Urbandale) we are working on what we call our Flex Shell drill. Basically, we swing the ball from one side of the court to the other as quickly as we can and then try to cut the offensive player off a screen towards the ball. The defensive man must jump to the ball as quickly as he can, or he will get screened and won't be able to defend the offensive cutter. I thought we did okay with this today but we don't set great screens like some teams.

Our four-out-and-one-man inside, man-to-man offense was not really good today. In fact, on my notes to myself I said it was really ugly. I thought we would put in our Louisville play today, but we didn't.

The one-on-one, full-court drill was adjusted to make it more of a fast-break drill, both offensively and defensively. It's different than the one-on-one ball-handling, defensive-movement drill. Really, I guess they are two different drills. But I like this one, too. The defensive player is stationed at the free-throw line and the offensive player takes the ball at the baseline and then attacks the basket at the other end of the floor. The defender can stop the ball early or drop back, his choice. We added another man later and made it two-on-two. One of the things we are trying to do is at least speed-dribble the ball up the court after every shot, even if we don't have a true fast-break.

We did not use any of our presses (ever) on Friday. On Saturday we work on all of our presses. Mark feels as though we have to establish our quarter-court man before we do anything else. I like his determination with this way of thinking but there is a danger: by not pressing enough early it will take us lots of time to establish the habit of getting into the press immediately upon scoring. And if the ball comes in before the press is set, it's like getting caught in a quarter-court rotation (not a good thing), only now it occurs full-court (a terrible thing).

Justin Pothoven and Brandon Esterbrook played with the green team today. They definitely make us more athletic. Brandon is a pretty good shooter, especially from the outside. They also make us much less experienced. I'd like to look at them a little longer with this group just to see if they are quick learners. This is really Justin's first serious look. He really adds quickness and lots of energy to our zone offense and offensive rebounding. Though, he doesn't rebound defensively very well and seems to get a little lost in some of our other things. I need to get Justin in, and just he and I should sit down and make sure that he understands everything we are doing. Remember, if we spend too much time working with the players that aren't going to play we are losing ground to other teams. What to do, what to do?

Monday, November 27

Basketball's such a psychological thing; kids aren't pawns and don't want to be treated as such. We have met with various players off and on throughout the year for many different reasons. We have captains meetings throughout the summer that mostly deal with leadership rather than specific basketball things. Meetings of some form are things that a coach had better be doing on a consistent basis if he wants to be successful. The best meetings are usually ones that are casual and seem as though they are happenstance, but may be very intentional by the coach. Lots of learning goes on with these.

Today we had more of a formal meeting with Colin about his role as a senior leader on this team. It's my opinion that Colin is such a perfectionist and so hard upon himself that sometimes it comes out as negative towards his teammates. We discussed a survey that we had done on Colin's leadership skills and how he could improve upon them. I asked him to be very intentional about the way he is going to treat himself (in a positive manner), and I also think that he needs to be proactive about this approach. By that I mean he has to think ahead, before every game and scrimmage, and decide (before the emotions get involved) how he is going to act in given situations. He needs a game plan. Colin is a good kid (really smart, too); he was very much in favor of this.

Monday, November 27, Practice #11
Ratings, B-Mo, Jesse, the List of Contenders, Our Captains and Zone Offense

I woke up this morning, grabbed the paper, and read that we were rated the number four team in the state of Iowa in class 3A. What? Maybe with all of our seniors available we'd be a top 10 team but not now. One guy does ratings at *The Register*; he sends out a survey, asks a few questions about who is back, and then comes out with a rating. Ratings are fun for people to talk about; they tend to be pretty tough on coaches. Besides, sometimes these ratings are just foolish. One of our local sports writers (who is a great guy and a friend) was a wrestler. This guy truly works at his job and cares about being accurate, but

I think if you would ask he would tell you that his ratings would be mostly a guess.

We started practice with a number of warm-up drills. For a Monday practice we look pretty sharp, when oftentimes Mondays tend to be slow and sluggish early. Then it dawned upon me; we have a game tomorrow. Kids get tired of beating on each other in practice; even if we aren't really ready for a game the kids need one.

I am so excited to have B-Mo back. He immediately makes us better. He is out of shape and hasn't gotten up to game speed yet, but there is no question that we need him, and he will help us. B-Mo is starting on the white team today; this alone helps us. By making them better they make our green team better.

Jesse is out today with his hip-flexor problems. He will be out for at least a week, maybe more.

C.J. struggles all day with practice. He is an effort guy (I love those kind of guys) but to give great effort requires mental toughness and conditioning. He looks tired and is making mistakes he doesn't normally make. He is also a guy that is kind of a tweener, and that doesn't help. He gives up size at the post and he gives up quickness and speed as a wing. I hope that as he matures he gains in at least one of those areas.

Brandon Esterbrook started practice with lots of energy and good decision-making. He also finished that way. Brandon was a young man that I thought had a chance to play for us this year, but until you see them on a consistent basis you never know. If he would consistently practice the way he did today, there is no question he could be at least a first line sub off the bench, maybe more.

Justin was also on the green team again today. I like his energy, but his offensive game is a little bit loose. That comes from the fact that he doesn't play a lot in the summer. If he would play and lift, there is no question that he would eventually be a player.

This time prior to the NC drill we were more adamant about getting defenders back to prevent the long pass over the top for the offense. That definitely made the drill more effective. I just wish Kaleb had said something earlier about this. But, it is better late than never saying anything about it. Yet again, Brandon E. really stuck out to me in a positive way during this drill.

It's so funny, maybe that is not the right word; it is so strange that Tyler has come to play today, while he virtually took Saturday off even though he was there physically. We have spoken with Tyler often about paying attention and consistency in his play. Today he came to play. What are we going to do with this kid? When we had our meeting earlier today we asked them who they felt like we should play at one of the wing positions. Colin was most high on Clayton (if only we could get him back) but also said Tyler. Sometimes there is a tendency for players to favor other players in their own class, but Colin had some reasons. He felt that Tyler was a solid, on-ball defender and played with an offensive style that allowed others to shine while he played much more conservatively, something that Colin felt we needed from one of the spots.

Brock also looked pretty good today. He probably does better as an offensive player when he has at least two other ball-handlers with him on his same team. He really helps us as an extra ball handler in this situation. If we are playing a pressing team, he might be a guy that needs to play a little more. When he is the point guard and handles the ball the majority of the time he sometimes struggles with that. One of his major weaknesses however is his screen out; he is in a bad habit of watching the ball hit the rim on the shot rather than forgetting the ball and finding his man to screen out.

At the end of practice in preparation for tonight's game we ran through all of our offensive zone stuff and man-to-man stuff. Coach Core added a simple counter to the Cyclone play. I like it in that we don't have to call it; rather it is a read by the post player. The kids did a pretty good job with it.

I don't write much about Klarc and Kaleb it seems like. We just rarely need to say anything to them and rarely need to do major corrections with them. Man, when they were just pups on the varsity team, it was a never-ending dialog about things that they needed to do differently. My expectations for those guys is pretty high, and when they do something that is really just pretty darn good I probably don't say enough about it because of these expectations. At the end of practice I did. They have been very good captains this year, in both a verbal sense and an effort way.

One of the things that used to be a no-no in yesteryear was using the dribble against a zone. Nowadays it is the way to go, especially against a team that plays a laning zone or a zone that gets out into the passing lanes. The one stipulation about the dribble is that it needs to be an attacking dribble that drives the ball into a gap and at the basket. There is a tendency for kids to take a meaningless, sideways, one dribble that tends to reduce the offensive attack. We are adamant about the attack dribble.

If a team packs it in and allows easy swing passes, there is probably less need for it; the ball can move quickly with an undefended pass. A packed in zone is probably going to give you a few more open, outside shots because it is so concerned about protecting the middle. Nonetheless, during our zone work today we limited players to using the dribble drive as a means of offensive execution. It was an area that at one time was a weakness for us. I hope this year it will be strength.

Right at the end of practice tonight we added a very simple Louisville offense. It is an offense designed to spread and balance the floor and gives us just a bit of motion before we get into our motion O. I like it. We didn't add this to use tomorrow, but just to make it easier when we start practicing it later—they've at least seen it now.

We (the coaches) have decided to talk less prior to our games in the pre-game talks. So today after practice Mark told them about his desire to see a great defensive team and let the offense take care of itself. And I spoke of us being a smart team that is able to make adjustments during the game. Coaches are limited to the number of timeouts they may call, if players don't learn to think the game, it may be too late by the next timeout to make much of a difference. Besides, by thinking and suggesting during the game players take more ownership. When you can get your players to take ownership, they will put out their best effort.

Bus leaves at 5:00 for a boy/girl double header at Knoxville tonight—be there.

Chapter 3—The Regular Season Begins

Tuesday, November 28, Game #1, Pella at Knoxville

Knoxville snuck in a game before us on Monday night. For them now it works both ways. They have experience on us, but they also should have legs that are more tired than ours. We shall see. By the way, Knoxville opened with a win over South Tama by 25 points.

We are starting the three Korvers, (Kaleb, Kirk, and Klarc) along with Colin and Brock. This lineup is based upon what Coach Core refers to as Blue Collar stats that he has kept in practice. They are—the number of touches a player gets on the ball while he is on defense and the number of rebounds he gets.

I am currently watching the tape of this game the following day on Wednesday. As a coach you try to stat certain things and watch carefully for other things to give you a sense of what is going on in the game. But watching tape allows you to slow down situations and see what is really going on. Frequently it's the last thing you want to do because you are tired or just got done with practice and like your players, you want to get away a little bit, but really it is something you must do. And the more often you watch a tape of a game the better you will understand what happens and then hopefully make appropriate adjustments. It's like this, you go to work the next day after getting home late from the game. Then go to practice, then eat supper, then go watch film. Then it's time to go to bed, and the next day you can do the same thing all over again, and then you add on the fact that you must get ready for another game. Oh, by the way, you wake up in the middle of the night thinking of things too. Ah, the great life.

We started the game on a positive note with a good drive to the hole by Boswell. But then Kirk on their possession, gave up a baseline drive to the basket for an easy lay-up.

Then we got up five-two on a three from Brock. Our fast-break that we have spent a lot of time on is non-existent; the question is, why?

Our defense is trying to extend out against this patterned offense. But we are having a hard time finding the balance of getting into the passing lanes before the catch but backing off to keep them out of the lane after they catch. This continues to haunt us all night long. Brock is our best at playing the passing lanes, but he is also one of our worst about giving up the dribble drive. Knoxville makes us pay for this by getting to the free-throw line. They are not making a lot of shots but they are putting us in position to foul.

We, on the other hand, got to the free-throw line rarely in the first half. We got there more in the second half but shot only 38% from the line. Wow, some of our best shooters were struggling there!

What I liked about our offense was the fact that we did a good job of attacking their defense with the dribble. What I didn't like was the fact that we took too long to make a decision on what to do with the ball, we took too many dribbles to get to the basket, we attacked before we moved the defense (oftentimes this resulted in a one-on-two situation), and we tried to force difficult passes that weren't there rather than throw easy passes to a completely open man.

This is a quiz—why would a player throw a difficult pass rather than just make a simple play by throwing the ball to a wide-open man? And the answer is 1) They don't have the ability to see the floor, 2) They rush the offense and try to make a play that isn't there because they are impatient, or 3) The only passes they see on ESPN are the great passes. Those are the passes that players complete about one out of ten times. Unfortunately, they don't show the nine others that were thrown away. In a lot of ways these are selfish passes. Why? Because the passer is interested in drawing attention to himself with the pass, that's why. I digress. In my mind the answer is a combination of the three things, but I really think a lot of it has to do with #3: too much ESPN passing.

For the first half we shot 47%—not bad, just not enough shots. We only took 18 shots in the first half. Actually we took only 36 for the game; they took 29 but shot four more free throws, and they were shooting 31% at half.

In the locker room we talked about screening out on defense and about getting some ball movement. We came out and did just that. Both of our first two possessions ended up in pretty good shots because of that, but we just missed. From that point out we reverted back to our first-half style.

B-Mo has played in this game but sparingly. When he comes the biggest thing I notice is that we've added a defensive rebounder that helps keep Knoxville off the board. For a while the only guy getting any defensive rebounds was Kaleb.

With 4:16 left in the game we are down three points 37-34. With 2:58 left we are still down at 38-40. We run Cyclones down two with 2:27 left in the game. Kaleb makes a nice pass to Klarc, slipping down the lane after screening to tie the game up at 40-40.

To get back in the hunt we went to our pressing defense that seemed to make us a little better. We created some uncertainty for them and made us a little more aggressive because we turned them over. We had the ball with just seconds left in the game with a two-point lead but they turned us over. So with 2.9 seconds left Knoxville had the ball and called back-to-back timeouts to set up their play. They had the ball 84 feet from their own hoop. Thank goodness for us, they missed a half-court buzzer-beater, and we hung on to win 42-40.

Offensively, this was really an ugly game for us. Defensively, we did okay until they shot; then we forgot to block out and rebound.

Our unofficial shooting stats were: Kaleb 5-10, Klarc 3-9, Kirk 3-4, Colin 2-6, Brock 2-5, Tyler Linn 0-1, and B-Mo 1-3. Brandon E., Justin, and Zach all played, although not much, they did not shoot.

Wednesday, November 29

I got to school this morning and was really in kind of an ugly mood after thinking about the game. Yeah we won, but what made me the angriest was our lack of a fast-break. I spoke with both Klarc and Coach Core about it and suggested that we either make some position changes or we forget the fast-break and concentrate on a secondary break (this is really just an early offense as soon as the ball gets down the court) or that we not break at all. I hate that; I love to run, but it makes some sense. If we aren't going to run, we are wasting lots of time in practice doing things that we will never use. We could use that same time in the quarter-court getting better at that part of the game.

I knew my position changes weren't going to fly. I think Coach thinks this is the best spot for all involved. But to me, if we are going to try something, now is the time, not later in the year. As far as the rest goes, I don't want to give up on the break; I love that part of the game, and I hated to suggest it.

(Later that day) By the way, looking at today's practice schedule, we aren't giving up. Deep down, I'm glad.

(Later yet that day) Whoa, Coach Core just came in and said that maybe that radical idea I had this morning didn't seem quite so radical this afternoon. Mark is a good coach for this program. He is continually looking to become a better coach and make his team a better team.

Wednesday, November 29, Practice #12
Injuries, Clayton, Rebounding, Position Changes, More Break, More Press, Tyler Linn, Post Touches, and the Weather

The pickings are a little slim when we start practice. Kaleb and Kirk both were at the chiropractor. Kirk is having troubles with his foot, and Kaleb, his ankle. They got to practice at about 3:45 (practice starts at 3:30). Kaleb was not able to practice at all. The chiropractor thinks that he will be able to play on Friday. Kaleb doesn't sound quite as convinced. Brandon Esterbrook and Brock were both on a field trip with a class out of town, and the bus was running late. They got off the bus at about 3:30. Finally, Klarc had a slight physical problem as well, and our trainer Rob Blom cautioned him to be smart about it.

Because of these problems and distractions Mark's practice plan kind of went down the drain.

Clayton Boeyink has decided to try non-contact practice today. The doctors have been suggesting to him that his injury might be a sports-hernia. He says he has all the symptoms. He's got an appointment on the 5th with a specialist. I asked why he didn't wait until after the appointment, and he said, "If it's a hernia it's a hernia; I'm just getting tired of sitting, and I want to play." He looked a little out of shape. He told me after practice it was okay. I don't really think it was. He is such a good athlete; he would really help us if he could play. If for no other reason, for his sake I wish he could play.

Because of our deficiencies in rebounding during the Knoxville game Coach Core is putting the kids through a series of rebounding drills. We had four rebounding drills, all back to back. Unfortunately, later on I don't see much carry over into a five-on-five situation. We are still watching the ball in flight rather than finding our man to box out. This is a difficult habit to break, but one we must if we are to be a good team.

After our discussion this morning Coach Core has decided to try some position changes for our transition game. I'm really thankful for that; I don't think I can coach a team that doesn't at least try to run. In 35 years of coaching I've never done that; we've not always run well, but we've always tried. I still think this should be a huge strength for this team if we can get our problems ironed out.

We are moving Klarc to point guard, Colin to the wing, B-Mo to the wing, Kaleb to the middle of the floor and the first post down, and Kirk to a trail post. This is pretty radical, but I think this is the way to go. Klarc loves the ball in his hands, and he is a physically strong player that hopefully will look up court. Colin, who had been playing the point, knows the frustrations of wings not getting ahead of the ball on the break. Hopefully because of this knowledge he will run hard at the wing. B-Mo, who hasn't practiced all year, was one of our hardest runners at the wing (with no practice) and he loves the corner baseline area on offense so he will be sprinting there. Kirk who is still a maturing athlete that will gain speed as he gets older doesn't have to get to the baseline on the other end, as he will trail to the top of the key. Ultimately, I would think that Kaleb, who had been at the wing, would have an advantage in speed against a defensive post in the transition period. Moreover, this puts Kaleb in the middle of the floor on the baseline for a split second and thus will give us good screen angles for our outside players to screen down for him. Klarc and Kirk would just be opposite each other depending on which wing the ball ends up being passed to. Hopefully, we would get some shots in transition before we get to this point.

To further encourage the proper attitude about sprinting the floor (attitude is, after all, the most important thing we can develop about running) the kids are running our one-break with a rule that states they must shoot the ball within five seconds of acquiring the defensive rebound; now that is moving.

Incidentally, the one-break drill is a five-on-five drill that is both a quarter-court drill and a full-court drill. The offensive team's first possession is a fast-break, designed to encourage a quick aggressive, attacking shot. Regardless of a make or a miss, the same offensive team gets the ball back, and they run a quarter-court offense. Now the current defensive team becomes the new offensive team on the shot; whether they get a defensive rebound or they are taking the ball out of bounds they are trying to score on a fast-break to the other end, and then they will get the ball back to run their quarter-court offense. We run this drill to encourage the break and to work on our set offenses.

We then spent time working a little bit on the Louisville offense for the second time. This offense will give us some starting positions and help organize us a little bit. It will also set up some simple screens and cuts. At the same time it will allow the boys to just play the game rather than get into the option one, option two modes.

Just what we needed: Tyler Linn goes down with an ankle sprain. It looks pretty bad. Tyler had just explained to Coach Core that he felt that he was just now rounding out into basketball shape. What is it with all of these injuries? I learned a long time ago: you can coach the kids you have or whine about the ones that you don't. The better option is to coach your kids.

Mark spoke with the kids about our post feeds: the number of times we got the ball into the post with a pass. We had zero in the first half and three for the game. We did get the ball in the lane often with the dribble but obviously not often enough by throwing it into the post players. As I've mentioned before, it is important for our offense (any offense) to get the ball into the paint.

Our press defense was next. This was one of the keys for us against Knoxville. We didn't run it all game until the end, and then it worked for at least one turnover and created for us a more aggressive mind set. Even though we work on it a lot in practice we want to establish our defensive priority as the quarter-court man-to-man defense. We don't want any confusion about that in the player's mind. Hopefully we've done that now, and I'm guessing that it won't be long before we will be using this more in games.

We finished practice with some brief work on our out-of-bounds plays, which included putting in our 20 (odd) series. All of the out-of-bounds plays so far are initiated out of the same set so that our opponents will not anticipate the cuts we are about to make.

To add to the mix now the weather is bad outside. We decided we needed to stop practice early to get the kids home before it got worse. No day is wasted in practice, but this one certainly challenged our team and us.

Thursday, November 30, Practice #13
Two-on-Two Rush, Thinking, Holding the Ball, Block Outs, On-ball-screens, Kirk and Andrew, Press O and D, and Ankle Problems

Started practice with more rebounding and then went to lay-ups, the reach-back, and lay-back type. Next we went to three on two in the quarter-court.

We are always looking for good drills to break the game down in to small increments. We don't want drills just for the sake of doing something; we want them to pertain to what we are trying to accomplish with our team. But with so many kids that have been around for a while, Mark thinks that it is important that we try some new drills occasionally so they don't get bored. Thus a new drill called the two-on-two rush was introduced.

I got this rush drill from the men's coach of DePaul at a clinic. It is quite rare that I am smart enough to come up with a drill of my own. But I feel as though I am smart enough to recognize other coach's drills that we could use to get better. This drill is a good combo drill that we get a number of things accomplished: full-court speed dribbling, offensive tip-ins, conditioning, guarding a receiver, and finishing with a two-on-two, full-court attack. I like the drill, except like the NC drill, the defense has to be smart enough to stop the inbounds pass from going over the top of them so we don't just give up a full-court lay-up. Wow, that is not exactly a deep thought; sometimes I guess if we have to tell them things like that some of our players have moments of not real deep thinking as well.

After this drill we went to the one-on-one driving line and then partner-drill shooting. It just amazes me that for a guy that has been coaching this long that I don't see things sooner in our practice season; I must be a slow learner. We are just flat-out holding the ball too long before we make our attack in the driving line drill. We would like the players (in ball games) to move the ball within about two seconds. In this drill we are sometimes faking before we attack, and then at times we take two or three dribbles before we shoot. The dribbles alone have to take at least two seconds. We are actually practicing holding on to the ball too long—that is not good. It's working, too; that is definitely one of the things I've seen this year: we don't move the ball quickly enough. Within this drill, upon the catch, the next move (including the look at the basket) should be made immediately or in conjunction with the offensive move. We should never catch, stand, and then move.

We ran the shell #1. Added to this shell was a must-shoot rule if the whistle blew. This was done so that we get more work on rebounding and blocking out. During the first shot zero out of four players blocked out. That too, unfortunately, was very game like. Kirk really struggles with this. I jumped him about this, and he was about to give me all the reasons that he didn't do it, and then he stopped and just shook his head; he knew he goofed—I like that kid!

Knoxville also exposed us with their on-ball screens. We needed more work on handling them. We also made a change on how to handle them. The man being screened now is supposed to get in the back pocket of the dribbler and follow him around so he doesn't get caught up in our hedge help. We also added on the weak side of the floor (the opposite side of where the ball is) a back screen or a flare screen for this drill. This adds to the movement of the offense and creates more difficult circumstances for our defense.

I watched Kirk and Andrew specifically while we blocked out during a free-throw drill. They still play too soft. They are sophomores, and in sophomore ball what I'm asking them to do (which is to play more physically) would be a foul, but in varsity ball it isn't. We need them to play this way.

We are now shooting free throws and then dropping back into a full-court press. While our press doesn't look too bad our press offense by our first team doesn't look too good. This is a first for Klarc as our point and Colin as a wing. Brock didn't think he should break to the middle of the press while on offense because he said his defender was already there. That is wrong. The offense must break middle just if for no other reason than to squeeze them inside even further so we can make a quick swing to the other side of the floor if the pass isn't there. They need more time at this; I sure hope Boone doesn't press.

We then ran the one-break drill and tried the Louisville play against the zone; it didn't look too bad. We also practiced Open against the zone. One of the guys I noticed during this portion of practice was Zach Morgan. He seems like he's got a little more hop in his git-along today.

Coach Core puts the kids in last-second game situations at the end of practice. One time they are up in score, but it's close, the next time down close, and the next time it is tied. He does a side out-of-bounds situation. With this we conclude practice.

Kaleb and Tyler Linn both sit out practice with sprained ankles. Clayton continues in his injured way, but does have an upcoming appointment with a specialist. Even Klarc, who is practicing, has a discolored ankle.

We have a game tomorrow at Boone.

Friday, December 1, Game #2 at Boone
Our Record: 1-0; Conference: 1-0
Clayton, #33, Officials, New Coach, Bubble Guys, Rocket Ships, Block Outs, and Individual Stuff

Just an update before the game: Clayton Boeyink came in this morning and said he got an MRI set up. Now he can take the results to the specialist. He said his mom was on the phone almost all day convincing people to do the MRI before he saw the specialist rather than after.

Boone returns a really nice player, a kid that wears #33 and is one of their post players. Number 33 is quite an athlete. He is a good football player and track guy; therefore he rarely runs out of gas. He is a guy we have to slow down if we are to win the game. I think in one game last year we held him to around 30!

Wow, for the first time I recognize the officials at Boone. And we've got some of the best in the state. That is a real treat for us here; it seems like we've had some very strange calls at this place.

Boone also has a new coach. He is a guy that is definitely a type-A coach. I think that Boone would be a very difficult place to coach. Their shortest trip in our conference is at least an hour. Most of their trips would be closer to an hour and a half. For that reason alone I would think that it would be somewhat difficult to get all of your athletes out for the sport. The guys that really love round ball would be out, but the guys that are on the bubble would probably not. Those guys on the bubble and not out for the team could easily make a difference in how good the team is going to be.

When I was a young coach I thought that I needed all of my players to make basketball their number-one sport. Now I realize how foolish that is. Don't get me wrong; you had better have at least two or three of your starters feel that way. Those are usually the guys that will be your best scorers because they are out shooting and playing in the summer. But those other bubble guys are often guys that do so many of the other things. Getting those guys out means that you've added athletes. You need to practice against good competition or it will be difficult to be good. Secondly, a number of those athletes are the guys that do the other things besides score—again because this isn't what they are good at (they haven't practiced it enough). We have had a lot of success at ole PHS with these kinds of guys starting and playing important minutes for us.

Our line up tonight is Klarc, Kaleb, Kirk, B-Mo, and Colin. I asked Kaleb about his ankle before the game, and he said it's taped so tight I can't feel it, and I'm ready to go. This is B-Mo's first start, and remember too we've changed our positions. With this lineup we are moving Brock to the bench. I have been really pleased and pleasantly surprised by his play. He had good practices up to the Urbandale scrimmage, then really played quite poorly in that scrimmage. But he rebounded at the shootout and then again against Knoxville in our first game.

First play of the game is Colin attacking the basket on the dribble in a fast-break situation; he got fouled. This is a good sign, first a true fast-break and then the foul.

The first time down the court defensively wasn't quite so good. We weren't matched up with the man we were guarding. This seems so junior high to me, but it seems like we go through this almost every year. One year we had entering players hand towels to people they were going in for in an attempt to get them to communicate with each other about things like who they were guarding or what defense we were in, etc. This time there was no subbing involved; we just didn't get matched up because we didn't communicate with each other. Also, one of the things we've been emphasizing in practice is the block out; neither Kirk nor Colin blocked out, so within seconds of the opening tip they were both on the bench. Coach Core is making a point.

We get lost in our match-ups at least three more times during this game! This might be one of the weakest parts of our defensive game.

We are like rocket ships on our break. I mean, we are flying down the court. The kids have responded.

Unfortunately now we are having a hard time throttling back. Our quarter-court offense is way too rushed. We are taking quick shots, sometimes without any passing at all. At times we are one on five. I whispered this to Mark during the game, and like me he knows that the kids are doing what they were asked to do, and he doesn't want to confuse them now. I definitely want to talk with them about this at half.

We actually go two-three zone for about four possessions in a row. They hit two three-point shots while we are in it, and we get two stops. Even in a zone you can match up towards a good shooter. Kaleb (the old veteran) did that. On the other side of the zone we seemed to lose him. You don't see Pella High in a zone very often. I used to refer to this as the Z-word, like it was a bad word to say. I'm not doing that anymore, because it is our plan to practice and implement a zone defense into the arsenal this year. It will definitely catch other teams off guard; they usually just work on their man offense the week they play against us.

We started off the game by pressing during every dead-ball situation. But it didn't take long before we had to get out of our man/zone presses. We haven't practiced enough against various offensive sets, and we continually lose our men and give up something cheap.

During the first quarter we gave up only one or two offensive trips into the paint by Boone. That is a tremendous improvement for us. One of them was a runner right at the end of the first quarter when we didn't hedge out to help; the score is 10-9, our favor at the end of the first quarter.

I mentioned that we'd like to get Kirk to be more physical. Early in the second quarter he literally gets thrown out of bounds by their #54.

Kaleb (our best free-throw shooter from last year) was one-six vs. Knoxville. Tonight he goes two-two the first time he goes to the line.

Let me tell you about a good attitude. Brock had a breakaway lay-up, and he missed it. He had two options: hang his head or sprint back. He sprinted back. It's almost worth it to me for him to have missed that shot, just so I could see his response to it; he is moving up in my book. Now if only we could get him to stop giving up the straight-line-penetration dribble drive.

We have done a much better job this game of tracking down loose balls. I think this comes from a more aggressive mind set on both ends of the floor and with our attacking mode on defense.

The score at half is 20-17 Pella.

We are playing well on the defensive end, but still we spent a few minutes talking about that end of the court. Mark and I both talked about the offensive end. We want them to continue to be rocket ships on the way down the court, then if we don't have something right away, move the ball around, make the extra pass like we did this summer. We will see if the kids can make an adjustment. We allow, even encourage the players to speak up about what they are seeing. Colin mentioned the need to get the ball into the post. Good teams can adjust quickly to their situations. We shall see.

Speaking of Colin, he got hot in the third quarter and knocked down three, three-pointers. That extra pass that we are now throwing during our quarter-court offense caused all of these. We have a much better combination of running the ball up the floor and operating a quarter-court offense.

During the third quarter Brock had an amazing series of fakes at the ball. This really impresses me. These are the kind of little things that go unnoticed and the only reason a player would do this is because he wants his team to win. I promise you it will not make the papers, and the fans sure won't notice it; shoot, his parents won't even understand it. But this is a great way to slow an offensive dribbler and help your teammate. He also had a great hustle play in the third quarter where he tipped the ball away, dove on the floor for the recovery, and then passed the ball off of his seat to a teammate.

The score was 26-24 with about three minutes left in the third.

The Magic Move and the Brunner Move were both in evidence this game. B-Mo in particular has perfected this move, and it is turning into baskets and foul shots. Z-Mo came in and gave us short bursts of good minutes. He even had a spinner under the basket. He was so wide open when he came out of the spin I think it goofed him up, because he missed a wide-open bank shot.

We're up 36-32 at the end of the third.

I really like the looks of Louisville. We need to work in practice on a team taking away our pass back to the post so that we will know what to do if that happens. I know it will happen; the more effective we become with this, the more other teams will scout us and try to take it away. We also got a couple of post ups out of this. Klarc really likes this option. A smaller player is guarding him, and Klarc is used to playing in the post.

Brandon Esterbrook just had one of those games that nothing seemed to go right. He has times in practice when he can do no wrong. Needless to say, he is a bit streaky. Brandon was also matched up initially when he first came into the game with #33. That is not a good match-up. I was really proud of Kaleb because he made a switch with Brandon. Two years ago, shoot, last year Kaleb would have never done that. He didn't have the confidence to guard a good offensive player. I personally think he could be a shut-down defender this year if he would concentrate on the defensive end.

Klarc has done an amazing job on #33. He finishes something like 4-11 from the field, and I don't think he made any free throws.

B-Mo is the only guy that took a charge. I think last year he had at least double the amount of charges taken than the number-two charge taker on our team.

We are up 47-40 with three minutes left and finish the game with a 51-42 margin.

We shot 35% compared to their 54%, but we only turned it over five times while they turned it over 20 times. We also held them to one offensive rebound and one made free throw!

Kaleb didn't shoot well but he sure did a lot of good things for us, not the least of which was rebound on the defensive boards. Kirk was three-five with his shooting. B-Mo didn't shoot especially well but hit some huge three-pointers and went to the line often. I really liked Klarc at point; we got a great push, and I liked Colin at the wing. He ran the floor and got shots because the defense wasn't focused upon him as a main ball handler. Brock didn't shoot worth a hoot, but I've already mentioned a number of things I liked about his game. Andrew and Zach just go out and do the dirty work and don't seem to mind a bit; they don't really look to shoot.

Meeting and walk through tomorrow at 10. It's 1:00 A.M., and I just got done writing up my notes. I'll need to be there by about 9:30 to get organized.

Saturday, December 2, 10:00 A. M., Meeting

We almost always meet on Saturday the day after a Friday game. Most of the time the meeting is a review of last night's game and a really short scouting report about our next opponent.

I'm not a big fan of the scouting report, at least not one that we would share with the kids. I especially am opposed to these reports early in the basketball season. I don't mind knowing a little bit about what our opponent likes to do on the offensive and defensive ends of the floor. And I don't mind knowing who their top-scoring players are or how they like to score (outside jumpers, or drives or post up, etc.) but that is about it. Once about a hundred years ago when I first got to Pella our next game was against Pella Christian, a really good basketball program right here along with us in Pella. This was my first season with Pella High, and along with the head coach at that time (George Wares) and the players—they had put together a lengthy and detailed scouting report about PC. It may have been even more detailed than normal because the players played against each other in the summer as well.

During the course of the week that first year as we prepared to play Pella Christian we discussed their personnel and went through all of the various situations that could come in the ball games as far as offenses and defenses that we might encounter. Then we would walk through their stuff and finally we would have our second team members try to simulate PC in live situations. By the time we played them we pretty much had them and the stuff that they did down.

What I found out from that experience was that because a player did something particularly well at an earlier meeting didn't mean that he would do that same thing well in this next game. I mean, these are high school kids, for heaven's sake. I couldn't get my own kids to clean their own rooms well twice in a row. So to expect 16-to-18-year-old kids to perform consistently as to what we thought they would perform like in front of about 2,500 people (this is a big game at Pella) is crazy. So the guy we thought would shoot well may not, and the guy that we didn't think could shoot might be hot for this game. Now, if these were the pros or this was deeper into the season where the kids might have learned to be consistent performers I might feel differently, but again not early season, and they definitely are a long ways from the pros.

Another thing that I found out was that we had talked about them so often that we forgot about us. We played like we were following a script, and the script had changed and somebody forgot to tell us. That is not how basketball goes; it is an act-and-react game.

I've said to the kids before that basketball isn't rocket science. There really are only so many things available for the offenses to do. Some offenses may do it in different order or they may do it quicker or better than other offenses, but the number of things to do, while many, are not infinite. As a result, if we prepare diligently for all of these options by drilling and simulating various offensive circumstances we should be prepared for anything, regardless of whom we play. This to me is a more sound overall approach to basketball than preparing one game at a time for each individual opponent.

Back to the meeting and what transpired there. First Mark mentioned a variety of subjects about last night's game. We (Mark and I) watch tape independently and come up with our own conclusions about what transpired; I like this.

Mark first talked about Nate and C. J., who had not gotten into the game. He congratulated them on the great attitudes they had shown their teammates in spite of the fact that they had not gotten on the floor. He really feels (and I think this is a good way to say this) that the bench raises the level of those on the floor.

His next message was to all players about their actions towards officials. Basically he said we would not tolerate any inappropriate actions towards them. What is inappropriate at Pella High might be okay at some other schools. We want absolutely no outward displays at all directed in any way at anybody. Now, I'm not saying we are perfect in stopping everything, but I will say there is very little of that type of thing going on. Hopefully, shortly there will be none.

He then talked about four-on-the-floor things. One was the fact we have to read and react quicker to what our defensive man is doing (I've been harping on this one). He re-explained the four-across alignment we used at the end of the game to get the ball in against hard pressure. We hadn't done it correctly, but we hadn't ever practiced it(this year) either. He mentioned how well the boys had done at protecting the ball late in the game and then compared our turnovers from the previous game against Knoxville (19) to this game, which were seven. We'd rather shoot it and go rebound it than throw it away; if we throw it away we've got no chance. At least a shot, even a bad one, gives us a chance to rebound it.

It was then that Coach Core realized that we were missing Brandon Esterbrook. I'm not sure how late he is when he does come in. What I do know is that while the rest of the team is going to have a meeting and some walk through that doesn't even require taping, Brandon will be doing some running and working up a sweat.

Next order of business was our lack of close-outs to the shooter with our hands up. This is a difficult thing for a player to do. A close-out is the term we use for our defender who has been in a help position when his man did not have the ball and is now trying to get back to guard his man that now has the ball. The close-out starts as a sprint, and then breaks down into short, choppy steps. We want the kids to have their hands up to disrupt an outside shot, but all the time while they are running out to the offensive player they need to anticipate that their man is going to drive them. Close-outs are tough.

Coach Core thought the two-three zone did pretty well, giving up only one basket in four possessions. He also told the kids that we would do a better job with the press, and that some of the things that Boone was doing to counter our presses were things we hadn't drilled enough.

Boone ran a set play that they didn't score with, but it looked as though they could have if they would have executed it better. We first talked about how we could have defended it better, and then we talked about possibly stealing it because of the issues that it causes for the defense.

There was one thing in particular that got our attention on the bench, and Mark wanted to walk through that situation as well. It involved Brock giving up a straight-line dribble. What really made it bad was the fact that the dribbler came from about half-court. We had 40 feet to get some help or at least fakes in at the dribbler—we did neither.

Mark next reviewed another play they ran. He then made mention of a great series of fakes, all within the same defensive possession by Brock. I had told Brock the same thing last night after the game and was going to mention this in my remarks as well; it was awesome; if only we could get everyone doing that.

The last thing he talked about was the Louisville offense, and for now, anyway he wanted them to stay in the pattern to get some motion going. Last night Klarc had stopped in the pattern to post up a smaller man, a good move normally, but for now Coach Core wants to run this all the way through—changes and improvising could be done later once we are used to the play.

It was then my turn to speak. I, too, spoke first of guys who didn't play. I spoke of Andrew Barber (stat man) and made fun of the fact that he thinks he can play, and he can't. He does understand the game, and I appreciated the chart and information he was giving me. I also mention Will Lubberden, our film guy and then pointed out by name the rest of the guys who didn't play. The guys that play get enough acclaim. I want our kids to tell those other kids how important they are to our team—I'm trying to set that example. After every game I tell the players that didn't play how much I appreciate their hard work in practice.

I told them how I liked our position changes for the break, and I liked Brock's response to the starting lineup, which took him out and moved him to the bench.

One of things that I let them know that irked me was the fact that at least two or three baskets came against our defense because we weren't matched up. That is not a talent issue; we just have to talk.

I also felt like we could do a better job in the zone of knowing where the opponent's best shooter was and cheating towards that guy. Kaleb did a nice job of that; he is a veteran and was leery of the shooter, while our rookies need to get better at recognizing this.

I gave Kirk a really hard time about something I had seen in the film. Kirk had been about four feet from the baseline with inside position on his man to the basket, and the next thing I know he was standing out of bounds. He had been thrown or pushed at least four feet. Now Kirk is at least 215 pounds. Do you see the issue?

I brought up: Brock's great attitude and his response to the blown shot, our team's more aggressive fast-break attitude, our team's ability to track down loose balls because of our attitude, and B-Mo and his spin moves.

Speaking of spin moves, Z-Mo's deserved special mention and brought up some good-natured laughing and kidding. It's good to get Zachary's name out there; I like to get him to smile.

I walked them through what would happen in the Louisville offense if the other team takes away the pass to the middleman, and then I focused on three of our seniors. Klarc had a great defensive game against #33, and I wanted everyone to know that. B-Mo didn't shoot well, but I wanted everyone to know that he hit some big shots the kind that were done during crucial stages of the game. And finally I wanted to talk about Kaleb and how much he had matured from last year already. He, too, shot poorly but this year, rather than hang his head, he led us with 14 rebounds and also had taken the responsibility of guarding #33 on his own when Klarc was out; he would have never, ever done that in previous years.

My last statement was to Andrew and Zach again; I just mentioned the simple fact that they were out there doing a lot of the dirty work that won't get the headlines, and I appreciated that.

I left the gym with the squeaking of Brandon Easterbrook's shoes on the floor as he was doing his sprints. I don't think he will be late again.

Monday, December 4, Practice #14
Pella Perks, Ball Handling, Injuries, Good O or Bad D, Press, Offensive Questions and Norwalk

It seems like a lot of people both in Pella and in other communities think that the Pella High boys basketball program gets more than their fair share of perks, that somehow we are given preferential treatment. I believe that they think that because we have had a fair amount of success within the program. Ironically, this is one of the very things that seems to come up often when we (Coach Core and I) do ask for something. We are reminded of this perception and then told that it wouldn't look good and would simply add to the perception. First of all, it just simply isn't true. I have compared our situation with other coaches that I meet at clinics etc. and find out that we have about the same as they do or sometimes even less. Secondly we just really don't ask for much.

At any rate, the reason that this popped into my mind was the fact that our intramural program was in the gym with us when we started practice. We have two gyms: the older one, which is also the smaller one, and the newer one. We are in the old one with the curtain dropped, separating us from the game going on next door. This forces us to practice the short way or cross-court if we want to go full-court. We are also limited to three baskets for about eighteen players.

I am not opposed to the intramural program; I'm all for it. It is well run and well attended by our kids not out for ball. It is also just as important to the school as our basketball program is. I'm just wondering how many other programs in the state get trumped by their intramural program.

Again, I'm not complaining; today we started at 4:00, forty minutes after the end of school. It used to be that if we had late practice with only one gym we might not even start until 6:00 P.M. and not go home until 7:30 or 8:00. This is a vast improvement; I'm just saying that the perception of getting all of these perks is just flat-out wrong!

We are opening almost all of our practices now with two-ball tennis-ball dribbling followed by two-ball basketball dribbling. Mark feels that if we all can improve upon our ball handling just a little bit it would help our team.

One of the things that a good team needs is ball handling and court awareness. Without them you don't get the ball up the court, and you don't get into your offense smoothly. But this is a skill that we as a program seem to be somewhat short in. The natural tendency is for guys to go out and shoot the ball when they are little. But the very thing that would assure more players of time on the floor is something that they don't seem to want to work on, the handling of the ball. Again, is this part of that glory issue or lack thereof? I really think so.

Tyler Linn is back from his ankle injury, and for the first time since showing up on the 25th of November with a hip-flexor injury, Jesse Wineland has returned.

As we get into our layups I reflect back upon our Boone game and think of at least four of these moves occurring during that game. Two were by B-Mo and one each by Z-Mo and Klarc. By the way, three of the four turned into baskets or fouls on the opposing team.

The latest shell drill is designed to put pressure on the safety man who is the last line of defense to the basket in case the ball gets penetrated. It's called give-and-go-with-a-flash-shell drill. See the following diagram.

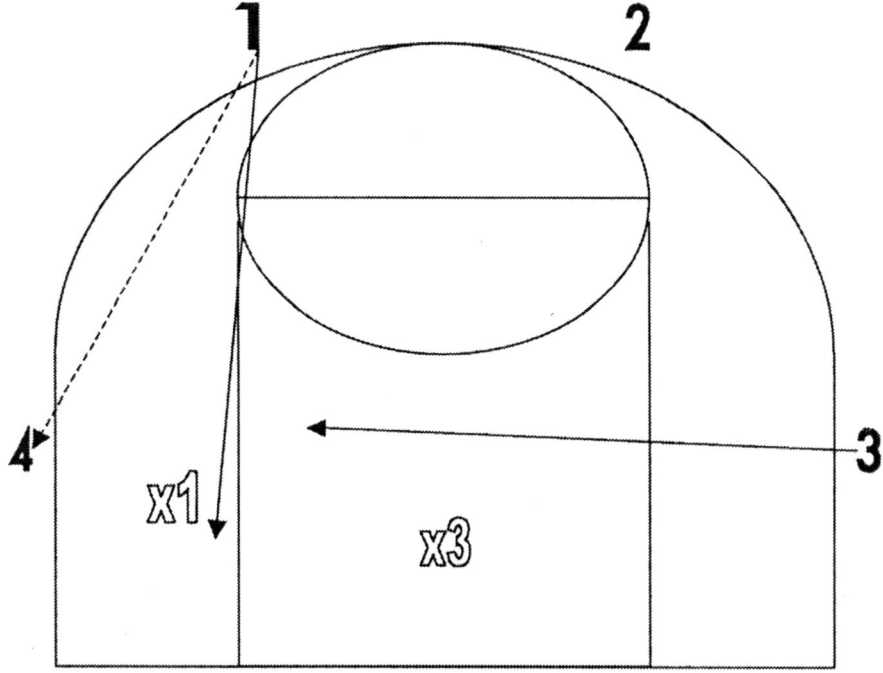

In this shell we ask x1 to defend the cutter #1 by being between his man and the ball. Since #4 just received a pass from #1 and #1 made the cut, x1 must be in the position shown. Our safety right now is x3. x3 must be in a help position (shown) in case #4 throws the ball over the top of x1. But then in this shell #3 cuts into the post area (shown)—we don't want x3 to give up that pass to his own man either; he must get in front of #3's cut. Then, if this is accomplished, we rotate people around quickly (the kids know the rotation) so that the cutters and the defenders find themselves in different positions and must react to that situation.

We always try to make things more difficult in practice situations and put kids in a position to learn to compete when it seems almost impossible to be successful. The really good players will compete ten out of ten times; most of the others won't. The really good players will go ten times, and maybe only one thing positive will happen with all of that effort; but that one thing might be the difference between winning and losing, the difference between a state championship and second place. There usually isn't a lot of difference between the two teams fighting to win a championship.

Amazingly enough we did pretty well with this shell drill. As a young coach I would have been very pleased, but now as an older coach I'm wondering why we did so well. Were we that good on defense or did we just do a poor job on offense? That is a question I continually ask myself at practice; it is also one I will often ask the kids. As a coach I don't think that you can ever be completely satisfied with what you're doing. If you are, you aren't checking both sides of the ball often enough; it would be rare indeed if the offense preformed perfectly and the defense did as well.

We are getting better at getting back in the NC drill. This is a perfect example of what I just mentioned. Earlier in the season I thought our fast-break was really good; one of the reasons for this was our performance during this drill. But it wasn't our offense that was good; it was our defense that was bad. We just weren't doing a good job of covering the long touchdown pass.

We tried placing three defenders under the basket with three offensive players surrounding the three-point arc. In this drill the manager threw the ball out to an offensive player who could catch and shoot or pass the ball. The defenders then had to make the adjustment; as one defender closed out, the other got on the line up line, and the third was a weak-side helper. We also got work on blocking out. It was a good drill.

We continue to work on both our press offense and our press defense. I would like to do something just slightly different from what Mark is asking from the defense. I will talk with him about this tomorrow. We are getting beat with the deep, over-the-top pass, and I think we could correct that if we rotate back under the basket correctly. Don't get me wrong; I believe that in order to be a good pressing team you had better get beat for a layup once in a while, or you aren't being aggressive enough; you're laying back, not taking any chances, and I think presses often necessitate taking chances.

However, I don't think it's a lack of aggressiveness as much as it is our rotation. This rotation would be more like our rotation in our man-to-man defensive rotation. The more similar we can make our defensive rules (regardless of the place on the floor) the more simple to learn, and therefore react to. Also, I would think that you have verified in your own mind that your rules are sound and logical if they are applicable most of the time regardless of down and distance (football joke).

During the next series of drills we are reviewing the various offenses we have against both the man-to-man defenses as well as the zone defenses. We tried a three-out-and-two-in offense against a man-to-man defense today. One post was at the free-throw line looking to screen on ball and the other at the block looking to post.

One of the things we haven't done against a zone yet this year is what we term as a "flash" to the open area. We actually originated a zone offense that we have used for years called "Flash." The name was derived from the thing that we wanted to occur the most—flash into the gaps that are created when a zone shifts. Our kids have run this at the lower levels as well as the varsity levels.

This year so far we have done very little; really I guess we have done none of this flashing. Just as with our man-to-man offense in years past we have done much moving and setting screens this year; we are not doing that. Rather we are spreading and dribble driving the ball in the gaps.

Offensively then we are (other than the fast-break) really doing some different things than we have done before. And how have we done? Well, based upon points, not that well. We have gotten 42 and then 51 points for an average of 46.5 points per game. This leads to a variety of questions. Is it our lack of offense, or have we played a couple of good defensive teams? We have worked hard on defense; is it just a matter of working more on the offense before they come along? Is it time to work on the offense, or do we want to establish the defense even more? While the average isn't great we did improve on points scored in our second game. Is it coming along already? Is it the quarter-court offense that we struggle with, or is more our lack of the break that is hurting our point production? Are we running the type of offense that best fits our personnel? Should we try to reintroduce some of the previous offensive things we have done? And would it be the right time now or would it just serve to add confusion to what we are already doing? Are we playing the right players for the offense that we are running, and if not, why not? Is the defensive contribution enough out of the ones we are playing? I'm sure there are more, but that's enough for right now—I'm starting to get a headache just thinking about it.

We finished practice with a twenty-minute walk through of what Norwalk does offensively. Coach Core says that he spends more time watching film and deciphering what Norwalk does offensively than any other team in the conference. They do a lot of stuff offensively. I believe that a coach has to decide where to spend his time. I think defense is more consistent than offense; I think ours is the better philosophy.

Mark and I decided that we would do more trapping against Norwalk's offense than we usually do against other opponents. They are so in to running their offense we want them to need to react to our defense rather than us to them. I guess we will see tomorrow night if we were correct.

Tuesday, December 5, Game #3, Norwalk at Home
Our Record: 2-0; Conference: 2-0
Number Two, Pre-Game, Kyle, BVH, Fans, End of Quarters, the Game, After the Game, and Klayton Korver

Oh yeah, by the way, we are rated number two in the state in class 3A. I hope to be number one at the end, but I know right now we are nowhere near number two.

The pre-game in the locker room is usually a review of things that we want to accomplish in tonight's game. One of the rituals that Coach Core does before every game is to check that the numbers the players are wearing match with the numbers in the book; we don't need to start the game with a technical foul.

Kyle Kramer has dressed the last two games due to injuries. It is good to get him and Nate into uniforms as often as we can. Kyle is a big man. He is wearing Clayton Boeyink's uniform. Clayton is not a big man—see the problem? Last game we all had a good yuk (along with Kyle who has a great sense of humor) about the fit. We decided when Clayton got his stuff back it might fit a little looser than when he lent it out. This time Kyle's stuff fits better.

Coach Core then discusses pre-game match-ups. The players are told whom they will be guarding and what to guard against. Kaleb and Klarc are assigned Norwalk's primary scorers.

I walk out onto the floor and immediately see Bill Van Horn. He is our athletic director and all-around good guy. It is hard to have a good program without the support of your administrators. Bill is one of the best; he has been more than supportive. He is also one of those guys that will sweep the gym floor at halftime if it needs to be done, and nobody is around to do it.

This is our first home game. There is a large crowd here tonight. At least in part a lot of the people have come to see the girl's game. Our girls under head coach Mike Vint are rated fifth and the Norwalk girls are first. The atmosphere is nice; some schools never get this kind of support from their fans. We are lucky.

What was interesting (I guess that is the right word) to me was sitting with the fans during the first quarter of the girl's game. Normally I don't do this but for a change I thought I would keep my wife happy. While the Pella people in general are knowledgeable and appreciative, people that are positive in their support, tonight I was sitting in front of one (there always has to be one) guy that I could hardly take. First he thought he was really funny with his comments—he wasn't; and then he thought he'd help coach from 40 yards away by yelling at the kids. He also didn't have a clue about that. I couldn't wait to leave the stands and get with the team.

Tonight again is a new starting line up; the three Korvers, B-Mo, and Colin are starting.

So far we have not seen a zone defense or at least not for any length of time in any one of our games. Tonight Norwalk starts in a man-to-man as well; so do we.

Our first offensive possession started off with a lot of ball touches by all of our players. They are moving the ball well but not really using the dribble to set up their passes. We end up with an uncontested perimeter shot that we miss.

They score first as Kirk was late getting back to stop a pass into the post. Kirk is young, and as he gets older and hopefully gets into the weight room this will not happen because he will become bigger, faster, and stronger.

Norwalk starts off incredibly hot. They are four for four from the field with 2:00 left in the first quarter. We are down 10-8. But all of a sudden Kirk hit three threes in a row from almost the same spot, and we end the first quarter up 14-10. This is a good thing, but at the same time a scary thing. If Kirk doesn't hit these shots we have barely scored. What are the odds that a player is going to make three threes in a row even when he is shooting by himself with no one guarding him?

The score is 17-17 with 5:42 left in the second quarter.

The Norwalk offense is very patient. They are swinging the ball from one side of the floor to the other quickly, and we are playing long periods of defense. They get patient at the end of the first and second quarters. When the clock reaches 1:00 they want to hold the ball for the last shot of the quarter. A lot of fans don't understand this, so let me talk about the philosophy behind it. First of all, it's a momentum and psychological thing. If you hit the shot right at the end of the quarter it just gives you a boost. Secondly and more importantly, it's a points thing. If Norwalk has the ball to start the second quarter and also scores at the end of the first quarter they get two possessions in a row against us. If they score both times that could be anywhere from a one-to-eight-point swing! Even if they don't have the ball to start the next period and we do, they certainly don't want to give us the opportunity for the same situation I just described above. We would rather have our kids not get a shot off at the end of the quarter than let them get the ball back. Unfortunately, other teams seem to be stealing our thinking, and now Norwalk is doing it to us.

What we haven't talked to the kids yet about is the mind-set they need to defend this situation. Put yourself in the opposing team's situation when the coach calls for them to take the last shot. Those kids know if they shoot before this they are in trouble. What should that tell us? Go get them! Take chances, go crazy; they're not going to shoot. We don't even have to guard for this. Then in about the last 10 (the time most teams are about to try to score) get solid and play regular defense.

In the first half defensively/statistically we had a mixed bag. We either turned them over, they had 11, or they scored. They shot 75% in the first half!

In the first half we got the ball into the paint/post about six times. That is just not enough. When we did, something good happened five of the six times. We either scored or got fouled. We haven't really taken any bad shots, but all of them have been pretty quick. We are shooting 46% at halftime, which is good for us. Kaleb is playing very unselfishly setting up others for a shot, but he hasn't even shot the ball yet.

At half we are up 28-24. Even though it is a low-scoring game, there just weren't a lot of possessions by either team because Norwalk was so patient with their offense. We actually took 26 shots compared to their 16.

With 3:00 left in the third quarter we are up 34-28. This is another low-scoring affair. With 3:30 left in the third quarter our all-state guard (Kaleb) has not yet shot the ball!

We are up 39-32 early in the fourth quarter, and while this has been a struggle it looks as though we are somewhat in control. Oops, it is 39-34 with 6:00 left in the game. Now we come down twice in a row and turn the ball over. They are unselfish turnovers, the kind you make when you are trying to set up a teammate for a better shot than you had, but you probably had a "good enough" shot that you should have taken rather than throw it away.

Kirk gives up an easy basket in the post. He tried for a steal rather than let the ball come into the post against him. He knows that we don't want that.

What we have, as coaches, failed to tell him is that he either keeps the ball out of the post with early defense by getting position to deny the pass in, or if he goes for the steal he must get it. If neither of these things happens, just get behind, get big, and make the offensive player shoot over you with your hands up.

It's now 41-40. They went inside against Klarc in the low post. Klarc is giving up size to the man he is guarding. We have a unique situation with Klarc; he plays point on offense and is guarding a post on defense.

Kaleb comes down and hits a big three that puts us back up by four with 3:30 left; that helps.

For the first time, Klarc takes a forced shot. This is a bad time for that. At about this time it would have been good for us to hang onto the ball and have Norwalk chase us a little bit. Not necessarily stall, but just open the floor and create areas to drive as the defense came out to guard.

They again go into the post against Klarc, and again he is just giving up too much size; I also think he is getting a bit tired. When you are at a disadvantage in this game, you have to work harder. That is what he has done all game, and he is tiring, but it's late and we can't take him out; we need his play and experience.

The score is 44-43 Pella, with 2:19 left and our ball. Kaleb is looking for his shot now but since he hasn't shot all game he doesn't have any rhythm to his motion. He shoots an air ball!

The smallest guy on the floor between both teams' rosters just got two offensive rebounds against us. We had to foul him. He misses the first free throw and makes the second; it's tied with 1:37 left in the game.

We get a good look from three by B-Mo, but he misses badly. Should we be shooting a three there? Boy, that is a coach thought; if it goes in I don't complain, do I?

We got the defensive rebound after they miss and call a timeout. We run a play that I set up in the huddle. I did a poor job of explaining what I wanted, and they didn't come close to doing what I was trying to explain, but we did get a pretty good post shot from Klarc off of what they thought I wanted; we just missed with about :40 left.

With 21 seconds left and their ball we can't turn them over. So with 1.7 seconds left. B-Mo, trying to make a defensive play, fouls and they make both free throws and go ahead by two points. We take a timeout to set up a full-court play, but it doesn't work and we go down to defeat 46-44.

In the locker room after the game the kids always gather to have a brief post-game meeting. When teams lose often coaches will come in and berate their players or at least the way they played, and when teams win they will often come in and cheer and congratulate those same players. I think that the good coaches never berate their players, but if they are going to be critical the time to do it is after a win not a loss. After a win kids are feeling good about themselves. They can handle some criticism then; it also helps them to understand that there is still work to be done. But after a loss the kids already are at least a bit down on themselves. This is the time to point out some of the good things they did, try to give them a perspective on the game, and build confidence, not tear it down. They need some reassuring at that point that everything is not as bad as they think it is.

That is what Coach Core did. He was positive and tried to encourage them in about a two-minute talk. He then, like most head coaches, had to go talk with the media. I assume he will now go give Norwalk credit for the things that they did and try to console our fans as well regarding the loss.

One of the things that really did make me feel good that night was when I walked out of the locker to get my wife and go home. She was talking with Klayton Korver, Kaleb and Kirk's brother. Klayton is playing for Drake University in Des Moines, and in my opinion is one of the most important players to their program. He is also one of the nicest people you would ever want to meet. He plays for a coach by the name of Tom Davis, a very successful coach who once coached, among other places, at the University of Iowa. I had coached Klayton when he was just a little boy as one of the players that played together with my youngest son, Luke. I used to tell those kids, "If you panic, if you're going to throw it away anyway, I want you to look up in the stands, find your girlfriend, and throw her the ball. Because then we can get back and play defense; we can't get back when you throw it away out front, and they are off for a layup." I used to try to come up with kind of goofy things like that to try to make my point. It seemed to stick better. Anyway, Klayton told me that he had quoted me to coach Davis. That's my claim to fame; I've been quoted to Tom Davis. But what really made me feel good was that Klayton said he remembers all of my quotes, which is very nice of him to say even if it's not maybe 100% true.

That night it was home to watch film and make notes about what I saw so I could pass them along to Coach. I knew that the next day (as always) we would find time (usually before school at about 7:30) to get together and talk over what we saw. I got to bed about midnight; I woke up a lot, always with the game on my mind.

Wednesday, December 6, Before School
My Little Darlin'

My wife, Tricia, is one of the many blessings that have occurred in my life. I learned a long time ago that she is the brains of the outfit, so I should probably listen when she speaks; not to everything—that would be impossible for us guys, but about the important stuff anyway.

So Trish takes a look at me in the morning and says, "didn't get much sleep did you?"

I said, "No," with that what-do-you-think? look on my face. She pretty much left me alone for the rest of the morning, as we were getting ready for school.

Then right before she left for work she came around the corner and said, "I know that you guys will figure out what is going on with the team on the floor. That's not going to be an issue; you always do (is that confidence in us, or is she just not as bright as I thought she was?), but what I really liked was how the boys handled themselves. It was a tough game that they lost, and they conducted themselves like men." Then she left.

Thanks, honey; that was a great thing to say.

Chapter 4—Losses Are Part of the Season— Practice, Practice, Practice

Wednesday, December 6, At School
Searching, Player Input, Seniors That Care, and Panic

When you win you feel pretty good about yourself, even if they are close wins like our first two. Now I've not felt especially good about them because I really felt like we were way off on the offensive end compared to what I thought we would be, but still I wasn't as hungry about improvement as I am now.

When you lose you search. You review what you did right but mostly what you did wrong and how you can improve on those things. That is what I was doing. I always do that and so does Mark, but today definitely we were even more determined; and that is probably a good thing.

Another good thing that just kept happening all day long was that players were stopping in to my office to discuss the game. That to me means that they are searching as well; it's important to them. I've been with teams that it was obvious to me that the coaches cared more than the players did about the team, this definitely doesn't appear to be the case here. I value the players' input. I don't always agree with it, but I value it. I want to know what they like about what we are doing but I really want to know what they think we are doing wrong. I encourage open discussion about all of our concepts and ideas. I figure if the kids understand why we are doing something they are more likely to be able to perform it better. And, if I can't give them a credible explanation about the why we do what we do—maybe we shouldn't be doing it. Maybe I'm wrong. I don't care about who is right and who is wrong; that is a coach's ego thing. What I care about is that we get it right. I spoke with all four senior starters today; they came to me, I didn't ask them to come in to talk about the game.

I told them about my own questions and doubts about some of the things that we were doing. I told them of the various random thoughts that I had concerning how to correct these things and then asked for feedback.

Mark was concerned about showing a panic reaction to the kids. I wasn't. If this was a young team and we had changed things every game for the last six games or seven games, then yes. But as it is, the only people I might be a little concerned about in this regard would be a younger player that might be struggling to learn some of the previous things that we are changing. But again to me, if you're going to change, now is the time. Eventually you've got to find what you believe in most and stick with it.

Wednesday, December 6, Practice #15
Know It All, Swing, Attitude, Passing Lanes, Jesse, Change Drill, Baseline, Partners, Duke., C.J., and Tricia

We start practice today with some basic stuff, rebounding with two hands and then we did an over-the-back rebounding drill designed to toughen up our positioning during the block outs. We added to that a put back, which means we got the rebound and put it back up as an offensive rebound. Then we went to partner shooting. Mark came over to me and said we probably need to do these maybe two or three times a practice. Some of our offensive woes could just simply be that we don't spend enough time in practice just shooting the ball.

I heard Mark asking Andrew (stats) and Will (video) if they thought we are starting the right people and if we are subbing the right people. I love that; he doesn't do that because he is unsure of himself as a coach, no way. He does that because he values their opinion and hopes that he will gain insight into the team. When a coach thinks he knows it all and doesn't at least listen (he needn't agree) to others' opinions he is not giving himself an opportunity to grow. You never know where you are going to get your next good idea.

We then do some power layups and two-on-one with a chaser. Our full-court push is definitely better. Making our position shifts from that consideration was good. But it also took our best offensive rebounder (Klarc) away from the basket; we got two, that's right, two offensive rebounds last game.

Clayton Boeyink thinks that maybe we should be swinging the ball more and faster. There is the fifth senior (probable starter if healthy) checking in with an opinion. I agree. You can almost never go wrong swinging the ball from one side of the floor to the other. Without the swing the defense can load up against the ball, with the swing the defense tries to load up on one side and then has to quickly regroup onto the other side. It's during that regrouping that mistakes can be made and offenses can take advantage of the defenses.

Practice drills are very short in duration. But the attitude on the floor is great; another good sign. The kids could be "licking their wounds," feeling sorry for themselves and complaining about being tired. It's not happening.

Last night we did a good job of getting into the passing lanes the first half of the game. Norwalk wants to run a pattern rather than being attack oriented. When that happens we want to destroy the timing of the pattern by getting out into the passing lanes. For some reason in the second half we didn't get it done. I think part of that reason was due to the fact that we didn't feel like our subs were playing well last night and therefore didn't sub as much. Which meant that the starters played heavier minutes and maybe got too tired to get into the lanes the second half. We are running a drill called "man drill" which simulates us getting into the lanes so next time we understand better what is meant by taking away the passing lanes.

Jesse is struggling tonight. Just about everything we do is difficult for him, and he isn't really doing it correctly. It isn't that he is not trying; no question he is. It's the simple fact that it is difficult to be good without repetitions, and because of his injuries he hasn't had enough reps.

We will rarely if ever go through a practice without a shell drill. Apart from the loss this day is no exception. We believe in defense. If we don't defend last night we are blown out; the way it is in spite of our offensive problems we definitely could have won that game. Playing defense does not guarantee a win, but it does give you your most consistent chance to win.

Nate Klyn suggested that we haven't done three stops in a row for a while. Mark immediately incorporated it into the practice. Can it be bad if you've got your players asking to do more defensive drills?

The "five-on-five-change drill" that we run tonight is designed to work on communication and improving our ability to match up with offensive players while on the run. The drill starts with one team with the ball running their offense until the coach yells, "Change." At that time the man with the ball puts it on the floor, and the other team picks it up on a fast-break to the other end of the floor. The original offensive team must get back on defense and they are not allowed (due to the confines of the rules of the drill) to guard the same player that was guarding them. Therefore they must talk on the way back, yelling out who is guarding who. We've given up enough cheap baskets not knowing whom we are guarding.

Now we again work on our press offense/defense drill. The switch we made in our defensive rotation seems a lot better. Even if we never get good enough to be a great pressing team, it will make us a better pressing team in practice allowing us to get better in our press attack on offense.

I asked Mark earlier if we could just stay in the quarter-court and work on our quarter-court offense with no fast-break involved. That's a switch. Mark tends to pay attention more to the quarter-court while I probably pay more attention to the full-court break. I just felt like we needed a number of reps in a row.

We decided we were going to experiment with a number of things during this time including trying some new stuff on the offensive end. One of the most obvious things that we felt we needed to do was add some screening to the man-to-man offense, and yet we wanted something simple.

One of the things that we tried and the one that the kids seemed to like best we are going to call, "baseline." In our goals were twofold: 1) to get Kaleb some screens and 2) Make it simple; this fits in both areas. Kaleb simply runs along the baseline while the offensive players are posted at the blocks setting screens for him. He may use the screen in any manner he sees fit and may go in any direction.

Our design to get Kaleb the ball more often is not always getting him a shot, although we certainly want him shooting more than three times a game. We want the ball in his hands more so he can make decisions with it. In our offense, since it is quite a bit of freelance, the guy with the ball is making decisions on the run. We think Kaleb is good at that.

The screeners along the baseline oftentimes will be Kirk and B-Mo. After they screen it is their job to step back towards the ball and look for a pass, ready to score. It is crazy how often the man setting the screen is the guy that gets open, especially when the guy running off the screen (Kaleb) is someone that the defense is very concerned about stopping. Many times the defense will help so much against the scorer they forget to guard the guy that is setting the screen.

I found this out with a great kid when I first got into Pella. I was coaching the junior high team of my oldest son, Josh. His team had a player (you know who you are) who was a great kid and a not so good player. My plan was to find a way to use him and at the same time get the ball to one of the better players, who happened to be Josh. We did this by having him continually screen for Josh. What I found out to my dismay at that point was that it was this player who was the guy that was always open!

This concept of the screener getting open also hit home with Kirk and Kaleb's older brother, Kyle, who is now with the Philadelphia 76ers. He was a blocker or a screener when he was playing for us in high school. His favorite move was to back screen then pop out after the screen and shoot the three. He was/is pretty good. Just as a side note, Kyle couldn't shoot a lick until I became his shooting coach. Just as a side note to the previous side note; that may not be 100% true.

We also worked on what we are going to refer to as the "Partners" offense and the "Duke" offense as well. I liked all three of the offenses, but the partner offense requires just a little more practicing so it's probably my least favorite right now because of that. If we start running those a little bit I will explain them in more detail later. Right now we are just looking at all of these.

We spent quite a bit of time in the quarter-court today. We got better today. If I were a betting man I would bet that our offense against the man-to-man has improved dramatically.

I liked C.J.'s practice tonight. You haven't heard from C.J. lately. Here is one of the reasons why—he has started thinking of himself as a second team player. The mind-set of the player often determines their play. If he thinks of himself as a player, he has a much better chance of being a player, again no guarantee, but it gives him his best chance. C.J. is not a finesse player, but he is a guy that is a great effort player. I'll bet C.J. would have gotten at least one offensive board in the last game; remember we only had three total.

At the end of practice I told the boys my "Tricia Story;" I could tell they appreciated it.

We always huddle after practice and somebody has to come up with a word that they all shout in unison before they leave the floor. Today's word was "Tricia."

Thursday, December 7, Practice #16
Andrew, Josh, Game Speed, Two on One "D," Brock, Tyler, Your Man, Duke, the Star, Partners, Creighton, B-Mo and Kirk, and Game Situations

One of the concerns about bringing a young player up to the varsity level is the amount of playing time that they will be getting. Prior to our last game

I felt like Andrew Ter Louw was getting an adequate amount of time. But last game Zach Morgan was (in our estimation) playing better than Andrew, so Andrew's time was reduced. Now the question is—if Zach continues to out play Andrew, should we consider moving him back to the sophomores? So we called him over before practice and asked him what he was thinking and how he was feeling about himself and his position on the varsity so far. All was good in "Andrew land." He says he really likes it and even if his time were to be reduced because of Zach moving up he would still rather play varsity. I'm not sure I agree with this whole-heartedly; I had a similar situation with my own son. I think this is a subject we need to revisit if his playing time does go down (it may not).

I've lived this setting to a degree with my oldest son, Josh, as he was also a varsity player as a freshman. He didn't start either his freshman or his sophomore year, but he was with the varsity in a back-up role and did play some. Towards the middle of his sophomore year we decided to move him back to the sophomore team just to get him more time on the floor. He was opposed to it, but we thought it best. His entire disposition changed after that move. I don't think he realized how much fun it was to be on the floor for long periods of time. Once he moved he realized how happy that made him. It was also the right thing in the long run for our program; you cannot sit a player long periods of time during his ninth and tenth grade years and expect him to be a player as a junior.

Once again, all of those advantages that the Pella boys' basketball team is supposed to have are not obvious to us as coaches. Upon entering the old gym there is a blood drive on half the floor. So we get to drop the curtain and use half the gym width ways and are limited to three baskets and 18 kids. And oh, by the way, then for the next twenty minutes we get to practice with the door on the far end of the gym wide open to the 20 degree weather as the blood drive people haul their equipment out to their van in the parking lot. But at least when all the stuff was finally taken out the door and the curtain was raised we got to practice on a dirty floor! Okay, okay, I know; I'll quit whining. It's just that I hear so much about all the things that we supposedly get—I'm telling you we don't!

We start with lay backs and reach backs. It is amazing how often we need to remind the players to go game speed when we are doing drills. I promise you that you will never, ever, ever shoot one of these shots unless you are under duress from a defensive player. Why would you? If there were no pressure in a game from a defender you would shoot a normal layup, not a lay or a reach back. I also promise that you will not have time to think about your footwork and make it just so. So we need guys to practice what will occur in games (game speed). The footwork will usually catch up once you go game speed.

We have worked very hard on trying to get our two-on-one fast-break situations better. Now Coach Core is talking about defending this situation. The best thing that a lone defender can hope for is to slow down the ball until the cavalry arrives. If the defender can make the offense pass the ball more than once in that situation usually a hustling defense should get back. In order to get that extra pass to occur the defender must fake and then make a decision. Fake a fake and just stay there and try to take a charge or get his hands on the ball. Or fake at the ball and jump into the passing lane to tip or intercept the pass if the ball handler makes a mistake. The farther away from the basket the defender can be when he starts this little ritual and still be able to get back to the basket; the better this will work. He may even be able to get two fakes in by the time they get to the hoop.

Getting a player in a stance *may* and getting him to focus on the hips *will* be the quickest way to make that player at least an adequate on-the-ball defender. Sounds simple; it's not. That whole stance thing goes away pretty quickly when the athlete gets tired. Sometimes it never gets there in the first place because an athletic stance isn't an easy stance to be in even when you aren't tired, but if the athlete wants to move quicker it's something he/she must get into. The eyes on the hips. This isn't a skill; it's decision to do it. We are still trying to combine those two things in our shell drills.

Brock sometimes appears to be one of the quickest kids we have on the team. His athleticism has really improved from last year. I've also got to believe that maybe some of what appears to be athleticism is his willingness to buy into our push about being aggressive and his ability to anticipate what may happen next.

Tyler Linn started today with a good practice. In order for him to play more he must become a more consistent practice player and show that he has the ability to put together at least one or two sets of good back to back practices.

Defensively the less we help each other the more we are ready to guard our own man. The more ready we are to guard our own man the more ready we are in anticipating his next move, and therefore, denying that move. The more we deny that move the more we wreak havoc upon the offensive team by being in passing lanes. And should the offensive player make a catch the defender would be in better position to defend if he were not forced to help. So what do we do in practice over and over? We practice helping. We are practicing for the times that a defender makes a mistake. It's our last line of defense; we don't want to help, but sometimes we must. The other end of this is that we must spend adequate time at becoming good on-ball defenders so we don't have to help.

The beginning of practice is ugly. We are throwing the ball away a lot. It's like we don't care. Is it great defense or poor offense? In this case I think it is terrible offense.

While practicing our new baseline offense Coach Core starts to define offensive roles for the players. It just makes sense; do what you do best and do more than the other things that you do. If you shoot better than you pass, maybe you should shoot a little more and vice versa. That doesn't mean you shoot every time. In truth if you are hot you should shoot more, and if you're not you should shoot less. In the latter situation you don't give up; you check once in a while to see (it may change) but if it doesn't, do something else to help your team.

"Duke," the play that we are very intentional about screening for Kaleb, is a simple yet hopefully effective way to make sure that what happened the other night doesn't reoccur. We want Kaleb to be involved on the offensive end. This offense looks okay again today; I think we are on to something here. The additional benefit of Duke has been an amazing increase on the offensive boards. I think everyone is so interested in stopping Kaleb that they are leaving their guys to help and allowing us a better shot at the boards. I also think our added offensive movement created by more screening puts us in a moving and more aggressive position to get to the boards.

In practice the coach will often have a player on the second team simulate an opposing team's best scorer. What has happened more than once in the past has been an amazing transformation of that second team player into a guy that can score and create shots for others. Again, it's a mind set. Now this guy thinks of himself as a scorer. He doesn't let all that other garbage jump in to take away his confidence; he just does what the coach wants him to do and lets the other stuff go away. Coach Core threw both Jesse and Tyler into the Duke offense as the scorer (not the opposing team's guy but our own Kaleb). I thought it was a great move; two guys we are trying to get to be more assertive—they were.

The Partners offense is a disaster. It's a very simple offense, but it requires attention, and we just haven't run it enough. We will make this a five-man shell drill and practice it prior to any game time that it may get. Right now I like our other stuff better.

"Creighton," a play we used to run a few years ago, is still a work in progress, as is another set called "Spartans." Neither of these sets will be used tomorrow.

We've moved B-Mo and Kirk to new spots in the Louisville offense to try to take advantage of their individual skills. Both look a little uncomfortable right now, but I'm convinced that this eventually will be a good move. Besides, now they will be able to run either position and make us harder to guard because of it.

The next part of practice was spent working against various defensive zone sets. Seems like in years past we haven't spent enough time against zones in practice, and every team we played came out and played us in zone. This year we are being very proactive and working against zones consistently in practice, and now no one is zoning us. Of course, why would they? Coaches find out what works and what doesn't against their opponents, and then they try to attack the weaknesses of the opponents. Right now our weakness has been our man-to-man offense.

At the end of a game you've got to have a plan for all situations. Down close, up close and tied with various amounts of time left on the clock are all things that could happen to your team. The option we like best right now if we are down close, is to run Duke. We want to put the ball in one of our best offensive player's hands, and let him make a decision. If we are up close we want to run motion. Normally when we are up close, depending on the time, we will tell our players exactly what type of shots they should take. For instance we might say only layups or free throws, no outside shots. The timing of this type of instruction is important. If you go to this too early you can make your teams tentative and play passively. It should only be a late-game move.

Game #4 Friday December 8, Pella vs. Newton
Our Record: 2-1; Conference: 2-1
Trapping, Clear out the Press, Double Klarc, Kirk the Outlet, F.T. Box Outs, Time to Shoot, Hedge, Half-Court Presses, Guard Your Guy, the Game, Flopping, Flashing, and Out-of-Bounds Plays.

Mark's point of emphasis before the game in the locker room was to get the ball into the paint on offense. Mine was to guard the player you are responsible for and don't be the cause of defensive rotations that hurt our defense. I am feeling stronger about that all the time. We are almost helping too much and definitely staying too long, creating our own problems and rotations.

We will open with our new baseline offense regardless of Newton's defense—man or zone. The zone defense is designed to cover areas of the floor, and if we can get our screeners on the baseline to slow the slides of the defensive players into their areas we can create open shots for our offensive players with this offense even against a zone. Then after that screen if they open back to the ball they, too, may be open. One of the things I've just recently learned (I know—I'm a slow learner) is that the more our offensive players understand how a zone slides, the more they will understand how to disrupt those slides.

Our first two possessions on offense are quick shots. B-Mo gets one inside, and Kirk a quick three-pointer from outside. B-Mo scores first for us later on, and Kirk again takes a three. Kirk is coming out. Kirk shot quick three-point attempts last game as well, but he was making them. This game so far he hasn't. If you will remember Coach Core's pre-game talk was about getting the ball inside.

Klarc gets a bucket with a nice drive right down the middle of the Newton zone. It's 4-4 with 5:30 in the first quarter.

We are doing a terrible job of attacking the Newton two-two-one zone press. We are either passing into or dribbling into the most trappable positions. These positions are the spots just before and just on the other side of the half-court line and nearest the sideline of the court. This is the last place we should enter the ball. In some ways the two-two-one zone press, while it starts three quarter-court, is actually almost a half-court trap designed to encourage the ball up the sideline and then trap at half-court. We aren't doing a good job of recognizing this, but so far we have been big enough (literally height wise) to throw out of the trap area or strong enough with the ball to dribble out.

Most people seem to think that the press will create a faster tempo for the offensive team. I don't always agree. I think that the three-one-one press where there are three defenders up court looking to trap the inbounds receiver will quicken the offense because once the ball comes out of the trap the offense has the advantage and will often attack the fall-back defenders. But I think the two-two-one zone press actually slows the tempo, because there is no initial trap usually and the offense must take the time to throw reversal passes (backwards or sideways) to beat the press rather than attacking passes to beat it.

B-Mo, that son of a gun, just has an ability to draw a charge that most guys don't have. He does so, and we are up 6-4 about halfway through the quarter.

I'm not sure if it's good news or bad news, but Kirk comes out and hits a three. I like the points, but I hope this doesn't mean he is just going to run to the three-point line and look to shoot rather than post up some. Kirk has a pretty good-sized derriere, and it would be nice if he would use it down low.

Later on B-Mo hits a three and gets fouled after the shot, so we get the ball right back under our own basket. I never thought I would say these words, but I think Kaleb might be more active on the defensive end than he is on the offensive end! I'd sure like him to move more; that is the idea behind the baseline offense.

One minute, 44 seconds in the quarter: 12-6 PHS leads.

Tyler Linn comes in and almost immediately gets the ball on a break away and misses a contested layup. That's a tough spot, to come in cold and get the ball in that situation.

With a 14-8 lead and :09 seconds left it is Newton's ball out of bounds. They get called on a violation, so we get the ball back, and B-Mo scores with a short bank shot as the buzzer goes off to make it 16-8 Pella. This was potentially at least a four-point swing.

They start with the ball the second quarter and hit an open three; Kaleb misses a dribble drive shot, and they come back and hit another three-pointer.

Right now Kaleb, in this game as well as for the year, is struggling with his shot. He is shooting a poor percentage from the field and from the free-throw line. He is too good a shooter for this to continue, I'm hesitant to say anything to him because sometimes too much advice can mess with the shooter's mind. I do think he might be leaning back a little too far on his shot, and he is leaving the line a little quickly once the ball leaves his hand from the free throw. Balance is often an issue with a shooter.

I had mentioned too much lean to Kaleb in practice late last week, and I think he knows it, too, because he immediately imitated what I meant and said he was working on it.

We miss, and they get an offensive put-back rebound, and our eight-point lead is gone.

Kirk misses a three; Kaleb gets the rebound and gets fouled. Unfortunately he misses the free throw.

I also think part of Kaleb's shooting problems come from not shooting enough in practice. He has been the ultimate passer, but doesn't shoot all that often in practice. We need to get his scoring mentality back.

Tyler Linn hits a three and gets fouled on the shot, misses the free throw.

C.J. plays for the first time this year. He comes in and within seconds puts up a three, misses, gets his own rebound, puts it back up and gets fouled. He makes the free throw and we are up 21-16. Like his older brother, Brett, who played last year, C.J. is a high-energy player. Wow! In limited minutes C.J. will finish with four rebounds, two of them offensive.

We are doing a pretty good job of pressuring the Newton guards and making it difficult for them to get shots or run their offense. If we can destroy the timing of an offense even if we don't make steals but make the offense catch the ball a little bit out of their normal range or slow the passes a little, it can disrupt Newton's ability to score.

Coach Core pulls Kaleb with 4:30 left in the second quarter. He still doesn't see enough effort from Kaleb at getting the ball and himself inside. He will sit for the rest of the half.

Kirk is starting to flop a little bit as he tries to draw a charge. A flop is kind of an act where the defender gets hit and exaggerates the contact in order to draw the official's attention. That will actually work against us, because if the officials even suspect we are flopping they will hesitate to call even real charges. Kirk just needs to toughen up. When he came to the bench I asked him what he needed to do. He said, "Be more physical." He has heard the message at least.

I told him, "Kirk, you're just a pup, but if you don't learn to bite now you may never learn."

Wow another C.J. three-pointer!

Colin gives up what little body he has diving on the floor for a loose ball. His effort play gets the ball back for us. The score is 26-18 Pella. Colin then makes a free throw to put us up by nine.

We come out with our own two-two-one press and immediately give up a layup. This is our 53 defense, and the guys at half-court didn't rotate back correctly.

Tyler Linn makes one of two free throws, and B-Mo misses a bunny underneath the basket on a great pass from Klarc.

One of the few poor plays Klarc makes is the next possession when his man beats him off the dribble down the middle of the floor all the way to the hoop for a basket. How can a dribbler go 20 feet without anyone there to help support against the drive? Vision, effort, or lack of rotation or all of the above is probably the answer.

Score at half is 30-22, us.

Even though Kaleb isn't shooting well he is a beast on the defensive board. Last game he had 14 rebounds; I wouldn't doubt that he might duplicate that again tonight.

The half-time discussion (that is probably not the right word) was about getting the ball inside. It's interesting (is that the word) that coach's pre-game point of emphasis was to get the ball inside. At halftime we are 4-19 from the arc. You can imagine that stat didn't go over very well.

They must have heard as Klarc came out and got fouled with a dribble penetration that led to made free throws.

About midway through the third quarter Newton starts throwing the ball into their post players. Newton's #23 (one of the posts) in particular starts to score on us inside. I thought our defensive post players had established their position a couple of times and got rooted out by the Newton "bigs." If the officials aren't going to call it, you can whine (which rarely does any good) or you can push back.

Colin shoots an early three on the next possession down the floor. He is coming out.

Our next offensive possession ends with a layup after Klarc penetrated and brought two defenders to him, and then he dished to Kirk for the easy inside shot.

In the middle of the third it is 34-24 Pella.

They are now starting to go to #23 harder, getting him the ball at the high and low post, and he is hurting us. Two things we could have done would have been to do a better job of denying the ball initially and secondly helping a little more off of their non-shooters.

I also think that we need to take a look at Kaleb guarding a post inside. It would have to be the right type of non-physical post, but Kaleb has height and is quick off the floor. It would also put him even closer to the defensive boards. The question: should we do some of this? Then what would this do to our other match-ups?

Kaleb ends up with all of his points in the second half. Some from free throws after he attacked the basket with the dribble and even a couple of threes.

It's 40-30 with 3:35 left in the third.

We are finally starting to get a middle flash against their press. But when the ball is reversed if we don't hit that first flash guy, the second guy at half-court must flash; he isn't. This last time it was Brock that didn't go. They tend to want to stay on the outside and ask for an over-the-top pass; we definitely don't want that, but unless the flash is made to the middle the passer sometimes has little choice but to try it.

B-Mo draws yet another charge.

Colin subs to get Klarc a little rest time as a point guard. Colin seems to know his limitations here and is smart enough to think *pass* rather than *dribble* against this press. I think Klarc needs a few more breaks during the game—very short but more.

It continues to amaze me how poorly we run our out-of-bounds plays. It is as though we've never done them before.

If the officials would have had the guts to call it, B-Mo would have just drawn back-to-back charges against Newton. I think they choked a little on their whistles.

45-30 with a minute and a half left in the third.

When you go for a steal and make it, you are a hero. If you go and miss it becomes an advantage for the offense because they now outnumber the defense. We missed, and they hit a three.

We follow that with a turnover, and then they get another offensive put back. But B-Mo scores on an out-of-bounds play. Hey, maybe I was wrong about the out of bounds plays. I remember once that I was wrong years ago.

It's 47-37 after three quarters.

Klarc and B-Mo sandwich a couple of threes around another two-pointer for them by #23. Unfortunately B-Mo then picks up his fourth foul.

We have done so much better about getting the ball inside, but now we revert, and four of our last five shots have been three-point attempts. The good news is that we are making some now: it's 57-43, and Colin hits a little floater for two to make it 59-43.

Mark wants more traps now late. I'm not really sure why or what he was thinking. He might be using this as an opportunity to use this game as a practice to get better at this part of the game or maybe he sees something. Anyway, we get caught in some bad rotations that hurt us. We also foul and stop the clock 30 feet from the hoop so they can score points, with no time running, from the free-throw line.

They go man late to try to get the ball, and we go zone late to try to do a better job of protecting the paint against their big guys.

We continue to shoot threes, some leading to a fast-break against us, and some we make.

They also go man-to-man in their press. Against a man-to-man press we just simply need to clear out and give our point guard room to maneuver without the fear of being trapped. We didn't recognize this very well and stayed back to help, which also brought the other defenders into play.

Kaleb fouls out with us up 13 points.

Newton is now starting to double Klarc on the inbounds pass against the press. This calls for our other guys at half-court to break back to the ball. They are late recognizing this, and Klarc is just plain tough enough to get open and handle the double team.

As we play keep away from the defense with a substantial lead we want our big boy (in this case) to be the outlet man. If we get our big guy to run out front, I know that their big boy is not interested in guarding him 20 feet from the hoop; they just don't like it out there. Kirk is doing this, but he needs to learn to go back inside when he doesn't have the ball and pop back out.

Final score is 66-57, Pella High.

Klarc had a terrific game. He was the glue in handling the ball. He made terrific decisions with the ball at the point. He scored for us, made free throws, and rebounded. This is one of Klarc's best games. Klarc is very composed as a point guard.

That composure issue right now is also the reason to give Zach a few more minutes than Andrew right now. Zach has the experience and is more comfortable than Andrew. He was steady for us this game.

One of the areas we need to improve upon is our box outs against an offensive free throw. We want our best rebounders closest to the basket and their job is to block out and step up towards the opponent's rebounder who is stationed right next to him. Our defenders above our opponent must step down on our opponent, and finally, our last man is responsible to block out the shooter.

We also need to work on when to shoot at the end of the quarters when it is our ball. I would like them to attempt to score with about :07. This way we get a shot, maybe a put back, but even with no put back we won't be giving them a defensive rebound that turns into a shot at the other end of the floor. Remember, we would rather not get a shot than to have them get the last one.

During the game Coach Core is frustrated with our ability to finish our layups under defensive pressure. That, to me, means we need to shoot more power layups. If you recall, this drill simulates that exactly. It also always reminds me of Klayton Korver. We were in the heat of a state championship game, and late in the game while holding a slim lead, Klayton sealed a championship with a tough layup under pressure that also resulted in a foul on the opponent and made free throw for Klayton. So after the game we are all jumping around enjoying our win, and I told Klayton how huge that play was. He just smiled and said, "Power layups, coach; power layups."

It's obvious that we need to go back to our on-ball hedge-shell drill. We had a number of times that we didn't hedge out on the dribbler. Remember we want the man guarding the man setting the screen for the dribbler to step out and impede the dribble, draw a charge, or make the dribbler go high so his defender has a chance to catch him after getting over the screen. Our hedges are flat and incorrect. I've noticed both Kirk and Colin in this regard, but I'm sure after watching film there will be others.

We also need to work on our press offense against a half-court trap—that is really what Newton was running against us, and we haven't spent any time yet in practice attacking half-court presses. Again, there is only so much time in practice before the coach loses the player mentally; as a coach you have to decide which things to emphasize and which things to let go.

We won three of four critical areas during this game. We didn't shoot as well as Newton, but we took, unofficially, eleven more shots. We accomplished this by getting more offensive rebounds and turning them over more than they turned us over. We also attempted and made more free throws than they did.

Monday, December 11, A.M.

We didn't meet on Saturday, and that is a rarity. It did give me little more time to review the tape and make some notes.

Coach Core came in, and we had a brief coaches' meeting. One of his concerns was Kaleb and the lack of play that he had against Newton. The baseline defense was designed to get Kaleb open off of screens set along the baseline. Kaleb didn't move along those screens during the game, although he had during practice. We concluded that maybe he was just open and didn't feel the need to move.

We feel like Kaleb is very satisfied to take three-point shots, and we are definitely not opposed to the three. However, we both feel that Kaleb will sometimes get into a shooting funk because he relies too heavily on this shot and not enough on his other abilities. He also has the ability to get to the line and attack with the dribble. We need to build off of what he accomplished the second half of the Newton game rather than be too critical of his first half performance as a stand-still shooter. We also talked a bit about him possibly playing some defensive post and will use some drills tonight to take a look at this.

Another thing we discussed was the possibility of using some more zone. We packed in a two-three against Newton. We might also consider a bit of a match-up zone; we will probably look at that a little bit tonight.

Monday, December 11, Practice #17
Clayton, Colin, Kaleb, Improvement, Tyler, Billy, Pressing, Match Up, and Brandon

It's amazing to me to realize that this is only our sixteenth practice; the basketball season is a long one. Clayton Boeyink is going to try a full practice today. He is getting really frustrated with the lack of progress in diagnosis of his injury, so he is just going to jump in and go.

We start with quarter-court layups, both floaters and power layups and then go to the Michigan full-court lay-up drill. The Michigan drill is designed to get the kids moving up and down the court. It also incorporates passing with an outlet pass (simulating a fast-break outlet) and a catch and immediate pass up court.

The North Carolina drill is going great. We have reemphasized the idea of defensive balance and not allowing the offensive team to throw "the bomb" (over the top of the defense pass) during the fast-break. The kids are all being very aggressive during the drill; we have had some good defensive plays and some nice offensive ball movement. We are making some extra passes and getting back on "D." The only thing we haven't had much of is an offensive rebound. It's hard to do both: get the boards and get back on defense; we would like the players to do both. Remember; is it bad offense or good defense?

The basketball game of old, where there is very little contact is a thing of the past, and in most situations there is at least some contact. This drill is no exception. And with contact there can be kids going down on the floor. This is part of the game. Most kids (probably adults too) over dramatize their little hurts and small injuries for sympathy of others; we don't have time for sympathy. Our players are taught to bounce back up and get back in the play. During this drill there was crashing of bodies to the floor, but true to our desires, most players bounced up (even though I know they all experienced at least some small amount of pain) except one. I watched as Coach Core ran to check on the player and then to get a towel.

By the time I got there, Colin Boswell, who was trying to literally crawl off the floor was sitting up. His face was streaked with blood; he looked like one of those guys that get shot in a war movie. I asked him where he was hurt and got a towel on the back of his head where he was pointing. When I looked there was a gash back there that appeared to me like it needed stitches. He also complained somewhat of being dizzy. But one of the first things he wanted to know was if he could play in tomorrow's game!

Coach Core wants to take no chances in this situation, so after fruitless efforts to contact a family member, he had Andrew and Will drive Colin out to the hospital. It's really amazing to me that with the size, speed of their bodies, and effort that these kids put out that we don't have more of this. We are all hoping that Colin is okay.

We have moved Kaleb over to the "big boys" in our rebounding and defending-the-post drills. He gives up weight but is making up for it with his quickness and height; I think he might be able to help us there on the defensive end. That would also put him closer to the defensive boards; he is already a monster there and might even be better if he were to guard a post.

Our one-on-one-stuff is better, with the kids making quicker decisions on offense when they get the ball. We don't want a lot of faking, and if they do fake, it needs to be on the catch and quick. If each individual can be quicker on the offensive end with their decision-making our overall ball movement will improve.

That kind of thinking is true in all cases; the concept of individual improvement improves the team. I'm not a stats guy, but I've got to believe that there is some validity to this. As an example, if each starter moves just one percent more on offense we will gain five-percent movement! That is one of the ways teams can improve. If each starter gets one percent more offensive rebounds than what they normally get, our team would improve in this area by five percent. Asking a player to improve by one percent is something that most feel like they can do. It gives them something real to shoot for; to me it's much better than saying, "Hey, you need to be a better passer," or something like that.

I send Mark an evaluation of the last practice or the last game that we play as soon as I possibly can. I feel like it is my job to say what I think even if I don't agree with the head coach. If I were the head man I wouldn't want a "yes man." What good would that do? So I've already sent my list to Coach Core, and he is implementing one of the drills I think we need more work on—the shell that covers hedging.

The other side of my job is to accept the fact that not everything I think is going to be something Mark agrees with. I will try to say what I have to say once or twice, and if it's something I really feel strongly about maybe three and even four times. But after that I know that I've been heard, and Coach has made a decision; it is just different than mine. After all, ultimately he is the one that takes the heat; he'd better believe in what it is that he is doing.

One of the players I've noticed again in practice is Tyler Terlouw; he is just a pretty good athlete. I think he is actually a better player than what he gives himself credit for. Sometimes kids get in a mind set about themselves, and it is hard for them to see themselves in any other way. In order for Tyler to be a player (starter or sub that plays big minutes) he must first allow himself to believe that he is worthy of that. Athletically I really think he is capable; I need to share with him more about this, and I will, then it's up to him to believe in himself. I can't tell you how often I see this. A kid that believes in himself or herself beats out a kid that is a better athlete but just absolutely refuses to have faith in himself.

Billy Fox played for us when we won two state championships. He was not a starter, but he was the first guard off of the bench. He was not always that first guard; he actually started at about third or fourth guard off of the bench. I think Billy had to overcome that feeling of *I'm not good enough* to move up like he did; he learned to think differently about himself. Billy not only became an invaluable sub off the bench for our high school team but became a college football player as well.

96

Our press offense improves as our defense improves. Again, it just makes sense. Don't be upset with the offensive players for not performing the drill or the play the way that you want. Get upset with the defense; make them defend the cut or the pass that you don't want made, and it will force the offense into something else. This is what we did today. We took away passes up the sideline and trapped in the corners as Newton did to us. This forced our offensive team to attack the middle of the floor and make appropriate cuts so they would be open for a pass.

We also simulated what Newton did to us by denying the ball into Klarc on the initial inbounds pass against the press. This forced our guys at half-court to break back to the ball to receive the pass; it forced them to pay attention to what was going on. It also necessitated some different cuts by various players to get open. This isn't a problem in our press offense.

Our zone-press offense is probably the simplest offense any team could run, but in my mind that is a superior thing, and it also allows us to be more flexible in whom we play where. If the players understand the concept of the press they can fit into any spot. And the concept is simple; when the ball comes in to the receiver we want a man on the same sideline as the receiver, a man in the middle of the press, and a man to reverse the ball to whichever player is somewhat behind the receiver. That's it! And when or if the ball goes to the other side of the floor we want the same thing. I'll show you what normally happens in the following diagram.

The #1 man receives the ball, and #5 steps in. #5 must be away and behind the ball so in case #1 wants to pass to him he doesn't have to throw through defensive arms. #3 is on the same sideline and #2 has broken to the middle. If the ball goes back to #5, #2 goes to the sideline and #3 breaks to the middle. This is our zone-press offense.

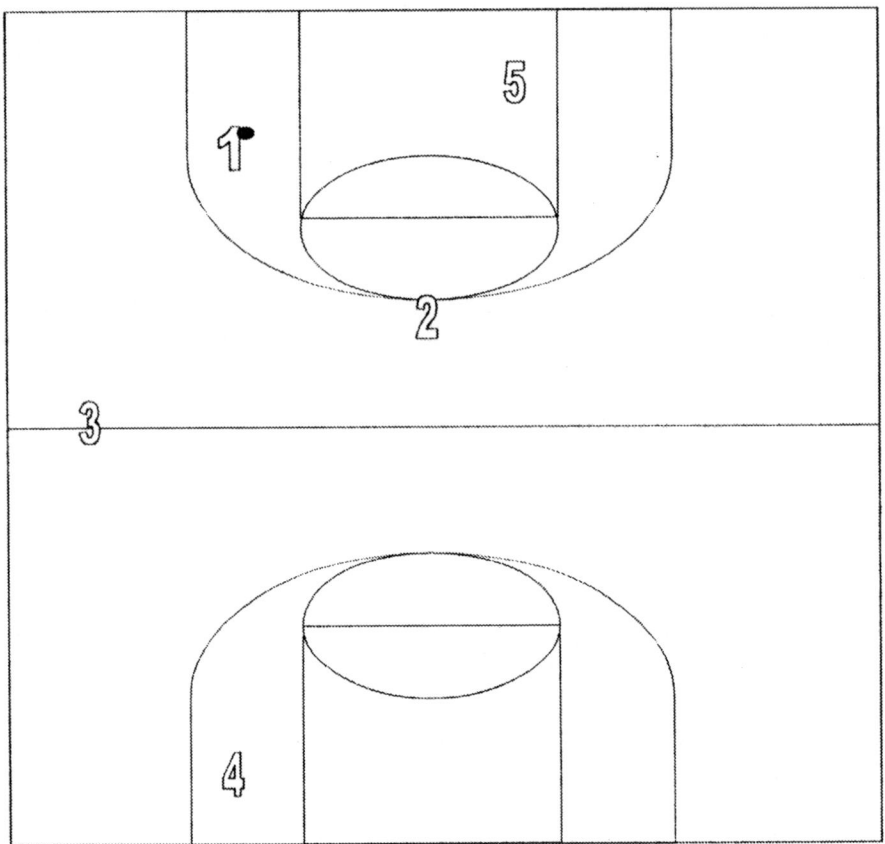

The man-press offense is even simpler. Throw it to your best ball handler and get out of his way. Give him the entire court to work with by sending the other players to the other end of the floor. I say best ball handler: that is really not always the case. Give it to the player with the greatest advantage against his defender when dribbling and clear for him. Often this is the point, but it doesn't have to be.

Now the key to breaking a press is to recognize what kind of press it is because teams should do different things against different presses. As I just explained, teams should clear out against a man and flash against a zone. Sounds easy but there are defensive teams (like us) who try to disguise which kind of press we are running. We may actually change from a man to a zone and back to a zone all within the length of the floor. Now here is a key to that—

don't confuse your own players when you are the defensive pressing team. They had better know what they are doing, or that team will be giving up layups. Some layups are to be expected if the defenders are playing aggressively. But too many will get the team beat.

Towards the end of practice I talked very briefly about a match-up zone that we may take a look at. A match-up, much like the press, is designed to look like a zone but is played much like a man-to-man. Again part of the battle for the offense will be to recognize what we are running before they attack it. If we can make them indecisive or confused this will help us. We will not run any of this tomorrow; this was just an introductory run through.

Brandon Esterbrook and the white team really did well with the baseline offense. I think Brandon got one shot, but everyone else got a lot of good looks. The question is—why doesn't our green team look this good when they run it? Maybe it's Brandon. I'd like to see him play more, but he can't until he takes care of the ball a little bit better and plays better on-the-ball defense.

We finish with out-of-bounds plays, Duke offense, and rebounding defensively out of a free-throw situation. And finally, game situations are practiced with us up, down, or tied in points and what we will do.

Chapter 5—A Work in Progress

Mark's pre-game emphasis was the following: on offense get the ball inside, on defense block out. He also talked about #33, the University of Iowa football recruit and fine basketball player that is one of Osky's starters and leading scorer. Finally, he wanted the kids to run our 43 press after a made shot and the 53 press after a made free throw.

Our opening possession offensively is encouraging, as we did a nice job of swinging the ball that ends up inside for Kirk and an easy basket.

It's 7-7 in the middle of the first quarter.

We are playing a lot of kids in the first quarter. Zach, Colin, C.J., and Brandon Esterbrook have all been in the game.

C.J. and Colin each hit threes, and Klarc a two-pointer, but we didn't cover an out-of-bounds play well and gave up a three to #33. We've also given up way too many dribble drives to the basket, and we are down 12-16 with a minute and a half left in the first quarter. Kaleb hits a couple of free throws and Klarc a shot right at the end of the quarter to keep us close at the end of the quarter; we are down 16-18.

The score with 6:30 left in the second quarter is 19-20, Osky, after Kirk gets a nice pass from Colin for a score and a foul inside under the hoop. Colin later makes a nice steal in the press and also hits a runner for two. Kaleb attacks the hoop and makes a couple of free throws. Then C.J. gets a put back basket to make the score 25-27 halfway through the second.

The score doesn't change much, as with about :40 left we are down 25-29. We have gone for about 3:30 without scoring, but they haven't scored much either. Osky holds the ball for the last shot, and we do a good job defending, as they end up with a tough, last-second shot that doesn't come close.

After Colin hits a three we are down 28-29 with 6:40 in the third. They have run the same out-of-bounds play before with #33, and he has made us pay for being late in our help by hitting a three; he does so again. B-Mo had a nice pass to Kirk, who turns it into a basket and a foul to make the score 31-32, still in the early third quarter.

From here we miss shots and start turning the ball over, and all of a sudden we are down 31-39. Finally, after what seemed like forever, B-Mo hits a three-pointer to break our scoring slump; a quick swing pass created this during the second part of the fast-break with 2:45 in the third.

Osky now goes to their high-flex offense. This is a continuity offense that cuts different players into basically the same spots on the floor at various times as the ball swings from one side of the floor to the other.

The score is 35-36, Osky, late in the third quarter. From here things go from bad to worse as we drop to 41-48 with about 7:00 in the fourth quarter. Kaleb draws a foul and makes both free throws, Klarc forces a turnover, and the next possession Kirk scores on a layup, and all of a sudden we are back in the hunt, down 44-48. What felt like was slipping away is coming back.

Kaleb gets a layup, but then we give up a straight line to the hoop for a score. Colin then hits a three-pointer. We are down 53-54 after a series of back-door cuts by Osky. We just didn't defend this very well. Our safety was out of position, and we were losing vision of our own man. Kaleb hit a deep three, or we would be losing ground again. There is three and a half left in the fourth. The score remains the same with two minutes left. #33 hits two free throws with 1:30 left. Kirk returns the favor and makes two free throws. We are down 55-56, and C.J. fouls. The young man he fouls (you can tell by his form) is not a good free-throw shooter and misses both. We miss an inside shot; they take off on a break and get fouled. The shooter makes one, and it is 55-57.

Our next possession after a timeout is to run Cyclones for Kaleb. It's not exactly how it was designed, but we did get a shot. It's a miss. But B-Mo is there for the board and gets it back up with people all over him and scores! We are tied 57-57! The game goes into overtime.

Osky starts the O.T. with a three-minute possession that turns into a forced three-pointer by #33. Our defense was more patient than their offense.

We get the ball into Klarc and he throws it back out. The ball comes back into him and he hits a step-back two-pointer, and we are up two, their ball. Number 30 for Osky is fouled. He misses the first and makes the second; it's our ball, up one. After a timeout we've told the kids only layups and free throws, so we are trying to eat up the clock when Kaleb gets fouled. Kaleb is the guy I would want at the line (I still would) but he misses the front end of a one and one with 1:22 left in O.T.

In a quirky situation, Colin trips, and Osky ends up with an uncontested layup off of our missed free throw. In the next possession he is fouled. He makes the first and the second is halfway down (it looked good) when it came back out. It is 60-60 with :47 left. Osky does a good job of running the clock down and attacks with about :03 left. We foul; #33 goes to the line and makes both. We do get a desperation shot at the end, but it is no good.

Wednesday, December 13

I stayed up late last night "licking my wounds and feeling sorry for myself."

Today (again) I did lots of searching and discussions with players and Coach Core. I also did a blow-by-blow written description of plays that each player made during the game. I made three different lists of these plays. One list was in order, play by play. The next list was in order by player. So for example I listed all of Klarc's plays separately in order by quarter. And then finally I tallied up all individual plays and listed them in order together for four quarters.

What did I find? I don't know! I looked at it so many different ways I got more confused as I went. The one thing that seemed somewhat obvious was that our problems aren't a one-player issue. There doesn't seem to be someone that is the main culprit on either end of the floor. It would be easier to fix if there were. We would simply reevaluate that person's job and the number of minutes they were receiving. But when everybody seems to be part of the problem, it is much more complicated.

I gave all of these play-by-play sheets to Coach Core and asked him to take a look to see if I had missed anything; he took them home with him.

The best things (so far) that have come out of these discussions today are a couple of different points. One is the fact that had we scored six more points in two games we would now be five-zero rather than three-two; we are close. This normally would indicate either no change or very small changes (and maybe it still does) but we do have a number of kids that have played varsity ball for at least two years and maybe there is a little more call for change than normal. The other thing that came out of our discussion was a question, a good question. The question is—is it a personnel issue or is it a system issue? Are we playing the right guys, and are they playing the right number of minutes, or is our system the right one for this group?

As coaches we like to run the ball up the floor and play man-to-man defense. This has been for years a very successful system at Pella High. Maybe (and this truly is a maybe) this group might be better at doing something else. Maybe they should play zone and walk the ball up. I would hate that! But if it would give us the best chance to be successful then that is what we should do, period.

Wednesday, December 13, Practice #18
Give It All, More Shots, Safety, Last Second, Huggins, Swings, Match-Up Z, Adam, and Roles

The boys that played a lot last night have tired legs. In order to accommodate them we are going to change up practice a little bit. We would rather have the boys go 100% for a short time at things that they can do than have them go 90% for a long time and do things that they can't do.

I worked today in pre-practice with our post players while Mark had the outside players shooting the ball. Initially we worked only on drop steps to the basket against a man holding a blocking dummy. Both of our young players, Andrew and Kirk, stand up too high prior to catching the ball. They need to lower their center of gravity so that they don't get pushed out of position on the catch; that was a point of emphasis today during our drilling.

The team then does the "Brunner" and power layups and then follows up with power put backs. The power put backs are new and are preformed the same as an offensive rebound put back, but again, a man with a blocking dummy tries to disrupt the shot by banging them with the dummy. Nate and Kyle are the guys doing most of the banging.

We follow these two drills with three-on-two in the quarter-court and then block outs from a free-throw position. The perimeter players then went back to do some partner shooting while I took the posts again.

The second post drill was a catch-and-spin drill where the player would rebound off one side of the glass, do a spin dribble to the other side, rebound again, spin back again, and score. This will make them better at spinning, rebounding, and will give them a better sense of where the basket is as they improve. Mark also wants the outside guys shooting the ball more. He just thinks that part of our problem on the offensive end is that we are not doing enough shooting in practice.

The safety position was exposed against Osky. They did this in a somewhat unique way by moving their weak-side (the side away from the ball) offensive player up to the level of the free-throw line extended. By doing this it forced our safety to cover a greater distance to get himself under the basket. When a greater distance is involved it means more room for error on our part, and the fatigue of getting in and out of that spot also becomes a factor. In the shell drill today we tried to simulate that by moving everything up away from the basket. We also added an open post by making the offense try to guard five offensive players with four defensive players. One of those offensive players was stationed under the basket and couldn't move. Every pass that the offense could throw into him was considered a defeat for the defense. The point is this—we need a safety regardless of where from, how far they must run, or if they are tired; we must fill this spot.

Once again we are working on controlling the last few seconds of a quarter. Our kids still have not bought into this way of thinking, and we are again practicing all of the possible scenarios that could come about and practicing especially hard on the situation where the other team has the ball and is holding it for the last shot of the quarter. I thought Clayton really made a good point during this drill. He said we are just making bad traps, by making bad traps the offense can get the ball out quickly and easily. We are putting ourselves in a position to end up just chasing around the floor. That in my mind was a good point. A good trap gives the advantage to the defense, a bad one to the offense.

Bob Huggins at Kansas State asks a simple question. It goes something like this: defensively would you rather have the ball at the wing or in the center of the court. To me that is a no-brainer. Defensively we want it at the wing. If it's at the wing we know where the help is supposed to come from and who is responsible to be there. When the ball goes to the center there is no help side, and kids are confused about who should help and who should stay with their men.

So Huggins's next point is this. If you want it on the side of the floor, why would you deny the wing pass? When a coach (such as myself or Coach Core) can't answer a question with a good answer that makes sense in terms of making us better maybe it's time for that coach to consider making a change. The other thing that this change could make for us would be to get our off side wing (usually the guy that ends up as our safety) closer to the basket and make his coverage area less. I think this is what we are going to do. We are going to start giving up wing passes and deny more the swing pass back to the point. I'm in hopes that this is a major move to help our somewhat questionable defense so far this year.

I've coached for about 100 years; I know one simple way to make your offense better is to get the ball from one side of the floor to the other a few times. I call this swinging the ball. That is the reason behind our next drill. We run the Duke offense, but this time the offense must make 10 passes or shoot a layup whichever comes first. I like to do this same thing by whispering to the offense something like—the ball must get into the lane twice from each side of the floor before we can shoot. I just think it's easier and more effective than counting passes when the defense knows what is coming.

Finally we worked on our match-up zone a little bit more. If it's the personnel, that is one thing, if it's the system that isn't fitting the personnel, it's our job to change that so we continue to look at this.

I was about to leave the floor when Adam Miller came over and told me that one of the things that he noticed a lot last night was that our kids were looking at the bench a lot and especially when they made a mistake. He thought maybe they were playing afraid of being pulled. I look at this as a positive. Really, in some ways I think Bob Knight does this on purpose. My guess is that he feels that if his kids can learn to handle his heat then handling the heat of the game will be easy. It makes some sense; if you crumble because one guy got mad at you even though he is your coach, how well equipped are you to handle 2,000 people screaming at you during the heat of the game? I do, however, think this was a great observation by Adam; I also think we need to bring it up and talk about the positive side of handling it. This again is an opportunity to practice mental toughness.

After practice was over I mentioned to them that we just finished practice #15 out of approximately 80 practices. We aren't expected to be perfect or even excellent, we have time. But I also asked them to consider the question of what their role is on this team. I do think that by now they should have a pretty good idea of what they can do to help us be as good as we can be. The rebounder is just as important as the scorer, and the screener is just as important as the ball handler. It is not the best five players that win games: it is the five players that play the best that win. Mark finished by asking each player to bring to him a list of two things that they are best at and will bring to our team.

Thursday, December 14, Practice #19
Seals, Blocks, Charges, One on Two, Paint, Knight, Box and Diamond, Two-One-Two, Match Up, and Jason

To open practice the outside players did some shooting while the inside players worked on post moves. One of the things I found out while working with the posts is that they are not doing a good job of sealing the defensive player off with their butt. Their initial move and seal is good, but then they lose contact with the defender. I want them to maintain the contact and continue to seal.

We followed that with power layups and then power put backs. We want the boys to lean into the bag; we are leaning away from the contact. By leaning away it allows (in a real game) the opportunity for a taller player to have room to block a shot because there is room for him to operate. Leaning into a bigger player takes away his space to jump and puts him back on his heels; it takes the operating area away from the defender and gives it to the offensive player.

Coach Core added a lay-up drill that also incorporates the use of the blocking dummy. He put the dummy holder on the inside and a manager reaching for the ball on the outside and has the offensive player drive between them for a layup. We have just missed too many inside shots in our first five games, and I think Mark is trying to simulate the contact that he feels is creating our miscues.

For the first time this year we are doing a take-a-charge drill. The defender starts at the free-throw line elbow and rolls the ball to the offensive player stationed at the three-point line and across from the defender. The offensive player retrieves the pass and attacks the basket while the defender goes down to set up to take a charge. Coach Core, after watching film of the Osky game, thought that there was at least five times that we had an opportunity to take a charge that we didn't; thus the reason for the drill. I did think it was kind of cool that he told B-Mo (who is far and away our best at this) to go get a drink and relax while everyone else was going through the drill. He felt that B-Mo has already proven himself and wanted the guys to know that.

We then went one-on-two full-court. One offensive man attacks two defenders with the dribble as they harass and try to steal the ball from him. If the "O" can handle this situation in practice, going one-on-one should be okay in a game. One of the worst things about this drill was not the drill itself but the fact that it looked like a drill. Drills should be a microcosm of something that happens in a ball game, and we should respond accordingly. So when the ball gets knocked away and is loose on the floor with one guy jogging after it, I know that the kids are working this as a drill. Because in a real game I would hope that if there were a loose ball we would have bodies sprinting for and diving after it. We are actually practicing what we don't want to do when the kids treat this as a drill. Why would you practice that?

The NC drill was next and then the free-throw block-out drill followed that, so that the players are shooting free throws while they are tired.

The one-on-one driving-line drill drives me crazy. The last thing that Coach said to the guys was, "Keep the ball out of the paint." I got in a position where I could see all the baskets at one time and I'll bet not one person was able to accomplish that during the first minute of the drill. We got a little better as it went along, but certainly not good.

I really get the feeling that our players are not doing a good enough job of guarding their own man, and our next drill was created with that in mind. Two offensive players are placed in a quarter-court setting. They are guarded by two defensive players. We place a manager with a blocking dummy in the middle of the lane where the drill occurs, and he is assigned the job of setting random screens against the defenders. When there are only two defenders it is much more difficult to get help when guarding your man, and when we add a screener to this drill it creates even more problems. I took the big guys while Coach Core took the guards. On my end we weren't very good.

Another drill we used to do quite often that we are doing for the first time this year is named the "Knight Drill." This drill was named after Bob Knight and integrates screening and cutting to get open for shots. The drill also has an open passer (Andrew and Will were our guys) who stands at the top of the key as an outlet if the offensive players can't find an open cutter. Shooters must get their shots coming off of screens; they are not allowed to dribble drive into a shot. Remember the player from my son's team? He is the guy that taught me that the guy setting the screen is more likely to get open than the guy screening. Remember Kyle Korver? He is the guy that made a living out of setting back screens and then coming open off of those screens. I call that separating form the screen. Our guys in this drill are waiting too long to separate; it's screen and then separate with no hesitation. We are screen, standing, and then finally moving to the pass, and that is too late.

Next comes the five-on-four open-post drill again. The kids do a good job of covering that post with hustle and communication from the weak-side defenders.

We ran just a multitude of presses when we did our press offense and defense segment of practice. We worked against the three-one-one press, the two-two-one and half-court presses. The following diagram shows the difference in the three-one-one press and the two-two-one presses. The names of the presses originate from the formation that they are originally set in. With two players up and two players at half-court and one player all the way back, the two-two-one is also sometimes called a box press. The three-one-one press formation is often called a diamond or a one-two-one-one press. The normal trapping areas are shown in gray. The three-one-one press is the more aggressive of the presses; it is a press that takes more chances for traps. It also is more likely the one that will give up some lay-ups at the other end.

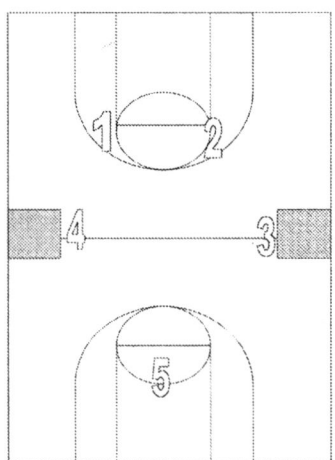
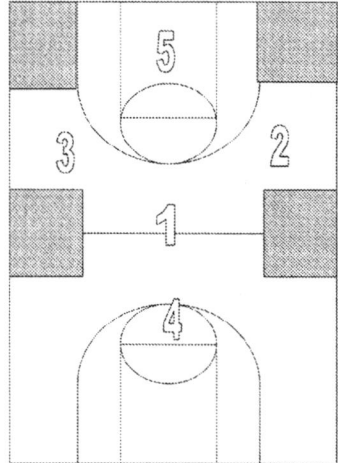

We also experimented with a two-one-two half-court press of our own; we are just taking a look at something we may come back to later.

We then go to the end of quarter situations and how we plan to handle them. After that we go to the one-break drill, which at the end of each fast-break we ran one of our set plays. We ran this against both man and zone defenses so that we practiced all of our sets.

We finished practice with more work on the match-up zone. I hate to admit it, but I'm starting to like this defense. It's simple and includes many of the principles that we use in our straight man-to-man defense.

Jason Dole (2005/06 graduate and ball player) came in to visit today, and I asked him to stop by practice and tell me what he sees. After practice we also had Jason talk with the players about what he noticed during practice. Jason, while an excellent speaker, struggled a little bit to tell the kids what he wanted to say; I think I know why; he was trying to explain the intangibles that I spoke of earlier. Why? Because that is what he did. How important are those intangibles? Last year Jason was injured and didn't play in all but 12 games. We were 11 and 1 with him and those intangibles, and about a .500 team without him.

Friday, December 15, Practice #20
Kirk, Stop-Score-Stop, 4:00 Scrimmage, Transfer, Rebounding, Lynn Swann, and Who Cares

The outside shooters were shooting outside shots, and the post players were working on their post moves prior to going power layups and then our newly formed layup drill against a blocking dummy and a defender reaching for the ball. Then came the Michigan drill and the 10 passes or a lay-up drill, the latter drill a five-on-five drill.

After this drill Kirk steps out. His feet are hurting him—another injury. He sits for the rest of practice with ice on his foot. Clayton got what we think is good news from the doctor. He doesn't think Clayton's groin or hip is the problem; he thinks it's his back. He also said that he thinks that Clayton can go full speed, and they will be able to correct it to ease the pain that he has had.

The stop-score-stop drill is another five-on-five drill intended to simulate a possession-by-possession mentality about building a lead. In order to get a lead a team has to do just what the drill says; you must stop the other team, score yourself and then stop them again. If you do that and you do it more than they do it to you, your team is going to win. We play that the winner of the drill is the team that accomplishes this first.

Something that we haven't done this year is a 4:00 scrimmage. After running these drills we set the clock and divide into teams and scrimmage for four minutes. The plan calls for us to have four of these scrimmages that will occur throughout practice in between drills.

After this first scrimmage we work on stopping the drive into the lane. I think we did a little better today. We then went again with the two-on-two and manager-in-the-middle, with a blocking dummy setting random screens on the defenders. We are trying to get the kids to guard their men and not rely on help. It's tough to help when it is two-on-two. And there is no help when it's one-on-one.

We went to war rebounding, and then we scrimmaged again.

Transfer, to convey, to carry over: it's the main purpose of a drill. We run drills, which are really small parts of the game isolated. The purpose of the drill, then, is to carry over into the big picture or the game itself. The best teams can do it and the teams that struggle, toil with the ability to transfer. We didn't begin to carry over our rebounding effort into the scrimmage. Coach was upset.

We did our shell drill with an open post; we didn't rebound. Coach was upset. We ran when we didn't rebound.

We did free-throw block outs and went back to scrimmage again. Again we didn't rebound; again we ran. Finally, after we got done running, we rebounded in the next part of the scrimmage—some.

We worked on out-of-bounds plays. We still have people that don't know what they are doing. We talked about it; they promised me they would have them down by Monday night. I asked them what would happen if they didn't. I wanted them to set the penalty. They said they would run.

Initially Coach Core said we weren't going to practice on Saturday; we'd get a day off. Wrong! We practiced so poorly he told the kids that it wasn't going to happen; we have practice tomorrow at 9:00 A.M.

Finally after Coach Core yelled, yelled some more, got mad, and we ran and then ran some more, we had somewhat of a decent practice. Why should the coach have to do that to get players to play harder? That is what I was asking myself towards the end of practice.

At the end of practice Coach Core told the players about his dream back in the 70s when he was a kid getting ready to play organized football for the first time in his life. His vision was of himself simulating the great Lynn Swann who played for the Steelers. It was all good, catching the ball and running for touchdowns with the people cheering him on. What he found out was that it didn't just happen that way. In order to be great and make plays he had to work, he had to sweat and he had to do the blue-collar things over and over again in practice. It took effort, work and sweat; touchdowns didn't just happen. His point was that he felt like some of our players thought that things would just happen without the work. They wanted the highlight film without any of the work. I thought it was a good point. I had another when it came my time.

I really like every kid we've got on the team; I really do. This is one of those teams that just doesn't have a turkey on it. They are all really nice kids. I told them that. I told them that what I was about to say wouldn't change that. But I did want to make a point. My point was about them caring.

I asked them to think of someone they really cared about. It could be their mother, their father, grandfather or mother, their brother or sister, anybody that they really cared about. Then I asked them to visualize that person standing under the basket in the paint. Then I asked them to compare how hard they would work to keep the ball out of that paint if it meant that they would forever lose that loved one if the ball got in the paint. I then asked them to compare that type of effort and attitude with the one they had for keeping the ball out of the paint for this practice. I just wanted them to know that there are different levels of caring and no matter how much they say they care, they weren't showing anywhere near that level of caring during practice. Right now I think they may care more about themselves than about winning. Again, that sounds bad, and I don't mean it to. I would be proud to have any one of these guys as my son. I'm just saying that they don't understand fully where their own priorities lie, and they must before or if they choose to change them.

Friday, December 15, Scouting at Pella Christian

After returning home at 5:15 from practice I found myself sitting in a warm gym across town at 6:30 watching the Pella Christian girls play the Knoxville girls in a basketball game. I wasn't there because I wanted to see that game; I was there because I was going to watch the PC boys play the K'ville boys. But if you wanted to see that game you had better get there early because this gym was only built to hold so many people, and my lovely bride and I were trying to make sure that we were two of them.

I haven't scouted a game in a long time. There are a number of reasons. One of my reasons is the simple fact that there really isn't much new in the game of basketball. We try to prepare for everything, and almost every team I know runs some part of that everything. Second, I think it detracts from our team. Coaches start coaching to beat certain teams rather than to make their own team better. They take short cuts to be ready for the game rather than to get ready for the season. Third, it takes away from me. The time I spend scouting is time I take away from preparation for our team and time that I take away from my family and my home. And adding scouting to a long season of basketball is just another thing to wear me out and not make me ready to coach our guys. I also think scouting at the high school level can really be misleading. Sometimes a kid gets hot who normally doesn't score, sometimes the scorer is cold; one time the team plays a zone while your team might play a man and the opponent may do something different against this team than they plan to do against you. Teams match up differently; a small, fast team will play differently and look different when it plays another small fast team than it would if it played a big slow team. And I tend to overrate or underrate teams based upon a one game performance; it's difficult to keep things in perspective.

With that said I went to scout because Coach Core asked me if I would like to see PC play. Coach has been very kind to me and has never ever said that he would like me to go scout. We've worked together maybe ten years now; I figured I owed him at least this. Besides, while the games that have been played between conference teams have been relatively close, Pella Christian has not only been winning; they have been killing their opponents. I really kind of wanted to see them.

You know that part that I said I tend to overrate or underrate teams? Well, I thought PC was awesome. They have speed, size, quickness, and I've always thought their coach, Larry Hessing, has done a great job of coaching his kids regardless of his talent level.

PC presses in a variety of presses. Mostly they showed a run-and-trap press very similar to our 34 press, something they haven't done before. Normally they are a two-two-one press team if they press at all. They also ran some three-one-one press. In addition to the press, they dropped back and played hard pressure man-to-man defense. They played with great effort and looked to intercept passes and trap.

Offensively they are very talented. Their point guard is very quick and very aggressive, and as usual their post players run the floor like guards, straight to a position under the hoop. The big kids they have can attack the basket inside or shoot from the outside. They still run some Kansas secondary break. This is a secondary break that many teams run—it usually goes something like the following.

The point will pass to a trailing post who swings the ball to a wing. This wing may now look to lob to their trailing post man who is now cutting to the hoop after getting a back screen from the low-post man (located at the baseline) on the opposite side of the floor. The post that sets the back screen may also be open for a shot after separating from the screen or he may throw a high-low pass down into the blocks or a flair pass to the point guard who receives a screen from the opposite wing.

If the point guard gets the ball (remember he flared out into the wing area) he may then shoot or try again to enter the ball to the post located at the block.

The PC big kids are big and they go deep into their bench; this allows them to place continuous pressure on their opponent on both the offensive end by running at full speed and the defensive end with their full-court pressure.

The Pella vs. Pella Christian game is a big game for the town of Pella. The Central College gym where we play the game, because it holds more people, will be hopping with around 1500 people. We will definitely have our hands full this year.

Saturday, December 15, Practice #21
Short Practice, Rebounding, Scouting, Ball Movement, Press "O,"
Tyler Terlouw, Wings, and Posts

We are going one hour today for practice. Our normal practices are usually about one and one half hours in length, even at the beginning of the season. We would rather have the kids go really hard for a short time than go too long and lose their intensity. If the kids know that they won't be going for two or more hours they are more likely to play hard all the time.

Because time is limited all of the drills are limited in time, and today they are even shorter. Coach Core and I got together prior to practice to compare our notes about our scouting reports. Mark watched Grinnell and Norwalk last night, and I spoke with him about what I saw at Pella Christian.

After yesterday's practice Mark was adamant that today we make every drill a rebounding and loose-ball drill. In other words, regardless of what drill we did we would make sure that we emphasized rebounding as part of it.

We opened practice with the perimeter players shooting outside and the post players working on their post moves. We followed that with a rebounding drill, then followed that with power layups. Even the power layups we yelled about going back to get involved with the boards.

We then drilled with the three-on-two, two-on-one drill where the players make two trips up and down the court. The first phase has three players attack two defensive players and the second phase back down the court has the two offensive players (who were the previous two defensive players) attacking the one man dropping back, who was the shooter during the first trip down the court.

After that we drilled the two-on-one drill with a chaser. This drill has the boys separate into two teams. One team strikes with two players attacking the other teams one man back on defense. Once the ball crosses half-court the team with only one defender sends a man onto the floor, but he must sprint to put his foot in the center circle before he tries to get back into the play and help his partner stop the offense. The drill is full-court, so upon completion on one end the rebound is taken, and they go to the opposite end where the first offensive team now has one defender back with another trying to get in the play as a chaser who must get to the center circle first.

We then went from shell number one where the kids are just practicing moving as the ball moves—we call it jump to the ball and then went to a shell where the offensive players were running give and go cuts or screening down for each other to get open.

After watching Knoxville last night, who was PC's opponent, I realized how much faster they move the ball than we do. I've known we hold the ball too long, but they gave me even more perspective on this. That was my main coaching point (from an offensive standpoint): move the ball. I made that call, "Move the ball!" to almost every player as they caught the ball. I think that really helped our offense. I know this is supposed to be a defensive drill but if you make your offense better, that alone will make your defense better by being more difficult to guard. Moving the ball faster and swinging the ball from side to side more often is going to be an even more important point of emphasis from me from now on.

We then went one-on-one full-court, two-on-two full-court, three-on-three full-court, four-on-four full-court and finally five-on-five full-court. While Mark was working hard on making the defense better in these situations by stressing fakes at the ball, trapping areas, and positioning, I was trying to work on the offensive end. I wanted the kids to first of all recognize the press for what it is and then make the correct response to what they see. Much like football teams that disguise the types of coverage their teams are using, so too do basketball coaches try to masquerade their presses. Offensive players cannot clear out against a zone press, and they should clear out against a man press. And if the press is a combo press like our 33 and 34 presses the players have to clear out, but if their defensive man turns back to trap it's the responsibility of the offensive man who left him to come back to the ball as a receiver for the man being trapped. We need more work on the press stuff, especially the offensive end.

Earlier I spoke of Tyler Terlouw. I'm feeling it again. I just see a lot of things I like about him. I really like his effort and attitude. I need to sit down and talk with him. There are also a lot of things I like about Brandon Esterbrook, I mean besides the fact that he seems like a good guy. But with Brandon, the number one thing he must do is keep his man out of the paint. He helps well, but he often loses his man when he helps.

Coaches have to decide how they are going to use their time in practice. When you practice more in one area you take away from another area. I think one of the things we haven't done enough of lately is the baseline-sink move on the weak-side defensive position. I'll ask Mark to incorporate that into our next practice.

We worked more on the match-up zone today to end practice. I need to speak with all of our wing players and remind them of this idea of sinking on the weak side, just like you would if you were playing man-to-man. About the only exception to this sink would be an offense that uses an overload set against a zone. I also need to remind them that we are never guarding a space without a man in it unless they are in a weak-side help position.

Offensively I think we need to work on our post-entry pass to start our offense. A post-entry, especially one that comes from a back screen first, is a terrific way to alleviate hard ball pressure by a defense.

Chapter 6—What Kind of Team Are We? Searching

Monday, December 18, Practice #22
Out of Bounds Plays, Mr. Bensink, Press Offense, Looking at the Hoop, and the Juniors.

We started with ball-handling drills and then shot Brunner lay-ups.

Based upon our discussion about our lack of ability to run our own out-of-bounds plays (that occurred on Saturday) we then ran every out-of-bounds play we had with each player occupying all of the various positions available to them with each play. The kids had made a commitment to get better at the plays by studying them over the weekend. I could see that they had done so; we were much improved in this area.

We then went to power layups, two-on-one with a chaser, and shell drill number one, which is a daily drill for us. We ran some back-to-back shell drills that integrated on-ball screens and then a shell with a give and go and a flash from the opposite side to the post area. During this time of the practice I was all about moving the ball and encouraging a great effort to rebound the ball. Coach Core was watching the defense and trying to make sure that the offense was running the shell properly.

We then stole a drill from Dave Bensink, our freshman coach, and used it for our varsity players. The drill has three offensive players on one side of the floor—one of those players is a post player while the other two are at the wing trying to enter the ball into the post. We work hard on both sides of the ball, denying the entry as well as making a hard post up. We also are emphasizing the rebound when the shot goes up.

We ran the Knight drill again and then went to our driving-line drill at the quarter-court highlighting the point of protecting the lane area.

From that point and for the next extended segment of the practice we went full-court, building in progression from one-on-one full-court all the way through five-on-five full-court. It is during this time that we are working on both the press offense and the press defense. Coach Core's point of importance is more toward the defensive aspect of the press while mine is more toward attacking the press with our offense. We are making progress in both areas. It's my opinion that the offensive end will be especially important during the Pella Christian game. The actual offensive attack is getting better, but during our next practice, which will be Thursday, we will need to stress the recognition of the press so our kids use the correct attack against the press that they see.

All of the one break drill that we use today is run from the out-of-bounds plays that the kids have been working on. This is a good reemphasis of getting better at these plays.

We worked really hard at getting the kids to look at the basket on the catch of each pass. In theory I think this makes a lot of sense. But in reality I think this has just served to slow our ball movement. Our catch and decision making has to be almost spontaneous. We need to be thinking ahead of what may happen upon the catch of the ball, and if nothing is there, move it quickly. This is two days in a row that we have moved the ball more quickly; there are times that I'm thinking to myself—*wow, that was awesome! I like it.*

Generally speaking the juniors don't: screen out, they don't break to the middle against the press, and they don't screen out on the defensive boards. This is a broad statement to include all of the juniors, but I do think that it tends to be more true than false.

We've had two really good intense practices in a row. The challenge is now to keep this going.

Tuesday, December 19

Clayton Boeyink (of all days) missed first period today; he over slept. Tonight's game was to be his first back since his injury, but our school has a policy (one I definitely agree with) that states that the athlete must be in school all day in order to be eligible to play. Clayton will not be playing tonight; he was scheduled to start. Speaking of Clayton he just at this moment walked into my office. He looked like a whipped pup the moment he walked in. He said he just forgot to set his alarm. I feel badly for him and his teammates, but I told him that mistakes happen. I mean that. I told him that I have made so many mistakes in my life that it is hard for me to be too critical of the one he just made. He apologized to me again and took off to talk with Coach Core.

Tuesday, Dec 19, Game #6, at South Tama
Our Record: 3-2; Conference: 3-2
Back to Back, Kaleb Our Post, Lane Zones, B-Mo, Patience on O and D, Stealing the Post, and Juniors

We come into this game after two of our better back-to-back practices, and I'm feeling really positive because of this. I also feel positive because (at least on paper) S. Tama has been struggling to win games. The down side is the loss of Kirk and now Clayton.

We've decided (with player input) to start small, so Brock will open at the guard spot, and Kaleb for all purposes, will be one of our post players. Actually I like this move; hopefully we will be a little quicker because of it.

Mark's point of emphasis in pre-game was to rebound the ball while mine was to move the ball. They actually work very well together because we are much more likely to get more rebounds of the offensive nature if we make the defense move and get them out of position by moving the ball.

Tama came out in a laning type of zone that tries to tip passes by extending into the lanes. Against this type of zone we needed some more dribble penetration to bring defenders back into the lane and create angles to pass the ball. This is something that we have struggled to do. Klarc penetrates pretty well, but this is not a strength for many of our other players. Once the penetration has been made then the decision-making comes in. The decision goes to the ball handler as to if it is wiser to pass out to an open man or go ahead and shoot the ball. We don't make a lot of good decisions during the course of this game. That is bad enough but when we do make the right decisions we are having a hard time finishing. The man that receives a kick-out pass from the guy that drives can't seem to make an open shot, and the times that the driver shoots, he seems like he has a hard time completing the shot as well. This can be a deadly combination for us.

Kaleb, because he hasn't had enough repetitions, is catching the ball in the post and kicking it right back out without taking a look at the hoop. If there is a place to hold the ball, this is it. I rarely complain when a player holds the ball in the post and takes his time either bringing an extra defender to him or going one-on-one four feet from the hoop.

B-Mo starts slowly again for us for the second game in a row. He doesn't appear to be playing as confidently as we would like him to. He can be such a good player, but sometimes he doesn't believe it himself. Brock, too, really struggles with this early season start. He gets beat with back cuts following his man into the lane. He too seems insecure about his play.

We do get some good fast-break push of the ball early in the game and a nice hoop. That puts us down 2-4 with about five and a half minutes left in the first. Colin hits a runner, and it's a tied game.

Hey, we ran our out-of-bounds play correctly and got Kaleb a wide-open look from three, he buried it to put us up 7-4. Andrew follows that up by drawing a charge, and it looks good for ole PHS.

Tama continues to pressure the wings, making it difficult for us to run our one-four offense against their zone. The obvious answer is to enter the ball to the post players, but Kaleb lacks experience there, and B-Mo is just not being very assertive. Fortunately one of the things that B-Mo is an expert at is drawing a charge, and once again he does so early in this game.

Kaleb gets a steal and a break away that ties the score back up at 9-9 after they had made a couple of free throws. Next Jesse draws a charge on the defensive end, our second one of the game. Finally Brock hits a shot late in the quarter, and we are up 12-9. B-Mo gets on the board with an inside shot on a nice pass from Kaleb. They score, and we come down and hold the ball for the last shot of the quarter. We turned the ball over with about :01 left, the score is 14-11 at the end of the first.

We open the quarter with a nice fast-break and a good pass from Klarc to Colin, who makes both free throws. B-Mo off of an offensive rebound gets fouled and makes two free throws; we are up 18-11.

We are moving the ball well, making Tama play defense, but our offensive patience ran out before their defensive patience did, and we threw up a poor shot that they rebounded. Next time down we got another offensive rebound and Kaleb had a great assist to Klarc under the hoop, and that makes the score 20-13. Klarc then makes one of two free throws on our next possession, but off of the missed free throw they come down with an easy layup.

With the score 21-15 we come down and throw the ball away. We then had a nice play that resulted in a missed layup; they then convert that rebound into a break and the score is 21-17.

Two juniors get together for the next hoop as C.J. finds Jesse under the basket for two points for the good guys. After some good "D" we throw the ball away and then give up dribble penetration to make it 23-19. We just can't seem to get a lot of good things in a row going all at the same time. If we would, that is how blowouts occur.

It is 23-21 with about 2:00 left before half when Jesse makes one of two free throws. Kaleb gives up dribble penetration and a score, but then comes down and hits a deep three; it's 28-25 late in the second. Again we throw the ball away but get it back and are holding to take the last shot of the quarter. But as C.J. tries to get the ball to Klarc it is tipped away, and they get an easy lay-up. C.J. didn't hang his head, though; we rush the ball down the court, and he hits a three at the buzzer to make it 30-30 at the break.

We started Jesse the second half to reward him for some good minutes in the first half. Kaleb hits one of those three point shots that roll around the rim about three times before it goes in. And then Klarc ties it up with two free throws early in the third quarter.

It's 38-38 halfway through the third quarter. We then give up a basket and a foul. With 1:29 left in the third they make a couple of "throws," and we are down 40-45. Colin hits a big three and that puts us within two.

Kaleb is trying to use his quickness in the post because he is not a large muscular player. He has made some steals in there, but when he misses he gives up layups or at least put backs off of the offensive boards. In Kaleb's defense—this is really his first live defensive post assignment.

At the end of three it's 43-48.

We played one possession of match-up zone, the first time we've tried it in a game, and we lost their man, who hit a three. We tried the zone simply because they are lighting up our man defense. Coach Core didn't like the looks of the zone and called a timeout. Later he also said that he knew we only had so many possessions and so much time left in the game, and he didn't want S. Tama to get too patient running their zone offense. We went back to man.

We are down 43-53 with 6:43 left in the game. It definitely is not looking good for us.

Kaleb finds B-Mo for a hoop, and then S. Tama's leading scorer comes down and misses badly on two free throws; they aren't close. Kaleb hits one of two free throws, and we are back in the hunt 47-53 with 4:02 left. We get a steal and Kaleb gets a layup; here we come.

Ah oh, Kaleb rolls his ankle and has to come out. Coach Core tells him that it is his call as to if he can play. In the meantime Klarc gets an offensive board and puts it back in. It's a two-point game! Klarc gets a steal, but they get the ball back.

Again our two juniors get together on the next defensive possession, and it's big. Jesse does a great job of hedging on an on-ball screen. This hedge is so good it allows C.J. to get a steal and score. It's 53-53.

B-Mo fouls out trying to pick up another charge with 1:03 left, and after they make a free throw we are down one.

C.J. gets an inside shot blocked, but again doesn't hang his head. Instead grabs his own offensive board and puts it back up and in; Pella 55-54!

They've got the ball back with :17 left after a timeout. We decided we were going to scramble on defense. We were going to play very aggressively and look for traps rather than let them run something that they set up during the timeout. During the scramble they do make a nice back cut, but Colin is there to make a huge help-side play. He is also there when they do get an off-balance shot up towards the board to get the loose ball and seal the game and the win for us.

Wednesday, December 20, 2006

Even though we came back to win it kind of felt like a loss to me; I am searching today again.

I got an email from Klayton Korver at Drake who saw the score and has been to some of our games and practices. As he is a former PHS player and current college player and one of the smartest players we've ever had, I really respect his opinion; I'm glad he sent me something.

I've also had discussions with Klarc and Coach Core today. They were good talks. We kicked around a lot of stuff. The best thing that Klarc said to me was that he and the rest of the guys were feeling really good and very confident about our PC game on Thursday.

I spoke with Colin, Jesse, and Clayton during the day. Colin feels like sometimes we coaches stress something so hard that the players overreact to what we say, and that is all they concentrate on doing. I know what he means, and to a degree I agree with him. However, as I explained to him this has not been a team that reacts very well to indirect or what I like to call "subtle" coaching. If we as coaches aren't fairly direct with this group they tend not to hear what we say. But I do think that there is a fine line with being really direct and trying to control what the guys are doing too much. Colin's complaint in this regard was that he felt we moved the ball too fast and we lost some rhythm last night. I really think that it was more a terminology thing on my part. I have been yelling, "Move the ball!" What I want them to do is to make quicker decisions when they get the ball. There is a difference, and I need to do a better job of making sure I'm saying what I'm thinking. I loved the fact that Colin came in to talk about that. We want them taking ownership of the team; we want them making suggestions and weighing in with their opinions. I've always asked players to be critical of what we are doing (to us not to others) so that we can talk about things. I figure I can't go wrong with this. If I can't justify what I've said I need to change my thinking or clarify my terminology. If I can justify what I think, it just makes it more clear to both the player and me as to why we are doing things by discussing it.

As an example last night, as the zone was a laning zone we should have driven it more or attacked it more and swung it less. That's what I wanted. They heard me say, "Swing it," rather than "Make a quicker decision."

I thought Jesse was closer to hitting on something more important, however. He just felt like we weren't making adjustments very well. If something happens in a game and it happens over and over again, the players need to make adjustments and not wait for a timeout and specific instructions from the coach. "Adjustments:" that is a word I used to say constantly when coaching; I'm thinking maybe we need to bring it back.

Clayton felt like there might be too much control on the offensive end. I think that is another consideration. Coaches have a tendency to over coach the offense and under coach the defense, rarely the other way around.

Wednesday, Dec 20, Practice #23
Legs, Klarc, and Kaleb, One-Four, Set Plays, High-Low, PC, Recognition, and Laugh with Coach Core

Coach Core and I made a decision even before the South Tama game that our practice on Wednesday would have to be an easy one just to save the players' legs. I was hoping that the previous night's game would be one that maybe some guys could rest, but it went to the wire, so there was no rest available.

We started practice with post and perimeter shooting and then went to floaters.

We put the kids in their press offense and asked the defense to vary the defense they were in without telling the offense. We also tried trapping late in the possession. If I were PC, I would try to press us by making someone else besides Klarc handle the ball so we tried to take Klarc away as well and made an adjustment when that happened. We also put Kaleb in the reversal position for Klarc to pass to rather than a post player. Kaleb will give us an extra ball handler against the press. That was the last thing we did full-court, and it lasted only about 10 minutes.

We then worked on the one-four across offense against both the man and the zone defenses in the quarter-court, adding a point-cut through the lane. Then we worked against the man defense by running our four-out offense as well as Duke.

I take it back; we are working full-court, just getting back on defense. One of PC's greatest assets is their fast-break. We are also going to send two back on defense when the shot goes up to try to stop the break. Normally we send four to the offensive board and only one back.

We worked on our set plays; our three main ones are Cyclone, Bulldogs, and Creighton.

The rest of practice was some short drill work on defending the high-low pass (the pass that goes from the high post to the low post) and working on various sets and plays that PC runs. If we can keep the ball out of the high post it really stops this part of the game for them. Or at least if we can make them catch it up higher it will be a slower and more difficult pass for them.

Their offense (in addition to the high-low-post pass) includes a flare screen for their guards. We want to switch the flare screen so we can occupy the safety position with the same player consistently without moving him in and out of the spot. The other thing that the switch will do would be to allow us to take away the point pass back from the wing.

There are two things that Pella Christian will do out of a one-four-low set. A one-four-low set means that they set up with the point guard at the top of the key and the rest of the players along the baseline, two at the blocks and two out in the corners. The first thing they do is just simply clear the area for their quick and talented point guard to attack one-on-one against his defender. By putting everyone else low they take away help from other defenders unless they come up and off of their own men. If someone helps defensively off of his man, the point then throws the pass to the open man. It's dangerous to help up from the baseline for the obvious reason that the offensive players are closer to the hoop.

The second thing that they do out of this set (on the right side) is to set up a back door cut. So actually they sprint from a one-four-low position into a one-four-high position. By that I mean they sprint up from the baseline position to similar positions but now across the width of the floor from the foul-shooting line extended. When they get to this position, whichever post player is open receives a pass from the point guard and that post then passes to the wing on his side who has immediately cut back door looking for a layup.

We will attempt to stop both plays by first of all recognizing the set as initiating from a one-four-low set. This should tell us that one of the two plays is coming and should really help our ability to defend it. Secondly we must fake at the one man as though we are going to help or double team him and then quickly recover to our man. And finally against the back cut, if the defensive wing recognizes the initial set he would anticipate and stop the cut.

The following diagram shows one of Pella Christian's out-of-bounds plays underneath their own hoop. The passing goes from #1 to #5 to #2. After #5 passes, he cuts off of a screen by #4 coming across the lane (shown in **Diagram a**). In **Diagram b**, #1 cuts off a staggered double screen set by #3 and #4. #2, who has the ball now, may pass to #1 or #5 coming off of screens or may look inside to #4 or #3 after the screen.

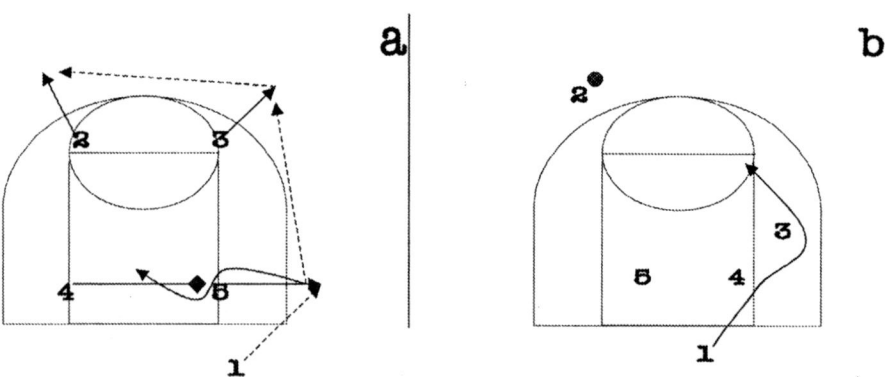

Finally today we had a nice laugh with Coach Core as he was teaching the kids how to beat some of the screens that PC will set during their offense. He wanted the kids to beat the screen before it was ever set, in other words, get closer to the ball and beat the offensive player to the spot he wanted to occupy on his cut. That will effectively defeat the offensive man's cut.

Coach made the mistake of trying to demonstrate the defensive move against one of our players setting the screen; I gave this idea of a live demonstration years ago when I realized that it made me look even dumber than I normally look (that is hard to do, I'm pretty natural at that dumb look). At any rate, being the young coach he is, Coach Core tried. He said of himself (after a less than stellar performance), "I know I'm not exactly poetry in motion (he definitely wasn't), but if I can do this you guys surely can." He made a great point, but the poetry in motion thing was pretty funny.

December 21, Game #7, Pella vs. Pella Christian at Central College
Our Record: 4-2; Conference: 4-2

In our pre-game I talked about the ability to pay attention to the things we are supposed to do. I asked the kids not to "time travel," during the game. I asked them not to think about something bad that just happened (that is past time travel) or something bad that could happen (that is future time travel) but to stay in the moment of the game to pay close attention to the play at hand. I tried to give them an example by pointing out how well we remember what to do in practice. For example when we tell the kids to run our one-four they get into it and for the most part make the right cuts, although not always the right decisions. But in games so far we sometimes don't even know how to set up or cut in the one-four set.

Now I ask you, is that a physical ability? Of course not; that is the ability to do what you are supposed to do when you are supposed to do it. It's obviously a mental ability. In tonight's game we have all sorts of reasons not to pay attention to what we are supposed to do. We will basically choose to pay attention to something; it could be the people surrounding us (moms and dads and friends or even the opposing crowd) or to shiny white uniforms we have on or even the bright lights. That is the down side; we've got all sorts of reasons not to pay attention to each possession. The upside is that this also gives us a chance to get better at paying attention (to what we are supposed to pay attention to) when there are all of these reasons not to. We can practice at this and get better.

I'm trying to do two main things with this little talk. One is to really make them see the importance of our concentration, and two is to ease the pressure of the game. I ease the pressure with the thought that we are practicing to get better (not to be perfect).

Also via Klarc's request we broke out the bear drill in the locker room. This has been a great drill to alleviate fear or to get the guys pumped up. It's a pretty tough drill, but it always leaves the guys laughing and shouting. It goes like this. I have the boys line up in two rows facing each other. I then had a veteran of the drill like Klarc growl like a bear growls, right in the face of his partner across the way, loud and snarly. So after the example I have one line do it all at the same time to the other line, and then the opposite line does it back, and the big finish is with both lines growling at the same time. It's funny to watch and it's crazy to see how excited and relaxed it seems to make our guys.

In spite of the bear drill both teams started off with some early game jitters. The game is held at our local college because they have more seating available to the public. This gym at one time held about 2,000 people but now is down to probably around to 1500-1600 fans, still a sizeable group to watch a Thursday night high school ball game. Naturally the Pella vs. Pella Christian game is a big game within Pella. This one is no exception. The place is packed with a frenzied atmosphere that has both teams turning the ball over and missing shots.

We started the game by having our first two shots blocked, then B-Mo scores, and we turn it over. They started with two turnovers themselves and missed a shot on the next possession.

Klarc hits a hoop, but in the meantime they have a two-pointer and come back with a three; we are down 4-5. Kaleb gets a dribble drive and a basket.

The PC press is not effective against us early in the game because they have chosen to guard Kaleb with their point guard. Kaleb is taking him down the floor and out of the area where he could help in the press.

After some nice ball swing Colin drives in and scores and gets fouled for an old-fashioned three-point play, and that puts us up 9-7 halfway through the first quarter.

Clayton Boeyink is in our lineup for the first time all year. He really has only had about two really hard practices, and this is the first time he has competed in a sport since somewhere in October. I know he will add intangibles to our team even though he may not be ultra sharp. He brings hustle, speed, and quickness along with a willingness to battle for loose balls and the unselfish pass-first attitude that all good offenses need. He is also the man assigned to control their point guard. He is our quick guy, and we've got him on their quick guy. Clayton is stepping up to the challenge.

Jesse, Brock and C.J. are to play in short spurts this game. The college floor is 10 feet longer than the high school floor, and there is no question that PC has a deeper bench than we do. We've got to get these kids in the game not only to get them some time but also to get our starters some rest time. Jesse hasn't played much but will do some subbing at both the point and mostly wing positions. Brock will fill in at the wing, and C.J. will sub mostly at the wing but possibly some at the post.

With 2:29 left in the first we are down 9-11. After Klarc draws a charge with 1:00 left in the first the score is 11-11, and fans are into it, loud and clear. Now with :30 left in the quarter, and PC up 13-11, we are looking for the last shot. We did get it, a little runner by Colin, but he missed, and the score remains the same.

B-Mo needs to make quicker decisions on the offensive end. Oftentimes he is going one on two, he must be a little more patient until the ball has moved before he shoots the ball. We really want him to be more of a scorer for us, he hasn't been really even looking to score, so he is in a bit of a foreign situation tonight and may struggle, but he is willing to try.

When we're 11-15 Clayton draws an offensive foul to prevent further damage.

Pella Christian is the best team we've played. They just squeaked by Osky the other night when they jumped out to a big lead but didn't finish well. Other than that they have been blasting teams by 20-30 points.

Kaleb hits a couple of free throws, and then Colin gets the ball back for us with a steal; we are down 13-15. When they get the ball back it's Klarc's turn to poke the ball away, and Colin, again while going for the loose ball, gets fouled. We can't score, but they come back with a three against us.

Kaleb makes it 15-18 after a score with another dribble drive. PC misses, and Brock Pope ties it up with a three. Again there is a scramble for a loose ball that after a tie up goes to us with the possession arrow. Kaleb then makes a nice pass to Clayton, and all of a sudden we are up.

After a couple of exchanges by both teams they hit a three, and we are down one point. It doesn't last long, though, as Colin really attacks the press with a drive that puts us right back into the lead. After they turn the ball back over B-Mo hits Jesse with a nice pass, and he makes two free throws. We are up 24-23 with 1:49 left in the quarter.

We want our defensive players to help each other, but they can't stay when they help. They must help a fraction of a second to slow the opponent so the original defender can catch back up and then recover to their man. Colin did a great job of helping but either expected a complete switch with Clayton picking up his man or he stayed too long, and his man hit a three.

Kaleb misses a short shot but stays with it and gets a put-back basket. It's 26 all, and we get the ball back with a steal. We run our Creighton play for Kaleb, and Klarc sets a terrific screen for him, he buries the three. After a wild scramble for a loose ball they end up with a three-on-one break that Kaleb is back trying to defend. He ends up fouling the shooter, who makes one of the two free throws.

With :25 left and leading 29-27 we will attempt to hold the ball for the last shot. At the buzzer we get a wide-open look from three but miss the shot.

At halftime we talk about trying to slow the ball swing of Pella Christian and defending their screens as to whether we will switch them or stay with our man. I personally feel really good about how we are playing and tell them so; I tell them to go out with a positive attitude and feel good about themselves.

They open with a quick basket—there goes the lead. We then turn the ball over, and they hit a three. Great half-time speech, huh? We are down 29-32.

They have moved their point guard up to the front to get him involved more in the press. This move will make them stronger in the press but should weaken their defense against Kaleb.

Colin scores with an assist from Clayton, and we are down one.

I have a fear about the depth of PC's bench. I know that between the extra length of the floor and more players to play, PC will try to tire us out.

B-Mo scores; we're up 34-32 with 6:00 left in the third. Unfortunately they come back and hit a three. We took a tough shot and missed. They then miss from three but score with a put-back basket. With 5:00 left in the third it's 34-37. Kaleb makes two free throws, and we're down one.

When we take Clayton out the PC point guard almost immediately takes advantage of this by creating for his teammates.

As the game goes on we have some guys trying too hard to do too much. We are also holding the ball too long as our decision-making right now is slow.

We are down by five with 2:40 left in the quarter. We have hit a bad spurt in this third quarter. We are hurrying on offense and taking some shots too early without a real advantage. A number of these shots turn into a break for PC. B-Mo then turns the ball over with a charge. I'm also afraid Klarc who has worked (always does) really hard looks like he is a little tired, as he has trailed his man a couple of times and has made some bad choices that is uncharacteristic of his play.

Then the real cap to a poor run for us is a simple inbounds pass we make from the sideline that turns into a fast-break layup for them and an easy score. I also think that B-Mo looks a little tired. He gives up quite a bit of size to their posts and is working hard both running the floor and playing defense. They are running four different posts in and out during the game; this requires great effort from B-Mo to stay up.

We are down 10 when Kaleb cuts it to eight with a little runner in the lane. We then got a break when they turned the ball right back over to us, but we returned the favor to them when we didn't take care while dribbling and had the ball poked away. We got the ball back but then Klarc gets hung up with no place to go, and they once again regain possession of the ball.

The officials that we have for this game are the best of the best. They have worked state championship games, and there is no doubt that these guys are the ones I want. With that said even the best make a few mistakes, and during Pella Christian's next possession one of the very few mistakes Clayton made all game took place when he gave up a drive to the basket and (in my opinion) the official also called a bad foul on Clayton. We are down 38-48 with less than a minute left in the third quarter.

Within a couple of more possessions there are both missed shots and turnovers, but following a poor inbounds pass on our part and a steal by PC, Clayton made a huge play by stealing the ball back and going full-court the opposite direction for a bucket and a foul. Going into the fourth we are down 41-48.

That Clayton was like a rocket on the steal. He is our best athlete and can really get out and go. One of the things that I said during halftime was, "Welcome back, Clayton; it is good to have you back!" He makes a difference in our team!

PC picks up a charge against Kaleb trying to get to the basket. And then they come down and power the ball inside for an easy two.

There is a fine line for a team that wants to play fast-break basketball between the times we should attack and the break is still on and when we should realize that the break is over and now we should swing the ball and move the defense before we shoot. Good fast-break shots will come very early before the defense gets set. But bad quarter-court offense shots also come early too, when the break is done and we haven't moved the defense. Right now we are in the bad-shot mode. There is plenty of time left in the game, but we have lost a bit of composure and are rushing our quarter-court offense and taking quick shots that oftentimes then will turn into a fast-break offense for the opposing team. During this stretch because we are shooting too early in the offense we haven't moved the ball to the opposite side of the floor at all prior to our next shot.

When the shot goes up, we miss and they run down and hit a three-pointer and that puts us down 12 points early in the fourth quarter.

The next time down we do get some great ball movement, and Colin hits a three to bring us back within nine points. But then we get mixed up on a switch on the defensive end and PC responds with a three of their own.

Clayton makes a terrific entry pass into Kaleb cutting into the lane, and he scores a two to cut the lead to 10 points.

With 5:30 left in the game we are down now 45-56 when PC misses, and Kaleb, who has been a man on the defensive boards, makes a great outlet pass to Clayton, who in mid-air makes a touch pass to Klarc for an easy layup off of the break.

As the game gets near the end, PC takes a timeout. They come back out with a lot of patience on the offensive end while we are trying to scramble a little bit looking for a turnover. They do shoot and miss, and we get the rebound. We can't take advantage, as we throw the ball away, and it turns into a fast-break going the other way. Once again Clayton comes to the rescue by drawing a charge to stop the layup.

Then (in my mind) we have a tired mistake as Klarc throws the ball out of bounds. The kid has worked really hard; this is not a normal play for him. I just believe that he lost his concentration for a moment because he was pooped and threw the ball away.

We've changed now to a two-two-one zone press to try to look for a way to pick up the tempo and create a turnover. With their little point man this will be difficult to pull off, but we must do something.

Regrettably it was difficult and resulted in a bucket and foul against us, as we didn't rotate back to guard the basket correctly. Now with 3:48 left we are down 10 and again turn the ball over. Further into the quarter we miss a three, but Klarc is there for a put-back hoop.

We did everything but turn them over on the next possession but they managed to not only hold on to the ball but we eventually fouled them. They did miss one of two free throws to help keep us around. B—Mo gets a hoop on a drive, but again they go their post man for two points. Kaleb is defending in at the post (remember we want our defensive post players to either get the steal or play behind, they cannot go for a steal and miss or it turns into an easy two) makes a mistake by going for and missing the steal. Kaleb will get better at this decision the more he plays inside, it will just take some time. Additionally if you are going to take a chance now is the time because it is late in the game.

This has been a highly competitive game that has given the fans their money's worth. While it hasn't been picture perfect it has been close and both teams have shot the ball relatively well. These defenses have been putting forth great effort but in this game it's the old question of, "Is this good offense or bad defense?" I think it has just been pretty good offense especially on PC's part. We haven't been an amazing defensive team this game, but we haven't been bad; they are just really shooting well.

We came down and probably got the most open three we've gotten all game, and not only missed but air-balled the shot. We did go to a more aggressive type of scramble defense, and turned them over, and we did get another look from three, but again we couldn't make the shot.

After a couple of turnovers and missed shots on the part of both teams along with some missed free throws by Pella Christian and even a miss of the front end of a one and one by Kaleb, we are down 52-61 with 49 left, and we must foul now to get the ball back. The final score is 52-62.

One of the things I started doing a few years back and have since given it over to Coach Core is a shooting camp during the summer. My idea of this type of camp was to give the kids a chance to shoot the ball during the summer. It was designed to get a lot of shots up during about six hours of time commitment. I am no shooting expert (although I always kiddingly take credit for making Kyle Korver the shooter that he is today) but one of the theories that I do buy into about shooting is that a good shooter shoots on the way up, probably earlier on the way up than an average shooter does. We used to work on this during this camp time, and I remember it really seemed to help B-Mo in particular. I wonder if we need to stress this a little more during practice because B-Mo has been complaining about his shooting lately and seems to have lost some confidence in it.

Coach Core was very positive with the kids after the game. He said that he felt like in this game we had taken a step forward in spite of the loss. I agree; I was really pleased with the boys. I read a quote by Coach K at Duke, and he said that "sometimes in a loss your team may not have played badly; they may have played well, but the other team might just have played better;" I think that happened tonight.

For the game we shot 4 out 19 from three-point range (25%) while PC shot 7 out of 18 (39%). From inside the arc we both shot 30 times, they made 18 (60%) while we made 16 (53%). Pella Christian missed some free throws only making 5 of 12 (42%) and helped us to stay close because we made 8 of 9 (89%). We had 17 turnovers compared to only 12 for PC. We also lost the battle of the boards 28-22.

Our leading scorer and rebounder for the game was Kaleb, as he had 17 points and eight rebounds. Colin chipped in with 10 points, and Clayton had an amazing game for his first game of the year, with seven points, two rebounds, and he led us in assists with five.

Friday, December 22

I found out today that Klarc might be a little banged up. One of the boys came in and said that he thought he might have gotten hurt in the second half when he was diving on the floor for a loose ball. I sure hope this is nothing serious. It has been a really unusual season this year for that sort of thing. We have yet to have our entire team together. We've gone from early season injuries to B-Mo, Clayton, and Jesse, to finally getting Clayton back, to now losing Kirk. And now comes Christmas break. This year our band takes a trip out of state during break, so we still won't have everyone around once practice begins again because at least two or three of the guys will be on the band trip. Hopefully someday soon we will put it all together and have everyone around at the same time.

There is no practice tonight as we are off for break.

Chapter 7—Stats and a Break After Our First Seven Games

Team Stats

Record 4-3
Offensive% from three—28%
Offensive% from two—45%
Overall shooting%—38%
Defensive% from three—28%
Defensive% from two—51%
Defensive overall shooting%—44%
We have attempted 61 more three-pointers than our opponents
We have attempted 27 fewer two-pointers than our opponents
We have made 5 more free throws on 6 more attempts than our opponents
We have outscored our opponents by 9 points
We have 23 fewer rebounds than our opponents
We have 32 fewer turnovers than our opponents
We have one less foul than our opponents

Individual Stats

Most made threes—Kaleb 12
Most attempted threes—Kaleb 42
Highest three-point%—Colin with 35%
Most made twos—Klarc 27
Most attempted twos—Klarc 52
Highest two point%—Kirk 60%
Most free throws made—Klarc 16
Most free throws attempted—Kaleb 27

Highest free throw% with ten or more attempts—Colin 69%
Most total points—Kaleb 80
Most rebounds—Kaleb 63
Most assists—Klarc 29
Most steals—Klarc 12
Most charges taken B-Mo—7

Conference Standings

Pella Christian 7-0
Oskaloosa 4-2
Grinnell 4-2
Pella 4-3
Newton 3-3
Knoxville 3-4
Boone 2-3
Norwalk 2-4
South Tama 0-6

Chapter 8—That Was a Break?
Let's Get Started Again!

Thursday, December 28, Practice #24
Bad Practice, Players Gone, Kyle and Nate, B-Mo and Kaleb,
Brainstorming, Carry Over, Partners, Hot Shooting, and Brandon

The first day back after Christmas break is always an unbelievably bad practice. The kids are usually in bad shape physically because like me they eat poorly and stay up until all hours of the night with friends or just because they can since there is no school now. The ball itself seems like a foreign object to the players too when they get back. What seemed so effortless prior to break (things like passing and dribbling) now seem to require supreme concentration that takes away from things like running plays and other basic basketball stuff.

Today is no exception to the rule; the kids are trying. We just aren't very good. And to add to our woes we are without six players. Five players are on the band trip in Florida, they are; C.J., Jesse, Andrew Ter Louw, Tyler Terlouw, and Justin. One player Klarc is seeing relatives in California. So once again we still do not have our entire team together. And it looks like we never will this year. Kirk showed up today with a boot on his foot and fracture in his foot; the doctor says he is out for six weeks. It's one of those years!

While Kyle and Nate do a lot of standing in practice they are always ready if called upon. If you're a coach you can't help but love these guys who have amazingly good attitudes. They are called upon today because they are one of only 10 players that we have available to practice. But once again it's not a problem for those two guys; they are always willing to help if they can.

B-Mo and Kaleb have struggled with their shot the first seven games of the season. Because of that I thought I'd take them aside and work with them a little bit on their shot while we were doing our partner shooting. I'm not a shooting guru, but I know that being on balance has got to be one of the basics that is important so I asked them to do two things today. One, I wanted them to shoot earlier on the way up in their shot, so they would be using their legs. And number two I asked them to finish with their toes pointed down towards the ground! I really believe that the lower body might be more important than the upper body and to a degree the shooting arm. The bigger muscles of the leg are much more consistent (because they are bigger) than those of the arms and this leads to more dependable up force on the shot. Also by asking them to point their toes down to the ground I'm encouraging them to be straight up and down and reinforcing the concept of using their legs.

Prior to practice Mark and I talked about any brainstorms that either one of us might have had over the break. Interestingly Mark and I both had some similar thoughts in a couple of things. He mentioned using a five-man substitution system by sending in all the juniors at one time. I had thought about a five-man subbing program (North Carolina used to do this with pretty positive results when Dean Smith was there) but not necessarily with just the juniors. He also said something about going zone. This is truly amazing because both of us believe so much in the man-to-man defense, and I had been thinking along the same lines. I suggested that maybe we look at our Partners offense without the Cyclone option at the top, but just create Partners on one side and work with a point guard at the top.

Practice started with ball handling—tennis balls and two-ball dribbling drills and then progressed to three-line passing and the Michigan drill. We then played three-on-two full-court and dropped back into a two-on-one situation.

We went to our one-on-one drill at the quarter-court and reminded the guys to keep the ball out of the paint. After that we extended the drill to one-on-one full-court. It was about now that the men looked mighty tuckered out. In fact, Nathan stepped out the door and visited the "urp monster," he chucked up his cookies—literally. But like a trooper he jumped back in and went back down to the other end of the court.

Then in order to review and give the guys a bit of a chance to rest the players did two step block outs from a standing position and then moved back to create a close-out drill that finished with a block out.

It's amazing to me that we just worked on keeping the ball out of the lane and blocking out, but almost immediately when we go four-on-four we first don't keep the ball out of the lane and then we don't block out. The carry over from drill to live play is still something we struggle with. About this time we had to go to free throw shooting, because now it was Tyler's turn to visit the "urp monster." That makes two times for Tyler, as he also had made a visit earlier in practice. But just like Nathan, Tyler is back and ready to go within a few minutes.

Remarkably our Partner offense with just an unguarded player on top to swing the ball looked about as good as we've looked so far this year in our man stuff. It slows the movement a little bit; that allows for the cutters and the screeners to be more aware of their jobs, and it also guarantees court spacing and balance; maybe we are onto something here.

B-Mo is on fire, he can't miss. I'd like to think the little shooting lesson before practice helped, but I know this can't be all of it; he is just in one of those modes where he isn't missing—he is hot. It is fun to see and hopefully will help his confidence. Kaleb is still kind of a mystery; he is still passing up shots. We have tried to encourage him to shoot more, but almost always his first look is to pass. That would be a nice thing to have if we had more shooters around him, but on our team he needs to shoot.

After the Partners offense we set the players in a couple of different four-man zones and worked on attacking them as well; B-Mo stayed hot.

Finally, to finish our team stuff we went four-on-four and turned it into a full-court game. One of the things I've noticed with Brandon E. is how often he ignores an easy pass to make a tougher one. Tomorrow I will ask either Andrew or Will to chart this for me so I can show him after practice. Brandon, too, has an ability to shoot the ball and isn't a bad player, but he must reduce his turnovers and make better decisions about when to shoot to get more time.

All in all for a first-day-back-from-break practice this one in comparison to others wasn't too bad. Oftentimes the second day is much better than the first; we shall see tomorrow.

Friday, December 29, Practice #25
Ten Guys, Set Plays, Louisville, Jump to the Ball, Get Closer to the Ball, Weak-Side Guard, Man Drill, and Kaleb Shooting

It is strange to walk into the gym and see only 10 players there to practice; once again it is the same 10 as yesterday.

Our initial drills consisted of two-hand rebounds followed by partner shooting, followed by free throw block outs.

We then went through all of our set man-to-man plays, which consist of Louisville, then Cyclones, then Creighton and finally Bulldogs.

Louisville is a simple set designed to get a little motion. The set is moved up high away from the baseline to allow for back cuts from the 3 and 4 players. A good way to originate the offense is to make a guard-to-guard pass first so that the weak-side defender must make a long run into the help side after he guards his man up to the free throw line extended.

Louisville

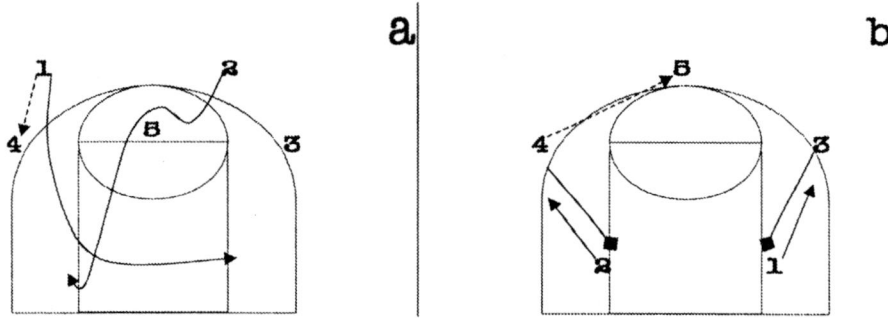

#1 and #2 will end up simply cutting through and ending up on the baseline while the man who caught the initial pass (in this case #4) reverses the ball to #5 as he steps out. The two original wings will then screen down for the baseline players. There are many options off of this such as using back screens rather than down screens or hitting the middle man (#5) and running a cross cut off of him with other options. But for now we don't even run this really well, so we are stuck here until we do.

With limited numbers of players it is difficult to do lots of full-court stuff, so we must try to get into this while the players' legs are fresh. With that in mind we progress from one-on-one full-court up through four-on-four full-court, adding one player at a time as we go.

We then did some more partner shooting sandwiched around some lay-back layups.

From that point we went into our shell drill. We worked on jumping to the ball. As the ball moves we would like every defensive player to move with it. There would never be a time that someone on the defense doesn't move with the pass. In some ways that is why it is harder to become a great defensive team than a great offensive team. On offense, when someone gets hot, you can be pretty good at scoring points, while on defense if all five guys aren't doing their job the defense will immediately break down; on defense it takes all five working together.

Good help-side defense is really pretty simple. You can call people safeties or give names to patterns, but really it's this—the guys not guarding the ball need to get closer to the ball. Now if you get too close to the ball the offense will counter with flare screens, but that is kind of what defense is. You have to pick your poison. I guess I would rather give up the flare screen than some of the other stuff if you don't get close enough to the ball. There is one exception to this rule of getting closer to the ball for us, however, and that is the weak-side man guarding the guard area when the ball goes to the opposite corner. He doesn't get closer. He must drop straight down the lane line to the weak-side post area; if he doesn't, if he does get close to the ball side he is very susceptible to flare screens, and there is also a lack of weak-side rebounding in case the shot goes up.

We added to the shell drill by incorporating a couple of offensive moves designed to make it more difficult on the defenders. The moves were a down screen on the weak side and a basket cut on the strong side.

I really liked the next drill where we ran man drill, and we allowed everything, including screens and dribbling. In essence we worked on guarding our own man with no help. I've felt for a while now that the more of this we do, the better defensive team we would become. What I really found interesting today was that initially Clayton scored on Colin twice, easily, and then all of a sudden when we announced who was scoring on whom it became more important to Colin to get Clayton stopped. When it did become more important he got him stopped! I also noticed that Brandon E. gave up a shot to his man and that he was probably about 20 feet away from him when he caught the ball. Remember, Brandon wasn't supposed to help at all, but as I've suspected for some time now he helps too much. He needs to learn better to stay with his man.

We then finished by running our Partners offense and shot free throws for sprints.

After practice I asked Kaleb to stick around for about five minutes to work on his shot. Of all the things we could have worked on I just told him the only thing I wanted was for him to have his toes pointed down when he goes up. I don't want to mess up a good shooter; I just want the guy that can shoot to be on balance when he shoots it.

Saturday December 30 Practice #26
The Head Coach, Parents, Assistant Coach, Chemistry, Schedule, Kids Decide How Good, Winning at PHS, Post "D," B-Mo, and Next Practice

It is just flat out easier to be the assistant coach that it is to be the head coach. The head coach is always the guy that gets criticized, and it really doesn't matter if he is right or he is wrong he is going to be criticized. I know I've seen it. We've won two state championships, and it didn't have a bearing: there was still criticism. I read a quote a long time ago from a coach who said if it came down to a parent's kid doing well or the kid's team winning the state championship, the parent is going to choose his kid's success over team's success.

As a parent myself I can attest to that form of parental thinking. When my two boys, Josh and Luke were playing, while it may have been some of the most fun I've ever had in coaching, it was also some of the most stress I've ever felt. It was tough because if we won and my son played poorly I was not quite as happy, or if we lost but my son played well I wasn't happy then either; it had to be both—my son played well and we won before I was ever truly happy.

Hey, this is what parents do. Remember, I am a parent. Our job is to try to do what we think is best for our kids; there is nothing wrong with that. It is what most of us have tried to do from the moment we had our children. But for coaches it can't be that way. All decisions must be made with the good of the team in mind first, and the good of the individual (if possible) second. Parents will never think that way, nor really should they think that way; again, that is not their job. But that is the job of the coach, and he must think that way if he is to be successful.

Another thing that most parents don't truly understand is that the players are really the ones who decide how much they will play. It's not a personal thing; we, as coaches, are too selfish for that. We want to put the kids on the floor who we think give us the best chance to win the game, and our goal as always is to win the last game we play. We see these kids every night in practice and make decisions about playing based upon that information; the fans see the players usually about once or twice a week. Like all coaches we are looking for players to make us better; we evaluate and reevaluate, sometimes daily, looking for the right answers.

And the assistant coach…is like the back-up quarterback on a football team that is struggling. Everyone thinks he is the greatest, which he is until he gets in and becomes the starter, and then they want the next back up. That's how I feel sometimes when someone says something about how much the boys like me. While I appreciate the comment, I also realize that it is a lot easier to like the assistant because (while I've been blessed to work with a couple of head coaches that gave me a lot of input) ultimately the head coach makes the decision and like almost every decision in every business you aren't going to please everyone. Coaching is no exception.

And so while I feel like Coach Core hears me, I also appreciate the fact that he will be the guy that takes the applause if it works, but he will also take the heat if it doesn't work. And with that in mind, in my approach with Mark, although not scientific, I do kind of have some basic ground rules for myself. First, I know that not everything I say will be used. Second, I might be wrong regardless of how much I believe I'm right. Third, I have to come back with another thought later on, for what good is it to have a "yes man" for either one of us? Fourth, I have to come back with that suggestion regardless of whether Mark used my previous idea or not. I might suggest ten things and any number could be used or ignored, and I still must give Mark my thoughts and ideas. And fifth, there comes a point when if I've mentioned something that I'm really sold on more than, say, three or four times, and Mark still chooses not to implement that thought, that I must now realize that he has heard me and chooses not to agree with me. Then it's up to me to stop—I don't want to drive him crazy. I must rethink my theory or idea and decide if it's worth another shot.

Chemistry—the spontaneous reaction of individuals to each other, especially a mutual sense of attraction or understanding. (That is the dictionary's definition of chemistry.) That is also something that goes into building a good team, and some teams search all season long and never find it. But in order for us to be good, we must find the right players, the right amount of playing time for each, and give them the appropriate amount of time in both practice and games to develop this chemistry. The late Red Aurbach said that it is not necessarily the five best players but rather the five players that play the best together that win games.

Part of this chemistry matter we are trying to improve upon as well, is helping the players understand that it is just as important to know when not to shoot as it is to know when to shoot, which players should shoot a little bit more and which a little less; we must do this without destroying the confidence that each player has. Confidence is the father of achievement. If we take that away we have really hurt the player, and unfortunately, sometimes that is exactly what we (unintentionally) do. Coaching is as much mental, actually probably more about the psychological side, as it is about the physical side. I heard one coach say that any idiot can get up and draw up plays on a chalkboard; you must do much more than that to be a coach.

Most kids are too insecure to recognize their own potential. I've told many a player that if only they could see the pictures that I have in my head for them that they would be shocked at how good I think they could be. The problem is getting my pictures of them into their heads. The best players we've had here have had a great belief in their own ability, and I'd like to think that we helped to nurture some of that. They've also had a burning desire to improve and were open to coaching and to trying new things, to breaking bad habits and replacing them with more productive ones. The problem that most players have with this is the fear of letting go of the old habits; I guess you could say that they don't always believe that the coach's way might be better especially if the initial results aren't as good. That is where that element of trust has to come in to play. The player has to trust that the coach is correct, or if he isn't the player has to trust that the coach is "good enough" to say, "This isn't working, and I was wrong; let's do it your way."

Wow! What an upcoming schedule. First we don't have many people here for practice, then three days after the band kids get back we play Friday and Saturday against the number one and number two teams in our league. This is really going to be a tough start to the New Year.

We did toss-out shooting until someone hit thirty shots. Toss outs are exactly what they sound like—each player has a ball and tosses it out in front of himself with backspin so that it comes back to him as though he is catching a pass. Upon the catch the player shoots the ball. We then paired up and tried to make seven in a row from the free-throw line. About five minutes later we gave up on that since we still had not accomplished the streak and went to the next thing in practice.

That next thing was a new rebound drill followed by the Brunner lay-up drill.

We then went two-on-two with an extra offensive man in the middle setting screens with a blocking dummy. My group, while not terrible, wasn't great either. As we got tired we came up out of our stance defensively and made passing and ball-handing mistakes offensively. Evidently the same situation was going on at the other end of the floor with Coach Core's group, because it wasn't long and all the players were being called to the line (that's the end line) which means that we are going to run. While we have talked about not making basketball into track practice Coach Core was really upset with the effort that the players were making.

After doing some running Coach Core talked to the kids and then so did I, but ultimately it goes back to the players as to just how good they want to be. The players have to be willing to pay a steep price. At times they must be willing to suppress some of their own individual wishes and talents. They must be in outstanding physical shape, be being willing to sacrifice vacation time and even be willing to be criticized repeatedly, in both games and practices. And I'm telling you, that it is tough to be really good, but it should be; if it weren't, everyone would do it!

While our normal approach at PHS is not to emphasize winning but to underscore getting better, with this group we may need to put more premium on being triumphant. Normally our teams at Pella seem to be under the gun about winning so to talk more about it just adds to the stress that the players already feel. Conversely, with this group of players they don't seem to be nearly as concerned about being successful as a team as they do about their individual accomplishment. I don't mean that to sound bad; each and every player on this team has been a great kid both on and off the court. I'm proud of them in that way and I think just about any parents would someday be very proud to have one of these boys marry their daughters. I just don't think that they are aware of the greater picture. They are like me or you, we just sometimes get caught up in our own world until something comes along that gives us some perspective; that is what we are trying to do, give them some perspective.

We worked on post defense then went to the open post drill so that we could continue to get better at guarding the post area. And then went back to the no help four-on-four (man drill) that I definitely feel we need work on. We have worked so hard on help that I fear that our players aren't worried enough about stopping their own guy. That is what this drill is designed to do—stop your man without help.

After that we went back and worked on the Partners offense. Both our defense improved and there was some carry over from the previous drill or our offense just wasn't very good. Balance: balance in life and balance in basketball, there is always that perfect balance that we are seeking to find.

Yesterday it was B-Mo, and today it is Kaleb. Both those guys have gotten really hot shooting the ball at practice. That is a good thing and something that we have sorely missed. I hope we can carry this over to game settings.

We finished with some zone work and a reminder of a 10:00 A.M. practice on January 1st. B-Mo thought we should move it back a little, and since B-Mo is a man of few words, Coach Core decided that since he was willing to speak up we would move it back if it worked for everyone else; it did, practice at 11:30 on the first.

Monday, January 1, 2007, Practice #27
Tennis Books, Klarc Is Back, Draw a Charge, Swing Your Partners, and Nate

Prior to practice Mark was telling me about a book that he read written by a tennis coach. This book (according to Mark) talks about the best mental outlook a tennis player can take when playing the game of tennis. Coach Core felt like there was a lot of transfer over for any athlete, including a basketball player. Mark's short version goes like this when describing the correct outlook; the worst mental talk you can use is negative, the second worst is positive!

The negative thinking is an obvious; the positive I will attempt to explain. By thinking too positively you set yourself up for failure because eventually you will not perform at the current level (assuming you are performing well) and then you will fall into negative thinking. Rather the best thing an athlete can do is a neutral way of thinking, non judgmental but detached and observing. It would be like watching a movie of yourself and looking for ways to get better without passing judgment on your play. It's about staying in the moment and making adjustments as you learn about yourself. Mark gave the book to Kaleb and asked him to read it for himself.

This reminds me of the child learning to walk. He doesn't get upset with himself. He just learns from his mistakes and moves on until eventually he is walking. He doesn't criticize himself; he doesn't give up. He just stays in the moment and tries to get better.

Klarc makes his return from his trip to California. Kyle is gone today visiting family over break.

We went from two-hand rebounding to toss-out jumpers, which, of all people, the guy who hadn't shot the ball in a week, Klarc won! We then shot floaters for layups and got up and down the court a little bit with the Michigan drill. We continued up and down the court by going full-court one-on-one.

I asked Mark if I could put in a "take a charge layup drill," and he readily agreed. I'd like us to be so much tougher than we are, and I'd also like us to be more team oriented. This drill was designed to create both things. Taking a charge to me encourages a tough attitude. I also made it a competitive drill that kids scored extra points for helping a teammate up off the floor. The drill met with limited success. As we are in games, we are hesitant to step in to take a charge and would rather run around someone on the offensive side as well; that makes this drill difficult to run.

We worked on our Partners offense really for the first time in a five-on-five situation. Partners is a simple offense. We put two guys on one side of the floor and make them partners and two guys on the other side and make them partners. The Partners work together to get themselves open as well as the teammate they are working with. Right now the fifth man on offense stays at the top of the one-two-two set. His job is to penetrate with the dribble and or swing the ball. Clayton appears to be a natural for this spot. He is quick with the dribble but also really likes and promotes swinging the ball from side to side of the floor.

Now what happens if the defense takes away the swing pass to Clayton? The temptation is for Clayton to back cut the defender but really this just tends to plug up the lane. Instead, we would like Clayton to actually move himself and his man away from the basket. I'd love to play four-on-four rather than five-on-five. Think about it; when you're in the driveway is it easier to score when there are 10 guys cluttering up everything or when there is only one defender and one offensive player? The same is true here as well; if we could figure out a way to play three-on-three and still keep everyone happy and involved we would. Swinging the ball shouldn't be a problem either; we just make the pass from side to side rather than through the point man.

After running Partners we went though all of our man-to-man plays and then spent considerable time working against zone defenses.

Nate Klyn is really a sharp player. Here he is playing five-on-five (because we are short of players) after rarely ever playing at all during practice and looking like he knows pretty much all of our stuff as well or better than most of the guys that play all of the time. If we could combine his mind with someone else's body he would be a very fine player. Nate is an in-betweener, a player not big enough to play post nor quick enough to play outside, but a smart, smart player.

Practices over break have been only an hour in length. The amount of up and down the court that we are doing is much less; so is our defensive work. We are spending more time now trying to get better with our quarter-court offense.

Tuesday January 2
Thinking (If You Knew Me You Might Not Believe That) Pictures, and Kids Making the Decisions.

Funny how this whole coaching thing worked out for me in my life. Here it is 3:00 P.M. during my Christmas break, and instead of out having coffee with a friend or my wife or watching TV or going to a movie or taking a nap I'm thinking more about basketball. I don't think that there has been a day in my life since I first got into this coaching gig that I haven't thought at least a little bit about the game. I even wake up thinking about the players or the game during the night—that is truly sick!

One of the things that this warped old mind of mine has been thinking about lately is the amount of credit that coaches seem to get. In my opinion it is too much regardless of how we are doing as a team. If we are winning we get too much credit, and if we are losing we get too much blame. We were at the state tournament one year, and I don't remember the exact situation but I think it had something to do with the other team running a zone defense. We took a timeout to discuss some of the issues that we were having in regards to this defense, and then the players took the floor. Nick Mulder (03) took the ball out of bounds for us on the sideline (this was a crucial part of a close game) when the other team had changed their defense into a full-court press that we didn't even mention during that timeout. Nick threw a perfect over-the-top pass to one of our guys down the sideline that turned into a lay-up. It looked so good that I'm sure many in the crowd thought that we had designed that very thing in the huddle. We hadn't. I remember I turned to Mark on the bench and whispered, "Just like we drew it up," and we both laughed at how the players had handled that situation without one word of input from us. Then I told Mark how everyone in the auditorium right now was talking about what a great job we did with that timeout; again we laughed.

But the other end is true as well. We get too much criticism when something isn't going well. When I was coaching at a little town called Underwood there was a fan that would always yell, "Rebound," as loud and as often as he could. The advice was good; I will never argue that, but you could tell that he thought just by the way he yelled that we had never coached that before and that by him yelling it, we would magically become a great rebounding team. In truth, we worked like crazy to become a better rebounding team; almost every day in practice we worked on it, but we just never really did become a good rebounding team.

But I'm not above some input if it could help our team, so I invited that fan in to help with our little guys' basketball program and asked him to coach one of the teams. I wish I could tell you I learned something and that he had a magical formula to make us a better rebounding team, but alas that didn't happen. He yelled it a lot (just like at our games) but I think he found out that it takes more than just yelling it to make it happen. I go back to the fact that the kids are the ones that really decide if you are going to be a rebounding team or a team that plays defense or a team that passes the ball; coaches can try to sell, they can try to influence, but ultimately it's the kids' decision.

Tuesday, January 2, Practice #28
They're Back, Up and Down, 11-Man, the White Team Guys, and Good at the End

We are one player away from being a whole team but unfortunately that player is probably five weeks away from his recovery. The band is back from their trip, and Kirk is the only player we are missing because of his injury. Prior to practice the guys suggested that we bring up a few extra trash cans for our returning players in case they have a need to throw up. I hope it doesn't come to that. Kirk is trying to get into shape by swimming; I think he is going about an hour a day.

We started with dribble tag and then went to full-court dribbling up and down the court. We made about 10 trips up and down the court, handling the ball with various forms of dribbles. We have opened almost every single pre-practice by dribbling tennis balls and two-ball dribbling. If we could make every player just a little bit better in their ability to dribble the ball, we, as a team, would become a better ball-handling team. Amazingly, Nathan won the second game of dribble tag!

We really hadn't gotten up and down the court that much over break; we just didn't have enough guys. This practice appears to be one where we will be trying to get some of our conditioning back and will be going up and down the court.

We do full-court stuff with the Michigan drill and then come back with the three-on-two and two-on-one full-court drill. We then go one-on-one full-court. Actually, everyone looks pretty darn good to start. I'd assume that the guys that just got off the bus a few hours ago are tired but happy to be moving rather than sitting on that long trip.

The next drill is called the 11-man drill. It is really a drill to improve rebounding and loose-ball recoveries.

Diagram O 11-Man Drill

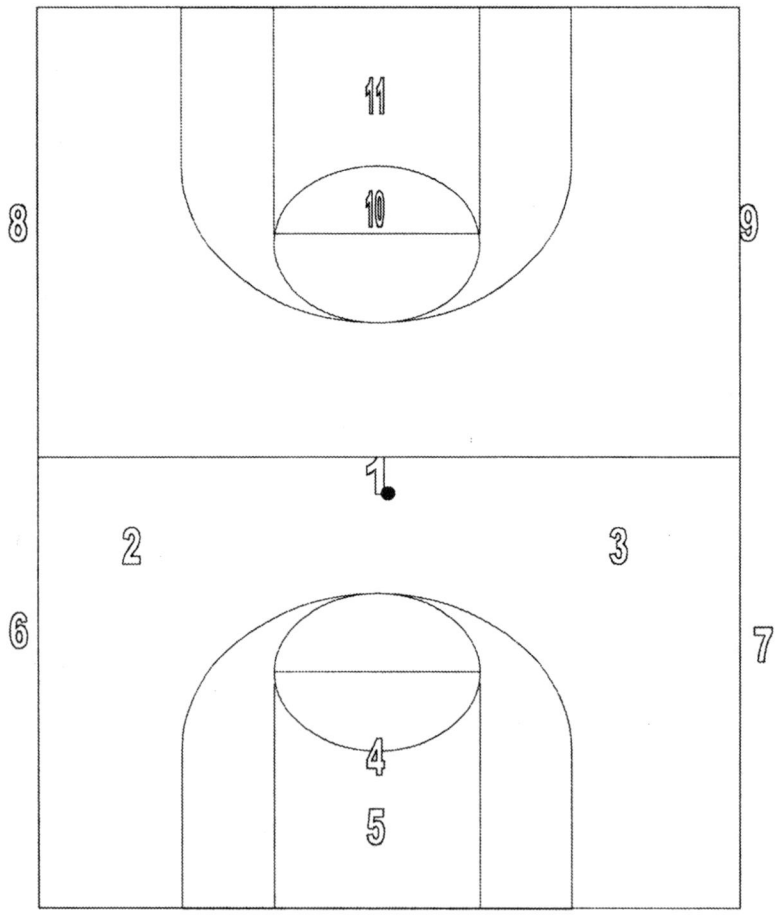

The line up of the drill is shown. #1, #2, and #3 are attacking #4 and #5 in a three-on-two situation with #6, #7, #8, and #9 standing out of bounds waiting for an outlet pass. #10 and #11 are back waiting for the offense to attack them. Upon the shot from #1, #2, or #3 the ball is rebounded by any one of the players, including #4 and #5. The man that gets the rebound outlets the ball to #6 or #7, who then become part of a fast-break the other way along with the man who got the rebound and made the outlet pass. The drill continues back and fourth up and down the floor. Each player counts the number of rebounds he gets, and at the end of the drill the winners do not have to run.

It is astonishing to me to watch the vigor and aggressiveness in which we both attack the basket and rebound the ball during this drill; this is the exact way that we would like them to play, but when we go out of this drill we become a much less assertive team and really don't attack the boards at all; it is a strange phenomenon.

We then ran our press offense/defense game. This, too, was a full-court drill that we do in a five-on-five setting. I know for sure that Pella Christian will press us; I'm not sure of Grinnell, but it does make sense to prepare for a press regardless of who or when you might see one.

We went into our Partners offense from the one break drill. The more I watch our Partners offense the more I'm starting to like it. Now it is up to us to anticipate how other teams might try to defend it and prepare the kids so they can make the adjustment during the flow of the game. And with a bit of luck do it without the use of a timeout.

Again we ran, from beginning to end, all of our man-to-man and zone offensive plays and also ran all of our out-of-bounds plays. Repetition and more repetition are two of the big keys to remembering and performing.

The white-team guys played exceedingly well tonight. In many of the drills and the five-on-five things that we did, I think those guys won or tied the majority of the drills. Almost every player on that team played well—both Zach and Tyler Terlouw did very well, and so did Jesse. But the three guys that really did well were Tyler Linn, Brandon E., and C.J. was even better than those two guys. I'll bet he made about 90% of his shots, and rarely did he turn the ball over. If those guys would play like that all of the time we would definitely become a better team. First of all, they would get better, so from a personal standpoint that would be a good thing for them; it would also give them a chance to play more in games and maybe even challenge for a starting position. And secondly, it would force our green-team players to improve or they would lose some playing time. Actually, it wouldn't be a bad thing to reduce some of their playing time if we could. I've mentioned before that I think we get a little bit tired during games; we would love to develop confidence in our bench players and use them more, but to do that they first have to become consistent in practice, and then they have to carry this over into games.

One of the really interesting things that happened tonight was caused by the good defense that the white team was playing. They made the green team play offense for a longer period of time than they wanted to or at least were accustomed to. I know it sounds weird to say that the green team didn't want to play offense, but it happens. There is a certain rhythm that offensive teams get into, and I'll bet most teams will shoot the ball somewhere within the same time of that rhythm almost 99% of the time. But the green team, which is used to getting a shot up fairly quickly (sometimes too quickly), was forced to continue to pass the ball looking for a good shot for much longer than they normally would. And when this happens, almost inevitably someone will get impatient and take a poor shot because they get tired of waiting for the opening; they aren't patient on the offensive end. That is exactly what the white team did to the green team tonight, and that is way cool!

The unexpected thing that comes about when your second-team guys play that kind of defense is that it forces your first-team guys to play smarter and better offense. So as your defense improves it will also improve the offense. It truly is an amazing game, this game of hoops.

It was a good practice tonight. We've got an extremely difficult schedule coming up immediately upon our return to play, but I can see improvement in our team; that is always what we are looking for, improvement—not perfection but improvement.

Our goal at least since I have been at PHS is to get to the state tournament. Shoot, I guess, really it's been to win the dang thing. The odds are stacked against us 63-1 to be exact, but why would we shoot for anything less? Some guys want to win the conference; I'd be happy about that if we did, but it isn't my number-one goal. We (Mark and I) want us to be good at the end of the year; we want to be playing our best at the end of the season, and if that means we don't win the conference, so be it, if it means we struggle early but get better late, then that is okay too.

Wednesday, January 3, 2007, Practice #29
P.C., C.J., B-Mo, No Help, 42, Partners, Duke, Tyler Linn's Birthday, Mrs. Korver, and Team Meeting

When Mark and I got together this morning we talked a little bit about the Pella Christian vs. PCM game he went to watch last night. He was surer than ever that we would need to clear the PC point guard out against the press. In order to do that each of our players must recognize whom he is guarding and then take him away from the ball.

We also spoke with C.J. about his play in yesterday's practice. Coach Core likes to reward the players from yesterday's white team that played well an opportunity to play with the green team but he also felt like moving C.J. from the white to the green would seriously hinder the white team's ability to compete. So Coach spoke with C.J. about the quandary he felt, and C.J. indicated that he would like the opportunity to work with the green team about once or so a week to develop chemistry with them, but he didn't mind one bit if he stayed on the white team the rest of the time. C.J. is truly one of the best team players we have.

Kaleb's progress on his book reading assignment isn't so good right now. But he assured us he would get it done. Clayton seems to be hurting a little bit today. His injury is one that seems to come and go, one day not bothering him and the next affecting his play.

We then broke up into "bigs" and "littles," Mark taking the guards while I got the bigs and worked with them in regards to keeping their seal when posting up. We went Michigan drill, followed by two-on-one with a chaser, and then to the 11-man drill.

During the 11-man drill the players were to count their loose-ball recoveries as well as their rebounds. Our leaders today were B-Mo and Klarc. B-Mo, during yesterday's practice also led us in blue-collar points with 13. The next group down was Andrew, C.J., and Kaleb. I would sure like it if we could get Andrew to play like this all of the time. He is doing what we need most in this drill, just showing toughness, hustle, and rebounding.

We worked on individual defense by running our driving line drill and then worked more on rebounding with free-throw block outs.

With our suspicion that the boys are relying too much on help from their teammates we ran the shell drill today with no help. In other words the players set up in their two-guard and two-forward set and just simply went one-on-one with very little ball movement and no help; when the shot went up, it turned into a rebound game. This drill then progressed by adding some screening on the weak side and then some on-ball screening later on. Now some minimal help was allowed, but again we encouraged each man to guard his own man. The managers and I were asked to watch all of the offensive players when the shot went up to see who didn't go to the boards, and if they didn't go, they were pulled from the drill, and they ran twice up and down the court.

I've been thinking maybe we need to run a little bit more of our half-court-trap stuff, called 42. The four indicates the type of defense we are in (trapping) and the two indicates the pick up point (half-court). What I'm trying to help the players understand is that it's a simple defense with some simple concepts. One, we want to trap in the corners of the floor, not so much in the middle. Two, the guys that are closest to the ball handler along with the man guarding the ball handler will probably be the guys trapping. Three, the man coming to form the trap should surprise the ball handler. Four, the guys not in the trap must be looking to pick the next pass off. And five, in the end, the guys looking to pick off the pass must be extremely aggressive. If the pass is completed the defense immediately becomes outnumbered, so the odds favor us when we are looking to pick rather than if they complete the pass.

Our Partners offense was a thing of beauty today. The players had to get an offensive rebound individually (like the 11-man drill) or they had to run. But out of three minutes of running this offense, we didn't ever turn the ball over, missed only two shots and got one of the offensive rebounds from the two misses. Good offense or bad defense? I really think our offense is coming.

We followed Partners with Duke, and I believe that there was carry over into this offense from Partners. I saw more and better use of screens, passes, and cutting with this offense as well. Our quarter-court offense has improved.

Again we went through all of our set plays individually. And again we seem to have a better handle on how these plays might work for us.

During the course of practice today Tyler Linn's mom stopped by with an assortment of doughnuts and sweets along with orange drinks. It is Tyler's birthday today. We all gathered around Tyler and sang happy birthday to him.

We had a second mother, Mrs. Korver, show up at the end of practice today. Wow, two mothers in one day! She was trying to get the boys organized for their afternoon team pictures. Mothers in general are truly an amazing group; the stuff they do for the guys is incredible and most of the time they don't even get a thank you; this is definitely a group that is over worked and under paid.

To finish the day the boys had a players-only meeting up in Coach Core's room. They were given Tyler's treats and asked to write down their goals and aspirations for the remainder of the season. Then if they all agreed with these goals, they were asked to sign the document indicating that they would, to the best of their ability, try to uphold these objectives.

Thursday, January 5, Practice #30
Tape, Kirk, the Rim, Bones, NC Shell, Grinnell, Press "O,"
Signals, Match Up, Separation, Clayton and O.B.

I haven't taped an ankle all year long. Things have changed from when I first got into this. It used to be that I always taped ankles, but now we have the convenience of having trainers that take that job from us coaches on many occasions. We (coaches) have had classes and training in the care and prevention of injuries, but these guys (the trainers), this is their job. They really know what they are doing. Anyway, I got to tape one today before practice, as Justin Pothoven tweaked his ankle a couple of days ago. I'm glad to report that it's like riding a bike; once you learn to tape you never forget, and I got along just fine.

We did two-hand continuous rebounding and then toss-out shooting to start practice.

Kirk (on injured reserve) came over and told me that Brandon Esterbrook was watching the ball when he shot; what a great thing for the "ole Kirk meister" to do! He is being the kind of teammate we would like all of the guys to be by finding a way to make someone else better, as well as himself.

Great shooters do not watch the ball when they shoot; they focus on the rim. There is lots of discussion on what part of the rim; some people say the front, some the back and some the entire rim, but all agree that they maintain concentration on the rim and not the ball. I think this will help Brandon shoot better. It's ironic because it seems that both Kaleb and B-Mo have started to shoot a little better, and now I was trying to figure out why Brandon wasn't shooting that well. His form etc., looks good, so I knew there was something else; I just didn't know what it was, and Kirk saw it.

I spoke with Kirk a little bit more about his foot. Prior to this I had spoken with Luke (my son the upcoming chiropractor) and he told me about the breaking down of bone, somewhat similar to the breaking down of muscle when lifting weights. I just think Kirk has to be smart about his workouts when he gets back. He may need to take time out of some things that we are doing. That puts him in a tough spot; first of all he needs to condition. Second, he needs to develop both his own personal rhythm and a team chemistry, and lastly, he needs to put the time in to get better. We have to be smart and balance this out when he gets back.

We went to the Magic layups followed by power layups followed by two-on-one full-court with a chaser. It's during this two-on-one segment that I noticed Klarc telling people where to go and what they could do. Talk about a balance: Klarc is one of our captains, and that is something we would like our captains to do, take responsibility for the betterment of our team. But there is a fine line between helping a peer and reprimanding a peer, and the captains have to walk that line. I think Klarc is very appropriate today and I think each day he gets better.

We ran the NC drill and stipulated to the kids that they must get an offensive rebound during the drill or it will cost them a sprint. If you haven't noticed, there is a push on offensive rebounding for this team by the coaches. I think we are getting better at that; I do have concerns on the other hand about our defensive block outs now.

We then run the NC shell drill, which is a combination of a give-and-go cut on the ball side and a flash from the weak side to the ball side.

We want the man guarding the give-and-go cut fronting this cutter so that the wing that he passed to can't throw the ball into him at the post area as he is cutting through. This drill then puts tremendous pressure on the man guarding the weak-side forward, as he must first help against the lob available to the give-and-go cutter and then step up to prevent his man from receiving a pass into the post area, as his man will try to flash at the instant that he sees the help being provided against the lob. We swing the ball to the other side of the floor quickly and then run the same thing to that side so different players end up in different spots. They must react; no, actually they need to anticipate the things that they will need to guard.

We spent time in post defense, both one-on-one and two-on-two. Grinnell has two big (one is six foot four, 265 lbs. a football first-team all-state linebacker and the other is a six foot seven, all-conference basketball player and their leading scorer) post players and we worked on switching screens and trying to deny the ball in to the post area in the first place. The best defense a player can play is before his man gets the ball. Deny or make it tough for him to get the thing will help destroy the offensive man's advantage but also the offensive flow of the team. In order to encourage the concept of denying the post we then put four defenders against five offensive players, one of which was a man in the post who is not guarded. It becomes the job of all the players to help in the post now and not just one man, but again, the idea is to deny it into the post.

The press-press-offensive segment started against the 54 defensive press (that's our three-one-one press) and evolved into the 44 press (that's the man press that tries to trap like a zone). Both Grinnell and PC have shown the ability to press, and we would like to be prepared for it.

Something new that we are trying to put into practice today is the ability to change our defenses through hand signals. We are trying that today during this pressing segment. We have three different hand signals that the players must react to, and they will each mean something different. We must be careful using these because it is important that all of the players are playing the same defense at the same time or we are really in deep doo-doo. We shall see. I think, if we call these during slower parts of the game we will be okay, but if we try to call them in the middle of fast and furious action it will hurt us more than our opponents.

For the first time in quite a while we are working on our match-up zone in hopes of using it a little bit more during the next two games. I'm not sure we've had enough reps to use it yet, but we have talked about it and practiced it sparingly throughout our practice season. In game time play, however, we have only run it one time, and that time was against South Tama. We gave up a three-pointer.

We tried to release out of our screens quicker today in the man segment. A good screen followed by a quick and distinct separation from the man being screened is difficult to guard. I don't think we've been separating quickly enough.

In practice today, Clayton almost immediately banged a previously injured arm. From that point out he didn't practice. Nuts! He was such a huge asset for us in his one-and-only game this year. I'm starting to think that not only is he snake bitten, but so is this team. We just cannot seem to get everybody together for this year.

We actually put in a new out-of-bounds play tonight! It has taken us until the middle of our season to know our other out-of-bounds plays well enough to learn a new one, but we made it. We also worked on stopping some of Grinnell's out-of-bounds plays.

When we were running our Partners offense and the rest of our man-to-man stuff tonight we really struggled without Clayton. He is a guy that likes to swing the ball from the point spot and has the athletic ability to create something off of a dribble drive. We miss that tonight. Who would think that getting the ball from one side of the floor to the other could be that tough?

We really do have a difficult weekend. Playing back to back against the two teams leading our conference will be a grueling challenge for us all. Even if we have improved, it may not show; honestly, we could be a much better team, and at the end of the weekend still drop to four and five.

Chapter 9—Finally, It's Game Time Again

Friday, January 5, Game #8 Pella at Grinnell
Our Record: 4-3; Conference: 4-3

This is our first game since break and our first game at Grinnell's new gym. Their old gym was a cracker box; this one is state of the art. One of the best things about this gym is that we have our own locker room instead of sharing one with the Grinnell girls. We used to have to wait until after halftime of the girls' game to get into our locker room because the Grinnell girls were in there. Then before our game their girls would come in as their game ended and we were finishing our pre-game talk. It was a fiasco.

Clayton is not going to play tonight although his arm is not broken but severely bruised. Return time is up in the air.

We have held an opponent to just 36% shooting in the first half. Now that is defense, the kind we've been trying to play since the beginning of the season. We have also been much more of an inside team as we took more two point attempts than three. for one of the few times this season.

Score at half, 31-25.

Kaleb played pretty good "D" on #10 but he hit a three on us anyway to pull closer, but B-Mo comes down after a few blanks by both teams and scores, we are back up 33-28. Then they pound the ball inside and draw foul number three on B-Mo; it's 33-29 after they make one of two free throws with 5:40 left in the third.

Our first possession of our match-up zone wasn't exactly a thing of beauty in the way that we ran it, but it turned out as a miss for them.

After some empty possessions we end up in an out-of-bounds play, and Kaleb pops out for a two-pointer. We are up six. We got a stop, and then Kaleb scores on a layup after a B-Mo screen, and we are up 37-29.

We've got them on the run, and they call a timeout. We came out of the timeout in the match-up zone, but C.J. just completely lost track of his job, and they ended up with a three. We got the ball back and we ran a sideline out-of-bounds play that Colin made a really nice read for a layup, and we are up 39-32.

Now Kaleb picks up foul number three, and the foul trouble is starting to mount up.

B-Mo misses a good look from three, but C.J. makes a really nice hustle play to throw the ball off of an opponent as he was saving an offensive rebound going out of bounds. B-Mo makes the play pay off by connecting on a three. We are up 42-32 with 2:32 left in the third.

B-Mo picks up foul number three.

Kaleb losses #10 on an out-of-bounds play, and it is 42-34. We follow that by turning the ball over against their press. Both teams shoot blanks, and we end up with the ball on the next possession when the ball is poked away from C.J. as he was bringing it up the court. Their next possession is a layup by their big guy. Colin got a great look from three but just misses it; there is 1:17 left in the third and now Colin fouls. That is his third. The fouls continue to mount.

After some more play it is 42-37, and B-Mo charges. That is his fourth. This is serious trouble. First, he is probably our leading threat on the offensive end right now and second, although he gives up about 80 lbs. to their big guy, he is our big guy and one of the few players that we have that can play with their posts physically. All of a sudden Kaleb picks up four, and both of our main scorers are out. After they hit two free throws it's 42-39. With around :40 left in the third we have four subs in because of our foul trouble.

We proceed to give up an offensive rebound and a put back and then follow that with a turnover against their press. Again we fail to block out, and Klarc picks up his third foul. After they make two free throws they are up 42-43 at the end of the third quarter.

Bulldogs turns into a turnover and a foul on our part (Klarc's fourth) and two free throws for them. Things are going right down the crapper. With 7:20 left in the game they are up 42-45, and all of our guys are in serious foul trouble with four apiece.

We are trying too hard now, and we travel on the next possession. The roof starts to cave in as one of their big guys scores on a jumper, and Colin fouls their other big guy trying to keep him away from the offensive boards, so Grinnell goes to the line and tacks on another point.

With 5:44 left we are down by six. We have just kind of quit playing aggressive defense now because of our foul trouble. We aren't giving them shots, but we aren't doing much to stop them either, and they score again to take an eight-point lead.

B-Mo tries to keep us close with a put-back of our own.

We are in a panic mode now, and we are caught out of position going for a steal that turns into a lay-up. C.J. hits one of two free throws on our end, and with half the quarter left we are down by eight.

Klarc gets us to within five after a fast-break basket but then loses his man as they get an inside hoop. We then come down and just don't look the pass into our hands, and it goes out of bounds to them. We followed that by being late in our help, and they score inside again. It's a nine-point game with 2:00 left.

We are out trying to pressure the ball, and it turns into dribble penetration for them. They penetrate against our guards; our big men come up the lane to help, and it turns into another layup.

B-Mo slips a screen for a layup, and they get a bunny of their own on the next possession. Kaleb comes back with a three, and we are down by eight. They hit two free throws, and B-Mo scores a three. They score the final points of the game with two more free throws, and the final score is 55-64.

We had two players foul out—Klarc and Colin, and two of our other three starters had four.

Saturday, January 6, 10:00 Meeting
Walk Through, Talking Too Much, Not Talking Enough, Inspiration, Trust, and Nine Points.

I got a bit carried away at the meeting today, and it wasn't very fair to Mark in spite of his assurances that it was okay.

Mark started the kids off with a bit of dribbling and then we did some loosening up with some shooting. During that time Klarc came up and said that his wrists were hurting him because of a fall he took in last night's game. So what is new? Another injury!

After the warm up Mark took the boys through some Pella Christian stuff in preparation for tonight's game. Then he asked me to go first with my notes from last night's game. That is when I got carried away; I talked so long that I really didn't give Coach Core much of a chance to speak.

My points? I asked the kids, "In 32 minutes of play or however much you played, how many times did you box out?" I knew the response that they would give if they were honest so I asked them to just think the answer to themselves. I pointed out that we took nine free throws in the first half and only four in the second. We also took six three-point shots in the first half and 16 in the second half after Coach Core's halftime emphasis was to be more aggressive than they were the first half. I pointed out to the kids how incongruent their response was to his coaching.

I then asked them how many times they spoke to one another or had a teammate talk to them during the game. They gave me a few examples—all of them positive. I asked them why so few? Why did they refuse to talk to each other during the course of the game when we need teamwork and chemistry so badly?

I asked them to name the things that inspired them about their teammates' play. They named a number of things that their teammates did that moved them. I asked them why they didn't tell each other about it, why it would take until now to bring it up and say it not only to them but to each other. I asked if anyone was offended when someone said something good about him? Obviously, they weren't offended, but inwardly very proud and appreciative of their teammates' comments.

Finally I brought up trust, which is what I feel is one of the biggest issues on this team. I told them that was extremely important to me that when they come to my office and they talk with me or want something from me that I will be very honest with them one way or another as to my agreement or disagreement with their comments or requests, but I would always try my best to do what I say I will do. I'm not perfect—I don't expect them to be either, but I try to make my actions match my words. Then I asked them if they do the same. Are they doing what they say they are going to do, with each other or with the coaches? And if not why not? Do they trust each other, will they?

My point is this: nine points (our margin of loss) can be made up in a heartbeat. We screen out four or five more times because it is a priority (we've made it that by promising each other that we will do it and because of our mutual trust we will) and it's already a tie game. We talk more because we trust each other, and we don't make so many mistakes about being in the wrong defense or not being matched up with the appropriate man, and we make up more points. We play more inspired and better because now we are talking and encouraging each other, now we are together, we trust and our mutual communication and commitment inspired by trust creates a sense of oneness and belief; anyway you get the idea: nine points is doable.

Saturday, January 6, Pella at Pella Christian, Game #9
Our Record: 4-4; Conference: 4-4

The opening tip goes to Pella Christian in front of another full house at the Central College gymnasium. I thought maybe since this was an early game (7:15 rather than 8:15) on a Saturday there might not be such a big crowd; I was wrong. It was packed, and the people were here to see cross-town rivals go at it.

Jesse starts for us tonight since Clayton is out of the game with his injury. That will put Colin on their quick little point guard. Colin is neither strong (he is actually quite slim) nor fast, nor quick, but he is determined, and he will compete as hard as he can. B-Mo is actually the one who suggested this match-up; he said that Colin was just so darned stubborn that if he decided on something he'd do it.

Our defensive start was not a great one. We had worked on two things in this morning's walk through, recognizing and stopping both the PC flex cut and their high-low passing game; their first basket comes inside off of a flex cut.

One of the other things that we've worked hard on is to recognize where their point guard is when they are pressing us to move the ball in such a way as to not allow him to be part of the press. When we take the ball out of bounds after their score, we have recognized this and made an appropriate move to use this counter.

B-Mo gets us on the board with a three, and the next two possessions for both teams came up empty.

They score inside (with a high-low); we miss, but then we turn them over, miss again, but then get on offensive board to get the ball back. With that, B-Mo now shoots a pull-up in the middle of the lane; it's B-Mo five, Pella Christian two.

The Partners offense that we run in practice looks very little like what I'm seeing early in the game. In practice, there are numerous picks both down and back screens with lots of movement and ball reversal, tonight we seem content to set one screen and not swing the ball; where does this come from?

They score again inside. Early in the game everything they have attempted has been an inside shot.

Kaleb hits a three as the defense was in transition, and they come down and miss (another little inside shot) but they rebound it and put it back in. Our counter is another transition play as Colin takes it to the hole with a difficult left-handed layup, but it goes in.

Both teams, and especially PC are being patient with the ball when they are on offense. Some of that comes from the fact that both teams are trying to play defense, and it takes time to break down a good "D." But PC is just flat out bigger than we are inside, and they are trying to take advantage of that by forcing the ball into the interior. Wait, they are not only bigger than we are inside, they are just flat out bigger than we are, period.

They score, and we travel with the ball, the score is 10-10 with 2:16 left in the first.

Both teams have some empty possessions; then they get two free throws and so do we, when Kaleb dribble drives the lane.

Late in the first quarter we ran some match-up zone that seemed to slow them down.

I'm guessing that Zach won't play a lot this game, but he did come in late in the first.

Early in the year when I watched PC play Knoxville I thought there were two things we had to do; one was to handle their press and two was to stop their break; so far we have accomplished both.

The score at the end of the first quarter is 12-12.

We started the second quarter in man-to-man, and it really didn't look like PC recognized what we were in, but they scored anyway. Colin comes back with a runner in the lane. PC hits a three that puts them up by three.

One of the things that I talked about this morning was trust, I wanted them to trust us as coaches, that we knew what were talking about and that I wanted to trust them by knowing that they had heard and responded to what they were being asked to do. During a timeout I told Klarc to quit dribbling into the trap areas against the PC zone—he looked at me nodded and the next possession we had I saw him headed up the sideline back into a trap area. But before he got there he switched directions and attacked the middle of the floor; Klarc had listened and responded.

Kaleb had a terrific "Magic" move to the hoop, but they called it a travel. Looked to me like a basket and a foul, but I might be just a little bit prejudiced, and I was only about 60 feet away from the call, so I might not have seen it quite as well—ya think?

We've pushed the PC offense farther out from the hoop right now. That is good; it will help destroy their timing and give us more time for recovery if we make a mistake. We turn them over. We got a shot out of Louisville, but we miss.

We run a trap defense but they hit a 10-foot bank shot; we are down 14-19. We miss, but they turn the ball back to us with five-seconds. A closely guarded call goes against them. B-Mo turns it over, but without missing a beat and without feeling sorry for himself he sprints back and knocks the ball away from them to get PHS the ball back. That is one of those intangible things. Most people when they make a mistake want to take the time to feel sorry for themselves; they want to hang their head or do whatever. Honestly, there is just no time for that because if you do that you've now made two mistakes, because the next play has already occurred while that little pity party was going on.

After running an out-of-bounds play we turn the ball over (we are experiencing one of those offensive droughts) and they come back with their flex-cut play for two, and with about 3:00 left we are down 14-21.

C.J. is in there fighting for an offensive rebound from our next possession after a missed jumper; he doesn't get it, but because of his effort tipping the ball Klarc picks it up and scores a put back. They miss. Now C.J., after some nice ball swing, ends up with an open three and buries it. PC takes a timeout. We've closed it to 19-21.

Jesse is working really hard defensively down on the block trying to keep the ball out of the post area. He is giving up about a foot in height and probably 50 pounds in weight, but the PC player gets frustrated and fouls Jesse; we get the ball back.

We get a shot from the top of the key and miss, but a really good hustle play after an offensive rebound by Kaleb gets us the ball back, and Colin attacks the hoop and draws two defenders in to him and passes out to B-Mo, who connects for three. They score; we are down 22-23, but we are in the fight.

Both teams come up empty, and then Kaleb (after some ball swing) hits a three. They miss and we are off on a fast-break, B-Mo throws such a nice touch pass to Colin out ahead of the defense that I think it caught him by surprise and he traveled before he shot the lay-up. They miss again and we hold the ball for the final shot of the half; we get a good shot but miss. Pella High is up two points at the half.

We get the ball to start the half. We are running our Partners offense but B-Mo is having a difficult time throwing the wing-to-post pass. As I think about it, it's really not his fault but ours. He is usually the guy getting the pass in the post rather than throwing it; he doesn't get enough reps in this. Also, it might be a good idea to move B-Mo away from Klarc's side in Partners. Klarc likes to post up; we should get a guy over on his side that is more comfortable with the post pass. Also putting a bigger player on Kaleb's side might get him some better screens to work off of.

Colin has done a good job on their point guard. We've played some zone, but B-Mo is right about Colin's stubbornness. Just as I speak this Colin fouls him. Now the foul is about 12 feet from the hoop, but for some reason the ref gives him the hoop and a free throw. Wow, that was a poor call; that is the old NBA continuation call. We've got good officials for this game; I don't mean that. It was just a poor call.

He missed the free throw. Colin attacks off the dribble and gets fouled hard going down to the floor. Immediately there are three guys there from PHS, including Kaleb (that was one of his performance goals for tonight's game, help pick our guys up if they are on the floor) to help pick him up; that is cool beans, man! That trust, caring for each other, all that sloppy stuff that macho men aren't supposed to do, that will do two things for you. You'll win more, but more importantly you'll enjoy playing with your teammates and friends more.

Colin hits one of two. They throw the ball inside; we drop down to help so they kick it out for a three. That is great offense on Pella Christian's part; throw it in, let the defense come down to help and then throw it out for an open shot. What happens if the help doesn't come? Play one-on-one from about five feet from the hoop.

We come back at them, beating the press with a power layup from Jesse, but don't get matched up defensively, and they throw inside to an open-post man. That is one of the dangers of switching back and fourth between defenses; an individual might be in a different defense than everyone else if he misses the call. I think that is what happened.

We bring the ball in against the press, and for one of the few times during the game their point guard got involved in the press. Prior to this he hadn't really been a factor. There is a thing called a flop in basketball. This is where the defender flops down like he has been run over by a freight train, when in reality he either hadn't been touched or the contact was minimal. They flopped; unfortunately the officials bought it, and we lose the ball.

We've played a lot of zone this half, and it has been very effective for us.

They miss the shot; we get the ball back. We miss, and once again they score on an interior pass to an open post in transition; it's B-Mo's man, and he is just late getting down the court. Remember, they run four post players in and out of the game; we basically have maybe two, and this is a high-intensity and hard-fought game. B-Mo may be just a little tired.

We miss on the next possession. Against PC B-Mo tried to draw a charge on one of their players coming down the lane. Now B-Mo may have flopped, but I know he got hit a whole lot harder than the PC player did about two possessions ago. I think most coaches know that basketball is an impossible game to officiate and that everything won't be called perfectly, so really all we are looking for is consistency; if it was a charge earlier on us, this should have been a charge on them! We are down 28-32 with about 5:30 left in the third.

After our timeout they shoot and miss and so did we, they miss again but this time Kaleb finds Klarc on a slip to the hoop. They miss an open outside shot, and then we miss as well. They miss again, and we get the ball inside to Klarc (our power point guard). He hits a little turnaround jump hook, and it's all tied up.

Kaleb—who has really done a nice job defending in the post because he gives up quite a bit of both height weight, loses his man and gives up a short jumper.

Now it's really getting frustrating for the coaches as they call Colin for a charge. Colin rarely gets all the way to the hoop and shoots little tear drops or floaters in the middle of the lane as he does now for us. Again, Colin must be 50 lbs. lighter and four inches shorter than the man he made contact with, who once again appears to flop to influence the officials, and once again they buy the act. The kid hit the ground like he'd been hit with a Mack Truck! Come on!

I say it's getting frustrating because honestly, we rarely say anything to any officials about any calls. But this is getting stupid, and we both (Mark and I) just simply lean back in our chairs and throw our hands up, trying to maintain our silence to show respect for the job we know is impossible to do.

B-Mo blocks a shot—our ball; we throw over the top of the press to Jesse, who got a little too excited with his good fortune, and he traveled. Once again we create a loose ball with our defense, and they recover it; there is contact, and one of our guys goes down, clearing a way for an inside hoop for them.

We missed a couple of free throws and then Kaleb does a nice job of helping one of his teammates in the post and causes a PC miss that we rebound. Kaleb attacks the hoop; once again another charge is called against us. That is it for Mark. He is one upset coach, and again I know I'm biased, but I feel he is right. I'm wondering if maybe the officials realize that they have made some poor calls, too, because Mark is letting them have it, and they don't even come over to warn him. They are just letting him go with his complaint. That is highly unusual behavior by officials. The good ones will ignore it for a while, then come over and warn the coach, and then if he still doesn't stop will give him a technical. None of the above happens, and Mark continues to vent.

I'm telling you that I think these guys are good officials. I do think, however, even good officials have bad calls or bad games just like players and coaches do. I think that for at least this quarter these guys have performed poorly.

We get a five count on PC and get the ball back. Colin gets fouled on the way to the hoop and makes one of two free throws. They get the ball inside for a hoop; we are down 32-38 and running time off the clock to try to get the last shot of the quarter when we turn the ball over with :03 left and we foul to stop the break (they are in the bonus) so they make two free throws at the end of the quarter—Pella Christian 40, Pella High 32.

We really make a poor play to start the fourth quarter with a simple inbounds play and turn the ball over. They miss an open three, and Kaleb hits a deep three for us. They turn it over again. Kaleb, when he realized his defender was cheating the screen to the top of the floor, changed sides of the floor and hits a three from the corner; all of a sudden we are only down two. The kids just keep fighting back. Time out, PC.

Kaleb makes three really good plays in a row as he covered out to the corner defensively to challenge an open shooter that resulted in a miss for PC. Our rule is: Closest man to the ball must cover the ball, and that is what happened. It wasn't Kaleb's man, but he saw that the guy was open, so he made an unselfish hustle play to cover out to the shooter.

B-Mo, off the dribble, finds Klarc underneath the hoop—it's tied. C.J. (Mr. Hustle) over hustles to prevent an outside shot and gives up a runner in the middle of the lane on defense. We miss a three; we are in the wrong cover in the match-up and give up an open three, but it's a miss. This time Kaleb and Jesse fail to block out, and we give up the put back.

We can't score; they again try to penetrate against C.J., but this time he knocks it loose, and it is our ball. We take a quick shot that turns out to be a miss, and a fast-break for PC. The next segment of play is wild. They pick off an inbounds pass, C.J. picks their pocket, they get it back, and B-Mo makes a steal. They pick it back off, and all of a sudden they are shooting a layup. We just must be tougher with the ball in our hands, but that was a flurry of action.

Again we take a quick shot—we've panicked a little bit on the offensive end. There is time, but we act as though we must get the ball up as soon as we can. Luckily they throw the ball away, and we are down by six with 3:30 left. Kaleb attacks the basket after a timeout, but we miss the shot. We get the ball back, and Klarc gets fouled as he makes the hoop; he misses the free throw. We are down four with 2:30.

C.J.'s defensive pressure causes a PC travel. We miss a three, but B-Mo is there for a put back; he misses, but Klarc doesn't as he gets our second offensive rebound of the possession. Time out, PC. We are down 44-46.

They spread the floor trying to keep the ball away, and we are scrambling, looking for traps. We are doing a much better job of being patient when looking for an opportunity to trap. The traps that we are getting just need to be set better and done in a more physical way to prevent PC getting the ball out. When the ball comes out of a trap you'd better pick it off, or your team is out numbered. That is what happened to us, and they get the ball inside for a hoop.

We come down and throw the ball away. One of our posts and probably our poorest ball handler is bringing the ball down the court—why is that? This is where we need someone to be a leader and come over and get the ball out of his hands. We had to foul; once again Kaleb and Klarc are there this time to pick up the PC player. PC misses, and we get new life. We miss an open shot from about the free-throw line but miss. We have to foul again, and now we can't be picky, as we foul their best free-throw shooter. He misses! We hustle the ball down, and Colin hits a three!

We are down with :07 left and foul with :01 left. They miss, but our long heave down court is knocked down, and we go down in defeat.

We are so close: so darn close. We need to keep the faith, not only keep but also grow the faith. What doesn't do us in, will make us stronger, and if we can hang in there and continue to get better (each and every player) by the end of the year we have a chance. Then if, and I do mean if we could get both Clayton and Kirk back, and we for once would become an entire team; well, then who knows what could happen?

Monday, January 8, Practice #31
Slip, Extrinsic Motivation, Tyler Linn, Tyler Ter Louw, Brock, Traps, Switching Partners, Jesse, Defending Late and Last-Second Shot

Slipping a screen in essence means setting kind of a fake screen. When the defensive players anticipate getting a screen they will oftentimes switch as they see the screen coming; slipping is a good counter to the switch. When the defense switches during a man-to-man defense they actually go into a momentary zone situation because they are both guarding an area that they anticipate the cut to be made into. The offense by slipping actually flashes (as they would in a zone) into an open area rather than set a really hard screen. We work on this now because PC did a lot of switching against our Partners offense, and we didn't react with enough slips.

The slip as described above is a quick cut into the area with no contact to the defender. Another slip method would be similar in nature but it could also involve a pin by the offensive player. The pin would look very similar to a screen out in that the offensive player as they slip might also spin in order to position themselves between the defender and the ball; we also worked on this.

We then did power layups. We had at least two or three of these in the ball game the other night. Our kids are getting used to protecting the ball with their bodies, and rather than taking contact, initiating contact with the defensive players. These resulted in defensive fouls against PC.

We got up and down the court with some three-line passing, and our three-on-two and two-on-one drill. I continued to push the concept of keeping the ball out of the lane during this drill; I am trying to help the kids with the concept of carry over from drills to game situations. Mark just stopped the kids and told them that they were going to do this drill for five minutes, and that if they didn't each individually get an offensive rebound those who didn't would run. Now here is the good news—they really started getting after the offensive boards. Here is the bad news—it took an extrinsic motivational ploy like that to get them to go to the board. The question is why? Why does it take an artificial reward rather than a genuine desire to rebound the ball? Are the kids still not convinced that rebounding the ball is important?

The 11-man drill is something we've decided that we need more of. It basically is a go get the ball drill, both off the boards and as a loose ball on the floor. Our kids are great kids, but they need to become more blue collar, more willing to do the dirty work, the work that this type of drill promotes.

Tyler Linn just took a shot to the eye. I walked him into the locker room and he looked okay; looks like a scratch and won't need a stitch, but he is doing some bleeding. Rob Blom, our trainer, just walked in and is now checking on Tyler just to make sure.

I spoke with both Tyler Ter Louw and Brock today. We had a discussion on both the ways they could get better and the ways that they could each contribute to making our team a better squad. Both conversations were productive; both young men are good guys, and both men have the ability to play more and make us better. It is important to me that I tell the players the exact truth as much as I can or know. That is what I tried to do here. It really (in my mind) comes down to them believing in themselves. Both players have some athletic abilities that we could use, but for various reasons they have limited themselves and their own personal way of thinking about themselves. In today's practice I can tell that they both heard what I had to say, and they are both trying to play accordingly. Now, they must improve upon this first start on a daily basis and must consistently practice this way in order to move up the pecking order. We shall see. I hope they do.

We worked on trapping in the next portion of practice; when to trap and how to set the trap in the correct way. We are not trying to steal the ball out of the hands of the man being trapped; rather we want a steal or a deflection of the pass that he is throwing out of the pass. We would like the players that are setting the trap to have their lower body forward and up against the man being trapped with their hands up and straight. This creates a sense of pressure in the man that is trapped and yet we won't be fouling him. I think our traps would be a lot better if the guys that were doing the trapping were more confident that this next pass would be picked off. They would both look for it more and apply it harder if they knew it would create a turnover. Right now we rarely create the turnover because the players outside of the trap aren't aggressive enough in their pursuit of the ball.

Our press-press offense consists of the white team running a full-court, hard, overplaying, man-to-man press looking for traps (similar to PC) while the green team works on various half-court defenses, called by our hand signals. Our green team really had problems with the white team's press—much more than what occurred the other night. Hmmm.

We switched B-Mo and Klarc to opposite sides from each other in our Partners offense. We also had the white team play very aggressively in the quarter-court defense as well. I'm hoping this will simulate what we see on Friday night when we play Knoxville.

The one-break drill is next with the white team running a regular zone while the green team attacks it with our various zone offenses and the green team running our own zone defense. We still have some gaps in our zone defensive system that we need more repetitions with.

One of the things that I asked Tyler Ter Louw to do was to play more aggressively and more physically against the green team. He must be doing that. I've seen him get a good post feed with a very physical post up, and now I've seen another player push him out of frustration. I walked over to him and said, "Tyler, you must be playing more physical because I saw someone get mad and push you. Are you going to back off now because you got pushed?" He told me he wouldn't. Here is the thing: if he backs off because he is afraid of hurting a teammate's feelings or making him momentarily angry, he will back off in game situations too; again we shall see.

Jesse's effort and play has picked up in practice since his extended minutes against PC.

Our last part of practice was dedicated to how to deny the ball in-bounds against an opponent when time is running out during the game and how to attack a full-court defense with a quick-set play with just seconds left. Both circumstances occurred against PC, and we didn't handle either one of them really well. Honestly, both situations are ones that the odds are against success, but nonetheless there are times that they work. How much time do you dedicate to practicing these things when they happen so infrequently? That is the question. By the way, just now in practice with about :03 left we hit a half-court shot out of the play—a good place to stop.

The Boy's Athletic Association of Iowa sent us a letter that they received from the officials of the first Pella vs. PC game. Coach Core is reading it to the kids. In essence it says that the officials really felt good about the community spirit and the atmosphere of competitiveness between the two teams. They indicated that they would like to send a copy of this cross-town rivalry as an example to all teams, coaches and communities as to how to conduct themselves during the game of basketball at any level. It was a nice note and one I'll bet a lot of high schools never receive. Once again, win or lose, I'm proud of our guys.

Tuesday, January 9, Practice #32
Andrew, Clayton, Scrimmage Notes, Kaleb, and Playing the Zone

About a week ago we moved Andrew Ter Louw back to the sophomore team. He just wasn't getting the minutes on the floor he needed to get in order to make it worth it to play with the varsity. He needs game time, and this was the best way to do it. He was such a good young man about it; he listened to what we had to say, and he then indicated he understood the decision and went without a complaint. I would have expected nothing less from Andrew.

While we want him to practice as often as he can with the sophomore team because he really has a different role with them than with us, we also would like him to practice with the varsity if it works out okay for him. His priority in both practice and games is now with the junior varsity ahead of the varsity. But tonight he is at our practice, and he really is adding athleticism and quickness to the white team. He looks much more excited about basketball and more sure of himself, I'm guessing in part because of the move to the junior varsity team.

We opened with some shooting, the Magic drill and then went full-court with the Michigan drill.

Since it is Tuesday and we normally have games on Tuesday, Coach Core decided that today's practice would be a lot of scrimmaging rather than a normal practice, kind of designed to give the guys that game feeling of Tuesday night. The scrimmages will be 8:00 with a running clock.

Clayton makes his return tonight.

I am coaching the white team while Mark coaches the green team. We are both trying to officiate as well; we'd like the boys to play and not listen to quite so much coach talk today.

The Partners offense seems surprisingly hard to guard when the defense is zone, this offense was designed for man-to-man defenses.

The following are just my thoughts about individual players during the scrimmage:

Tyler Terlouw continues to show that he isn't going to back off for the white team. That is two days in a row that he has upped his performance.

Clayton looks pretty rusty. He has missed a number of layups and is turning the ball over. I would think that he would be; during the course of the year he sure hasn't had many practices.

Brandon Esterbrook is shooting the lights out for the white team. I asked him if watching the rim rather than the flight of the ball on the release has made some difference in the way he is shooting. He got this really big smile on his face and said, "yeah." Unfortunately, Brandon is also leading us in this practice with turnovers. That is the next step toward playing: cut those down.

As I mentioned earlier Andrew just really had a lot of energy, rebounded well, and made hustle plays.

Klarc was Klarc, a solid player that showed leadership, ball handling, and toughness.

Kaleb continues to pass up shots. I feel as though his game-time shooting is much better. He is looking more, I think, because he is more confident in his shot. But in practice he continues to look for others first. That is a nice and unselfish trait, but at the same time he needs to practice shooting in scrimmage situations in order to continue to improve his shooting during games.

Tyler Linn is not a natural point guard, even though his size gives him the look of a point guard. But he was forced to play point today and did a pretty good job out front. Tyler would prefer to play wing where there is a little less dribbling and ball handling. While he isn't a bad ball handler, he just doesn't believe in his own ability and therefore doesn't handle it as well as I would expect him to.

We got Nate Klyn in a little bit today. He took himself out a couple of times; I think the conditioning is a factor.

Justin took a shot in the nose during scrimmage. Somebody's head got him when he was trying to rebound—who says this is a non-contact sport? Justin is an athlete. He can run, and he can jump. If only he would play the game more in the off-season! His court awareness and his composure with the ball are the only things that prevent him from becoming a player. He could improve in both of those areas by playing the game during the off-season.

I didn't really notice Colin during the scrimmage. That is good from the standpoint of not doing something bad that causes attention but it is bad in that I would think that a starter would be a bit more noticeable.

B-Mo shot the ball well from outside, which created some room for his inside drive. The white team had Zach on him, and that would be a difficult cover for Zach. For example, in football B-Mo played quarterback while Zach played linebacker. They just have different athletic talents. Zach is strong as a house but B-Mo is quicker and faster.

One of the reasons that I think the players like Jesse as a teammate is that he knows what his role is and plays it. I think that is okay to a degree. Jesse tries not to make mistakes and works on defense. However if you never step outside of your comfort zone, you will never get better.

After practice I spoke with Mark and Kaleb about the book that Mark wanted Kaleb to read. The short version of what Kaleb found through the reading was that he played this game for two reasons. One was to prove himself, and two was to have fun. We (all three of us) would like him to increase in the having-fun department and forget the proving-himself department. That would be a difficult way to play—needing to prove yourself and trying to live up to the expectations brought about by having two older brothers play college ball and one of them in the pros. Kaleb has lived with this kind of pressure for quite a while for a young guy; I wish we could do more to alleviate this. He said that some of his most fun on the basketball court comes from talking to/at B-Mo. He said they have fun with the things they say to one another as they play. I'm going to start looking for and encouraging that.

As I watched the scrimmage I noticed something about our zone. One rule that I think we need to add to the zone is to make sure that the offside wing player drops down into the offside rebounding position when the ball goes away from him. I think that would help in both rebounding and playing in the correct position to cover.

Wednesday, January 10

We had a nice meeting with Kaleb today. He is a good guy. Coach Core had asked the captains to check with the other players for their reasons for not rebounding the ball as hard as they could. The players had some good responses, and we discussed them, but eventually it led to other things concerning the team.

An additional area of conversation we had with Kaleb was about Tyler Terlouw. Yesterday Tyler made Kaleb mad by how hard and physical he was playing against him. We then told Kaleb of our discussion that we had with Tyler. We told him that we had encouraged such play because we are just not a very strong physical team. We then challenged Kaleb and asked him to not only accept Tyler's play but to embrace it as the kind of play that we would like from him.

Our poor captains have heard lots of coach talk from us; Kaleb is kind enough to at least pretend like he is still listening (I'm kidding). I know he listens.

Wednesday, January 10, Practice #33
Spy, Colin, Kirk, Clayton, Nowhere Dribble, Three Stops, Z-Word, Signals, New Plays, Jesse and Valpo

We always "spy" on something during practice. Today Andrew Barber is watching just Colin to see what he does with every possession of the ball during any four-on-four or five-on-five situation. We've charted a variety of players this year in such areas as rebounding, turnovers, and shots attempted, etc. By the end of practice we will know how many times Colin caught the ball and what he did with it.

Kirk was sick yesterday, and Brock is taped up with a jammed thumb/hand. Clayton told Coach Core his arm was sore today, but he is going to practice. Klarc is late for practice; I'm assuming maybe he went to get his wrist checked out.

We opened practice with 30 made shots and then divided up into two and three-man teams to make six free throws in a row. We followed this with Brunner and then power layups. Then we went to three-on-two and back to two-on-one. Our lack of effort and concentration caused the players to do some running and also put an end to this drill. We will try some shell now.

The shell drills go from simply jumping to the ball to a dribble-penetration drill. During the penetration segment each man is told not to help the other on defense. Our rotation (our help) should be only in emergencies; we are trying to find out if one guy can guard the other.

If you want to guard someone, the first thing that the boys are finding out is that they must get in a "stance." The stance is something that isn't really that comfortable, and it's tiring, but it is necessary. The second thing they must do is learn to focus, specifically on the mid-section, and the third thing that they must do is have a deep desire to stop their man.

The defense is getting better at this, but I can't tell you how often our guys go no place with their dribble; that helps the defense. We want the offense to be great so it forces our defense to be great.

The next fifteen minutes of practice was really cool. We did the three-stops-in-a-row drill, and we really did this drill hard. Just to remind you, not only must the players stop the offense from scoring, they cannot allow the following: a loss of vision, the ball in the lane, an uncontested outside shot, or lack of a block out. Should the defense allow one of these things to happen, regardless of the ball going in or not, the possession is not perfect, and therefore, the stop is not made. At any rate, the effort in this drill was phenomenal! Both teams would battle to two stops but neither team would allow the other to win. The kids were adamant offensively about going to the boards and getting the ball in the paint, and from that we get all sorts of great looks from the outside offensively. This is the kind of mentality that could make us a good offensive team. The by-product of that would be an improvement in our team defense. In other words, we would get better.

We did the three-stops drill in the quarter-court. As soon as we went to our full-court work we didn't look the same. Our intensity and effort went down, as did our overall play. I wish I knew why. Maybe we should be a walk-it-up team offensively and play just in the quarter-court. I'd hate that personally, but maybe it would be best for our team.

We incorporated some new rules in our match-up zone and then added a regular zone set in a one-two-two formation. Peculiar. I used to say, "the Z word," implying that it was a swear word when we talked about zone. I wanted our kids tough and felt like a zone was not a good defense and wasn't the way to go. Now we are working on two different versions of a zone. Are we as coaches changing with the times and using our personnel more wisely by doing this, or are we giving in and using the zone as an easy out?

We are trying our one-break drill with the new hand signals. The players are having a difficult time making the switches to the various defenses. I don't think we can switch this much this quickly. I think we will need some dead-ball or walk-it-up situations in order to change defenses.

We put in a couple of new offensive plays towards the end of practice today, both named after Jesse's girl friend. The first one has her first name, that features a flex cut and the second has her second name, which features an on-ball screen from the baseline up, Klarc screening for Kaleb.

We finished practice again with a quick review of "Valpo," our full-court-score-with-:03-left-at-the-end-of-the-game offense.

By the way, Colin came out pretty darn good with his charting. Andrew tells the player at the end of practice that he was being "spied" on and what the results were. Colin is making more of an attempt to set other people up for shots, and it proved out statistically. The thing that he didn't do was set a screen for anyone—Colin is not the most massive of all people. I can see why this might be the area he needs to improve upon.

Thursday, January 11, Practice #34
C.J. Physical, Clayton, Point of Emphasis, Rebound, T.O., Paint, Inside Triangle, K'ville, Kaleb, Quick Shots, Tyler, and Home Late.

Going back to the whole physical-play thing that I was talking about earlier—our "band guy" C.J. is setting the most physical screens we set. C.J. is really a bright student. In addition to that he is an outstanding kid (when you get to be my age you can call 17-year-olds kids). I appreciate the fact that he heard us ask for more physical play, and he has responded.

Clayton is almost a one-armed player. We spoke with Rob before practice to double check but he said it is most likely a deep bone bruise, and they hurt like crazy. I know Clayton really wants to play; he is choosing to gut it out.

We did some shooting and then free throws to start practice. The post players worked on inside moves and the perimeter players shot jumpers. We then did some floaters and then power layups.

At one time a while back Coach Core had asked that the kids to consider every drill a rebounding and loose-ball drill. Because the ball is bouncing around and lying loose on the floor during the initial warm ups the boys are going to run as a reminder to rebound the ball.

In addition to the running reminder the next part of practice is the 11-man drill.

It is amazing how the point of emphasis seems to affect the players. We have really emphasized rebounding the ball, and that has improved. Earlier in the season we had emphasized taking care of the ball, and that was pretty darn good. Carry over was supposed to have set in; we should be taking care of the ball and adding rebounding. It hasn't. We are rebounding, but now we are throwing the ball away, not only in practice but also in games. Again, running is the method as a reminder to value each possession.

We did two shell drills. The first was jump to the ball and the second was dribble penetration. During the second again we asked the players to guard their men, to not expect help—they were on their own. I've seen improvement.

C.J. is in the head stance during the shell drill. Again, the human head weighs about 12 lbs. We want our players with their heads over their shoulders, not ahead of them leaning forward. The latter stance seems to be the easier one, however. This head-out stance is easier because it allows you to straighten your legs and still gives the athletes the appearance of being down and low as if they are ready to move. This is not true. With 12 lbs in front of your shoulders and your legs straight, the last thing you are ready for is movement. As C.J. gets more tired he comes up even more out of that ever-important stance. He and I spoke about this off to the side of the shell; he knew immediately what I was saying—told you he was sharp. Now, will he carry over?

Both the green and the white teams tried running Louisville as delay with :30 left in the quarter as one of our practice segments with various degrees of success. I'm not sure that I like everyone up so close to the half-court area; this could lead to a quick steal and layup at the other end. I like having the man at the free-throw line if he is a good ball handler, but I don't like this offense in this situation if he is not a ball handler because it limits the area that the guards (when they have the ball) can use to penetrate. However if the player at the free-throw line is good with the ball, he can pop out as an open receiver and operate as a guard usually against a big, slow post.

Almost my entire practice dialog to the players has been, "Get the ball in the paint." I'll bet the players would like to come over and tell me to quit saying that; I'm probably driving them crazy. But I saw glimpses of really good play when we do that in our three-stop drill—I'd like this to carry over. It is not that I think all the shots should come from the lane, not at all. But I do think a lot of plays that start in the lane end up with shots both inside and outside.

Much of the second half of practice we are working on various forms of zone offenses; there is no reason not to get the ball in the paint during this phase either. We then tried to simulate Knoxville's defense (man-to-man) and ran Partners and our set plays against it as well.

Mark allowed me a little bit of time at the end of practice to have some more repetitions with our match-up zone defense. Where we need work is recognition from the outside players as to who should be guarding whom. The interesting thing to me since we've tried implementing this defense is how much more I've learned in regards to attacking it. Again, if you make your defense better it forces you to make your offense better and vice versa.

Knoxville runs an inside triangle as one of their offenses. The concept is simple; the results can be very effective. A wing and two post players screen and cut for each other within the triangle formation that they form with each other. This triangle usually takes the form of one player at the free throw line and two players positioned along the baseline in the post areas.

The other two players (normally their guards) may slide up and down the sides of the triangle on opposite sides of the floor looking to catch and shoot or enter the ball to the low-post player on their side or at any time into the high post. The movement of the triangle players, if done correctly, is meant to confuse the defense or pin the defenders behind the offensive players. We counter this with some switching between the players defending in the inside spots and help down into the lane area from players guarding their outside shooters.

Again defensive basketball is making decisions, choosing options that seem least harmful to the defense. Knoxville has made 17 three-point shots in 10 games. Our players that are guarding guards should be able to help off of their men into the lane area.

I thought Kaleb really had a good practice, and I told him so in front of his teammates. He really attacked the lane area. Because of that he got fouled, played more assertively, rebounded offensively and set his teammates up for outside shots. What's not to like?

Clayton just plain adds to our team.

We have taken some quick shots today in practice but not as many; I know this because they are more obvious when we do shoot them. Quick shots are fine if they go in, but if we miss them, oftentimes they turn into a fast-break going the other way. The only quick shots we want are off of the fast-break, otherwise we want some ball movement.

Tyler Terlouw keeps showing me he wants to play. He is rebounding and continues to play in a physical manner.

We walked through some out-of-bounds plays that Knoxville runs and then went home.

I was home for about an hour. I went back to watch our freshman and our sophomores play. I did finally get home for good at about 8:00 P.M.

Friday, January 12

This would be my ideal game plan against Knoxville tonight.
On offense:

We would get the ball in the paint

We would be very aware of their over play and make some back door cuts. Louisville would be ideal for this; the pass to the middle man would key a wing cut or the pass from guard to wing could be a back door cut.

On defense:

We would keep the ball from the lane area and make them shoot from outside.

We would make numbers 0, 2, and 4 handle the ball and help off of them when we trap.

Chapter 10—Can We Turn This Season Around?

Friday, January 12, Pella vs. Knoxville, Game #10
Our Record: 4-5; Conference: 4-5

This game starts the second swing through the conference for us. It is a game that we really need to win for our confidence.

A player that played on the first team that I was a part of at Pella High called to see if he could get some second-grade kids involved with our guys for tonight's game. So the little boys sat with our guys during the girls' game and then came in the locker room for our pre-game meeting. We had all the big boys and the little boys together for a picture before we left the locker room. Then the little guys sat behind our bench during the game. When the second graders took off their top shirts, as the varsity took the floor, we saw that each boy had a green letter on his white shirt. They sat in such an order that it spelled out GO PELLA!

I think that the little guys really enjoyed the locker room and hanging out with "real players." But I also think it was good for our guys, too. It helped get some perspective back about playing and being childlike in our appreciation for the game.

During the pre-game talk Mark talked about rebounding the ball and playing hard with composure. He drew up and reviewed on the board a couple of our plays as well. I talked just about us getting the ball in the paint and keeping them out of the paint and making a team shoot that has a hard time shooting from the outside.

Clayton is back in the starting lineup for the second time this season. Jesse will not start tonight.

Man, our opening possession is a thing of beauty, with a ball swing from one side of the floor to the other and then back again, which leads to penetration and a short jumper in the lane by B-Mo. The next time we get the ball back we get a ball swing through dribble penetration by Colin, and again it's B-Mo with a hoop.

Out first two defensive possessions were both man-to-man, and we pitched a shut out. The third possession is a match-up zone. Our shut out continues.

Klarc had a really nice pass that results in another hoop for B-Mo this time off the break, and once again we are in the match-up. I really think the official was almost feeling sorry for the Knoxville team, as B-Mo was called for a blocking foul even though he seemed to be set and the offensive player from Knoxville initiated the contact. That makes the score 6-1 after they make one of two from the line.

Knoxville travels on their next two possessions, and for us Kaleb had a really nice penetrating dribble but missed an open layup. Then Jesse came in to be at the top of the Partners offense, which moved Clayton into the wing, and he ended up with a nice dribble-penetration layup. Knoxville timeout.

We get another stop and we also missed another layup attempt by Kaleb, but K got his own rebound and Klarc had a miss as well; we are attacking the boards better. They threw the ball away again, and we had another miss. The next possession, Knoxville was really baffled as to what defense we were in, and they took a long time to shoot and then miss, but they got the offensive put back for a hoop. We've given up three points with 2:30 left in the first.

Pella makes a careless turnover the next time down; there was no pressure. We just didn't look the ball into our hands, and we missed the pass. They scored on dribble penetration, but we came right back as Colin really made a nice catch on a fast-break pass that resulted in a layup.

Knoxville missed, and then Brandon E. had a sneaky little back cut that resulted in a layup. They turned the ball over against us and Klarc had one blocked as he tried to attack off the break.

One of the things we must do out of both of our zone defenses is rebound better than we are. Zones can be tough to board from because you don't have a man assigned to block out but must just go get the ball. We ran Louisville for the last shot and came up empty; the score at the quarter 12-7.

Our first offensive possession of the second quarter is not a terrible shot but one that we could have gotten any time, we just didn't take much time to get a good look, and we missed. But they get a technical foul for having six guys on the floor, and we make one of two throws but get the ball back. Clayton beats his man off the dribble for a little pull-up jumper for two.

Knoxville was running their man-to-man offense against our zone defense on the next possession; they are confused. We actually got a trap out of our zone defense rather than the man we are trying to trap from. But they came out of the trap and hit a three. But Klarc had a nice assist to B-Mo, who scores from three for us. We run our straight zone for the second time in a row, and for the second time they hit a three. They are back in the game.

Our ball swing is not what it was at the beginning of the game. We are getting the ball into the paint, but we aren't getting the swing. But our changing defenses have confused Knoxville. Unfortunately our offense isn't what it was either, we are putting up contested two-pointers off of a secondary break.

They score, and it's 18-15. We miss another quick shot, and they come down for a layup off of a break and it's 18-17 with 4:24 left until half. Clayton, again with dribble penetration, scores from an out-of-bounds play and gets fouled. We fall back into the match-up for a stop. Another quick shot, this time from three, is a miss.

After Kaleb hits a penetration layup we seem to be getting it back together. This is Kaleb's first basket of the game. Tyler Linn makes an appearance for the first time in a number of games. His teammates enjoy Tyler, and they are in favor of his playing but they also understand his inconsistent play in practice has been an impediment to his playing time. Brandon E., who is playing post defense, gets caught behind the post and must lunge for a steal, giving up a straight line to the hoop for the Knoxville player who gets fouled—he misses both.

B-Mo scores with a spin move on a break that brings me out of my seat. A number of our fans reacted that way as well. It was way cool. We had a stop, but the ball bounced the opposite way of three of our guys and ended up going to their lone player under the boards for an easy two.

B-Mo again scores with a little jumper on an assist from Brandon. Tyler comes out after about a minute of play. He did fine while he was in there. The score is 29-19 with 5:10 left in the half. They throw it away; we get a ball swing, and Kaleb ends it with a runner in the lane. We actually ran our Fist and got a trap the next time down that resulted in a turnover for Knoxville. Sorry to say we carry the ball and turn it over, but they miss the last shot of the quarter, and the score at half is 31-19, the good guys.

Our halftime was just a moment to reinforce all the good things that we were doing. We shot only four three-point shots and made only one, but we made something like 11 of 16 from inside the arc.

Kaleb caught a post entry pass to start the second half and attacked the basket to get fouled on his way to the hoop; he hits one of two. But they come down and hit a three and then turn us over under our own hoop for a five-point swing within seconds. We again have an empty possession, and they come down with another hoop. Colin answers as he gets fouled on a fast-break attack. It's 32-26 early in the third.

Colin makes two free throws. Our match-up has been really an effective defense when paired with our man-to-man defense. We are starting to recognize and react better to open men. We fouled a shooter, and they make two free throws, and then Kaleb misses a runner in the lane but scores on his own put back.

Their secondary break scores and B-Mo misses, but Kaleb is there to put it back in the hoop. It seems to me that for the game almost every time we have swung the ball from one side of the floor to the other we've scored, either with a hoop or by free throws.

We were the ones confused on the next defensive possession as Kaleb lost his man and gave up an open two out of our match-up zone. That is one of the very few mistakes Kaleb has made on the defensive end. Clayton comes back with a little runner off of an out-of-bounds play, and they hit two free throws after C.J. doesn't hedge out quite hard enough and ends up fouling.

Knoxville tries a zone full-court press for the first time but we threw over the top to Brandon E.; he is so open he misses a very short jumper in the lane. There are a couple of empty possessions by both teams, and they finally score on a put back. It's our timeout, and we talk to the kids about calling too much zone. The plan going in was to run about 70% man, 25% match-up, and 5% straight zone.

Colin hits a three! Colin follows that up with an old-fashioned three by scoring a bucket and getting fouled. I've encouraged B-Mo to use his spin move and he has used it consistently during this game. He came down one on three, and I thought he should pull it out, but he attacked with the spin and just about pulled it off. He missed, but it was truly a great move. Then on the next Knoxville possession he picks off a pass and is off for a semi-breakaway but this time just flat misses a little bunny layup. It's 46-36 with a minute left in the third. They turn it over, but we turn it back to them by setting an illegal screen. That is almost a joyous thing for me, getting called for setting a screen—illegal or not we don't set many really hard screens.

They miss, and we get the last shot but get a little confused on our Louisville offense, so B-Mo goes from the center spot to set an on-ball screen for Kaleb, who gets a good look but misses at the buzzer. I liked that option.

Our turnover turns into a Knoxville fast-break basket. Their press turns Clayton over. (He hasn't had many). Klarc had a tough shot off of a break that he could connect with. They score on a post pass. Time out, PHS. The score is 46-40 with a bit over six minutes left.

Klarc came down and called Duke for Kaleb. I liked this call. We've been running Partners, and Duke is a great counter. K gets fouled and makes both. They score on an offensive put back.

Kaleb has to feel more involved than when he gets satisfied and just stands to shoot the three. He is attacking the basket with the dribble; he is getting offensive rebounds, and he is getting to the line.

We miss but get a steal on the other end that turns into a two-on-one break that we don't handle correctly but get the ball back out of bounds. B-Mo cleans up a missed shot off of our offensive board. Kaleb now gets a break away two after a nifty steal. They get another post score, and we get to the line again with Kaleb. It's 53-44 now with four minutes left. On the next possession we secure the rebound, and it turns into a run out for Jesse for an easy two.

Knoxville throws in one of those shots that just has no business going in and gets fouled to boot.

We are not attacking their press very well, but they are not a very good pressing team. They are used to being pressed (because of their lack of a ball handler) rather than doing the pressing.

Some empty possessions for both teams follow when B-Mo makes an impressive steal of a post pass when Kaleb got stuck behind his man and couldn't prevent the entry pass. B-Mo left his man and darted in front of the incoming pass; this leads to two more free throws from Kaleb at the other end.

Clayton makes a steal, and it's time to take some time. We are taking time off the clock with this possession that results in a really nice pass from Kaleb to cousin Klarc who scores and makes the free throw as well. At this time of the game we are looking for nothing but layups and free throws. Klarc and Colin finish the scoring with three more free throws, and the final score is 62-49.

Saturday, January 13, Meeting and Walk Through

The guys loosened up some stiff muscles with some easy jogging, dribbling, and shooting for about ten minutes before we meet. Clayton is so sore that he cannot even do this; he sits out. Kirk is over on the sideline working on the stationary bike for the second time in two days.

Mark announced that our two managers/stat/video/assistant coaches—Will Lubberden and Andrew Barber, each got the highest scores on his government semester test—the boys cheered the good news.

He also reminded the players to seek out and thank the cheerleaders for again providing the players with some goodies and the pep band members for their excellent play during last night's game. His final thank-you reminder was for the fans and parents that came to the game last night. Lots of people were at the game last night, almost a full gym.

Personally I still miss seeing one of our biggest fans at our games. My father-in-law used to be at every one of our games. He was of the "fearsome fivesome" (5 older gentlemen who used to line the front row opposite our bench) at all home games. He and those guys were true fans, biased for Pella with all their hearts. They coached, officiated, and helped the kids play all without leaving their seats and they were always with us win or lose. I think Tom is still there with me somewhere.

Stat-wise, our leaders from the Knoxville game were Kaleb with 10 rebounds; Klarc, five assists; and B-Mo four steals. We also had balanced shot attempts between the players and proof we were getting the ball inside as we had only nine three-point attempts compared to 38 two-point attempts. We made 21 of those 38 shots and attempted 20 free throws, making 14 of them. Additional proof of our inside-attack mind set was the fact that both of their post players fouled out; that definitely is a first for us this year.

Win or lose we are going to talk about some of the things that we need to improve upon. Two of them that Coach talked about were our lack of success or even attempts in regards to our Fist defense (the man-to-man-into-a-trap defense), and the poor job of hedging on ball screens that we did. If we hedge really hard, we will rarely switch into bad match-ups such as our guards defending their posts. Last night Colin, had to switch (onto a man probably 100 lbs. heavier than he is), and we would like to avoid that situation.

Mark had the same question for the team that Klarc had for me yesterday during a little meeting we had. Are we flopping when we are trying to draw a charge? It seems as though we haven't gotten a charge call in forever. If an official sees a flop he is likely to think that all of the attempted charges we take might be flops, even when they are legit and should be called in our favor. The boys said that they were not. They said that they were taking hits that honestly were charges; hopefully we will start getting some calls in this regard.

The next area that we talked about was our offensive attack against a zone press. Last night we did not flash into the middle very well against the two-two-one press that Knoxville changed into late in the game. We didn't turn it over much against the press, but again neither Mark nor I thought Knoxville's normal game plan would be as a pressing team. Our fear is that up against a team that lives with an aggressive press we might struggle, so we would like to prepare with them in mind.

In my mind our problems with the press start with one of two things; we are either lazy when it comes to flashing into an open area or we don't recognize the zone until it is too late. Against a man we want to clear down the floor while against a zone we must become receivers.

Mark also thought that defensively our post players were not "up line" enough in the post. The defender in the post is in correct position if his relation to the ball is closer to the ball when it's at the point (this is up line) and farther from the baseline. In this way he can easily get in front of the post when the ball goes to a wing to defend the pass entry. If the defensive post is closer to the baseline than the point he is in trouble; by the time he realizes the pass is coming in to the post he is already pinned behind the offensive player.

I once again asked the boys about the amount of talking they gave or received from each other last night. It sounds like there was more than before. On the floor I think it starts with Clayton. On the bench it seems to be Tyler Terlouw who is really stepping up.

I also asked about inspirational plays that they saw out of their teammates last night. They mentioned basket and fouled plays, one by Clayton the other Klarc. I mentioned Colin's smart play and B-Mo's spin move. The hand slaps between teammates was mentioned, as was the talk of starting the game with a half-court shot and the giggling that caused.

We then changed subject areas by going on to our next opponent, Boone. Their leading scorer is six feet seven inches, and they also have a state-class athlete that almost all of their offense revolves around. Their basic offense is a three-out-and-two-in offense designed to get the ball to the high post and then work the high-low offense against our defense. They will try to get the ball into the paint by throwing a post pass from the free-throw lane down. In fact, if we do struggle with this on Tuesday it will be more the fault of the man guarding the high post man and letting his man catch it too close to the lane than the man guarding the low post man.

Boone also runs some good set plays that we must prepare for. One of the ways to handle a set play is to recognize it before it happens. The players can do this in a couple of different ways. One is recognizing the original positioning of the offensive players if it is different from their normal set up. The second is to try to pick up the verbal or non-verbal way they are making the call for the play. See the diagram below for one of Boone's set plays.

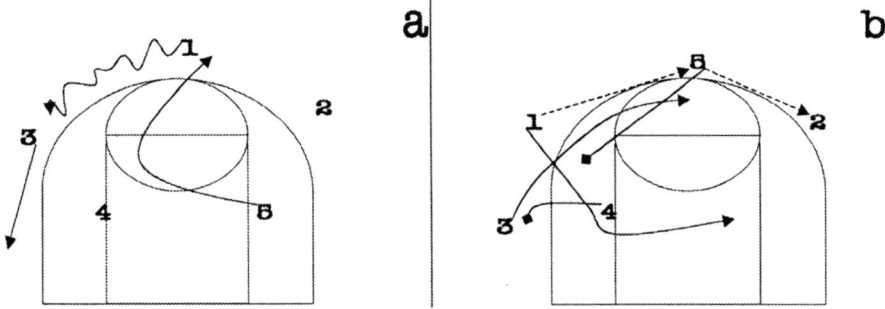

As I said, everything revolves around their athlete represented as #3 here. The play goes like this. #1 dribbles #3 into the corner as #5 flashes at the ball and then out to the top of the key all shown in **Diagram a**. #1 then reverses the ball to #5, who quickly gets the ball to #2. #2 now has the option to pass to #1 coming off of #4's screen or #3 coming off of a staggered screen set by #4 coming out of the post or #5 who, after passing to #2, screens down for #3.

Actually, in the diagram, another option 1 would have after he dribbles #3 into the corner would be to simply enter the ball into the post-man #4 because the entire back side of the defense is cleared out if the man guarding the #2 man errors by not dropping in to help.

These plays will be hard to recognize because they both start out of a three-out-and-two-in formation. We just simply must recognize the dribble down by #1 or be aware of a verbal or non-verbal call for this play.

The second play can be recognized by the original set. It is a box set, something not normal for Boone. We should immediately react to this, and if our kids talk we should be okay. A box set is exactly what it sounds like. Other than the point guard at the top of the key the rest of the players form a box around the lane.

Their athlete gets a screen from their best shooter coming across the lane along the baseline as the point dribbles to his side. The posts (located at the elbows of the free-throw line in the box set) then screen down for the shooter coming up after screening for the athlete. Those down screeners are now in great position to go to the offensive boards.

On any of Boone's sideline out-of-bounds plays it doesn't matter what formation Boone sets up in; their athlete will take the ball out of bounds, throw it in, step back in, and immediately get a return pass and will take the three or attack the hoop with the dribble.

And finally their out-of-bounds plays underneath are pretty straightforward. The point takes the ball out of bounds while the athlete lines up directly in front of him at the block. The post player lines up farther up yet and directly behind the athlete. On the slap of the ball the athlete screens up for the post, who dives into the lane, and then the other two players I haven't mentioned come over to screen for the athlete. They then roll back to the hoop or spread to half-court to become a deep outlet.

Interesting, as we were walking through these things and this last out-of-bounds play we had the green team (first team) guys walking through the defense. As soon as the green team came out to defend the cut Klarc went right over to guard the 3-man—looks like he wants their star.

We went home, finally a day off.

Monday, January 15, Practice #35
Time of the Year, Zirk, Rebounding, On-Ball Screens, Fist, Clayton, O.B., and the Xs and Os

Practice about this time of the year starts to feel like work to both players and coaches. This is an easy time to lose focus and start looking at this as something that you must do rather than something you get to do.

Practice started with some shooting and layups of various types that took place in the quarter-court. Both the post players and the perimeter guys are taking shots that they would normally shoot in a game. Then we progressed to some full-court layups in the Michigan drill.

The Zirk (Kirk Korver) is out in the hallway pedaling away on the stationary bike. By the end of practice he tells me he went 24 miles. I've heard that the mileage on a bike is equivalent to approximately 1/3 of what one would get as a runner. If that is true Kirk got in about an eight-mile run. He worked up a pretty good sweat, and I was teasing him about that. He just looked at me laughed and said, "Coach, this thing gives me a sore butt."

The practice continued with two-on-one with a chaser and then some one-on-one play.

We then got up and down the court with the NC drill. Coach Core's continued emphasis has been on rebounding the ball on the offensive end, and this continued today. As a reminder to the boys to rebound, they ran if all five guys weren't going to the boards. Coach Core walked over to me and pointed out how amazingly well we shoot when we start going to the offensive boards. What he meant by that was that the shooter felt less pressure to make his shot since he knew we had a chance to rebound his miss, and therefore, he actually shot the ball better. When the shooter feels as though we will get one shot and one only there is a fear of failure and an effort to guide each shot into the hoop—that makes for poor shooting.

Our two shell drills started with the one that we do on almost a daily basis, which is simply a jump to the ball on every pass. It progressed to on-ball screens. If you will recall defense against this type of screen was exposed as being less than appropriate against Knoxville. We are trying to tighten this area of defense up, not only for the upcoming game but also for any future games.

Our press-press offensive segment today is designed to give the green team more work on breaking a zone press (Knoxville) and equally important running our own half-court trapping defense. Out of approximately 20 calls and attempts to run this in the previous games we probably actually ran it once. Mark and I talked about how to improve this defense this morning. We settled on the one thing that seems to work with this group; they have an independent punishment associated with not performing the required deed. So today the players had to be involved in a trap or intercepting or tipping a pass or they would run. It worked; once again there was more trapping and rotating than I have seen all year.

It was about this time that Clayton came over and said his arm was really hurting him. We had him sit out from this point on. Poor Clayton can't seem to get over his arm injury. Again, that is bad for him but it is also really bad for our team. He has been a leader as well as a very good player for us.

Okay, I know you've been dying to know about these out-of-bounds plays that we are running, and I know I told you I'd have to kill you if I showed them to you, but I will let you in on one if you promise not to tell anyone. Actually it is really one set with two options out of the set. We do quite a bit of this; we read off of one man's move and react based upon what cut they make.

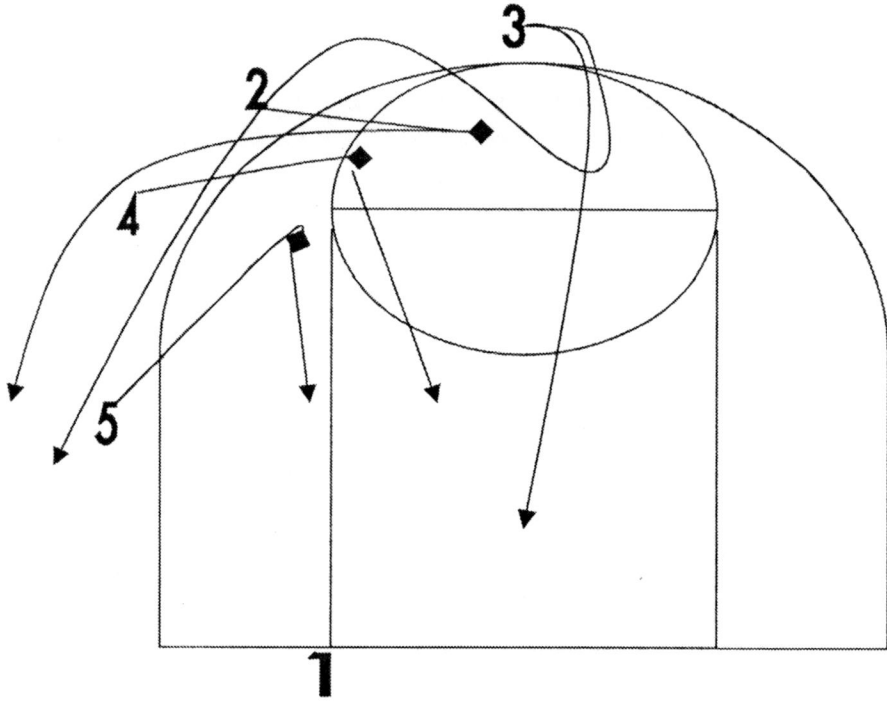

I assume this is self-explanatory (clear as mud) but for those that can't read this simple diagram I will explain. Actually I'm kidding; I know it looks complicated. It's not. We line up as shown and then #2 reads #3's cut. #4 and #5 are simply screening inside for either #2 or #3 coming around the screen to the baseline corner. After they screen #4 and #5 both separate towards the hoop looking for an open area. #2 watches #3; if #3 cuts hard to the basket #2 will come back and use the screens by #4 and #5. If #3 fakes the cut to the hoop and goes to the corner then #2 is part of the screen (along with #4 and #5) and then he goes to the hoop or an open area. I just drew it up this way so you would be impressed with all of the arrows and cuts we apparently make and it would look like a well-conceived play set up by coaches who really know their stuff.

Speaking of really knowing their stuff. That is my next gripe. Just about any coach can draw up some plays and move players around through a series of cuts and plays. Often people confuse that with coaching. Remember, the more you put in the player's mind the slower their feet get. We want simple yet effective offenses and defenses. We have to remember this so that we coaches keep our egos in check and don't start doing some of this kind of stuff just to show people how much we know. There is a substantial difference in time allowed and player commitment from high school to college to the pros; it would do well for most high school coaches to remember this.

We finished practice with some play reviews as well as some review of our basic zone defense. We also did some more shooting and free throw shooting.

Chapter 11—A .500 Team

Jesse will start tonight because once again Clayton is sitting out due to severe pain in his arm. Tonight's game seems to be a big challenge without either Kirk or Clayton. I figure both of those guys as either starters or one starter and a first guy off of the bench. Guys that would normally be players six and seven are now starters and the first guy off of the bench and so on. But the best part of this is that if we can handle this we are getting a lot of guys experience on the floor and making our team deeper because of it. I learned a long time ago that you really only have one option—you play the guys you have; you can make excuses, but that in the long run only hurts you; you play the guys you have.

In the pre-game warm-up we ran our offense against the second team so well that Coach Core told the team to stop warming up and shoot free throws. We opened the game the same way. Our first possession had ball swing and lane penetration and finished with a Kaleb Korver layup.

The two players we are most concerned about coming into the game are #33, an extremely good athlete and #55, a six foot seven post player who is their leading scorer.

Both teams have an empty trip down the floor, and then Boone comes down and hits a three. This three comes in something of a fast-break situation. Our guard or first man back needs to cover the basket to prevent a true fast-break layup and then react out to his man once his fellow defenders are back. The man under the hoop must read when it is safe to come out—I think our read was too slow.

We had another really nice offensive possession the next time down with a ball swing and an extra pass by all the guys that resulted in a three for Colin. Both teams are scoreless on their next possessions, but all of a sudden we are taking one-pass three-point attempts. Eventually they do hit another three in much like the previous situation where we are just late recovering out to the shooter.

Number 55 scores on a layup. B-Mo is trying to defend him but gives up pretty serious size. We want B-Mo to prevent the ball from coming in, but if he can't, to simply get behind and make the man shoot over him. Our next time with the ball results in a layup for Kaleb.

We hold them scoreless for two possessions in a row and score a basket of our own on a nice pass from Klarc to B-Mo under the hoop. Number 25 for Boone seems to be making all of their shots, as he hits a pull up jumper, but Klarc comes back with a hoop for us as well. We make a stop on the next series, but we turn the ball back over to them with a travel of our own. Colin gets a deflection on defense, but they get a shot up, and Z-Mo gets us a defensive board. We get the ball down on a break and miss a three. Out of our last five possessions, we have attempted four threes and one two-pointer. What happened to getting the ball in the paint and attacking the hoop, which was so effective for us early?

Kaleb attacks the hoop on our next possession, but draws a blank. We didn't give up any points on their offensive trip, and Kaleb hits a three for us. C.J. makes a really good switch out for us defensively, but #25 once again finds a way to the basket. Klarc finds a way for two for us. C.J. tips away their next pass and we go on a break, which results in a fast-break pull-up jumper for two points for C.J.

We break out our match-up zone on the next possession and get a stop, but they get the offensive board, and we immediately tie them up for a jump and our ball. Tyler Linn comes in as a sub now. Both teams miss in their next attempts and we end up with the ball for the last shot of the quarter. We attempt to run Louisville, and it ends up a little convoluted, but Kaleb penetrates and makes a great pass to C.J. under the hoop. If C.J. is an inch taller he scores at the buzzer, but instead six foot seven gets a finger on the shot, and we miss. It's 18-12, Pella High, at the end of the first.

Our offense has really looked good, especially early in the first quarter. Midway through we started settling for long and early outside shots or we would have scored more than the 18 we've gotten.

We've got a college coach here watching one of our players tonight. Seems like it might add to the pressure, doesn't it? On the contrary, as one coach said to me about a future recruit that he was watching at a high school game, "I plan on being at all of his games when he gets to college; he might want to get used to it." Makes some sense, doesn't it?

Kaleb attempts a three but misses to start the second. His attempt is rebounded by PHS, and we end up with a little runner in the middle by Colin. They miss, and Kaleb runs a curl cut out of our Partners offense that results in a layup, and we are up 22-12. They miss, and we return the favor with another three-point miss of our own.

Our match-up zone results in a foul on us, and they take the ball out, but again we force a miss and get the ball back. Jesse gets on the board with a three—we are really working on all cylinders on the offensive end; we are up 25-12. We ran our Fist trap at them, and we created a turnover from Boone! We miss, they miss two free throws then we've got two guys going for and securing the rebound, so we end up traveling, and they get the ball back.

It doesn't hurt us, however as Jesse now draws a charge against Boone. Boone goes back into a zone. They have been playing man-to-man for the first part of the game, and that is the only defense we saw when we played at Boone. But our attack tonight against their man has been really good.

We go to our one-four offense against the zone, and all of a sudden we look like a different team. Our attack, rather than being aggressive, is passive, with just perimeter passing and very little lane attack. We turn the ball over against the zone, and they miss as well, but the ball goes out off of us. We make a stop, and Kaleb gets fouled going to the basket.

The zone has slowed us down. Both our attitude and our cutting and moving have been slowed. Our defense is making stops, but once again we settle for a three (that we can get just about any time that we want) and miss.

Another quick three, another miss, but Klarc picks up our second charge of the game against Boone. Unfortunately we throw it away, and they hit a three. We turn the ball right back over to them, and then they turn it back over to us, which results in a fast-break layup for Colin.

Boone scores a pull-up jumper in the middle of the lane. We get the ball in the paint but try a shot after only two passes that is contested and miss, but their possession is a miss as well. Klarc makes an acrobatic running hook in the middle of the lane for two more for Pella, and once again they miss.

We attempt to run Open but throw it away before we can even get into the play, but Klarc makes a hustle play back to prevent two for Boone. Our out-of-bounds play results again in the last shot of the quarter; we got a good look but missed. The score is 29-17 at halftime.

The talk at halftime was mostly about attacking the zone defense that Boone was running. But we also talked about the need to do a better job on #25 who had scored most of Boone's points in the first half. This is a surprise scorer, but now we need to adjust.

We are trying to slip into the middle of the Boone zone early in the second half, and I see a lot of open players in there, but we just don't get the ball there very well. The zone is a laning zone, one that pressures passers and ball handlers, and we aren't creating enough space from our ball handlers to their defenders to find the open players.

We are getting some open looks but missing them from outside. B-Mo, however, gets it to Colin, who scores two more. Their adjustment at halftime seems to be to get their big guy more involved the second half as they go to him for a quick short hook for two.

We miss; they turn it over. We miss again, and so do they. On the last miss we end up on a two-on-one break, but we throw it away without a shot. For the third time in a row our defense is up to the challenge, and finally we score on a nice entry pass from Jesse to Kaleb, who bobbles the ball but recovers it in time to score off a break. The score is 33-19, with 4:30 left in the third.

We lost #25 on an out-of-bounds play; and he made us pay with a basket and a foul. Empty possessions by both teams, and then a turn over by us leads to another basket by #25. This guy is turning into all-conference against us.

We just can't make this easy, as we miss again and they creep within 35-24. A great pass by Klarc to B-Mo follows their turnover and results in two made free throws. We ran straight zone the next possession and forced a miss, but we missed too.

Boone goes back man. Why? We traveled; maybe it wasn't a bad idea on their part, especially now that they come down and hit a basket. It's 36-30 late in the third when #25 hits a three and gets fouled. Wow; he has gone from all-conference to all-state.

Kaleb ends Boone's run with two free throws. Our match-up is really good and forces Boone to run a lot of offense, but they are patient and eventually score. Our last shot of the quarter is a miss, we get a put back (also a miss), and it's 39-32, Pella High.

B-Mo is rebounding the heck out of the ball for us. But this one time he can't get it done, and they convert one of two free throws. Klarc hits a two, and they miss, and now Boone is dropping back into their zone. C.J. hits a three!

We blocked #25's shot (naturally right back to him); he gets to the basket for another basket and foul. Offensively we finally start to combine penetration with more passing, and we are starting to look like we are getting some rhythm back to the offense.

C.J. and Klarc both go to the offensive boards for us, and it's Pella's ball out of bounds after they foul us to prevent an easy shot. Kaleb ends up with an old-fashioned bucket and a foul. Number 25 is human, as he misses a free throw; B-Mo hits a shot in the lane during a break, and then blocks a shot, and we get the ball back.

Kaleb and B-Mo both draw two defensive players, which leaves Colin open for a three, and we are back up 52-36 with 4:30 left. Boone turns the ball over, but then so do we. For the second time in a row they turn the ball over, which results in a really nice pass from Klarc to Colin on the break, and he, too, ends up with an old-fashioned bucket and a foul.

They hit one of two free throws, and now they are trying to press against us. This is not what they do, and they are not very good at it; I think we will make them pay.

Kaleb makes two free throws.

Our next offensive possession we shoot both long and quick and that calls for a timeout. During that timeout we reminded the kids we were up 15, not down; play like that. We wanted free throws and layups. We came out and made them chase us for a little bit, then Colin makes two free throws after being fouled.

After fouling (who else) #25 on a three-point attempt, he makes all three. We did make Boone pay as C.J. makes a nice pass to B-Mo against their press that results in a hoop, and they then foul us going after an offensive board, but we miss the gift free throws.

An out-of-bounds play later on results in two more for B-Mo, but #25 gets fouled going to the hoop and makes two. Klarc gets loose under the hoop and makes two of his own. They miss the next shot, but we throw it away. Their inside shot is sent out with a B-Mo block and Kaleb finds B-Mo under the hoop for two more, and the score is 64-44.

For the first time all year we get are able to clear the bench with :48 left. Nate Klyn is in, and I know both he and the other guys like that he has this opportunity. Boone scores five unanswered points including a three by their stud athlete at the buzzer to make it 64-49.

Number 25 for Boone turned out to be all world as he scored 33 points against us. Our post defenders, mainly Kaleb and especially B-Mo, did a great job in there defensively, as the Boone posts combined for only 8 points total. By the way, B-Mo, while not having a great offensive game points wise, did have 15 rebounds. Even Tyler Terlouw got in the act for the first time all season. He came in during crucial game play and did a nice job defending in the post. And Klarc, pitched a shut out against a guy Boone looks to for scoring.

During post game in the locker room I thought Coach Core made a really good point in that he told the boys that they should feel good about playing five good games in a row; three of them against quality teams and two of them against teams that played hard. He felt that we are just now starting to come together; I hope he is right. I'd really feel good if we could now get the "Zirk" and Clayton back with us.

Wednesday, January 17, Practice #36
Legs, Kirk, Clayton, Flex Cut, On-Ball Screens, Zone Offense, Mental Toughness, and Norwalk Stuff

Mark and I got together earlier to discuss how long practice would be today. It is always a balancing act between the need for practice to improve on the fundamentals and the fact that we are just coming off a game, and the kids will have tired legs and will need to rest some to get those legs back for the upcoming game on Friday.

Kirk is riding like crazy out in the hall on the stationary bike trying to regain some shape. Clayton is going to do some light shooting stuff but will sit out of practice. Coach Core and I also talked about the possibility of letting Clayton play in games but limit his practice time. That is an unusual thing to do at the high school level, and I would say a fairly common thing to do at the pro level. Those guys in the pros take a beating and need to recover from injuries etc. We rarely have this situation at our level. Mark has spoken with the captains about this, and they seem fine with it. I think I am too as long as all the players are cool with it and as soon as Clayton gets over this "arm thing" that he resumes practice as soon as possible. The kids that this would affect the most are the kids that would lose playing time to Clayton. If this was close in terms of who was the better player, this might be an issue; I don't think it is close. I think Clayton has proven himself to the coaches and to his teammates. Besides, I know if he could practice he would. Who in his or her right mind would want to come to practice every night and not play but just stand around? These guys want to play.

We opened practice with the standard stuff of shooting, lay-ups, and three-line passing. The shell drill (flex cut) was meant to simulate the cuts we will see in Friday's game and the basic essentials that we need to defeat Norwalk and defend this cut. Jumping quickly in the direction of the ball side was emphasized repeatedly during the drill. By doing this the man guarding the screener will not be required to help out on the cutter and therefore can go out quickly to slow or stop the reversal pass to the other side of the floor (the second essential). One of the counters to jumping to the ball too quickly is for the offense to fake the cut and stay on the side that they started out on. The defender would then be caught in the lane or on the other side of the court behind a screen. (We call this a flare cut). But we don't think that teams that run this flex cut like to do that—they want to stay in their pattern; if nothing else we'd like them to go to plan B rather than beat us with their A plan.

We also ran the shell drill that emphasized the on-ball screen. We did this one in reaction to our poor response to it during the Boone game. This is coaching; even though we have reviewed this often you must review it as many times as needed until the players are in a habit of doing the fundamentals correctly. But again, there is only so much time; if we don't pick up things quickly we spend time in review rather than in breaking new grounds to make us better.

Our next practice segment was offensive-zone work brought about by some lack of execution during the Boone game. We worked on slipping screens out of the Partners offense, finding the open areas. We also worked on our one-four zone offense. The main focus here was to open the offense by passing to the post. During this option and this phase of our practice we are trying to be very intentional about looking for a high-low pass; a pass from the high post down the middle of the defense to the low post. We just kind of wander through the lane rather than post up in there—that is a goal for tonight, get more aggressive posting in the lane during this offense. I read a quote from a college coach that went something like this: for every three-second call we get, we get 68 shots in the lane; we don't worry too much about the three-second call. I asked our kids how many three-second calls we've had during the season; they thought maybe two or three!

We tried to implement some of the things that we had been working on into a full-court situation by doing the stop-score-and-stop drill. Then we walked through some things that Norwalk will attack us with. I have those diagramed in **Diagram W** later.

After practice we talked about coming back to practice the day after a game. We talked about the mental toughness that it takes to come back when the legs are tired and the body is sore. To me this is a great opportunity to practice mental toughness (something that is a difficult concept to explain). If a player has every reason to have a bad practice, to not work hard, to not hustle, and then can find a way to work through that stuff, this is a mental thing not a physical thing—that is mental toughness. We were not very tough tonight. Our kids gave in to being tired.

Diagram W

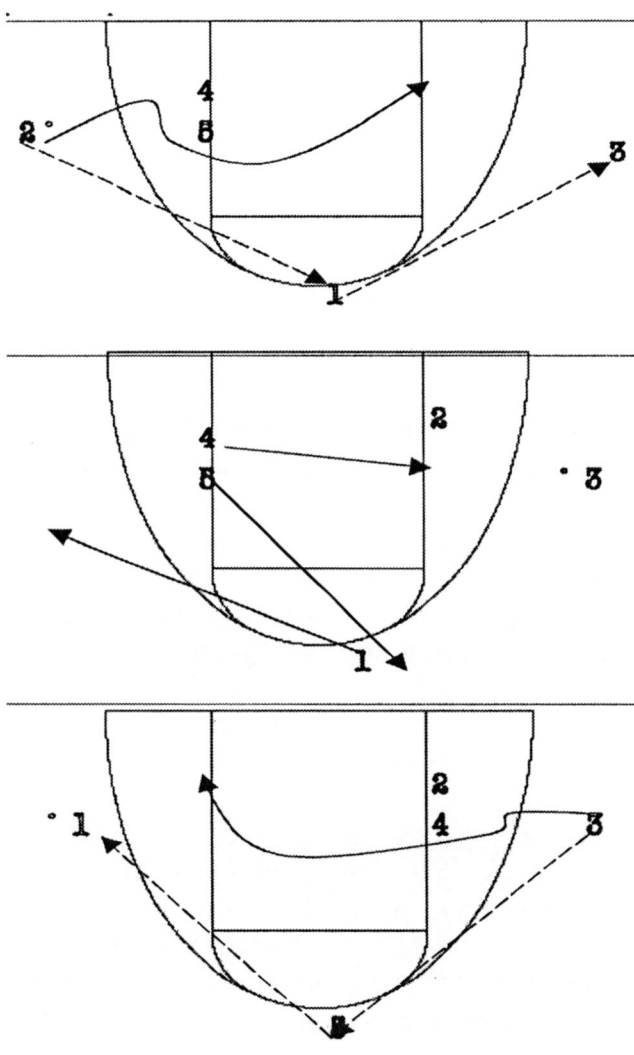

Diagram W shows the basic pattern to the Norwalk offense. The ball starts at the wing (top picture) with #2 and he passes to #1, who quickly swings it to #3. #2 then cuts off of the double screen (flex cut) set by #4 and #5. The man who swung the ball (#1) goes away (shown in the second picture) from his pass, and the top man in the screen (#5) comes to the top of the pattern. The bottom man in the double screen goes across the lane to become the top man in the new double screen on the opposite side of the floor. Then the pattern repeats as shown in the third picture.

We want the man defending the flex cut to beat the cutter across the lane so the two post defenders don't have to help, and then the post defender guarding the top post man (#5 in this case) can get out there and take away the quick-reversal pass. This will disrupt the offense and create some steal opportunities for us.

Norwalk did not score points against us with this so much as they controlled the tempo of the game and tired our defenders out by swinging the ball continually from side to side and making us chase the ball and fight through screens.

Another simple but effective pattern that Norwalk runs puts two shooters on one side of the floor: one at the baseline and one up around the free-throw line extended. These two players don't move a lot; they just get ready to catch and shoot. They then run another continuity pattern with their three remaining players. One man in the guard area passes across to another man in the opposite guard area and down screens for a player at the blocks who comes to the top. The player that down screened then changes sides of the lane. The man who just caught the ball at the guard spot now passes the ball to the man who comes to the top off of the baseline screen and the pattern continues. If the player coming to the top feels as though the defense is cheating and trying to intercept the pass across the top of the lane he back cuts to the basket, which has been cleared out of weak-side defenders. Again this pattern can be effective and time consuming, a way to control the tempo and the make-up of the game.

Thursday, January 18, Practice #37
Tyler Terlouw, C.J., Hedging—Trapping—Trusting, New Three-Man Drill, End of Quarter, and Confidence in the Match-up

When we got to our one-on-one driving line I really liked the way Tyler Terlouw and C.J. got after it. They were physical, dove on the floor for a loose ball and got back up and in the play in a hurry. Jesse, who was in a different group, did much the same.

Once again we continually must go back to hedging the on-ball screen. This is now a trust issue. It can't be a fundamental thing. We have done this so often the boys must know what we expect them to do. It can't be that. They just don't trust enough in each other that they will receive help if they give help, which is what they are doing when they hedge. What I mean is this: when the person hedges into helping his teammate he is temporarily out of position and would need help from a teammate if his man were to dive to the basket. If the "hedger" was absolutely sure he would get that help I think he would get out there. On the other hand, if he does get out there and no help arrives for him when his man dives it looks like he (the hedger) has screwed up—he looks bad. I think that is what we must overcome, not the fundamental. Now why would this "hedger guy" feel like this? It's obvious isn't it? He has been made to look foolish before because the help for his man didn't come, and he didn't like that feeling. What is the answer? It's twofold. One, the man must get help more often, and two, he has to be willing to look a little foolish once in a while (mentally tough) and know that next time the help will get there.

This to me is a similar problem that we have when we run our Fist defense. It's a chancy moment for both the men setting the trap and the guys rotating up for the steals. They leave their own man and must rely on help from others. This is almost the same situation with the same solutions.

It is ironic that the next drill that we do is the man drill; this is the drill that we use to teach guarding your own man and not expecting help. In this drill we don't want them to rely on help. When we hedge and when we trap they must rely on help. What is the answer? Know the situation and trust. Trust yourself and others that they can guard their man, but also trust when you trap or hedge that you will get help when you need it.

The next drill is a new one that Mark made up and I really liked. We just simply put three guys out on the floor guarding three offensive players and had them switch men continually, as we do in our match-up zone. This required a lot of communication and court vision. We struggled with this drill, but I think it will make us better. We also did this in a two-on-two situation, as our posts might play inside.

After some more practice we went to the end-of-quarter situations and practiced on them. What I don't think a lot of people realize (including some of our players prior to explaining it to them) was the five-second-rule violation when a player has the ball. When the player catches the ball he actually has four seconds to hold it, four more seconds to dribble it and then four more seconds once he picks it up from the dribble. That is 12 seconds a man could have the ball if he is closely guarded. If he breaks contact with the man and separates more than six feet from his defender the count will start all over again! It seemed as though once our guys realized this, our end-of-quarter work got a lot calmer.

Our confidence in our match-up zone wasn't very good against Norwalk's offensive sets. We lost men and didn't cover for each other very well. We may run more pure zone early in the game and then come back to the match-up as a way to counter this offense.

I gotta start calling C.J. Craig, which is his real first name. That C.J. stuff just takes too long to come out of my mouth. Klarc always calls him Craig (just to be recalcitrant); it means obstinate (I looked it up). I'm going to, as well, if I remember; when you get to be my age, though…what was I talking about?

Thursday Night at Home, 7:30 P.M.

I'm at home; I'm supposed to be relaxing and enjoying my evening. I mean, it's 7:30, and I've only been home for about two hours, long enough to eat and start my workout. It came to me, the way to guard this offense in the match-up zone. I really think it will be easy. I get on the phone like a kid in the candy store; I'm so excited, and called Mark. He liked the idea (sorry can't tell you) but with the voice of reason, he wisely said that he thought that we should wait with it until tournament time. I always think it's easy; sometimes it isn't. It helps to practice something before your team tries to do it in a game, doesn't it?

Chapter 12—We've Won Two in a Row

Friday, January 19, Pella at Norwalk, Game #12
Our Record: 6-5; Conference: 6-5

We should get a boost for tonight's game, as I just found out that Clayton would play. This is the good news; the bad news is that he hasn't practiced all week. Sometime this is probably going to catch up with him and with us. It also makes for a difficult situation as far as who should start and how this should affect both Clayton's and other player's playing time. Jesse will start, and we will find out how much Clayton will be available after he warms up.

Mark and I talked about being both mentally and physically tougher than we were the last time we played them. We start mostly seniors, and they start mostly younger players. The troubling things is that we really play a lot of off-guards and small forwards with little or no real point guard and center-type player; those are two areas of need that we have, and Norwalk has a true power player in their big, six foot, five inch, powerfully built sophomore.

The opening tip I hope is not a sign of things to come. Norwalk obviously got the tip, and he tipped it so hard that it went out of bounds and should be our ball. For some reason it goes to Norwalk.

One of the strengths of the Norwalk coaching staff is their ability to get kids to run their set plays well. Their opening hoop is just such a play that catches Colin by surprise, and he fouls. They are on the board after making one, 1-0.

Norwalk starts man-to-man and we go to our Partners offense. Kaleb appears to be fouled (I might be a little biased) as he attacks the lane with the dribble, and he gets a shot up that goes in with a whistle. I'm thinking basket and hoop—wrong. Within :30 Kaleb has a charging call against him.

Norwalk runs their double screening offense that we have been working against in practice. We really are doing a nice job of trying to pressure the reversal pass, and they end up with a turnover and we get a fast-break layup for B-Mo.

Next possession Klarc makes the steal and completes a difficult pass to Jesse, who can't finish the fast-break—great opportunity there for the power layup to come into play.

Klarc then makes a hustle play on a loose-ball rebound, and it looks like a jump ball, but instead it is a foul on us.

Our defense is giving Norwalk some problems early in the game, making it difficult to swing the ball. So they change their offense to a four-out-one-in, isolating Kaleb defensively against their big guy. Kaleb holds his ground and forces another turnover.

Clayton enters. We move Jesse to the wing, and Kaleb attacks with the dribble. Another whistle, another Kaleb charge! So with 5:45 left in the first quarter our leading scorer is sitting with us on the bench. Brandon Esterbrook (Kaleb's replacement) comes in, and they immediately attack him with a clear-out play that results in a layup. Our offense has some movement, but we are not separating from our screens very well, and Clayton tries to attack the middle with the dribble and gets called for a travel. We get the ball back with a Norwalk turnover.

We really got some nice ball swing, missed, but Klarc is called for over the back on the offensive foul; that is the first foul called that I'm in agreement with.

We come back and run match-up zone; they settle for a guarded three that is a miss, but put it back in with an offensive board. We are starting to hold the ball too long before making our decisions, which gives the defense a chance to catch back up with the offense; because of that we turn the ball over.

Our straight man is not good enough as we give up a three after helping down into the post. C.J. fails to adhere to our "closest man rule," which states that the closest man to an unguarded shooter must go to make the cover.

We get a point-blank layup attempt and miss; they return the miss favor, but because of a poor outlet pass off the boards they get the ball back. Norwalk is running their two-man screen again, and we force a miss and secure the board. But because we are holding the ball too long we are not getting very good looks on the offensive end. Finally B-Mo, with a nice spin move (Magic) in the middle of the lane gets two free throws.

Our Fist defense results in a good trap between C.J. and Klarc, but our guys on the weak side don't rotate up as the ball comes out, and now we are out numbered on defense four to three, but this time we didn't get hurt by it.

Norwalk is attempting to hold for the last shot of the quarter. We get what I thought was a really good trap set on their guy (just as we had worked on in end-of-quarter situations). They step through, and I guess it is another foul on us with :28 left; strange call there. They make both free throws but Craig (C.J., remember?) hits a tough shot in the lane with people on him. The officials wave off the shot and give it to us out of bounds. B-Mo gets it back for us with a jumper in the middle of the lane for two. With 1.2 seconds left in the quarter Clayton fouls the shooter by reaching in from the help position, and they make both.

We are down 6-12 at the end of the first. Our defense is keeping us in the hunt, but our offense is poor. We aren't moving, we aren't setting hard screens, we aren't separating from the screens quickly enough, and we have already accumulated way too many fouls. We've got eight team fouls; (they are already in the bonus), and Norwalk has three fouls.

We've got good ball movement that almost looks like the old-fashioned outside weave, and B-Mo hits a three. They miss, and then so do we. We get another stop, and then B-Mo makes a hard flash down the middle for a point-blank layup—he misses! At this point I think B-Mo is still thinking about his miss and is running, but not sprinting back on defense, and therefore doesn't recover back in time and gets called for a block.

We work on free-throw block out virtually every day in practice, but we don't get it done, and they end up with the rebound and an eventual layup. On our out-of-bounds play Clayton misses, but Craig is there for the put back. Right now Craig has really helped us on the offensive end, but a couple of missed plays have hurt us defensively; it's 11-16.

Kaleb comes back into the second quarter, and we run Fist. Kaleb probably went for a steal that he couldn't get to; he probably could have made a better read or anticipated the trap earlier and therefore reacted earlier, but I guess at least he was looking to pick the ball off. When you run a defense like this— you are going to give up something once in a while, but the element of surprise and good execution should prevent too many easy hoops.

Once again Kaleb attacks the basket, and a Norwalk player hits the floor, but this time it is a block. I can't tell you how often Norwalk has been on the floor trying to draw a charge. Klarc misses, but B-Mo is there to clean it up off the offensive boards (14-18).

Klarc can't prevent a straight-line drive, and Colin doesn't get over in time to help, and so fouls. They get two free throws. We pick up another foul. We do a nice job on offense this time, with a good look from three, but miss, and there is a long, loose ball with Klarc in pursuit along with a Norwalk player—another foul on Klarc! Man, this is getting ridiculous! Any loose ball or anytime a Norwalk player falls on the floor it seems to be a foul on us.

I'm not blaming the Norwalk kids or coaches. I am however starting to realize that we have either made the officials really mad, and they are favoring Norwalk (gosh I certainly hope this isn't true) or they are very poor officials (probably some of the worst we've had) and don't know how to call the game. Two of the three are older officials that don't seem to have made the conversion to the modern game that includes some incidental contact on both sides of the ball; it's no longer considered a foul but a part of the game.

Kaleb hits a three and turns to run back on defense and runs right into the official who is standing too far into the play area, signaling the three. Fortunately Norwalk is not into a break, and we are okay. They've gone to their four-out offense, being patient and looking to get the ball inside. I'm not sure what happens next, but it looks as though we are about to get into a trap (hadn't gotten there yet) but there is yet another foul on us.

Now for one of the very few times this season I find myself yelling at the official as we are out trying to create some havoc with our Fist defense. We force the offensive player to carry the ball while attempting the spin move, but to my frustration there is no call, and this results later in another basket rather than a turnover for Norwalk.

Norwalk is really starting to sag their point defensive man down into the middle of the floor, which calls for either quicker and easier ball swing on our part or a shot to keep him honest. Neither Clayton nor Jesse seems to doing extremely well at either. Jesse continually catches and holds the ball above his head (pretty tough to shoot or even appear interested in shooting from this position) looking to swing the ball, but we all continue to hold it too long. If nothing else we could penetrate from the top down, bring two, then kick the ball out as a method of swinging the ball. Clayton looks obviously rusty; I've been surprised previously by his good play with such little practice. Tonight it looks as though it is catching up with him.

They have a semi break and we are late recovering out to the shooter as they hit a three; the score 17-26.

With 2:24 left we have 10 team fouls (actually we have more, but the score board will only show to 10 for team fouls) which means lots of individual fouls as well, and Norwalk has been in the bonus since the end of the first quarter; we are not yet there.

We get a good look but a miss from three, and now once again we are late covering out, and they bury another three. Our screens on the offensive end are very unphysical—in essence they are interchanges rather than screens. So Clayton gets penetration, and he too comes in with a spin (Magic) move to the middle but is called for a travel. This is really maddening as the same move just occurred on the Norwalk side and was let go as a legitimate play. I'm 40 feet away from the call; they are right there. I am really struggling to keep my composure with the officiating. I know the kids are really frustrated too. We aren't great, but the officials are worse.

We drop back zone, and Norwalk travels. Against the zone Norwalk doesn't move as well. Colin in particular is holding the ball way too long on our offensive end. He is not the only one, but he is one that is very obvious. Hey, we got a foul called against them; unbelievable! We are still not in the bonus.

Clayton now attacks the hoop, and Norwalk hits the ground. Ah oh, it is a travel this time. I guess the pleasant news is that it isn't a charge. Our man-to-man defense fails to verbally communicate, and they end up with an open man behind our defense for a layup. We get an open three from Craig, at the end of the quarter, and an ugly first half comes to an end with us down 17-31 at halftime.

At halftime it is not a happy time in the Pella locker room. Our kids are playing poorly, and so many of the things that we have needed to do we haven't. Coach Core lets them know what he thinks and then asks for my opinion, but I want to know what the kids think so I ask them.

B-Mo is a man of few words, so when he speaks up people listen, and he did speak up. Since the beginning of the game this is the best thing to come out of tonight, real leadership from one of the guys. We are down, but B-Mo wants us to go out and compete. When he got done Coach said, "You can't say it any better than that, let's go out and warm up," and we did.

Jesse starts the second half and really holds the ball too long at the top of the key. Norwalk is really sloughing off of him as continues to be a non-threat offensively. Klarc comes over the top after a dribble handoff from Jesse (good move) and misses, but Kaleb gets a put back and a free throw. We've cut it to eleven points.

They again come out with their two-man-screening game, and we aren't paying attention on the weak side and give up a lob for a lay-up. We make just enough mistakes individually to really hurt our team "d," but in a lot of ways I think our offense is so out of sync right now and we get so frustrated there that we lose concentration on defense. Colin gets a wide-open layup on a nice move but misses (I think this is our third open layup we've missed), but B-Mo is there to clean it up with a put back.

What is with these missed layups? Were we not mentally ready to play or has all this charging, team fouls, and individual fouls gotten into our heads, and we are taking our eye off the hoop so we don't run over someone (or at least not get close enough for a defender to fall down)?

They throw the ball away, and then we come down, and there is another Norwalk player on the ground—no call, hallelujah! Again, it's not all officials; we are still not setting anything resembling a hard screen; we are just interchanging.

Klarc gets an open three and misses, and then he comes down and gets backdoored for a layup. Our little run seems done. We are down 22-35. Now our offense really is almost four-on-five, as our point guard isn't even up to the three-point line.

B-Mo makes a nice spin (Magic)—charge! These guys (officials) are absolutely terrible! The Norwalk player barely gets touched as B-Mo's momentum from the spin takes him directly away from the defender and towards the basket, but they have, in spite of that, called another charge.

Our match-up zone allows a good look, but they miss, and B-Mo gets a put back off of an offensive rebound and a free throw as well. We are trying to pressure, and in my mind (and evidently the minds of our fans as well by their voices of disapproval) the Norwalk player travels, but we do not get a call. In spite of that we do convert a steal into a Boeyink fast-break layup.

They run their two-man-screen game well and get a hoop along the baseline; that is our mistake. Along with the basket Norwalk is awarded a free throw; that is the official's mistake, as there is literally a foot of day light between our defender and their offensive player as the shot goes up. The crowd is getting ugly here from the Pella side. I've mentioned before what good fans we have at Pella, and I will stand by them now too. They are just becoming as frustrated as the kids and we are with this kind of officiating.

Klarc misses our fourth layup of the game, although this one was contested, but once again B-Mo is there to put it back in. Norwalk turns the ball over and then Kaleb hits Klarc with a nice kick-out pass and a three-pointer. During

Kaleb's drive the Norwalk players are again diving for the floor trying to draw a charge but no call. We've closed it to 31-38.

Norwalk comes out and runs a simple little cross cut out of a timeout, and Craig and Colin fail to communicate on defense and make an easy switch which results in two free throws for Norwalk. Offensively now Colin has the ball at the top of the key with no one on him, and doesn't even take a look at the hoop. Colin is usually not like that; he is normally very aggressive about seeking an opportunity to score. Man when it rains…

Craig goes for a steal in the post and can't make it that turns into a layup. C.J. gives up a lot of size inside and tries to combat that by taking away the pass. I can see his dilemma because he feels like if the ball comes into his man at the post he is too small to defend him. But I'd rather have the offense shoot over a small man than give up a drop-step layup.

My son Josh used to be the best defender against an offensive dribbler that used a cross-over dribble to change directions. He would just stay close enough to the dribbler to put his hand in there and pick the dribble off—that is exactly what happened to Klarc as the man who makes the pick shoots a layup at the other end.

Again, C.J. for a steal at the post, but Kaleb gets a block. Unfortunately, that sets off a rotation of our defense that turns into a Norwalk three. It is 31-45. They are on a seven-point run, and we take a timeout.

We took a timeout and moved Kaleb to the top of our offense so they couldn't sag back inside. Kaleb tries the dribble drive and gets the ball poked away but foul on Norwalk. Our out-of-bounds play ends up in a turnover; Clayton simply misses the pass. I don't know if it is his arm or his concentration.

They give us the ball back on a turnover, and Colin is off to the races on the break. He gets undercut as he attacks the hoop as the Norwalk defender slides in from the side. Unbelievable—a charge is called against Colin. There is absolutely no question, there is no way, not a chance that this is a charge, but according to the guys with the whistles that is what they are going to call.

I haven't counted along the way, but this has to be at least five charges called on us. When is the last time that has happened to us since I've been at PHS? Never. I can't wait to look at this film. Sometimes I find out I was wrong when I thought I was so right about these types of things.

I'm convinced. The officials are either the absolute worst we've ever had or they have decided that Pella High is not going to have a chance to win this thing. Why? The next possession we do get Norwalk trapped, and the Norwalk player throws it out of bounds with none of our guys nearby. What makes it even more obvious is that the Norwalk team is starting to head back up court (the man who threw the pass leading the way) on defense, not even waiting for the official's signal. You can guess what happened—Norwalk's ball, is the call. We are playing five on seven.

Bringing the ball up the court their guard uses his off hand to push Klarc off to advance the ball up the court on the dribble (no call—now that is an offensive foul) and because we can't stay with the man who pushed off they get a back-cut pass and hoop right at the end of the quarter. We are down 31-47 at the end of the quarter, and it is their ball back to start the fourth.

We fouled next possession. This was a legit call. We are scrambling now trying to trap as often as we can. We foul in the trap. They miss. Kaleb drives and misses a point-blank layup with no one on him and fouls out of frustration. Is that layup number five?

On our next offensive possession K hits a three.

One of the adjustments to the Partners offense for future reference might be to use Kaleb at the top and set on-ball screens for him or actually make any on-ball screen a new man at the top of the offense.

We cannot get the ball, as Norwalk is content to pass it around and play keep away…(smart play). Even when we do get a trap they call a timeout to avoid the turnover. Once again they run their little cross screen under the hoop, and Colin and B-Mo don't communicate so Norwalk gets an inside bunny. This has not been Colin's best game.

Okay, this is it. I am done with talking about this game. Kaleb just picked up his fifth foul with an offensive foul that saw him driving down the lane with the defender on his right hip (who then, what else, hits the floor) and picks up another offensive foul with 6:00 left in the fourth quarter. In real time Kaleb has played about one half of our game. Out of five fouls against Kaleb, three have been offensive. I believe that to be our sixth offensive foul of the game, of which I would say that maybe (and I'm giving the official the benefit of the doubt now), maybe one had an outside chance to be called by a tournament-level official. I know that I have made a great effort early on to be unbiased in my commentary about the officiating, and I know it will not get any better now.

The final quarter is a combination of us trapping, looking to turn them over, in a helter-skelter style of play, and them holding the ball and trying to be composed under our constant harassment.

Dean Smith, the Hall of Fame basketball coach from North Carolina, used to keep a points-per-possession chart. He divided the number of possessions by the number of points and came up with the answer. He said that if his team could average one point per possession they would win a vast majority of their games. He said the best way to do this is to get to the free throw line. Norwalk buried us at the free-throw line, final score: Norwalk 56, Pella 44.

Saturday, January 21, Morning

I watch the game on tape when I get home and talk to myself on the Dictaphone to get some perspective on the game. Usually, when I review the game on tape, there are a few things that happen pretty consistently. One, if we win, we usually aren't as good as I thought we were that night. Two, if we lose or play poorly, it's usually not as bad as I thought it was when the game was going on. And lastly, if I disagree with the officiating it's not as bad as I think it was at the time. Once again after watching the tape I found it to be true that we weren't maybe quite as bad as I thought we were, although we weren't really good. I didn't find it to be true about the officiating.

The officiating had to be some of the worst I've seen in years. Remember, I am writing now a day after the game, and the emotions of the moment of are now gone, and I was expecting to find out that once again the officiating wasn't as bad as I thought; but it might have been even worse than I thought it was at the time, and at the time I thought it was terrible.

As I have gotten to be an older more experienced coach I have realized how difficult the game is to officiate. Both Mark and I try to keep our mouths shut and let them do their job. Younger people are not getting into officiating in part because coaches and fans have been so hard on the officials in the past, and those guys are getting underpaid to take the abuse they take. So we really do try, and rarely do we complain, and our A.D., Bill Van Horn, has done a great job with our fans helping them to become some of the best in the conference and maybe the state.

But one of the most frustrating things for both coaches and players (I'm sure fans as well) to experience is the complete lack of input that we have into a game where the officiating is so bad. Both players and coaches just have to "take it." There is no recourse for a coach or player; the official is always right, regardless of how wrong he may be. The game of basketball changed dramatically on Friday night from what I know to be state-tournament type of play. If the state tournament is the ultimate and these are the best officials (they received the highest ratings and are asked to officiate the games because of it) in the state, then the officiating that we got last night had to be very close to the other end of the sport; they both may be fruits, but one is an apple and the other was an orange. If that is the way the game is going to be called at the highest level, I would have no problem with it; we as coaches and players would need to adjust, but if it isn't then the three guys in the striped shirts that we had last night either need to get out, because the game has passed them by, or they need to adjust their game. I could go on. I'm so mad for our guys; I'd better just shut up.

Monday, 7:30 A.M.

We didn't practice on Saturday or even have a walk through, so Mark and I got together to discuss our notes and thoughts from Friday's debacle.

My thoughts were many. One, I'm not sure we can play man-to-man defense. Is it time to look at something else or will getting both Kirk and Clayton back be enough of a change to make us better? How long do we wait for this answer, and at what point do we start to lose confidence if we wait too long?

About the only guy we haven't looked at much in game situations is Tyler Terlouw; is it time to take a longer look? By using a post rather than a wing will this give us some extra help at rebounding and playing a more physical game?

Are these panic moves? I don't know; they say timing is everything.

Other questions that we discussed were: why did Jesse play so passively? (As a note: later on that day Coach Core spoke with Jesse, and he just simply said that he felt like his teammates were better than him, and that he was trying to stay out of their way. That is pretty unselfish, but in my mind, misguided thinking). If we play more zone and less man should we look at incorporating some triangle and two and/or box-and-one? Why do we play harder in practice than sometimes in games?

During the remainder of the day I had a number of players stop by. Craig stopped for about 10 minutes. Klarc stopped as well, and so did Colin at the end of the day. (By the way, he isn't feeling well but will attempt to practice).

The best conversation I had though was with Clayton. Clayton wanted to know if he was hurting the team by playing; we discussed that, but I'm not sure we ever came to a great conclusion. We are better when he plays, but if it was a guarantee that he could sit out and get healthy I would vote for that; however there is no guarantee of that, so what do we do?

During my talk with Clayton I brought up the idea that maybe everyone didn't really care that much about making the state tournament. And if they didn't that is okay. It doesn't make them bad people, just not motivated people (in the area of basketball). If the worst thing that happened in their lives was not making the tournament that would be a pretty good life. However, I told Clayton that for me it was like when you were trying to tell somebody about how much fun something is, and you can tell that they just don't get it, but if they did it themselves they would understand the fun factor. That is what I think about the tourney. I've been there, and yes, it is fun. But for me right now the fun thing would be getting these kids there so they could get to experience the ride. You can't really describe it; you have to do it yourself.

I left Clayton with this analogy. If your parents said that you couldn't do something but you really, really wanted to do it, in the long run don't you think you'd find a way to make it happen—especially as seniors? That is the trip to the tourney. If you really, really wanted to do it (assuming we have enough talent) don't you think we'd find a way? I left it at that with Clayton. He is only one young man, but sometimes one man makes a difference.

Monday, January 22, Practice #38
Fluke, Spy, Rebounding, Screen and Re-Screen, Butt Work, Box and Triangle, Newton, Sub—State, Trust, Players Taking Over, and Adversity

Coach Core told me that he had spoken with Kaleb and asked if he thought about Friday's game—Kaleb's response, "It was a fluke, and we just need to move on." I don't know; he might be right, and Coach Core and I are making too much out of the loss. Again, timing is everything. If it was a fluke we need to treat it accordingly; if it wasn't we need to decide what to do.

Today we are going to "spy on" Jesse being more aggressive and Kaleb going to the offensive boards. But this time we are telling them prior to practice; this is a switch in our approach to this "spying."

We warmed up with shooting and dribbling drills, and then went full-court one-on-one. After that we did the Michigan drill and then drilled with the four-on-five open post.

We then go to a combination rebounding game that incorporates our offense. During this phase Coach Core is really pushing the rebounding, and I am trying to be more adamant about running our offense more correctly in the quarter-court. We are spending much more time in the quarter-court right now than we normally do (one of the ideas that came out of our earlier meeting) and it exposes the fact that we just are not taking care of the ball as well as we should.

During this phase I am really after our post players, Tyler T, in particular, about screening and then re-screening for the offensive man on his side of the floor. I would like him to do this so that he can then "seal" his man in the post area and not catch the ball so much on the outside where he is less comfortable. This would also put him closer to the hoop in a better rebounding position.

We break down the offense further by going two-on-two on one side of the court with an open man to pass to. There is no excuse to throw the ball away, and the two men are working together trying to get each other open and read the correct cut before and after the screen.

When the practice turns to more zone offense I am after both Zach and Tyler to seal their men within the zone. By this I mean I want their butt on the defender, and I want them to keep it there as long as they can regardless of where the ball goes. Even if they don't get a pass they will slow the zones slides and interfere with the defensive players' responsibilities within the zone. This is one of those things that doesn't show up in the box score.

After the zone portion of the practice the green team is called over and secretly runs a box-and-one and then a triangle-and-two defense against the white team to see how it looks. In my opinion the box-and-one is okay but I really kind of like the triangle-and-two better. Earlier in the year we were most concerned from an offensive standpoint about teams running a box-and-one against Kaleb, and we practiced it accordingly. Now we might use it for ourselves. The triangle-and-two is another combination defense that employs a man-to-man defense against two offensive players and a zone defense in the shape of a triangle against the other three. I'd like to tell you that these defenses are the answers to all of our problems; I don't think they are, but we are hoping for a jump start here, and during this time of year, just from a boredom factor it would be a good thing to give the kids something new to revitalize them.

Next we are working against a two-two-one zone press, the one that Newton employs, and then we try a one-three-one half-court trap of our own.

Again, the idea of a change up to help confuse our opposition and the fact that our current seniors had some success with this defense when they were young, might give them some confidence with this.

We finished the live portion of practice by reviewing the match-up zone defense and made the change that the wing will go with a ball-side cutter (it's not worth drawing up) so that it would be less confusing for our players.

At the end of practice we all gathered around and talked. Clayton spoke, Kaleb spoke, and so did Klarc and myself.

Coach Core finished the discussion pointing out a number of things. One of the things that Mark talked about was Norwalk. He feels like they are the best team in our sub-state and for us to make it to state this is the team that we probably need to beat.

He also went to the reoccurring theme of trust. He pointed out that trust is an earned commodity and that you earn trust by doing your job consistently to the best of your ability. He used Kaleb and Jesse and the "spying" on them that we did as an example. Kaleb was involved with 40 offensive possessions during today's practice of which he went to the offensive boards 27 times. Jesse was involved in 43 offensive possessions and was "really aggressive" 17 of those times. He pointed out that if we are going to trust, we have to be trustworthy.

Next Mark wanted to address the "fluke" theory that Kaleb proposed earlier in regards to the Norwalk game. He asked, "Is it a fluke that they were 13 of 17 from within the arc? Is it a fluke that B-Mo was the only player with multiple offensive rebounds for us, and is it a fluke that Klarc had nine assists the game before and zero against Norwalk?" Obviously Coach Core doesn't think that the Norwalk game was a fluke, and he feels like this is an easy way out for us if we think this way. I don't know if I agree, but I definitely see his point. It would be a whole lot better for us to assume the worst and prepare for it than go in with the idea that they were lucky.

He is begging the players to step up. He wants the players to take over this team. It can't be the coaches and coach talk; it must be the players that are going to turn this around. Mark is asking them to be tougher both mentally and physically and fight back when challenged with adversity. He wants them to even look forward to adversity and enjoy the challenge of recovering from misfortunes that come with the game.

I know what Mark is doing. He is trying to challenge them; he feels that we are too soft and that if we could just get over this, maybe just maybe we could find a really good team underneath.

Chapter 13—It's Still Only January

Tuesday, January 23, Pella at Newton, Game #13
Our Record: 6-6; Conference: 6-6

In the pre-game locker room we talked about a couple of different things. One was the idea of not worrying about yourself so much during the game. We wanted them to worry about their teammates. Ironically to take the focus off of self-play most often allows the player to play better because they are less anxious about how they are doing, and they won't judge themselves so harshly if things aren't perfect.

Coach Core relayed a story about his childhood and the things that he remembered when he played basketball. He talked about the need to enjoy the moment, because this will be a time of their lives that the players will look back on and relive many times. He also said that the friendships that were developed on this team might also be lifelong friendships.

We didn't do any review yesterday of Newton, and Coach Core said that was by design. We had reviewed pretty carefully with the Norwalk game plan, and it didn't really seem to help. Sometimes (in my view) a coach can plan too much about the other team, and by the time you talk it through over and over the kids are thinking so much about the opponent that they forget about playing themselves. I think this is what Mark had decided. So we briefly reviewed some things that we thought we see in tonight's game, and then the players stretched and loosened up in the hallway before the game.

Earlier Jesse had indicated that he was more comfortable coming off the bench and felt like it would be better if someone else started (don't get that very often). So Coach asked him whom he should start, and Jesse thought C.J. should be tonight's starter; that's what we did.

We got the opening tip and did a nice job of getting some ball movement prior to Klarc attacking the hoop and drawing a two shot foul—he made one.

Both teams start the game off man-to-man, which is a surprise to us as, Newton played zone exclusively in our first meeting. It's ironic because we are looking to do less man and more of our other defenses this game.

They come down and miss, but we turn the ball over, which results in two points off of a break for them. Craig gets a shot inside blocked, but then both teams turn the ball over to each other in their next possessions. Kaleb makes a steal and gets the ball to Colin for a layup. We then forced another miss, but they got the ball back out of bounds and score on their out-of-bounds play.

We miss and drop back zone; they seem confused and shoot a contested three that misses. We miss again in a secondary-break situation from three, and they get the ball inside the lane for a two.

Newton is trying to run their two-two-one zone press and drop back into a man-to-man. That is fairly difficult to do because the defender must cover an area and then cover a man. It works fine if the man you are covering is nearby, but if he is on the opposite side of the floor this is much more difficult and will probably result in some open looks for us in a secondary-break situation. By that I mean not a true out-and-out fast-break but in the midst of the defense getting organized.

We miss another three, get the board, but then turn the ball over; we are down 3-6. Klarc makes a steal; another shot is missed, but Jesse, who has come in off the bench, gets the offensive board. Craig has picked up two really quick fouls and is over on the bench with us.

Both teams have some empty possessions. What is interesting to me is that sometimes I'm not 100% sure what defense we are in. If I don't catch the signal I can be a little confused. That means one of two things: either we are camouflaging the defenses really well or some of our guys are confused, and we've got some guys playing one defense and the others are playing something else. I hope it's the former and not the latter.

Jesse picks up a charge on a Newton player, and B-Mo hits a pull-up. They miss again, and Kaleb makes a nice pass that results in two points for PHS. The game turns a little ugly (from an offensive standpoint) now as both teams have turnovers and missed shots, and then Clayton draws another charge against Newton.

We are up 7-6 when they make two free throws, and it is our ball and we are holding for the last shot of the quarter. B-Mo draws two defenders, and then passes the ball out to Colin, who buries a three at the quarter to put us up 10-8.

The officials are supposed to put the ball into play immediately upon the second buzzer after a quarter break, but it is rare that this occurs. It is a point of emphasis by the boys' union, however, and these officials must have listened because Newton was just coming out of the huddle when the official handed Kaleb the ball out of bounds and he fired a pass for an easy layup for us before they could get back. That is a gift.

Out of the quarter timeout we are determined to play some triangle and two. They missed but then scored on a put back. Duke ends up getting Colin an easy hoop, as all of the defenders were so focused on stopping Kaleb and switching screens that it cleared a side for his drive.

Jesse then comes down and draws another charge—I'm thinking that Newton looks confused as to what we are in and how to attack it; that is the reason for the charge. Again we run Duke, and this time Kaleb gets to the line converting one free throw, but we get the ball back with an offensive board. Again we get fouled, and this time we take it out of bounds. It is too bad that we are missing, but it is good that we are getting to the boards and creating team and individual foul problems for them.

Kaleb makes a hoop with a drive from the corner. From our triangle defense we fail to guard a shooter, and they hit a three, then we miss a two on the break. Both teams come up empty on the next possessions, but then they get a bucket and a free throw.

Kaleb gets a layup, Newton turns the ball over, we miss, they turn it over again, and this time Kaleb gets a pass in the post and gets fouled; he makes two free throws.

They score, but then Tyler Terlouw gets his first important varsity points with a rebound put-back shot. Newton misses again, and Klarc gets fouled on a break; we are up 25-17.

Both teams miss their shots, and then B-Mo draws a charge. Kaleb scores again for Pella, and Newton misses once again, but sadly we throw the ball away.

They are struggling to recover from playing a two-two-one zone press to finding our guys in their man-to-man quarter-court defense, and we continue to get some quick hoops in a semi-break situation. We are up 29-21 after we miss two free throws. They come back with two free throws, and we turn it over, trying to get the last shot of the quarter, that turns into a lay-up for them. We do get the last shot but miss it.

Newton finished with a 7-0 run at the end of the second quarter, so rather than have an 11-point lead we are only up by four, and it wasn't because of something they did—to be more precisely, it was because of our poor play and decision making.

Colin makes a steal to start the second half, but we miss a lay-up. You haven't heard much about Craig because he has spent considerable time on the bench; he picks up number four early in the third.

Kaleb has done a really good job defensively against a player that hurt us last time. So has Klarc, by the way, but now Kaleb blocks a shot and further intimidates the man he is guarding. We travel on our next possession, however.

One of the things we have done poorly is defending their out-of-bounds plays. Once again they get two points on a baseline play. Kaleb hits a three out of the Partners offense, and they miss, and then he hits another three out of a break situation—way cool!

Defensively we are playing a lot of triangle right now. It has effectively taken out their scorers; well, at least it's taken out one of their guys and slowed the other.

Kaleb now makes a steal but gets into a hurry and charges; that is three and the score is 35-27.

Colin misses a steal, but we cannot convert, and Klarc fouls going after the rebound. After Newton misfires, B-Mo gets a hoop with a give-and-go post-up move. We have moved to a ten-point lead halfway through the third, but Newton hits a three.

Our Duke play has become a Colin Boswell lay-up drill, as everyone chases Kaleb through the screens. Kaleb picks up foul number four with three and half left to go in the third.

Both teams have a couple of empty trips, and then Colin gets a free throw on a nice pass from Clayton.

Both teams draw a blank; B-Mo then gets fouled and makes both. They miss free throws, and we miss shots late in the third quarter when Jesse hits a hoop. Again they miss, but we make a turnover. They score on the old-fashioned three late, and that ends the quarter.

It is 43-35, and we start with the ball as the fourth quarter opens. We run Spartans for B-Mo, and he nails a three. They get an open look and miss, and so do we. The shot we took was probably too quick for this late in the game with a lead.

Colin must love to hear Duke being called out, as he scores another lay-up from this set. After they throw it away Jesse makes a good pass to C.J. (Craig) who makes one of two free throws, as he was fouled on his attempted layup.

They hit a three, and we miss a lay-up attempt. Both teams miss some shots, and when they get the ball back, Colin makes a timely steal for us.

This part of the game is not exactly a thing of beauty, as both teams turn the ball over and both teams are fouling. During this time B-Mo and Klarc get steals, and on Klarc's steal, it turns into a lay-up for Kaleb on the other end. In addition, a weak call by the official gives him a free throw as well. (See? I'm trying to be fair with officiating thing.)

Newton misses two straight bunny shots and then they foul us. It looks good for PHS.

At this point we need to milk the clock by moving the ball and completing passes.

A nice interior pass from Kaleb to Klarc yields a jump hook for two in the lane, and we are up 12. And once again, what I would call a poor call by the officials against Newton, gives the ball back to us.

It is 54-42 late in the game, and we are really trying to take time off of the clock. Newton makes a concerted effort to foul and to foul early to see if we can make free throws down the stretch and try to counter our foul shooting with two-point, and if possible, three-point baskets. C.J. hits a couple of free throws; Colin makes four, Klarc makes one, Kaleb makes four, and on the last foul (committed against Kaleb) the officials rule it is an intentional foul, so we get the ball back.

The end of the game seems to last forever, as we prove our ability to score at the free-throw line, and the final score is 65-51.

Wednesday January 24, Practice #39
Middle of the Press, Phil, One-Three-One, "Pointing," Number 33, Weak Side Drop, Hand Signals, OB Plays, Flex, and Playing Soft

After warming up with floaters and the Princeton shooting drill we walked through our zone press offense. Both Mark and I during the game and after reviewing the tape felt like our cutters in the middle of the press were open and should have received at least a few passes in the middle; they never did. Not one. To me, this again is a matter of trust. The players looking in there don't have the needed level of trust to throw the ball to the cutter.

Against Newton we got away with not throwing the ball to the middle against the press. Against a better pressing team there is no question we will need to attack the middle of the floor. Besides that, eventually, unless the cutter receives a pass in there once in a while, he is going to say, "What's the use? I don't get it anyway," and then he will quit cutting. That will make it even more difficult to attack the press. Why?—Because the mere presence of the cutter forces the defense to try to cover the middle of the floor and opens up the outside of the floor. Our guys quit cutting, and the outsides will close up as well.

Phil Hemming came to practice today to help explain the one-three-one half-court trap that we have incorporated into our defensive scheme. He came because he used to coach with us and because he used to coach our current seniors when they were in junior high, during this time they ran some of this defense. Phil did a nice job of reviewing the trap areas and the responsibilities of each player. I liked what I saw.

Next we worked on "pointing" our one-two-two zone. By pointing I mean adjusting our zone defense so that our guys know where to be and are close to a certain player (usually the opponent's leading scorer or best shooter) and almost play him like they are man-to-man with him while he is in the area that they cover in the zone. We are doing this because it gives us another look in our zone defense and in preparation for Friday night's game against Osky.

To remind you, Osky's #33 is the University of Iowa football recruit and fine basketball player, and leading scorer. We want to know where he is during all times of the game because he is such a big part of their offense. Osky has only been beaten twice all season, and both times it was Pella Christian. Currently, according to the *Des Moines Register*, the Osky team is rated as the tenth best 4A team in the state. While we are mainly a 3A league, Osky, Boone, and Newton are 4A members of the league.

Going back to the Newton game—one of the things that we noticed in the zone was the poor weak-side drop we got from our wing players. In our zone the players that are away from the ball (weak side) and up towards the free-throw line area (on the initial set) will slide straight down the outside of the free-throw lane to become weak-side defenders and rebounders until the ball comes back to their side, and then the opposite wing (who now becomes weak side) will do the same. It is now that we are working and revisiting this drop technique. It fits in well at this time because the same procedure is used in the one-three-one half-court trap defense that we are using.

We also review some things that gave us problems when we were in the triangle and two.

We are trying to change defenses on the run with hand signals, and if we can do this the change alone can be confusing to the opponent and put them in a thinking mode rather than an attacking mode. The danger lies in self-confusion, especially if there is a fast-break against the team making defensive changes. We talked about ways to handle this, got player input as to what they felt most comfortable with, and then went back to the Newton game.

One of the things we didn't do well was to handle Newton's out-of-bounds plays. Osky will run all out-of-bounds plays though #33, and we need to be prepared to switch out to him regardless of the defense we are in or who's man he is. Number 33 has 34 three-pointers in 12 games. His next closest teammate has made four. Regrettably, this is definitely not the only thing you must guard him for because he is such an explosive athlete he can get to the basket as well.

All this talk about #33 tends to minimize the fact that Osky is also a very good offensive rebounding team. We must rebound in order to have a chance to defeat Osky.

One of the offenses that Osky runs is the flex. The flex is an offense that fills five spots over and over again with different players cutting into the various spots. It's an offense that many teams use at least part of the time. Osky runs the flex in a unique way in that they move the offense up away from the baseline. Normally the offense is run down towards the baseline. It is a continuity pattern or repeats itself.

Because Osky moves this up from the baseline they make liberal use of back cuts if the defense overplays the wing players.

They also like to attack with the dribble from the wing because the help against the drive must come from so far away. For example, the weak-side defender and normal help man would be the guy that is guarding the opposite side wing when the ball is entered into the ball-side wing. So if the (left) wing were to get the ball, and he beats his defender with the dribble, the help man (guarding the right wing) must come all the way across the court to help. Additionally the right wing must drop down 15 feet to get into position to help.

We want our kids to play the wings softer to prevent the previous two offensive scenarios—the back cut and the drives. We'd also like to slow or prevent the guard-to-guard pass to destroy the timing and cutting of the offense as well as give us a chance to catch up defensively.

Thursday, January 25

We had a great meeting today with one of the players. I've spoken of trust often and our lack of it in regards to each other. This is just another way to say chemistry that we seem to lack this year. This player used words like "feeling appreciated" and "useful." He didn't want to be the star; he just wanted to know that his teammates appreciated what he did and that he was more than just another player—that he was one of them.

I think he is right on the nose. I use "trust," he used "appreciated," being one of "them." I encouraged him to talk with some of the others to repeat how he feels, to be honest with his teammates. If only we could get the guys to speak up. They've heard it from the coaches. It must come from each other now. I understand that it would be difficult and that guys sometimes more than girls will struggle with this type of communication. But—I guess we will soon find out just how important this is to them. To be good is going to be difficult; it is going to require sacrifices and the willingness to sometimes look foolish or vulnerable. We shall see.

Thursday, January 25, Practice #40
Re-Screen and On-Ball Screen, Switching Defenses, Lack of Trust, Mouth Shut and Ears Open, Rebound, and Composure

After warming up with shooting, ball-handling, and running-the-floor drills we get into some half-court two-on-two stuff that incorporates screening and moving without the ball.

During the Partners-offensive set we are trying to add our standard screens to the offense. Our tendency is to back or down screen and then separate. We will also occasionally post up and flash. Those are all good moves, and we encourage them. Today we are trying to add a couple of other wrinkles, those being the screen and re-screen option as well as the screen and then on-ball screen alternative. Both of those choices would add to the flexibility of our man-to-man offense.

From this point we moved into a full-court setting and worked on switching into various defenses through the use of hand signals. And then we went to end-of-quarter situations.

During breaks in the action I tried to speak with both Klarc and Kaleb and asked them what their opinion was about our lack of trust when throwing the ball into the middle of the press. I thought they both were honest, and I got a different slant from speaking with them. I really don't think it's a conscious lack of trust; I think what would better describe it would be a powerful belief in themselves and their ability to handle the ball better than the others who are doing the flashing. What I don't learn if I just keep my mouth shut and my ears open!

Brandon Esterbrook is representing #33 during practice, and we are trying hard to make sure that we know where he is as we change back and forth between various defenses. Even now we sometimes lose him, as we will #33, I just hope not too often.

Personally, our most serious worries about the Osky game are: slowing down #33, rebounding the ball, and our ability (from a psychological standpoint) to keep our composure in the midst of a big-game atmosphere.

Friday, January 26, 2007

In today's *Des Moines Register* there is a big article about #33, his career points, etc. In addition to all of the talk about this young man there is mention of the Pella game and finally a comment about a possible big showdown with Pella Christian for the conference championship. I guess this hit me as a slight towards our team. I hope it struck our players the same way, and they respond to it as competitors.

Friday, January 26, Pella vs. Osky, Game #14
Our Record: 7-6; Conference: 7-6

In the pre-game locker room we reviewed offenses and especially defenses making sure we were okay with all of our calls. We also reminded the kids of our main points of emphasis, which were #33, keeping the ball out of the paint, and finally, rebounding the ball defensively.

Prior to going out I asked the boys why this game was the most important thing in their lives. There was a lot of looking around and silence and then finally Klarc said, "Is this a trick question? It's not the most important things in our lives."

B-Mo spoke up and said, "It's only a game, but sometimes we make it more than it is." That was exactly what I wanted to hear, perspective on the game of basketball.

I also wanted the guys that didn't play so much to hear from the starters before we took the floor because I wanted the players both ways, starter to sub and from sub to starter, to hear what the others thought of their teammates. (If they are not going to talk on their own, I'm going to help them.) About Tyler Linn they said that he is the hardest guy to get around, and he blocks out every time. About Brandon E. they said he could really shoot. About Zach they said he was strong as a horse and would throw the starters around during practice. About Clayton they said he's just gotten cheated with all the injuries and stuff but just keeps coming back. I really liked what they said; I hope some of the guys that don't play as much were encouraged by their teammates' comments.

Osky got the tip and we went man-to-man, a decision we made on the bench prior to the game. They missed the first shot but got an offensive put-back for two. We came down and got two of our own when Craig (who missed the defensive block out) got free on a cut underneath and laid it in.

C.J. started tonight because Clayton did not practice again for the last two days. He will be available to play.

The place is rocking. Osky is only 15 minutes away, and they have a good team. Our pep band is terrific!

Our first two possessions on defense are man-to-man; on the third we went to the match-up zone. They missed, but we turned the ball over. Then they scored, and so did we, as B-Mo had an offensive board, and Kaleb finished it off with a spinner in the middle of the lane.

Both teams turn it over, then B-Mo blocks a shot to get the ball back for PHS. Klarc hits a fade away in the middle of the lane from an out-of-bounds play. Both teams miss when Klarc makes a steal, but then we miss a three. They travel, and Jesse who just came into the game rebounds his own miss and puts it in for two.

Osky has turned it over and missed twice more in their previous three possessions when they miss again. We charged, and they missed again but got an offensive rebound (almost more like a loose ball) and hit a two.

Osky is pressuring really hard out of their man-to-man defense trying to play tight on dribblers and overplay passing lanes. Klarc makes them pay for pressuring when he goes by his defender for a layup. We fall back and break out the one-three-one-trap zone for the first time, and B-Mo makes a steal.

Pella travels, but Colin makes a steal and gets fouled, making two free throws; it's 12-6, Pella. Once again Osky misses the initial shot but gets a bucket and a foul on the offensive rebound put-back.

We missed a short jumper and came back with our Fist defense, but Osky countered with a three-pointer to tie it up. We work the clock down, and Klarc hits a jumper from the free-throw line at the buzzer to put us up 14-12 at the end of one quarter.

We also got the ball back to start the second quarter. We drew a couple of fouls but didn't get the ball in the hoop. When they came down and attacked our zone with the dribble, B-Mo drew a charge.

Colin has attacked the hoop with the dribble and gotten fouled almost every time; it happens again on our next possession, and he makes them pay by hitting both free throws.

Number 33 made a really tough baseline reach back from under the hoop on the next play. Clayton was really too unselfish as he passed up a wide-open layup to get Kaleb an uncontested three, which went half way down and popped back out. Osky came back with a three of their own that went in.

But B-Mo says, "Right back at ya," when he nailed a three. The next time Osky had the ball we fouled a three-point shooter. We knew that they were really good at flopping and trying to draw a foul on a three-point attempt if we were even close to them physically. We had discussed this and warned the players about it, but they did it anyway. Fortunately they hit only one of three free throws.

Kaleb hit B-Mo with a nice pass for two, and Osky hit two of their own from inside. We missed a three, and they also had an empty trip down the floor. Kaleb misses in penetration, and Osky gets a dump-down pass into the lane for a hoop.

We turn the ball over, but Kaleb forces an Osky turnover with a nice hustle play. Once again Klarc has a penetration move for two, but Osky also scores.

All this time I've felt like our match-up has been pretty good. I think it has been good in conjunction with our other defenses and has created some confusion in the minds of the Osky players, but I don't know that we have made a lot of stops with it. We have made the offense work for their shots nonetheless.

Both teams miss, and we take a timeout, down 23-24. Duke for B-Mo doesn't result in a score, but Colin makes a steal that allows us another shot opportunity, which we failed to convert. Osky scored, and we missed the last shot of the half. The half-time score is Pella 23, Osky 26.

We started with the ball in the second half, ran a set play, and B-Mo scored two. We are starting the second half in a triangle and two, and our defense forced them to airmail their first attempt.

Kaleb makes a nice kick-out to Colin, who cans a three. B-Mo does it again and picks up another charge, but Klarc charges back.

Later Kaleb finally gets a three to go down, then they miss, and we travel. Our triangle isn't great, but it creates another miss, and C.J. sneaks inside for two. Osky scores at the free-throw line, and we have two opportunities to score, as both B-Mo and Jesse get offensive rebounds, but we can't get a hoop. Osky misses, as do we on a fast-break attempt from Craig to Jesse, but once again Osky misses a shot of their own but they put it back in with a rebound.

B-Mo drops a spinner (Magic) in the middle, and they also score inside. Colin missed, but Craig gets the board, and then Kaleb misses but rebounds the ball, and as he is falling to the ground kisses one off the glass for a huge hoop. The fans are up and screaming.

Osky's fans have something to scream about, too, with an old-fashioned three from an offensive put-back and foul. The score is now 37-31, the good guys.

With 2:15 left in the third we are up 37-33. Defensively we are playing more straight zone defense, and Jesse helps the cause by picking up a charging foul against our opponents. We miss, and they score, but B-Mo hits a big three for Pella. They came back with a three, and we miss a short inside shot at the buzzer, and it's 39-38 at the end of three.

Klarc has done a nice job on #33. He has had some help with our switching defenses, which seem to slow and confuse the Osky offenses. But Kaleb has also had opportunities to guard him when Klarc is out, and he too deserves a lot of credit for his defensive play.

On the bench between the quarters I was imploring the guys to be positive by telling them all we wanted was to have a shot in the fourth quarter to pull this out. I know they were a little disappointed because they missed a short shot at the end, and Osky had cut the lead to one point again. The crowd for Osky was feeling pretty good about now, and we needed to understand that we had already accomplished a goal by putting ourselves in position to win.

They came out with a miss, and Craig gets the board. Kaleb nails another three, and we take a 42-38 lead when Kaleb appears to make a steal, but it is called a foul, so Osky gets the ball back and connects on a three-pointer.

Offensively we are running a lot of Duke for B-Mo; Coach Core's idea not necessarily to get B-Mo a lot of points but to get the guys that are separating from screens some looks. We are down 42-43 after a five-point run by Osky, but Kaleb drains a three for us. They miss, and it is 45-43 with 4:13 left in the game.

Our composure is very good as we work the ball around, both milking the clock and looking for layups or free throws. Colin hits a two, and they miss, as Klarc brings down the rebound. Colin misses a three!

They shoot and miss, and it looks like they are going to come up with it, but Craig makes a terrific hustle play to secure the rebound and then has the presence of mind to call a timeout before he goes out of bounds.

It is 47-43, and we are really going to take the air out of the ball, but the officials call an illegal screen on us, and Osky gets the ball back. (It is never easy for us).

They miss two free throws with 1:23 left in the game, and it's our ball out of bounds. We attempted a very poor pass from an out-of-bounds play, but B-Mo saved the day with his ability to jump and haul down the pass away from the defense.

It's our ball out of bounds again, and we take a timeout. We made a bad coaching call by calling our Deb out-of-bounds play because it puts the ball in the corner (not a good place to have it at the end of the game), it is a place that is easily trapped; that is exactly what happens, as Colin has to call a timeout to keep from turning the ball over.

We continue to struggle just to get the ball in, but then they foul Klarc, who misses the front end of a one and one. (Remember, it's never easy for us.) The score remains 47-43, with :45 left.

We did a great job of identifying #33, so they took a three that misses, and then they get the ball back out of bounds. After a baseline drive by Osky it's 47-45, and we go four across, getting the ball to Kaleb, who is immediately fouled.

Kaleb's first free throw rattles back and fourth and pops up and then finally through the hoop. His second is nothing but net, and Pella High is up by four with 10.4 seconds left.

They shoot and miss, and there is a wild scramble for the loose ball, with Colin diving on the floor to secure the win for the Pella Dutch.

Zach Morgan goes to the radio after this game; we have different players do the radio all the time. I was really proud of Zach as he talked about the importance of his job to make the first-line players better. He saw his job as an important one. Believe me it is!

Saturday, January 27

Mark's two goals for the team last night were for our guys to be the most competitive team and to handle everything with class, both the good things and the bad. He told the boys today that they had done both.

Mark also told the boys about what he would call some blue-collar stats from last night's game. In rebounding, Kaleb and Craig both had eight, and B-Mo had seven. Kaleb also had six assists, B-Mo and Colin three, and Clayton two. B-Mo also took three charges.

For the season B-Mo has taken 12 charges, and in some ways an even more impressive number is that Jesse has taken six. Taking six charges in the limited time that Jesse has played is really pretty amazing.

We were eight of nine from the line, and Osky only had three.

One stat that Coach Core wasn't so impressed with was the ratio of three point shots in comparison to the number of two-pointers we took for the game. We attempted 29 twos and 17 threes, and Coach Core would like it to be more of a three-to-one ratio. Mark feels like we took some quick shots and settled for some shots when we could have gotten some better inside shots if we had taken a little more time and made a few more passes (I will confirm this in a moment).

The absolute worst stat for us last night was the fact that we gave up 12 offensive rebounds. I'm not sure of this, but I wouldn't be too far off if I said that all but two of Osky's third-quarter hoops were off of offensive rebounds.

Mark also tried to explain his thinking in the change he made in our Duke offense. He figured a number of things. One, he thought that when we run this for Kaleb it seems like we work too hard to get just him a shot, and we don't separate very well from the screens, looking for other people and having them shoot the ball. It also increases the likelihood that Kaleb feels more obligated to shoot the ball. And finally, (and I think the best point) Coach figures that if Kaleb is setting screens the man guarding him will not switch out to help against B-Mo even if B-Mo loses his man, because the defender will be more concerned about Kaleb than B-Mo, thus giving B-Mo a good look at the basket. Clayton also mentioned the fact that the opposing team's big man will probably be the one guarding B-Mo and will be overmatched running through screens. B-Mo gives up size and strength on the defensive end to most posts but he is quicker and a better runner too, and this should give him an advantage on the offensive end. This was good stuff, man; good coaching and thinking.

Our chances to get a better seed in the districts just sky rocketed. We have now beaten Newton, Osky, and Boone (all 4A teams) and moved from having virtually no chance of a good seed into being the leader for one of the top spots. A lot will depend upon this upcoming Friday's games. If we win and Norwalk loses we should be in. If this set of circumstances were to take place we would get the first game at home and (at least according to seed) would play a weaker opponent in the opening round.

Kirk has been working like crazy on the stationary bike, and today he is doing the elliptical in the exercise room. The doctors say he can go with whatever his pain tolerance will take, but Coach Core is being ultra-conservative. This is really a good move on his part, and one that most coaches wouldn't make. In the long run there is no question that this is the right move.

During my part of the meeting I confirmed what Coach Core had said about quick shots. Nate is keeping stats, and one of the things he is doing is counting passes and registering results in connection with the number of passes that we throw before we lose possession of the ball. The results are shown below.

1 pass	1/5 shots	20%	Fouled 4	5 points	0 Turnover
2 pass	4/13	31%	1	9	1
3 pass	6/12	50%	5	19	2
4 pass	3/9	33	0	7	1
2< pass	5/18	28	5	14	1
3>pass	9/21	44	5	26	3

The last two rows are the totals from the first four rows in the chart above. This is the second game in a row that if we throw two or fewer passes we are not nearly as likely to score as we are when we throw three or more passes.

I also thought that all of the work that we've done on end-of-quarter situations finally paid off last night, as we did a much better job in this area.

In our Partners offense we could have flashed to the free-throw line more often to get the ball. Furthermore, we need to add to our offensive options when we are in this offense. Hopefully we will be practicing these some more on Monday. Once again they include on-ball screening and the move to screen and re-screen.

Last night, by chance, we had a bit of a ball swing just from having Klarc and Clayton in the game at the same time. Clayton would come from the wing and cut behind Klarc at the point (to become the new point), and Klarc would head to replace Clayton at the wing. I think we could do this any time and told them so, regardless of who might be the point or the wing. Klarc and Clayton also had an exchange when Klarc passed away from where Clayton was playing wing and came down to set a screen for him to get him to the point. I like it. Another option for our posts would be to occasionally simply screen across and switch sides and partners.

On defense I was really pleased with our ability to point the ball out of the zone. I also praised not only Klarc for the job he did on #33 but also Kaleb. The two areas I was critical were first, when I pointed out that sometimes we guard air, which means that we are guarding a spot on the floor and not a man; I hate that; we need to match up. And second, our weak-side rebounding and the technique we need to use to improve upon this, namely we need to be in an open stance (butt to the baseline) at the weak-side wing rather than closed and facing the ball. When we are closed we end up not having the vision to see the offensive rebounder coming in behind (and then beating into the lane) the defensive rebounder.

There wasn't one guy that came in that didn't do at least an adequate job for the team last night, and I wanted to point this out. Jesse had a put-back, drew a charge, and caused them to commit at least one foul. Tyler Terlouw again gave solid minutes. Brock, while not playing, has been improving in practice. And while Craig was a starter last night, he is a junior and the least experienced starter we had, so I wanted to point out his hustle plays, his rebounding, and his decision making—all of them were done very well.

And finally I wanted to praise Zach Morgan for his interview. I had him stand up while I spoke about what a great job he did on the radio and the fact that I got a call about his interview and the person that called was really positive about him as well.

Chapter 14—After a BIG Win

Monday, January 29, Practice #41
Team Response, Kirk, Re-Screen and On-Ball Screens, End of Quarter, and Louisville

It is interesting to see how a team responds to a big win. Some come back to their next practice ready to go and get even better; they are inspired. Some come back feeling really good about themselves and have to be convinced to work hard in the following practice. Unfortunately, the combination of winning and Monday afternoon practice was not a good mix. We came out flat and really didn't get a lot better during the day. This sounds like a criticism of just the kids; it isn't—this is a criticism of me as well. I wasn't ready for practice either. I wasn't ready mentally to coach, and I didn't help much during the day.

With all that said, we did have some good news, Kirk makes an appearance at practice doing some minimal workout. He shoots; does layups, a little bit of up and down the floor, and then jogs on the sideline. We are really concerned that Kirk not re-injure himself, but we are also torn because we would really like to get him back and going ASAP.

After loosening up with shooting and lay-ups we go to a three-on-three drill and work on switching men as we would in the match-up zone. This was just the guard-type players while the post players were working on post-up moves at the other end. From there we put all of the guys into a zone concept but with only three players trying to match up with a moving offense. In both of these situations Coach Core was really after the kids to rebound the ball since that was one of the things we didn't do really well against Osky.

Then we went to a two-on-two set and worked on our Partners offense. We worked on the screen and re-screen concept and the on-ball screen move. Then we went five-on-five trying to do the same things while also using the flash move and the single screen and pop-out moves. Tyler Linn was instantly promoted to the first team when Colin shot a quick first pass rather than moving the ball first.

During the press-press offense part of practice Kirk and I stood alone down at the end of the floor while the rest of the guys were practicing. Kirk was unsure of some of the things that we were doing, and he wanted to review them. Why wouldn't he be unsure? How long has he been gone? Anyway, after just a few minutes Kirk seemed to pick up what we were doing. It is one thing to talk it through; it is another to react and physically do things, but that is not a surprise to me. Kirk is a smart player who picks things up quickly— I could tell that he had been paying attention while he was on the sideline riding that stationary bike. We talked about his role in the triangle defense, the match-up, the Fist, and finally the half-court, one-three-one-trap zone defense.

Then we worked on the end-of-the-quarter offense and defensive situations. Coach Core then got specific and worked on end-of-fourth-quarter stuff. We are up by four, and there are two minutes left in the ball game. There is a delicate balance in this situation. If the team gets too conservative they are sitting ducks, defenses will overplay and look to pick off passes and dribblers because they are alerted to the fact that we aren't attacking. But if we just shoot without moving the ball and without attacking high percentage shots we are playing into the defensive team's hands.

In **Diagram M**, I drew out the Louisville set and the cuts. We've added to the cuts by encouraging the guards to split the post and then go to the baseline. Today we changed the down screen into a back screen by the guards. I would like to eventually hand signal either move, but not today; we are simply adding the back screens.

We finished practice by playing some half-court scrimmage and working on changing-up defenses.

Practice was short today because there were intramural games prior to practice, and then there was a freshman girls' game early that evening. We don't have a game until Friday (different from the normal Tuesday-Friday routine) and maybe that was a reason for our lack of urgency.

Tuesday, January 28, Practice #42
Bronx, Clayton, Kirk, B-Mo, Craig, Learning, Blitz, S. Tama, and Zone Attack

After shooting and lay-ups we went to the Bronx drill. This is a drill that is a tough-guy-go-get-the-rebound drill. The guys are three at a time in the lane, and that is the only area from which the ball may be shot. Upon the shot they all rebound, and the man that gets the ball puts it back up regardless of the previous shot being missed or pulled out of the net on a make. With three guys in the lane, and their only mission is to rebound and put it back up, it is a physical, tough drill.

Clayton is going to work out with us today. Kirk continues to jog up and down the floor without doing any real basketball work—just making sure his foot can take it and gets some shape back before he starts to go live. The idea is to see if he is okay first by letting him dictate the moves that he can do on his injured foot, and then if that works out okay we will see if he can respond to another's moves (defense).

Ah-oh, could it be? Are we getting near to having everyone back for the first time in the entire season? Oops, spoke too soon—B-Mo is out sick today. That will give us a chance to look more at some of the other guys playing the post.

During the five-on-five-rebound game we are also working on our man-to-man offense. We continue to encourage re-screens and on-ball screens. While I like these, I also like screen and separate or post, so we have to be careful about our point of emphasis, that we don't overdo it. We would also like a few on-ball screens at the point position as well. If we increase our offensive activity at the wings it will open up more opportunities for the point guard because they will not be in as much help position and will not be as aware when the ball swings out to the top.

Craig is a great example of what we would like from our cutters. He does a terrific job of cutting about to the middle of the floor, looking for an interior pass from the opposite side of the floor from where he is working. He is really aggressively making that cut on a regular basis. By doing that, two things happen. He might get the pass and score, or, he really brings the man defending him deep into the lane and creates a great screen angle for his partner when he comes back out. Tomorrow I will be encouraging this from all of our guys.

It never fails to amaze me how much I continue to learn from players. After doing this stuff for about 100 years one would think that I've covered it all—not true. Every year I learn a number of things that work for certain players, and then I try to transfer that kind of learning into other players; it happens over and over again.

Again we go into the three-on-three drill that we have been using lately. It's paradoxical that regardless of what defense we are in we end up playing a lot of man-to-man. We may switch more, and it may be called something else, but it really ends up being a form of guarding your man in an area.

We tried a new defense in our press-press offense segment. We are calling it the Blitz, and it will be similar to our Fist defense. Essentially the defense creates a double team and an opportunity to steal the pass out or at least an opportunity to create a little uncertainty in the offensive team's attack.

South Tama's offense has many characteristics of the Louisville offense that we run, so we ran our Louisville in order to simulate Tama's offense against our match-up. We split the teams more evenly today, so it wasn't first vs. second teams today, but the white team's defensive unit handled this offense superbly. Man, if we can do that in a ball game, it will be tough to score upon.

South Tama (in our last game with them) played a three-two zone that extended out into the passing lanes, and we didn't handle it very well. Their post players stayed home under the basket, but their outside men tried to create havoc by aggressively attacking receivers upon the catch or by trying to deny the pass all together.

They also extended the top of the zone (the point of the defense) out to almost make it a half-court defense.

The player at the top of the zone pushes the offensive point guard one way or the other. The idea is that the defense would then only need to cover one side of the floor if they can keep the ball from being reversed. The theory is good if we let them do this to us.

There are some counters to this. One, the offensive point guard can go right at the defensive number one player and not let him dictate the side. Two, we could set a screen on the number one player, and then roll back to the basket, or we could simply put two guards back and pass back and fourth and force the number one player to chase the ball. Actually, I would prefer a combination of one and two. I like the idea of our guy making the decision as to where to go (not the defender) and I also like the screen just to let the point defender know that we are there; that also momentarily takes him out of the play, and if the screener rolls, it gives us a five-on-four advantage.

Once the offense gets the ball into the quarter-court attack area the defense tries to extend and take away passing angles and ball swings. Again, the counters would be dribble penetration into the heart of the defense for a shot, a dump down to the post, or a cross-court pass to create a side-to-side ball movement. And once again an on-ball screen would also cause some confusion to the defense.

Our one-four offense is a good one against this as well, if we would do a better job of looking high-low. But until we do this better we probably won't get many really good looks. The defense will be playing our wings if they know they don't need to help inside. B-Mo and Tyler Terlouw are the best we have at sealing the defenders in a post up position, but none of our post players do a very good job of looking for each other down there.

Wednesday, January 29, Practice #43
Sophomores, Scrimmage, Kirk, Clayton, B-Mo, Sprints, Point Guard, Lots of Zone, Meeting, and Screen Angles

Today's practice is a scrimmage with the sophomore team. Our sophomores are a nice group and have done well this year.

Kirk is going to get his first live play since his injury today. We will try to keep his playing time short. Clayton is practicing, but B-Mo is still sick. We warmed up and got ready to scrimmage.

Upon the opening tip the varsity went down and scored but failed to go to the offensive boards. We cleared the floor and ran a sprint. Then defensively, we failed to box out, so we cleared the floor and ran again. At that point Coach Core took the starting varsity team off the floor and put our second unit in the scrimmage. He was really upset with the guys for their lack of effort on the boards. That has been a point of emphasis to them throughout the year; it has been continually emphasized day by day as well. To the players' credit they have gotten better at crashing the boards because of this, but it is still not instinctive to them.

The second unit scrimmaged the entire four—minute quarter and started and played the majority of the second four-minute quarter.

The scores of both quarters were pretty close.

The last quarter was an eight-minute quarter, which was more of a controlled scrimmage. Coach Core took this as an opportunity to stop play and run sets against the defense that the sophomores were running.

Some of the things that I noticed during the course of this scrimmage— there were three or four sophomores that did a nice job. I was really pleased with one of the guys that was playing point for them. Klarc (our current point) graduates and (like most of our positions) he will need to be replaced. The point guard is a position that I played in my youth and so have both of my sons and I know that when we don't get good point-guard play that makes the game a lot tougher.

Back to the things I noticed—the varsity played a lot of straight zone, and I wonder why that was the defense of choice. Another observation was that we didn't anticipate very well when we are on defense, and that was especially true when we were in our zone defense. There is a huge difference between reacting and anticipating what the offense might do. We were reacting, which puts us at least a second or two later than anticipating.

The sophomores are quicker than we are. It was obvious that the sophomore team was quicker to loose balls and long rebounds than we are. They were also able to put the ball on the floor and beat us off the dribble. The varsity was the physically stronger team and probably (over all) the more aggressive group.

The game is moving a little too fast for Kirk right now. Getting back on the floor is one thing, getting used to playing in a game situation is another. But, boy, was it nice to see him out there again. Knowing Kirk, he will respond quicker than most to game speed. He has a good sense for the game and doesn't normally get too shook up regardless of the situation.

After the scrimmage we had a short meeting in the hallway to discuss a variety of issues. A couple of them were on-the-floor matters, the first being our screen angles. When we set on-the-ball screens we would like them to encourage the dribbler to attack the middle of the floor and not the baseline. Going baseline is an option, but it should be a second choice. I heard it said by one coach that if you go to the baseline, shoot it, because everything else that happens from there is much worse. I don't know if I would go that far, but there are just many more things that an offensive player can do when they go to the middle of the floor.

The second on-the-floor area of concern was more a South Tama thing that we could use at any other time as well. This is also a screen issue. We set some on-ball screens for the point guard (against the sophomores) as he got to half-court and then rolled the post right into the zone offense. It looked good and fit well into what we would like to do.

Finally, the off-the-floor things we spoke about again included communication topics. We didn't talk as much as we should have when things didn't go really well for us early. But we did see Kirk talking and trying to lead with his teammates, and we wanted to credit him for that. I personally also believe that one of the things we need to get better at is to become more active listeners. By that I mean that the people that are trying to verbally lead might not be receiving enough feedback that they are being heard and therefore may be hesitant to speak up. An active listener is one who shakes his head when he affirms, he has good eye contact, he may smile or even disagree or interjects things. He is not just simply staring at the speaker and then walking away. We (as coaches) get a lot of that with these kids—great kids but not very active listeners.

By the way, just to give you an idea of our rebounding Mark had the kids run a sprint for each time they didn't block out or go to the offensive boards. And the sprint number went up by one each time—as an example, on the first missed block out we ran one on the second two and on the third three, and so on. Our final tally was 21! And almost all of those were early in the practice; I don't think we ever ran in the last 8:00; it just became a higher priority for them.

Thursday, January 29, Practice #44
Zone Slides, South Tama Zone, Nate, B-Mo, Z-mo, Louisville, Four out Is Now Spread, Screen Angles, Colin, and Kirk

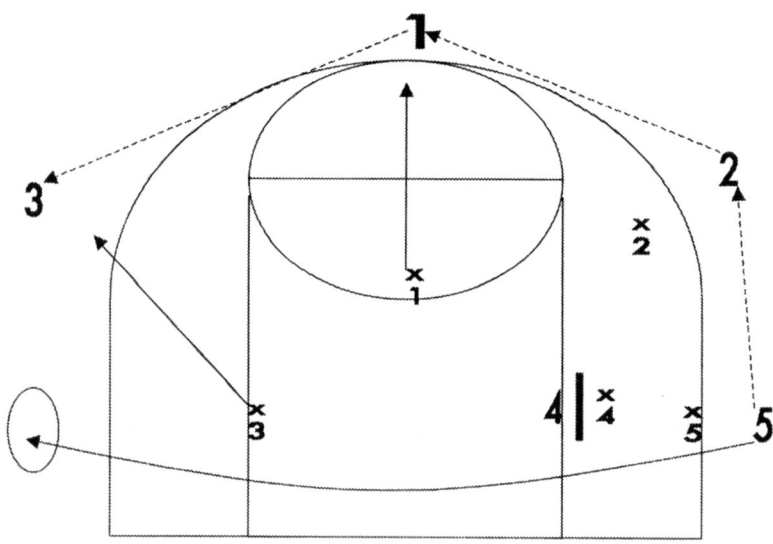

One of the ways to beat a zone defense is to help your players understand the slides that the zone will make in order to cover the various areas of the floor. Let me give you a for instance.

In the previous diagram (defenders have an x by the number) if #5 were to have the ball in one corner of the floor and then the offensive team were to quickly reverse the ball to the other side of the floor the defenders of a typical three-two zone might react as shown. But if #5 were to make a hard cut to the opposite side of the floor and #4 were to screen x4 the offense should get an open shot because often times in this type of zone it is x4's responsibility to cover out to the corner as x5 did when #5 was on his side of the floor. If our guys know the coverage by x4 in this situation, #4 (as shown) might be more likely to set a back screen against him to slow his slide to the opposite side.

I tell you all of this because we will be working today again against the South Tama zone defense, and we will be encouraging more screening against it.

One of the things that I forgot to mention yesterday during the scrimmage that I wanted to make sure to point out was Nate Klyn's willingness as a teammate. Yesterday when the guys were running for their mistakes Coach Core told both Kyle and Nate they didn't have to run. That did not stop Nate; he ran everything that anybody else did, and he didn't do it because he had to but because he wanted to. Now that is a great attitude, one that would make a more-talented player a star.

B-Mo and Z-Mo are both back. I think that this might be the first time in many, many moons that we have everybody here!

After initial warm ups we went to the shell drill and ran a basket cut on one side of the floor with a down screen on the other. This is a drill that forces the defense to move their heads as well as their bodies and if done correctly they must communicate with one another, as well.

For the first time we ran Louisville as an offense while we were trying to get three stops in a row. Both Coach Core and the boys seem to be getting more confidence in this offense as the season has gone along. Today we are allowing the offensive players to make hand signals to determine the type of screen we will set between wing and cutting guard; they can choose to set either a down or a back screen. We accomplish two things while we are working on this offense. One, we are actually working South Tama's offense or something very similar to it anyway, and two, we ourselves are getting better at running the offense and may do more of it now in games.

We know that #31 and #33 are Tama's best scorers. We will have different match-ups when we play the triangle-and-two (as we will guard these two players) than when we play our match-up zone, so we are working on this today.

We run a four-out and a one-four offense against the zone. Coach Core decided that we get too confused between the two names, and will now call the four-out our "spread offense."

Offensively we are running both Partners and Louisville today in practice, and while we are doing this we are also reemphasizing the screen angles and the appropriate ways to screen against South Tama.

I spoke with Colin right after practice; he said he didn't feel real good. He sounds like he is sick, but knowing Colin I wouldn't doubt for a minute that he is here tomorrow. I asked Kirk how he was doing and he said, with a huge smile, "Awesome; I'm ready to go." He is excited to play.

Friday, February 2, Pella vs. South Tama, Game #15
Our Record: 8-6; Conference: 8-6

For the first time all year it has happened, we have all the guys here; they are all back from the various injuries and sicknesses. Clayton is still not 100%, and I'm afraid he may never be, but at least he is able to play.

We are starting Craig again tonight.

Kaleb is on the floor almost immediately for a loose ball—that is always a good sign when our guys are diving for loose balls.

Craig starts us off with a little pull-up for two. Early it is evident on the defensive end that we are getting caught behind their post player in the lane area. This allows a post pass into the heart of our defense.

B-Mo doesn't get the points, but he is the guy that keeps one of our offensive possessions alive with a rebound and then kicks it out to Colin, who hits a two. Both B-Mo and Kaleb's initial shots of the game were threes—they were both open, but they were both misses. We would prefer to get them going at the hoop early.

About the third or fourth play of the game we ran Louisville (something we thought we should run a little more than we have been) and B-Mo goes right to the hoop for two. The defensive end is more of a struggle, as we are trying to change defenses too much on the run. Between that, our numerous substitutions, and the fact that South Tama is pushing the tempo (not giving us a lot of time to adjust to the various defensive calls), we are giving up some easy looks.

B-Mo sets an on-ball screen that gets Klarc so open that he missed it, but it was a great look at the hoop set up by a good screen.

The next time we ran Louisville we got fouled going to the hoop—that is two for two for this offense with something good happening.

C.J. is working in there as he always does. If he weren't an effort guy he wouldn't be playing nearly as much. One of those effort plays pays off for him with an offensive rebound and two free throws. The score is 10-10 halfway through the first quarter.

South Tama does not have the height that we do, but they are very athletic and quick. We normally do not have an advantage inside, but tonight we do, and both Kaleb and B-Mo have a block already.

Our new Blitz defense doesn't work because Klarc isn't pressuring the ball enough, and the point guard sees us coming.

South Tama also does a really nice job of swinging the ball from one side of the floor to the other—something we would like to slow down so it would give our defense more time to react. Klarc helps the cause when he comes from the back side of the defense to steal an entry pass into the post.

Our game plan was to change defenses every time that they scored, but they have scored so often we are changing every time down the court, and we just aren't handling it very well.

B-Mo scores on a dribble drive to the bucket.

After missing from three twice, Kaleb gets on the board with a dribble drive and scores off of a layup. We are down 14-17 when Clayton makes a nice dribble penetration and slips a pass to Tyler Terlouw, who scores to pull us within one at the end of the first quarter.

We gave up a lot of points in that first quarter. I think most of it stems from the fact that we are confusing ourselves more than we are them. We need to do a better job of communicating our defenses and not make so many changes if we are caught in transition.

Klarc gets us a hoop to start the second. That is our second possession in a row because we held the ball at the end of the first quarter and got the ball to start the second.

This Tama team has done a pretty good job of keeping us off of the offensive boards so far, and they also continue to get their post player in better position than ours, which is not good.

241

B-Mo has three blocks already; the third one turns out to be a fast-break, as it went from a block to Colin, who throws it ahead to Kaleb. Another fast-break came shortly as Craig gets fouled in the act of shooting. B-Mo misses a three later, but Kaleb tracks down the rebound, which unfortunately turns out to be a turnover.

South Tama has actually missed a few shots now. In the first quarter they were lighting it up. Kaleb picks up his second block.

Both teams have really gotten sloppy with the ball (especially us) and are taking quick shots; there is not much scoring going on all of a sudden.

Kirk makes an appearance.

Colin is holding onto the ball too long, and our guys continue to throw the ball away, but they return the favor with some poor passes of their own as well as missed shots.

Kaleb gets fouled on an attempted three and makes two of three from the line. Kirk was on his side of the floor and had pretty good position at the block; maybe next time. We are up 23-21 half way through the second.

The turnover fest continues. Either our defense is better, or they have come back to earth with their shooting percentages. It's probably both. It is a good thing we are doing a quality job on the defensive boards, holding them to one shot, or they might be taking more advantage of our poor ball handling.

It's incredible how poorly we have taken care of the ball for the last six minutes or so, but finally Jesse uses his body in a power lay-up-type mode and gets one of two free throws. Again Jesse makes a save on another possible turnover; he gets it to B-Mo, who cans a three.

We run our scramble defense and create a turnover with :20 left in the half. We do so much better at working the clock down than we used to. We do get the last shot of the half and even an offensive rebound put-back but we can't convert, and it is 27-25 at half.

We gave up 17 points in the first quarter and then cut that in half the second quarter, giving up eight.

The second half starts well for us, as we cause them to throw the ball away. C.J. and B-Mo do a great job of attacking the middle of the floor with on-ball screens and dribble drives that end up getting Colin a three-pointer.

B-Mo makes a steal from an attempted post pass by S. Tama that results in a fast-break for us. We miss, but get the ball back underneath (by Colin's penetration), and Craig gets a layup.

We are working so much harder at keeping the ball out of the post, and because of that they are not as efficient. Our own post entry from Colin to Craig gets us a hoop, and they call a timeout—it's 34-25, us.

B-Mo's on-ball screen allows Klarc to attack with the dribble, and the ball comes back to B-Mo under the hoop. He scores and also tacks on a free throw; it's 39-27 with 5:30 left in the third. We have definitely come out well in the third quarter.

I thought the officiating was really good in this game. I've never seen these guys before, and you hardly notice them out there. That is the way it should be; then you know they are calling a good game.

Klarc hits two free throws, and both Kaleb and B-Mo are preventing post touches.

We gave up yet another bucket to an inbounds play. That is going to happen, but we have stressed that if they are going to score it must be outside of the paint because we will outnumber them inside the paint (and we do)—their score came under the hoop; go figure!

Kaleb gets a three. It is 40-29. Our ball movement on the next series is really good; we miss the initial shot, but Kaleb is there to put it back in. Our defense seems to be picking up, and our changing defenses has slowed the S. Tama offense down as well.

Kaleb makes a long pass to Clayton on the run, and he is fouled on the attack, scoring one of two shots. When Kaleb comes out, and B-Mo continues to front at the post, our defensive rebounding isn't as good. These two guys are by far our best rebounders on the defensive end. With Kaleb on the bench resting, and B-Mo in a front position on defense, we are asking guys to get the boards that are usually not our primary rebounders, and we are only doing a fair job right now.

S. Tama hits a three with about 1:00 in the third, and we are trying to hold for the last shot (we are showing terrific poise), oops, spoke too soon, as Clayton throws the ball away, then he fouls. This turns out to be the right move, as they miss twice, and Klarc attacks the hoop and makes two free throws. With about :02 left and us pressuring the ball they throw in a half-court shot! Wouldn't you know it? It is 45-37 at the end of the third.

Kaleb gets a nice pass from B-Mo after setting and slipping a screen. He scores a layup to start the fourth quarter. Craig (later on) cans a couple of free throws, but they also hit another three.

Jesse is a pretty good free-throw shooter for us, and he makes two for two. Jesse scores again a little bit later on a pass out from B-Mo, who got another offensive rebound. He has come in and gotten us four quick points.

With 4:30 left we are up eight, and they are trying to pressure us a little bit harder, which allows Klarc to get into the lane and get fouled—he makes two free throws.

They won't go away, as they score and then Colin hits his patented "floater" from about 10 feet. It looks like a long layup—but he can make that shot and does often, maybe not from quite that far out, however.

After they turn it over we seem to get even smarter, as we do a nice job of moving the ball, and Klarc gets a turnaround shot in the middle of the lane, which forces a South Tama timeout.

We figured they would come out in a press, and they do. Big Kirk has reentered the game and is part of the press break. Kaleb hits a three, and Tama has to be feeling some pressure now.

Colin again probably keeps the ball too long but is pretty tough when the defense attacks him. He scores two free throws.

One of the keys to our second half run is keeping the ball out of the post. Another has been that I think our kids have figured out some of the offensive habits of the players that they are guarding and are making some adjustments of their own.

It's 64-47, and both teams go to the bench to end the game. We fail to score but defensively give up only one point ourselves, and the final is 64-48.

Now we need to start to think Perry. We play them tomorrow in a mid-afternoon game.

Chapter 15—It's a New Month and Our Kids Haven't Quit

Saturday Afternoon, February 3, Pella vs. Perry, Game #16
Our Record: 9-6; Conference: 9-6

We are coming into this non-conference game on a three-game winning streak that at least somewhat coincided with the time that we decided to start using various defenses rather than just the straight man-to-man.

At the time of this decision I know that both Coach Core and I felt like we were taking an unusual chance that might not be the best way to go. I guess what started out as initially a subtle change (going from 99% man-to-man to about 50%) has gone full gambit, and it didn't take long. Even in the first game, I know that we played much more like 50% man and 50% of something else.

Now I wouldn't have a clue about which defense we are actually running the most. I don't think we have one really good defense or a best defense, but what we are really doing is changing up enough to try to find out which defense it is that gives each opponent the most amount of difficulty or the one that they handle the poorest. And then if we've found a weakness we play more of that and less of the other defenses.

The other offshoot of the multiple defensive system is that the kids seem more interested in playing defense. Maybe they are revitalized (in some ways this has been an adventure for me, too) and I don't think our man-to-man has really suffered at all. The majority of our veteran players should know by now how to defend in a man-to-man.

We decided (based upon the South Tama game) that at least initially we should open in man until we all got settled in and knew whom we were guarding both individually and collectively.

The game is in the afternoon, and the crowd is pretty thin, but from a personal standpoint I love this early afternoon time. It actually gives me a few hours of a weekend on Saturday night rather than waiting around all day to play

245

and then no evening time available to relax. It also means that the visiting team can get back home before the evening is over.

Perry scores on a tough turn-around, fade-away shot—if we can make them take that shot all day we are going to be okay. Then they come out in a half-court one-three-one trap. Another advantage that running all of these various defenses has given to us is the opportunity to work against them offensively as well.

Kaleb is guarding the Perry team's best perimeter shooter, and B-Mo will be guarding the inside scorer. Klarc is guarding the point guard, who prefers to penetrate rather than shoot.

Perry's drop-back defense is also a one-three-one zone defense. They just extend the quarter-court defense to make their full-court-press defense.

Kaleb hits a three to score our first points of the game.

Perry's big kid inside will block shots, but he will also get in foul trouble because of this. Craig creates a foul on him when he gets a post pass and two foul shots. Our next scoring possession is a short shot from outside from B-Mo on an assist from Kaleb, and Craig gets us the ball back again as he is working for inside position on the boards and gets shoved by the defensive player trying to block him out.

Our defense has started man, and after a few possessions we are now showing some zone. Other than their opening possession they haven't scored.

Tyler Terlouw, who has come in for B-Mo, is working hard trying to seal and position the inside man of their zone.

This is a low-scoring game, as we are up 5-2 halfway through the first quarter.

Perry's next score is off of a set play (**Diagram AA**) in which the offense takes our zone defense to one side of the floor, then quickly reverses it to the other side of the floor and screens one of our baseline defenders away from the basket, which opens up a lob for a layup inside.

We make Perry pay for running the press against us when Colin receives a pass from Kaleb in the middle of the floor at about the free-throw line and finds himself open for a jumper right there, which he hits.

Offensively we got some really good ball movement, and our next shot is a two from Klarc at the baseline. Jesse draws a charge—he and B-Mo are our best at this.

Both B-Mo and Klarc are being unselfish to the point of passing up shots, and C.J. is still making hustle plays as he gets fouled while screening out against a Perry opponent.

When we switched out of a zone and went man-to-man it seemed to confuse the Perry offense, and this time instead of passing up a shot, B-Mo pulls up and hits a short shot in the middle of the lane.

Perry turned the tables on us when they changed their defense into a man, and we didn't react very well as they intercepted a poor pass, but what looked like a sure lay-up for them turned out to be a miss and even a miss on a follow-up shot, as Craig finally got the defensive rebound.

The set play that Perry ran is shown from top to bottom below. The pass swings quickly from #3 to #1 to #2 on the opposite side of the floor from where it started, stretching our defense out one way to create a better screen angle on our bottom man (x5) before he could cover the basket. In the next diagram down the ball is in #2's hands as #4 sneaks across to set a back screen against x5. The last picture shows the final result as Perry scores on a lob to their wing that had cut behind the screen from #4.

Diagram AA

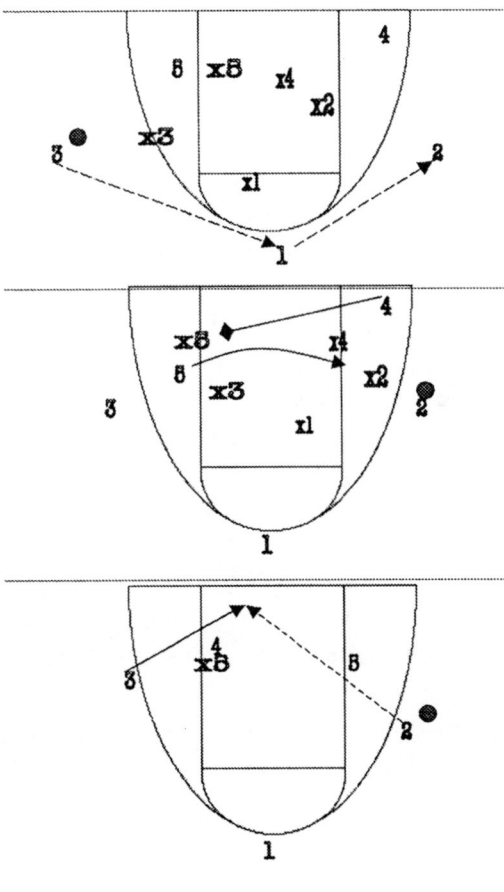

Perry has two high-scoring players that have been playing since they were underclassmen and who are now seniors. They both average around 15-16 points a game. From that point their scoring drops off considerably down to about six points a game. Their record in their conference is about the same as ours is in our conference, and they just played their conference champions to a three-point game, which would be similar to our play against our league champs.

With :30 left in the first quarter we are holding for the last shot. Remember the Open play that I described earlier—well we ran that to perfection, as B-Mo threw an almost double-play-like pass to Kaleb under the hoop and he scored right at the buzzer to end the first quarter, we are ahead 13-4. By the way, we also get the ball back.

Colin has really responded to my comment to him about holding the ball too long; he is definitely moving the ball more quickly now.

Our first show of the half-court trap results in a Perry turnover. We then threw the ball away, but Colin makes a deflection to get us the ball back.

Early in the second quarter after Perry throws the ball away again, their coach pulls the entire starting line up and goes with his second unit.

Kaleb has a nice assist to B-Mo, who cuts under the hoop for a basket and a foul; it's 16-4. Our trap creates another turnover, and now Kirk makes an entrance into the game—his second game in two days.

They finally a hit a three, but Kaleb has a good out-let pass to Clayton who makes a nice spin move in the lane to score. By the way, the first team for Perry has reentered.

There is a fine line between attacking off of the break and forcing up a shot. Williams at North Carolina says 7 or 17. By that he means either shoot in the first seven seconds or work it around for 17 seconds. We are still searching for that line, but Clayton makes a good decision to hold and wait for his teammates rather than attacking the hoop.

With the score 20-7 and 3:00 left in the second quarter both teams are missing shots and being very selective on the offensive end before they shoot. B-Mo creates a turnover by getting a deflection, but we give it right back to them, and they are off on a break. Jesse hustles back and takes yet another charge to stop the hoop.

The officials have done a nice job in this game. We've had one of them before but the other two are new to me.

Our offense this quarter has been very poor. We quit doing the things that got us going early, and now we are just standing and throwing long, slow passes that gain us very little in the way of an advantage.

Kaleb (early in the game) got a partial block against the Perry shooter, and I think intimidated him somewhat. He hasn't done a lot of scoring and has rushed a couple of attempts.

We had a nice play on defense when Klarc was pressuring the ball handler and got close to a five count when Perry set an on-ball screen, but B-Mo, who was guarding the screener, stepped out and hedged so well that it turned into a switch on defense and the five-second count continued which created a turnover for Perry.

We are up 22-12 at halftime. Offensively the game is exactly like it looks. Lots of missed shots. We have turned Perry over at least 13 times; shoot, they've only taken 17 shots. But our offense hasn't been very good either. We've put up more shots with fewer turnovers but we aren't making many of them.

At halftime we talked about using more on-ball screens against the zone and definitely using more dribble penetration within the offensive attack.

We ran our one-four offense for the first time, and B-Mo got a high-post pass, dribbled to the middle of the floor, and kicked out a pass to Colin, who buried a three. Later on Colin is also involved in a fast-break with a lead pass from Klarc, and he gets two free throws.

Kaleb has been on the Perry shooter the entire ball game (except when we are in a zone), and B-Mo has done an outstanding job against their big kid. The big boys for Perry (as we thought) have some foul troubles. As I speak, Kaleb makes a really nice play when he defends their shooter on the outside and then runs in to secure a defensive board.

Klarc is starting to do more flashing into the middle of the zone and ends up with about a 12-foot score. Next possession down Klarc does the same thing, this time from about 15 feet. B-Mo gets a steal and passes ahead to Kaleb, who is one-on-one in the open court and attacks the hoop. He gets fouled and makes both of his free throws.

We ran a lot of one-two-two zone in the first half with some man-to-man. This half so far we have run quite a bit of half-court zone trap and man-to-man half-court-trap stuff.

The score is 31-16 with 4:40 left in the third quarter.

Something subtle that most people will not see is Colin faking at the ball handler when we are on defense, and he is doing this out of our zone defense. Wow, that is really good!

The Perry set play scores again, but Colin comes back with a dribble drive and gets fouled for us. Our offense is being really choosy as far as our shot selection is concerned; this is part of the low score, but I do think that Perry is not a bad defensive team, and they don't give up anything really quick, either.

Colin comes back again with another dribble drive and misses but Kaleb gets the board and makes two free throws. The dribble drive creates problems for the defense—any time and any way you can get the ball into the heart of a zone it is going to be a problem for them; we should get some offensive rebounds if this happens.

They take a timeout. After the break we broke out our triangle-and-two defense.

Perry has come out in a man-to-man defense, and Kaleb gets a screen from B-Mo as he makes a ball-side cut which turns into a layup for PHS.

The big guy from Perry is out right now in foul trouble with four.

It's 35-23 late in the third quarter, and Perry shows a three-two full-court zone press after they score. B-Mo and C.J. each get an offensive board with B-Mo scoring the hoop.

C.J. picks up two quick fouls and comes to the bench with three fouls total.

Late in the third quarter #21 (the Perry shooter) scores, he has 12 of their points. When we get the ball back we are going to run some time off the clock to try to take the quarter's last shot. We did a good job, but Klarc can't connect with an open shot at the buzzer. The score is 37-25 at the end of three.

B-Mo's defensive block starts the break, and Kaleb's pass down court to B-Mo finishes the break for a bucket. Now that is a hustle play; make the block at one end and then score in transition on the other.

At the timeout we talked about running our trap just at the Perry shooter. It was a good idea, but we haven't done it, and I'm not sure why.

The next defensive board that Kaleb gets is his seventh one of the game by my count. Craig's steal of a Perry pass is his second of the game, and I'd say he must have at least three defensive rebounds himself and probably a couple of offensive boards too.

Perry got very few easy shots against us. Most of the time the Perry kids have been covered, and the shots they have made have been difficult.

Our triangle-and-two defense has not been as effective as some of our other defenses, and Perry is starting to gamble more in their press defense, which results in a down-court pass to Kirk, who makes a touch pass to Jesse, sprinting the other lane. The Perry defender must foul to stop the layup, and Jesse hits one of the two free throws. The score is 40-30 with about 5:00 left.

Our decision making at the end of games is getting better. We had some opportunities to attack the basket off of the press or kick it back out and look for a high percentage shot and run a little time off the clock. B-Mo makes a decision to pass up a shot and brings the ball out to run some clock.

Tyler Terlouw comes in for B-Mo, as he is having some shoulder problems, and we want Rob Blom to take a look at him. We are making Perry chase a little bit right now as we pass the ball around the horn.

Colin, the next time on defense, does come off of his man to trap the Perry shooter in the corner, along with Craig.

After Perry chases us for a while they get up out of defensive position and try to deflect our passes, so Klarc fakes a pass and makes a drive to the hoop. He gets fouled and makes one of two free throws.

B-Mo comes back in, Rob says B'Mo had a reoccurrence of a football shoulder injury, but it is minor in nature. B-Mo passes up a shot to take the ball back out. I'm not sure if that is the wise play or if the injury factored in here; I'm going to go with wise. I really like that B-Mo kid!

Colin again gets attacked when he holds the ball, but again, for a guy without much meat on his bones, he is just pretty darn tough with the ball and ends up making two free throws.

We are defending pretty well, and Kaleb makes a good fake at the ball, but that little fake got him just enough out of position to allow a drive by #21, one that results in a foul on us. He misses the first and on the second there is a line violation (that's great "D", we should have done this earlier). Just kidding.

Kaleb hits Colin, who hits a 15-foot shot. Kaleb will probably finish with at least nine defensive boards, and two more on the offensive end, and my guess is around four assists, counting this one.

With about 40 seconds left we get all the guys in that haven't played.

Tyler Linn gets on the board with a free throw, and Brock gets in the books with a steal. The final score is Pella 48, Perry 34. This is four wins in a row for us!

Monday, February 5, Practice #45
B-Mo, Clayton, Colin, Kirk, Post Entry, Press, Perry, Grinnell, Match-ups, the Match-up, Triangle, and Some Stats

B-Mo is sitting out this practice with his shoulder injury. He came in today before practice and said the soreness was waking him up at night. The odds are probably not very good that he will play tomorrow.

Clayton, however, is practicing with us. His lack of practice time is now showing up during game time. It had been pretty amazing to me how well he had done in games with virtually no practice, but it is starting to hurt his play now.

Colin is still hacking away with his cough. He has been fighting something for probably a week and half, but he won't give in to it. There have been a number of times I thought he would be out during the last three of four games, but he stays tough against this sick bug.

Kirk will be going pretty much full time now. I guess if we must lose B-Mo this is a really good time to get Kirk back. But a puppy sophomore going against one of the biggest, strongest seniors in our league is not a good thing. Kirk will not give up; I don't mean that, but he is giving up not only size but also experience. He can't be in terrific game shape, and I would guess he'd struggle if he played long periods of time with his conditioning.

After warming up we get into some post-entry passing as a drill. A good post pass should arrive as the post comes open, and it should be made in the area away from where the defender is stationed. We don't do either very well. But our offensive posts also don't do a great job of sealing the defender behind them either. Kirk (with his girth) should be a great target in there, but he hasn't had much work at this. He, like most of our posts, loses contact with the defender after making the initial contact. Tyler Terlouw is the best that we have at this on the team.

The white team today is simulating Grinnell. Grinnell's leading scorer and rebounder is a kid that wears a #10 jersey. Brandon E. will play his role today, and Z-Mo will play the big, bruising, post player that they have.

We worked on our press-and-press offense. Grinnell created a few turnovers with their press against us the first time. They, like Pella Christian, also run a run-and-trap press, which starts man-to-man and then, goes into a trap defense. Our players must realize that if their man leaves them to be part of a trap, they must come back to be a receiver for the man being trapped.

We also decided to work on some things that Perry hurt us with. First, they did an almost old-time-weave type of offense, and once again we didn't do a very good job of hedging the on-ball screen. We also worked on running at a hot player. When #21 got hot for Perry we wanted the guys to run at him as often as possible (and only at him) and trap him if he got the ball. We also really tried to deny the ball to him initially. This is a concept that, like the on-ball hedge, seems fairly easy to me, but we struggle with it.

Grinnell runs a flex offense as well. It is an offense that I explained earlier and one that many teams run, so our guys should know how to handle it. The key will be recognizing it when it is comes and then jumping towards the ball faster than the man making the cut can move. Grinnell, unlike some teams, isn't really patient with this offense; they want to score within one or two cuts and don't really want to continue to run it with a lot of swings of the ball from one side to the other.

Our match-ups to start the game will be: Klarc on #10, Kaleb will take their biggest three-point threat, B-Mo or Kirk will take their big boy, Colin will guard their point, and Craig will take the least effective offensive player they have.

Our triangle defense (in my opinion) might not be one that will be really successful for us tomorrow. The reason I'm worried about using it is because of their big guy. I'm afraid we will have some serious mismatches inside with him when we try to block him off.

I do think that our match-up zone will be a good defense for us to use, as well as our regular zone, and I'm interested to test out another new defense that North Carolina State used to run when Jim Valvano used to coach there. It is a gimmicky defense but one he had success with. The fundamental nature of the defense is a man-to-man defense, but we will guard the big guy from Grinnell by face-guarding him with one of our guards. He will completely ignore the ball and just be a pain in the neck to the offensive player. This is as much a psychological ploy as it is a real defense; we will see how the big man takes to being followed around like that for a while.

Our Partners offense is just flat out better when we do some on-ball screening. If nothing else it forces the defense out of position to hedge or even switch. We also worked on the Spread offense and then the One-four offense against the zone. B-Mo, who is at practice but sitting with ice on his shoulder, had an idea about changing this offense a little bit. This would be an adjustment for our post players. He thinks maybe we should have the better low-post player stay low and the better high-post player stay high rather than crossing them like we do now. His reasoning was that there are certain players on this team that would be better at doing one thing or the other.

Our new Blitz defense is a chancy play against Grinnell because it would mean that we would be leaving #10 open for a few seconds. The boys are not in favor of running this defense, but I kind of like it. I don't mean for long periods of time but just as a change up to all of our other defenses. The other option that we could use is to only do it when #10 is out. I don't think Coach Core is convinced either.

Finally, we practiced changing up our out-of-bounds defense a little bit. Wow, now that is something that we haven't changed since I've been here, and it's somewhat hard to make an old dog do new tricks. My preliminary reaction is to make the kids better at what we do rather than change what we are doing, but if we hadn't changed some other things a while back I don't think we would be on this streak of pretty good basketball. Maybe it's time.

Grinnell is giving up 49.1 points per game, and we are giving up 50.5 per game. Our offense is scoring 54.5, and Grinnell scores at 56 points a game. Statistically it looks like a close game.

Chapter 16—At One Time We Were
a Four and Five Team

Tuesday, February 6, Pella vs. Grinnell, Game #17
Our Record: 10-6; Conference: 9-6

Kirk will start tonight for B-Mo, but B-Mo is here and expects to play.

For the first time in many, many moons (at least since I can remember) we open in a zone defense. One of the biggest issues that there is with a zone is rebounding. Both Mark and I talked about it with the boys before the game in the locker room. It is difficult to board out of a zone because the defensive players don't have any direct responsibilities to block out specific people. The tendency is to not block out all together because of this mind set, or to accidentally block out one man with two guys and leave one open man completely untouched.

True to form our zone gives up two offensive rebounds in the first possession. Untrue to form, they come away with zero points in spite of that. Kaleb ends up blocking a shot, and C.J. finally gets a rebound to end their possession.

Grinnell comes out man-to-man, which is what they have played against us most of the time in the last few years. This is a departure from the Grinnell teams of old, as they were almost always a zone team. They took #10 off of Kaleb. I'm sure they did this to try to keep him out of foul trouble. In the game at Grinnell he was in foul trouble by the second quarter. He is guarding Craig, who statistically would be one of the weaker scorers not playing a guard position for us. But what they don't know is that Craig won't be an easy man to guard either. That comes from our guys. According to our players, it is not fun to guard C.J. because one just never knows what he is going to do because he is such an unorthodox player. I know for a fact as well that Craig will move, if nothing else, and keep #10 occupied.

Things didn't change on Grinnell's second possession—two more offensive rebounds but no points.

Didn't take Kirk long to get a three-point attempt. Right before the game Coach Core gave Kirk the green light to shoot it. We have been telling Kirk to get his rear down in the block area since he has been back. We need a presence down there. But tonight the Grinnell big kid will be guarding him, and Kirk's ability to make an outside shot will help take him away from the hoop.

Both teams are really being deliberate with the ball. Part of the credit goes to each team's defense, but part of it is just the way the teams are designed to attack in the quarter-court. We have pretty much proven to ourselves that if we don't have a quick early shot that we are better when we move the ball around and take some time exploring the defense.

Finally an offensive rebound and a put-back give Grinnell a 2-0 lead.

Colin hits a three for us to open the Pella scoring.

After opening straight zone we went into the match-up zone. It was effective except Kirk got caught on the side of the Grinnell post as he was trying to get in front and gave up a drop-step post shot.

It is almost halfway through the first quarter, and we are down 3-4. Man, it looks like this might be low scoring.

B-Mo comes into the game for Kirk and gets a defensive rebound. Offensively we are running Duke for B-Mo so that the big kid for Grinnell has to chase him and run through screens. We don't think he can do that very well or very long.

Both Pella and Grinnell look to run off of a defensive rebound, and Grinnell this time scores in just such a manner. Grinnell is also running a man-to-man, pressure, full-court defense and looking to jump Klarc as he brings the ball up the court.

Kaleb gets fouled in the act of shooting, but uncharacteristically he misses two free throws. That is not a good sign for us.

After they score again from an offensive rebound and our foul, we are down 3-9.

Jesse and Clayton are both in the game when B-Mo hits a three. We've got both him and Clayton out there playing without full use of one of their arms because of injury, and yet we are doing okay.

When we take Klarc out to give him a rest we move Kaleb to the point guard. Kaleb oftentimes guards post players on defense and plays wing on offense. Now he is the point. He also leads us in assists and rebounds as well as scoring. That is a pretty versatile player.

Clayton sets up B-Mo, who hits another three. Jesse also has a good hustle play later, saving a ball from going out of bounds and bouncing it off a Grinnell player as he was headed out of bounds.

We have to remember not to run B-Mo out of gas by running Duke too often. While we want to work Grinnell's post we don't want to kill off B-Mo. We've got to vary our offense a little bit and make sure we are getting everyone enough rest.

Colin has probably taken half of our shots in the first quarter. He hit the first one, but has been blocked twice since then. He is trying to get the ball in the lane but just can't finish in there right now.

Another offensive rebound leads to another Grinnell score. Grinnell is not scoring much with the first shot against our "D," but they sure are scoring off of the boards. We are down 9-13 at the end of one after holding for the last shot.

Klarc is back in at point, and we get B-Mo another hoop from three. The three-pointer right now is keeping us in this game.

#10 is helping off of Craig (that is part of the reason that Colin has had two blocked), but Craig just hit a three from the corner with a dribble penetration and an assist from Kaleb.

My favorite defense right now is our match-up zone. B-Mo is almost playing a one-man zone when the Grinnell big man goes to the top on the offensive end, daring him to shoot.

Kirk is trying to front the post, and Colin is late coming over to help, and they score. They've added two more offensive rebounds as well.

Klarc gets a steal and misses the shot, but Tyler Terlouw keeps it alive with an offensive rebound for us, and then Clayton also gets a long bounce-out recovery. Kaleb finally gets on the board with a drive to the hoop.

We've decided to play behind the Grinnell big man and make him shoot over the top rather than drop step to the hoop. Tyler and Clayton just kind of proved the point when they doubled him, and he missed badly.

Kaleb's defense against #10 in the match-up forces a turnover as he steps out of bounds. Right now K also has two defensive boards for us.

Clayton sets a nice on-ball screen for Kaleb, which gets him loose, and he draws a foul. Klarc rebounds a Kaleb miss and a really good on-ball screen and separation by Kaleb from his screen gets him the ball on the baseline, where he drives it in and gets fouled. He makes one of two free throws.

The officials have really done a good job so far in this game. They are calling what they must but allowing the players to play without taking them out of what they do well.

"Iowa" is what Grinnell calls their flex offense, and we recognize it right away and beat their screens to stop the offensive cuts they make. Clayton has a really good hustle play where he ends up on his belly on the floor but gets the ball back for us off of a defensive rebound.

Kaleb keeps trying to set an on-ball screen for Colin, and Colin just doesn't react to it. We need more work on these.

For one of the few times this half #10 gets loose in transition and hits a three before our defense is set.

Kaleb again gets an assist to Craig, who hits another three.

Both teams have had very few turnovers this half.

With seconds left we run Open, and B-Mo hits a shot from the free-throw line. But Jesse fouls a desperation heave from half-court that results in three free throws for Grinnell—they only made one. We are down 22-23 at halftime. We played an amazing first half defensive game. Our offense, due in part to their defense, was a struggle. Right before the end of the first half, Grinnell played some two-three zone; I wouldn't be shocked to see some more of that the second half because we sure didn't attack it very well.

While both teams have struggled to score, both teams have also defended hard. Our senior boys have never beaten Grinnell in any sport, so this is extra important to them. There is a great crowd that is into the game as well. While the game isn't high scoring it is intense and rugged.

B-Mo makes a steal after yet another offensive rebound by Grinnell.

Our match-up zone is frustrating their coach and their players, and their big boy tries a jumper from about 17 feet that results in an air ball. His range is limited to four feet—if we can get him to shoot more of those, we will win. While he is limited in range as a basketball player he is truly a fine athlete, going to UNI on a football scholarship; this kid is no slouch.

Surprisingly to me Grinnell does come out in a man defense—Kaleb hits a three-pointer.

Kaleb then gets an assist to Klarc, who scores two points. Grinnell calls a timeout as we go up 27-23.

We break out our new Freak defense now after the timeout. We've got Clayton (who gives up about 70 lbs. and five-inches) face guarding the big guy from Grinnell.

Kaleb has now pulled off three more defensive boards as Grinnell continues to miss shots—so what's new? So do we.

Klarc makes a nice dribble penetration then gets an assist to B-Mo, who cans a three. Wouldn't you know it, neither team can buy a shot, and then they come back with a three of their own.

They got two more offensive boards against the Freak, but we are up 30-26 halfway through the third. Kaleb's dribble layup (kind of a lean-away number) makes it 32-28 with about 3:00 left in the third.

Craig makes a good hustle play as he is in the middle of a scrum for a loose ball in the middle of the lane. This jump-ball turns into our ball on alternating possessions.

Probably our prettiest play of the night so far is a high-low pass from brother Kirk at the three-point line to brother Kaleb in the middle of the lane. Kaleb on the catch makes an immediate little jumper in the lane.

I can't tell you how selective both teams have become on the offensive end. This is like a war. Both teams figure they only have so many shots, and each one is important. The intensity is high, and the fans are noisy.

C.J.'s offensive rebound off a Kirk miss is really something. He comes flying in amongst two Grinnell players and backhands an offensive rebound with only one hand! Wow, now that was awesome! B-Mo follows this up with a sweet spin move that puts him on the line. He has shot the ball really well tonight and yet can't make either free throw; go figure.

What the heck, we haven't used the triangle defense yet so we are going to use this. And now Grinnell goes to their two-three zone; I was wondering where that was. There is 1:00 left in the third quarter. The score as the quarter comes to an end is 34-32, and it is their ball—it's a barnburner.

Fortunately for us Grinnell continues to miss on their offensive rebound put-backs, and B-Mo adds to their frustration with a block.

After they hit an inside shot and then a three, Klarc hits a huge shot for PHS as he drives the lane for a short pull-up jumper, and we are down one when we put the Grinnell post on the line (he misses both). He is only a 45% free-throw shooter, so this really isn't a huge surprise, but it is a good thing for us.

Kaleb and Craig are our defensive rebounders tonight. B-Mo's lack of mobility makes him look like a one-handed rebounder. It doesn't seem to have affected his shot, but it has definitely slowed his rebounding.

We run Open, and Kirk separates to the outside and hits a huge three for us! We are up 39-37, and then both teams have two empty possessions when the coach's son for Grinnell hits a two to tie it up.

With 3:30 left in the game Grinnell takes a timeout, and I figure they might hold the ball. They don't; they come out and run a play that gets the ball in the middle of the lane, but we are right there to bottle it up, and Kaleb controls the defensive board.

We miss, so do they; Kaleb gets the board again. With 2:14 left we take a timeout, and it is still 39-39. But it didn't do any good; we turn the ball over, but they miss again, and B-Mo gets the rebound.

With 2:00 and our ball, we tell the kids we want just layups. Grinnell has been playing the zone, and they refuse to come out of it. They extend the zone a bit, but not enough to really put a lot of pressure on our offense, so we are able to hold the ball until :22 left in the game, and we take a timeout.

We talked about team fouls (both teams had three), and I thought they would come out and foul us to take time off of the board; they did. But once we got the ball in again they didn't foul, and Klarc took the ball at the hoop with the dribble drive. No less than three Grinnell kids came over to get a piece of the shot, but Klarc shot a high floater (we practice these) off the board that seemed to sit on the rim for about an hour (okay a few seconds) and then fell in. The place went nuts. Grinnell called a timeout with 4.5 seconds left.

We told the boys to foul—especially the dribbler—because we didn't want anyone going for a pass and getting beat deep. Clayton fouled, and the clock is down to 2.3 seconds. The next pass that came in from the sidelines found the Grinnell point guard at about 22 feet out. He spun and let go again. For what seemed an eternity, I thought, *Oh, no, that thing is going in, and we are going to get beat by one!* It didn't; it clanged off the side of the rim, and the win was ours.

Man, I saw a little emotion here. Kaleb is in Klarc's face (in a good way), Kirk is being Kirk, jumping up and down, and even Colin is chest bumping someone.

This was a good win for us. Almost better than a pretty win, this was a gritty win, a tough, grind-it-out win against a very good team. This is the type of win coupled with the win over Osky that can give a team the kind of belief it needs to become a good team.

No practice tomorrow!

Thursday, February 8, Practice #46
Colin, Dance, Zone Offense, Seals, On-Screens, Cutters, and the Special

Colin is sitting out practice, as he stayed home sick from school and wasn't allowed to workout. He watched from the sidelines.

Kirk hit me up in the locker room about the basketball team dancing for our dance-team instructor. The boys did it last year, and it was a big hit. I think (even though they would never admit it) the guys had a great time doing it. Kirk keeps telling me how none of the other guys want to do it either, but they didn't really say anything. They just stood there. It was Kirk doing all the complaining. I think he might be just a little bit nervous about this, but he and they will be a gigantic hit. The dance is actually done in the gym in front of a lot of people. But the people won't mind if the boys aren't perfect; in fact if they are perfect, I think most people will be disappointed.

I went up to see Mark today about our zone offense. Yesterday I suggested that we might possibly need to put in some different kind of zone offense because we were so bad against Grinnell with our current stuff. He said that he really believed it had more to do with execution than what we run.

Normally I would agree, but I got to thinking about it and if we would have gone with that theory defensively we would still be playing nothing but straight man, and I think our season would have gone down the toilet. I threw that out to him today. After a moment's hesitation he decided we might as well give it a shot. It's always easy for me to suggest something, but he is the one who gets the heat if it doesn't work. I just really believe that we need some kind of preset movement in our zone offense. We just refuse to move on our own. I've never been a fan of a patterned offense, but maybe these guys need it.

After warming up we went into the two-on-two feed-the-post drill. I stayed with Kirk's group. I really want him to learn to seal. He likes to try to seal with his hip, and I would love for him to use his butt. In order to make this type of seal he must work and use his feet to keep position and not lose contact; both his footwork and his work ethic right now are not where they need to be. He will get better.

Our shell drill is live, four-on-four and we are working on the on-ball screen. We are working from a defensive standpoint, but my point of emphasis is on the offensive end. I think that this would really help us in everything that we do offensively in both the man-to-man offense and the zone. After we go four-on-four we switch to our Partners offense and allow them to set other screens, but we are still looking for on-ball screens. I am also after our post players (Kirk in particular) to seal the defense.

One of the things we do wrong with our on-ball screens is that our dribbler who receives the screen doesn't attack the basket very well; he just dribbles off the screen sideways. It's ironic that Craig probably gets to the hoop better than anyone with the dribble, and he is not really a great dribbler; he just has a more aggressive attacking mind-set.

Our movement off the ball has not really been very good all year long. This is also true when one of our dribblers creates some penetration and forces an extra defender to come over and help. When the defender comes over in the help position, the man he was guarding may need to adjust his position slightly to be an open receiver. This is something that we really need to work on, as most of our guys just stand if their man leaves and don't move to get more open.

Our One-four zone offense is something that we are going to change slightly. We are doing this because B-Mo suggested it. We normally cross the posts through the lane when the ball changes from one side of the floor to the other. We are going to stop doing that, and we will have one post stay high and the other stay low. B-Mo felt like this would be a perfect spot for Kaleb to be high all of the time. He could step out and shoot or be like an extra guard in moving the ball. It makes sense to me, and I know Coach Core wants the boys to feel like they've been heard and appreciates the input that he has been seeking all year long.

We put in Cutters offense as a continuity offense for our zone attack. Normally I don't like continuity offenses because they are too predictable and players tend to run the offense and not really look to score. I want most of our teams to score and run the offense in that order. But with this team, we need movement. It looks okay. If nothing else it certainly has movement.

Out of this Cutters offense we put in a special play that is set up to try to get a dunk. The most likely candidate to do this for us is Kaleb, but B-Mo could probably do this as well. The first time we ran this without the defense knowing it was coming we didn't get a dunk, but we got a great tip-in off of the pass; it was pretty sweet.

Someday I may draw these up for you, but not today.

Friday, February 9, Practice #47
B-Mo, Dance, Floaters, Rebound Ring, Easy Pass, Jesse, Kirk, Blitz, Coach Pressure, and Mount Pleasant

B-Mo has some kind of electrical stimulator attached to his shoulder for today's practice. The idea is to make the muscles work without irritating them.

The boys didn't show up for dance practice last night. They said they forgot about it because we were out of practice early.

The floaters that we are working on today simulate the exact shot that Klarc scored the winning hoop with against Grinnell.

We did the 11-man drill, driving line, and shell.

When we went to the five-on-five situation we split the teams evenly and did our man offense. Neither team was especially sharp. We tried to run three stops in a row, but the offenses were so careless with the ball that it was more a gift to the defenses than any form of a stop.

Coach Core broke out the old rebound ring. It's a ring that fits over the hoop and makes it impossible to make a shot, so there is always a rebound to be had. Seems like a good invention, but it just doesn't work very well. The rebound doesn't really bounce like it should, and you are in danger of taking away the shooter's confidence since he can't ever make a shot. We didn't have to worry about that too long, because the thing wouldn't stay attached to the ring, so we stopped that drill.

We practiced three-on-three like we were in our triangle defense and then like we were in our match-up defense.

Then we went through all of our zone offenses against our one-two-two zone defense. This included the Cutters (that we are still in the process of learning) and both of our zone specials.

One of the things that almost all kids refuse to do is just simply to throw an easy pass. If one man is open 10 feet away and another is guarded 15 feet away, we (like many teams) want to force the ball into the guarded man, especially if it is a pass that might lead (the key word here is *might*) to a basket. Sometimes you just have to pass up those passes and make an easy and open pass and wait for the defense to break down rather than try to force something that results in a turnover.

Jesse just has to be reminded to play aggressively on the offensive end. He tends to be passive, and sometimes he gets so passive that the offense is playing four-on-five. Today looks to be one of those days. Coach Core gets on him about it, and he immediately responds with a basket attack.

Kirk is pretty much lost in the Cutters offense. The inside post-position is a lot easier to understand, and that is where he played most of the time yesterday. Today he is playing in a different spot, and he isn't yet accustomed to the cuts he must make.

We run press-and-press offense drill, and I talk to the boys about a slight change in the Blitz defense. We haven't gotten anything out of it yet, but I still think it could work; once again today it doesn't look very good. Maybe it's time to give up on this defense; it might just be my stubbornness.

After practice is over Coach is trying to explain to the kids that sometimes he purposely tries to put a type of pressure and anxiety on them so they can practice a response to it, just as you might during a game. I don't really agree with this type of thing. I've always tried to help kids get comfortable with the game and have fun with it as well. But just because I would do it differently doesn't make me right. Bobby Knight certainly has had success by pressuring his players. He is the winningest coach of all time and in the Hall of Fame. Let's see; who am I?

This is definitely an upcoming game that we really don't know much about our opponent. I think that last year's loss to Mount Pleasant (a non-conference opponent) was one of the worst of my career, since I've been at Pella High. They were athletic. But, last year was also the first time that we've lost to them. We shall see.

Saturday, February 10, Pella vs. Mount Pleasant, Game #18
Our Record: 11-6; Conference: 10-6

Expectations are high for Pella basketball, oftentimes too high. We as coaches also put the bar pretty high for our players. When you do that your expectations for your players can lead to sounding pretty darn negative. Here is the scoop; we've got some really good things going on with these kids.

I don't think I'd be too far off calling both Will and Kyle two of the nicest boys I've met in a while. Nate, if he were six foot four, would probably be an all-conference post player. Tyler used to be a guy that didn't ever play. Then he became the guy that we hoped wouldn't hurt the team when he came in but just break even. Now he is a guy that helps the team when he enters the game.

Zach and Tyler are each seniors that come to practice every day, work hard, and don't complain even though they rarely get on the floor. Andrew Barber has a great imagination—because of this he still thinks he has the ability to be one of the best players in the locker room. C.J. and Kirk, while good players, are also two of the guys that are terrific chemistry builders for this team. Justin and Clayton are two very fine athletes who probably don't put a lot of time into this game in the summer, but still (because of this athleticism) have the ability to contribute to the program. Klarc is the only post player that I can recall in my coaching career that has had the ability to move from post to point guard. Brandon Esterbrook, if he were to have Andrew's imagination, would be quite a shooter, because when he becomes the other team's star in practice—he is really hard to guard. Brock hasn't yet gotten used to the idea that he is an athlete. He has grown (a foot?) but still thinks of himself as a non-athlete; when the realization sets in that he can play he will be fine. Jesse, for a small guy, is probably our best at using the power-lay-up move; he almost always hits a guy with his body before he shoots and gets to the line because of it. B-Mo is Mr. Steady. He comes to practice and games and just goes about doing his job, night after night. Colin's stubbornness, that at one time was a drawback, has been channeled into toughness, especially when he has the ball. And Kaleb, who usually can't do anything right by the "coach's standards", leads us in rebounding, scoring, assists, and has gone from the guy looking not to guard anyone to the guy who doesn't mind taking the other team's best player.

I guess what I'm saying is that if you put on the green and the white, you can't be all bad even if sometimes we coaches mistakenly put out those vibes.

This is a Saturday afternoon game against non-conference opponent, Mount Pleasant.

We start in our half-court trap defense. I really don't like this (although it's not the kids' fault, since we haven't really talked about it) because when we do go man we don't know whom we've got. Mt. P starts man-to-man; I'd be surprised if we see anything else.

We ran Louisville, and Klarc set a nice back screen then popped out for a 15-foot hoop.

Our next two defensive possessions we ran zone—still no man-to-man, but we got lost in the break (I think because of the lack of match-up), and they hit a three on us.

B-Mo's spin to the basket after attacking from the high post gets us another basket. Klarc also scores on the next possession for us with the Magic move.

We've been running the Partners offense prior to this, but this time Klarc calls Duke for B-Mo. B-Mo drives the ball into the lane and then finds Craig standing in the corner, for a three.

Mt. P hit a three on us last time and this time we overreact to one of their outside shooters and left the middle of our zone open, and they dumped it down for two points. A rare poor pass from Klarc also turns into a lay-up for Mt. P. The score is 9-9 with 3:40 left in the first.

Klarc gets an assist to B-Mo, who buries a three. Clayton's help in the post creates a jump ball.

We scored last time when we were in Louisville, so we run it again. This time we get farther into it, and Clayton makes a nice entry pass to Kirk for a low-post two-pointer. Clayton then makes a nice defensive stand and forces a double dribble.

To give Klarc a breather now we've moved Kaleb to the point. So now, besides all of those other things that I've already mentioned, Kaleb is also a back-up point. Kaleb also pressures the man at the high post so that he cannot throw a high-low pass (a Mt. P. play that is a staple of their offense) and thus creates a three-second call on them for a turnover.

Clayton creates a foul on Mt. P but can't make either free throw. Kaleb then fouls with a charge. Our help side breaks down because we are too quick to try to cover on the outside with our man-to-man defense and not as good about helping on the inside; we do this because they have hit some outside shots.

The Creighton play, which oftentimes ends up in a three attempt, instead is a dribble drive by Kaleb that results in a basket and closes the score to 16-17 at the end of the first quarter. I heard one of the kids as they were coming into the huddle say that 17 are too many to give up in a quarter. (I like that attitude.)

Colin gets a basket off of a straight dribble drive from Duke; it sure seems like that happens a lot. His basket gives us an 18-17 lead. Mt. P does go zone, but after B-Mo's offensive board that allows us to keep the ball, Kaleb hits a three with an assist from Craig.

Our match-up zone is starting to take effect now, as they seem to be somewhat confused on the offensive end.

Klarc attacks the hoop but gets the ball jostled from his hands. He gets it back and Magics his way for another hoop. We've opened up a 23-17 lead after Mt. P turns the ball over, and they now take a timeout.

Colin ends up with a dribble drive and kick-out to B-Mo, who misses the shot, but Kaleb gets the board. Once again we run Louisville, and once again a really good post entry pass to Kaleb from Clayton results in a layup.

Louisville has been good to us, so we run it again, and this time Clayton gets an assist to B-Mo, who steps out to the top of the key and hits a three. So far this game the Mount Pleasant team has guarded B-Mo like he doesn't have range on his shot, which is a mistake that B-Mo is making them pay for.

Klarc got good pressure on the shot, and Kaleb got his second defensive board of the game, and we come down again and run Louisville. This time it's a layup for Colin. All of a sudden we are up 30-19 with three something left in the first half.

Kirk draws a charge out of our match-up zone. Kaleb takes over for Klarc at point to give Klarc a break, and then he gets the break as Klarc comes in for him.

Our new Georgetown play, while I know to be effective over the course of the years of experience, results in a turnover when we don't do a good job of pinning the defender out. We've gotten a little careless with the ball this quarter as we've shuffled our feet a couple of times, resulting in travels as well.

Once again the Mt. P player guarding B-Mo lets him shoot a three from the corner virtually unguarded—again that is a mistake for them. B-Mo also saves us on the defensive end as he got a hand on a pass that looked like a sure two for them.

Klarc needs to start his dribble a little earlier, as he gets called for the five count. But we came back with Fist, and Craig and Clayton bottle up a Mt. P player in a trap, and B-Mo makes the play on the ball for the pick. He sees Klarc ahead, who hits the layup and we go in at halftime with a lead of ten—35 to 25.

Mt. P came out on fire in the first quarter, as they shot 73% from the field. They cooled in the second quarter (hopefully that had something to do with our defense) as they shot 22%. Our shooting was good throughout the first half, as we shot 60% from the field. Craig had three rebounds and an assist while B-Mo had four boards and an assist. Klarc had a defensive board, as did Kaleb, and Clayton had three assists, Klarc chipped in with one as well.

Klarc starts off the third quarter with a tip away from the man holding the ball, and he gets a lay-up. Next Kaleb jumps in front of a pass and picks it off. Klarc attacks with the dribble and scores, and they take a timeout.

We (in my opinion) have gone to the trap defense a little too much in this quarter, and while it's not a bad defense it can cost us some points if we don't do it right. But Craig makes a nice curl cut to score two points.

After they fast-break a hoop against us Klarc goes right back at them with a fast-break of our own that turns into a basket and a foul. The score is 44-31. Colin attacks the middle of the lane and hits his runner from about 10 feet.

Jesse got a defensive board, and he and Clayton combined for a good hustle play that resulted in a turnover for the Panthers. Both Jesse and Clayton got a defensive board, and Craig, while not getting the offensive board, draws a foul as he was battling for it and got pushed from behind. Klarc also got a tip-away steal for us that turns into a break and a three-pointer for Kaleb (Tyler T set an awesome screen to get K open for that shot).

With two minutes left in the third we are up 50-38. K gets us the ball back after Craig out hustles everyone to the loose ball. This turns into a pull-up jump shot for Kaleb at the end of the third, and we are up 52-43, and we will start with the ball in the fourth quarter.

The Panthers shot 64% that quarter while we shot 55%. They might have one or two offensive boards for the game so far; I'd guess we have around 8 or 10.

Bulldog ends up in an open look for B-Mo, but he can't connect. Now Colin gets an offensive board. B-Mo keeps the ball alive again with an offensive board. Coach Core has stressed going to the boards, and it is paying off.

Our defensive zone is getting to be pretty good at matching up even when we aren't in our match-up.

The officials, I think, have been pretty good, and they are young. That is a good thing. They have called it a bit soft compared to a state-tournament game, however.

Klarc gets a basket and a foul as he attacks the lane again. Defensively Klarc got another defensive board as Clayton made a nice close out on the offensive shooter forcing a missed shot.

It's 57-48 when Kaleb gets fouled attacking the middle of the lane. Klarc gets the call as he again goes to the rim in what could have been either a block or a charge. He makes two free throws. Colin gets the ball back for us with a tip away, and Kaleb has added to his defensive rebounding total by getting back-to-back rebounds. Kaleb also had a very unselfish play as he too made a Magic move into the lane, and rather than shoot it set his teammate up for a wide open three; unfortunately we missed the shot, but it was an unselfish play, nonetheless.

Colin gets another defensive board, and as the game is drawing down we start to get a little more patient with the ball. Kaleb set an on-ball screen and then slipped to the baseline, where Craig, after using the screen with the dribble, kicks it back out to him, and K knocks down yet another three.

Now Kaleb runs a really good curl cut, and he hits a jumper right in the middle of the lane.

Man, when there is a timeout (the score is 64-48) the first two guys off the bench seem to always be Clayton and Kirk.

We've played much more zone and match-up zone and a lot less man and trapping man in the fourth quarter, and I really think that has benefited us. B-Mo steals the ball, gets fouled, and strokes one of two.

Clayton, with good pressure on the ball, forces a turnover, and Colin gets doubled by the defense but is tough enough to get it out to Klarc. Klarc attacks with the dribble to the baseline and finds Kirk under the hoop. Mt. P wants him to earn it from the free-throw line as they foul him, and he knocks in both free throws (I think he might be 100% for the year).

With a 67-48 lead Klarc secures another defensive board for Pella. Brandon Esterbrook also gets a defensive board, as the guys that haven't played get an opportunity now. Z-Mo comes into the game, and Brandon, who had been fouled, makes both free throws. Tyler Linn is in as well, as Klarc gets another tip away and is fouled. Before he leaves the game he hits one more free throw. Justin is in now as well. With about 1:00 left we also get Nate into the game.

A good hustle play by Brandon forces a miss, and Justin gets a defensive board. Nate gets a good look in the middle of the lane but misses the shot. Justin again gets a board to keep the ball alive, as does Tyler Linn, who also gets a shot up as the game expires. The final score is 70-52, Pella High.

We gave up 17 in the first quarter and 35 for the rest of the game. In fact, in the fourth quarter they shot 25%.

Monday, February 12, Practice #48
Enough Traveling, Stance, Attacking Dribble, B-Mo, and Rover Defense

Coach Core has seen enough of the traveling call that haunts this team, and his intent to start practice is to do away with it once and for all. We start without the ball and work on moving forward without a false step. We work first with one foot then another. He has the kids partner up and watch each other to make sure their steps are correct. Then we went full-court, working with and without the ball, until finally all of the players go to a basket and work on performing dribble penetration without first moving their feet. That is the longest period of time I think we've ever spent working on this, but I think it will make a difference.

The driving-line drill is a live version of what the kids have been working on in regards to their attack on the basket with the dribble. Defensively we still want the ball out of the paint.

Our defensive stances have never been very good, and I mean all year long. Coach has the boys line up in the mass-slide drill to work on getting into a low stance. This stance thing to me is really a matter of want. To me it goes like this: the defender must want to stop his opponent, and he must want to do it without help. In order to do this he must be in an athletic stance to give him the most advantageous position he can be in—it will make him quicker. If he wants to make the stop, he will get down. If it isn't that important to him he probably won't be as far down because this is not the most comfortable position to be in. I'd like to think this drill helped, and maybe it did if for no other reason than a reminder that position is important, but I really think this is one of the reasons that we haven't been a very good man-to-man defensive team; the simple fact is we just aren't as concerned about man-to-man individual stops as we should be to play great individual defense.

Our on-ball screen shell is done for two reasons. One is continued work on hedging out on a dribbler (something we still don't do well) and continued emphasis on man-to-man defense. Our zone stuff has been working, but I think it has been working because of the fact that we continue to work on principles of the man-to-man. If we had started the other way around I don't think we would be very good at any defense. And two, we would like the boys offensively to "turn the corner" when they get a screen. We tend to dribble off a screen in a lateral mode rather than attacking the basket, and that is not aggressive enough.

B-Mo just took a charge in practice and came up bleeding. His cut is under his eye. It looks to me like he will need a stitch or two in order to close the wound; yet another injury (although minor) to our banged-up group. Kirk had been complaining before practice that his back was hurting but he wanted to practice and has. He says he is headed to the chiropractor tomorrow morning.

We worked on a variety of things as practice progressed. We worked on our press and our press offense; we worked on matching up out of both the zone and the triangle.

Then Coach Core put in yet another defense. We are literally going to not guard a man and use his defender as a "floater", a guy that really can't make a mistake. He can do anything, he can start showing some guard towards his man and then trap or look to pick off or become a one-man zone. We ran two possessions of something that I just can't believe would work, but in those two possessions it sure seemed to—now that is a defense I've never seen before, and I've been around this game for a long time. I'm not convinced, but if it works, I'm willing to give it a chance.

We also worked on Georgetown and Cutters and then did the one break drill. And then finally we worked on the end-of-quarter situations. Over the course of the year this is something that has really paid off; we are way better at this situation than we were before.

This practice was short but really had a positive feel to it. The kids have played well lately, and we have a game tomorrow against Centerville. Winning a few games certainly adds to a positive frame of mind, and it showed during this practice.

Tuesday, February 13

Initially we had a two-hour late start today because it snowed last night. Then that late start turned into no school. And now I just got a call from Mark telling me that the game is called off. We won't be able to make this up, as there is just very little time left in the season, so we are down to just two games left in the regular season.

Practice is at 3:00 today for those who can make it into school.

Tuesday, February 13, Practice #49
Tyler Linn, Layups, K-Pull Ups, Six Stitches, Scrimmages, and New Stuff

We started practice today at 3:00 since there was no school, and everyone made it except for Tyler Linn, who was still snowed in.

Brunner layups was our first drill, and as we were doing them I realized how much we had used these types of layups this year. Both the Brunner and the

Magic layup work have really paid off; we even won a game the other day when Klarc hit the floater against Grinnell. B-Mo has used this move almost all year long, and Klarc has used it for some time now, but the guy I see using it more and more is Kaleb.

Kaleb has also shot more pull-up jump shots than before. He is really starting to expand his game offensively. Kaleb has always been a good shooter from the outside, and during the middle of the season he got better at attacking all the way to the hoop, but now he is adding a third dimension, one that most guys don't do really well at the high school level, and that is the pull-up.

B-Mo came back to practice today with six stitches under his eye; six! I'd never make it as a doctor. B-Mo said that he didn't want to go to the doctor again (yesterday) but I told him I thought he should go because I was afraid it would split open again if he didn't get it fixed. I told him I thought maybe he'd get a stitch, but he'd better just go anyway—six stitches: I was close.

Tyler just showed up to practice. All these reasons not to come that would have been excusable with no questions asked, and he came anyway. He came in spite of the fact that he would probably not get any meaningful game time, and he is a senior with some talent. He came, and I really appreciate his attitude.

Klarc, before practice, indicated that he thought the work that they did yesterday in making the correct step without traveling was beneficial, so we did some more of that today, although we didn't spend nearly as much time working on it. We did carry over the concept, however, as we went immediately into the driving line drill that allowed some live attack steps similar to what we had just done.

From this point we went in to a series of three scrimmages. Each scrimmage was scored the same way in that the teams were awarded regular points on baskets but got no points if the shot was a "bad" shot regardless of if it was made or not. The teams also lost points if they turned it over. The guy in charge of determining bad shots was Andrew Barber. He does a good job with this. He is also the "spy" who stats people every night. He uses his judgment many times, and the kids are willing to accept his evaluation. That says something for both him and them.

The teams were evenly split and the scrimmages were about four minutes in length. All three scrimmages were pretty competitive. I liked Kaleb's pull-up jumpers that he made (at least two or three of them). I also liked the way Craig played. His confidence in his ability to score has grown over time. Many of his points came against B-Mo, who I consider a pretty fair defender. I was also really pleased with Tyler Terlouw. Not only did he rebound the ball well, he sealed on offense, and he also made three of four free throws. Tyler will not be with us on Friday, as he has a church duty. I like his priorities; I know he feels bad, but it is okay.

Mark feels like these guys have responded well to new stuff. He thinks that they may need the different things we do to wake them up and keep them interested. Coach Core added a new out-of-bounds play that is set in the same formation that our other out-of-bounds plays are run from. And I added a wrinkle to the Louisville play. The kids seem to be calling that play more and more, and we are continuing to have some success with it.

Wednesday, February 14, Practice #50
Sophs, Kaleb's Free Throws, Turn the Corner, Blitz, Kirk, and Dancing

Practice today is a scrimmage against the sophomore team. We determined prior to practice that the varsity should work on the things that we don't do very often in our games and in practice. We have played a lot of zone lately for instance, so today we didn't want the kids to run very much zone but work on some of our other defenses. We also wanted to practice many of our set plays and specials.

The sophomores have a nice team; they have good athletes and will be a good challenge for the varsity. It is nice for both groups to beat on somebody else rather than each other, especially late in the season. Today's practice is not an all-out scrimmage, but it is a controlled scrimmage. By that I mean that the coaches will call out the defenses and the offenses that they want to practice against, and the other team will comply. We will also stop and replay situations that don't go well.

Prior to practice I saw Kaleb down at the other end of the court shooting lots of free throws. While he hasn't been a poor free-throw shooter he has not been the outstanding shooter from the line that he has been in the past. I've been debating the merits of talking with Kaleb about his free throws. If a coach over talks something it may plant a seed into the mind of his athlete, and it may be a bad seed (like you are a bad free-throw shooter) but if the coach knows something that could help the athlete and doesn't share it then the coach isn't doing the job he could do. To me the psychology of coaching a player is much more important than the Xs and Os of the sport.

My decision to speak with Kaleb was based upon the fact that he seemed to be spending an inordinate amount of time practicing his free throws, so I figured it must have been bothering him. I also felt like the timing would be good because I wouldn't have much time to talk with him, and then it wouldn't seem like such a big deal, and I wouldn't "over coach" him.

I told Kaleb that I felt like he was aiming his free throws. I based that upon the rhythm of his shot in games as compared to his rhythm in practice. While in games it is slow, in practice it is quicker. The difference is not much, but I do see it. Also, almost all of his misses are short in games while his practice free throws are good. I told all of these things to him in the briefest manner I could while trying to make sure that he understood what I meant. Finally, I just told him that he is either going to make it or miss it, but aiming it and trying to guide it on the way will do him no good—then I walked away.

Prior to scrimmaging and after warming up we did work on post-entry passes and trying to do a better job of sealing the defensive player off, and we also worked on the on-ball screen. Normally working on the on-ball screen is a defensive move for us, but today and for the last few times we've done this drill it has been more about turning the corner with the dribble and being aggressive from an offensive standpoint.

Last time we scrimmaged the sophomore squad we ran for turnovers. We started this scrimmage running as well.

We tried the Blitz defense today again. It was ineffective. The first time we ran this defense we got a steal, and it worked perfectly. Since then (regardless of some of the changes we've made to improve it) it hasn't come close to working. I suggested to both the kids and Coach Core that maybe it is time to give up on this particular defense—there was some surprise that I saw register on their faces, but there wasn't a lot of opposition to the move; that should tell me something.

After our preliminary wave of turnovers we seem to have stopped doing that.

I just don't think Kirk wants to work hard enough either sealing his man or when we run our coverage when we are in the zone defense. I don't believe for a minute that this is an intentional move on Kirk's part; I just think that he feels like he is working really hard when he (in my opinion) isn't and has a lot more to give. That is part of coaching; helping kids to see that they can give more.

After practice the kids were talking about the possibility of the dance performance that is available to them. There was a lot of wishy-washy responses to the possibility of them dancing. Some are scared to death, some that went through it the year before had fun and would like to do it again, but are afraid to admit that—they had fun dancing; guys are just way too macho to admit that.

Thursday, February 15, Practice #51
NC Drill, Blitz, Duke for B-Mo, G'tn, Tyler T, and End of Quarters

We warmed up with partner shooting, some footwork as a reminder to the players to keep their feet still when they were faking or prior to attacking the basket, and then we did full-court one-on-one. This was followed by layups and then floaters. We then went to power layups and driving lines.

The shell drill was next, and then for the first time in a long time we did the NC drill. The NC drill was a staple of our early season practices, but as we went along we discovered that this team might just be better in the quarter-court than the full-court. It's important though to have the ability to run if we need to, just the threat of running against an opponent helps to keep them off of the offensive boards. If the opposition feels that we will never run they will crash the offensive boards with no thought of getting back to prevent our break.

During the press-press offense portion of the practice it comes up occasionally that there is a delicate balance of continuing to attack the basket when beating the press and pulling the ball back out when we don't have an advantage. In today's practice Craig had a two-on-one advantage when the ball came to him, and rather than attack the hoop C.J. took that ball to the corner baseline and then got trapped there by the defense. He came out and knew immediately what he had done; now he has to realize before doing it, not after, what he can and cannot do.

I spoke with Coach Core about the Blitz defense and apologized to him about yesterday when I announced to the kids that maybe we shouldn't run this defense. I try not to do anything that might appear as a conflict of thinking between Mark and me, and I felt bad that I hadn't talked to him privately before practice and before I said what I said. He, too, didn't seem to mind not running the Blitz and seemed to think that maybe we got the same thing out of the scramble defense. Interestingly enough in today's practice Klarc called the

Blitz when I thought it was a dead issue, and if the kids don't have confidence in it, then maybe I shouldn't either. Hmmmm.

We've been running Duke for B-Mo. It seems like it gets him more involved; it also means that if we can get Kaleb to set a screen for B-Mo that B-Mo will probably be open, because Kaleb's man won't leave him to help towards B-Mo. Well, today as we were running it I asked Coach to call it for Kirk—really just to get Kirk to move more in the offense. Funny thing happened, Kirk not only moved more but he moved very wisely. In fact, this clever movement that he showed might be because smart movement means less work on his part. Regardless of the reason—he and his teammates looked good when they ran this for Kirk. Maybe we've found a new offensive weapon.

As I've mentioned, Georgetown over the years has been one of our best offensive set plays against a zone. This group doesn't perform this play nearly as well (although it is early in the formative time with their experience in the play) and I think it is once again because we just don't do a really good job of sealing defensive players. Today we tried to help show the kids that this isn't only a play to get the ball to certain players inside, but it is a play that sets up well for offensive boards and that the outside guys must look to shoot if there is no interior pass available. If we don't seal well enough to get a pass, then the defenders have fought over the top of our interior screens, and that means that now we have inside position to rebound the ball.

Tyler Terlouw has been such a pleasant surprise; he reminds me almost daily of how pleased I have been with his play. He does seals as well as anybody and better than most, he tries to rebound and defend, and he almost never takes a play off but gives just about all he has. What's not to like? He is not a greatly skilled player, and he isn't really big, but he definitely does the blue-collar stuff.

While we are working on the end-of-quarter situations (by the way we have really improved upon this aspect of the game) Klarc got trapped. His response was to turn his back to the men trapping him and protect the ball with his body. The protecting the ball idea is a good one. Turning his back to the trappers is a bad one. When he turned his back he not only lost vision to his teammates, but this is also an invitation to the trappers to close up on him. Rather than turn, he must stay faced up to the men trapping and try to step through the trap with the dribble or pass by the defenders while pivoting or stepping at the defenders to create space.

Chapter 17—Nine Wins in a Row, Anyone?

Friday, February 16, Pella at PCM, Game #19
Our Record: 12-6

PCM is a 2A school, but it will be a team that is well coached. Their overall program has also been very successful as well. It was not too long ago, if memory serves me correctly, that they won a state championship. We were fortunate to beat them even when we had our back-to-back state championship teams at Pella.

Colin starts the game by going down on the floor and fighting for a loose ball; that is something you might not have seen out of him a couple of years ago. Prior to this play both Colin and Kaleb started the game with steals.

Our opening possession is a multi-pass possession that ends up in a dribble drive and pull up for Klarc. PCM opens the game in man defense, with #51, their post defender, guarding Klarc at the top of the key. This #51 is not a really tall player, about six foot three or four, but he is well built and very aggressive.

We decided that we needed to open in our man defense to make sure that we are matched up when the need arises to play man defense. Both teams are showing patience on the offensive end of the floor.

We got the ball in to Kirk at the blocks, where he has spent more time since his injury than before. Kirk is one of our best post passers, and he proved it as he fired the ball out to his big brother at the top of the key, and Kaleb bangs in a three.

Jesse and Clayton combined to create a turnover for PCM as Jesse bumped his man up to prevent penetration into the paint, and Clayton came over to pressure the dribble as well.

Kaleb spins (Brunner) from about 15 feet out at the free-throw line and gets all the way to the hoop for two. PCM has seen enough and calls a timeout.

Our next score came from Klarc, who attacks the basket with the dribble and scores as well as getting fouled. In addition Kaleb registers another foul on PCM, as he too attacks the hoop with the dribble.

Assist from Kaleb to B-Mo, who knocks down a three from the corner. Kaleb also knocked the ball away on the defensive end, but we got an unlucky break as the ball ended up in their hands under the hoop for a score.

Tyler Linn gets a little time on the floor with the score 13-10, with about 2:00 left in the first. PCM already has three offensive boards, and this is where they are doing most of their damage to us so far. In fact Kaleb's defensive board is the first we've had this game, and we are deep into the quarter.

Klarc's penetration off the break sets up Colin for a three-pointer. But even against our zone PCM's straight line dribble drive creates a rotation that Klarc must cover, and this opens up for a three-pointer against us.

Kaleb is really being aggressive with the dribble, and once again makes PCM pay as he drives, spins, and hits a six-foot shot.

At the end of the quarter we made a nice defensive play as the Mustangs were going to hold for the last shot, but we came out of a zone defense and jumped immediately into Fist to create a turnover, as B-Mo stepped in to pick off a pass. We, however, couldn't capitalize on it, and the quarter ends with our lead at 18-13.

We did get the ball back again, and ran Louisville; we didn't get anything immediately out of it. In fact we set it up and ran it again, but this time B-Mo made a dive to the basket and then received a down screen that opened him up for an assist from Klarc, as B-Mo sealed the deal with a three.

Our opening possession of match-up was not a thing of beauty, as we just simply didn't get matched up properly, and they hit a three right back at us. Clayton had a pretty Magic move but just missed the shot; luckily B-Mo got the ball back for us, as he was there to take a charge; it's 21-16 us, very early in the second.

We ran Duke for Klarc a couple of times just to try to move #51 and make him work on the defensive end. We came up dry with this, but it did move the PCM big boy. Alas, we still aren't matched up on the other end, and for a second time they drop in a three.

PCM went on quite a run against us; our five-point lead became a two-point deficit. But Klarc changed all that as we ran an out-of-bounds play for him that resulted in a fade-away shot in the middle of the lane for two.

Kaleb has a nice play on the defensive end by bothering a shot and then on the offensive end he penetrates into the lane and finds "the Zirk" (that would be Kirk) under the hoop with a nice pass that results in two made free throws for the big man.

Funny how this works; it seems like oftentimes I will write about someone doing something good, and then that same person comes back and does something else good. Jesse just did that, as at one end he got a defensive board and at the other end he ended up with an offensive board.

Colin saves Kirk's bacon as he comes over in help to force a miss from Kirk's man, and Kaleb pulls down a defensive board.

Defensively, since our little fiasco of not being matched up, we have played a bit more straight man-to-man defense. Once again PCM tried for the last shot of the quarter; once again we went to Fist, and that resulted in a Zirk block, and then a defensive board by the Kirk.

B-Mo had an unusual assist as he dribbled to the middle of the floor about to the top of the key and found Kaleb two or three steps behind the three-point arc, who then buried the double-deep three.

B-Mo screens in the defensive man, and Colin is the beneficiary as he hits at about 15.

While we initially didn't react very well to the flex cut that PCM ran, Jesse not only helped prevent a back cut but then recovered to his man and forced another turnover, the second turnover he has forced for the game. Jesse's minutes aren't heavy, but they have been very productive this game.

Klarc's last two plays of the first half were two I'm sure he would like to forget, as he got caught in a trap once and stepped back for an over and back call, and then the next time down threw the ball backwards to cause another over and back call. This is so unusual for Klarc to make these kinds of plays, that when he does, it becomes (unfairly to him) a glaring mistake. My feeling is that without him stepping up to play the point this season we would have been in deep chocolate.

At half we are up 30-27.

At halftime we talked about being more aggressive on the boards. PCM already had four offensive put-backs. We also talked about handling a screen that they were setting along the baseline that was giving our guys some trouble. Finally we talked about continuing our persistence of passing on the offensive end to get easy looks at the basket. But in my mind being more physical, especially on the boards, was a big key. So it just so happened that B-Mo and I were the last out of the locker room together, so on the way out I asked, "B-Mo how many defensive rebounds do you have?"

He replied immediately without looking at me, "None," and just kept walking—he knew he had to do better, and I would be surprised if he didn't.

Prior to the game, I had asked the boys how they were going to handle the mistakes that were bound to occur over the course of the game. They responded that they would just put them behind, and they would forget them and go forward. Now prior to the start of the second half, with Klarc sitting on the bench, I asked him the same question, and he looked at me and made a motion with his hand that went over and back of his head and he said, "Put it behind me and don't worry about it."

B-Mo starts the second half with a defensive rebound. That didn't take long.

An on-ball screen is such a good move for us, and I'd like to see more of it, as Craig gets one for Colin.

Klarc also responded with a good play as he picks off a pass and gets fouled, so we take the ball out of bounds. Craig gets one of the few offensive boards that we get—but we are shooting well so there will be fewer offensive rebounds to get.

What appears to be a good block by B-Mo turns out to be a foul, as he is now in some foul trouble. Tyler Terlouw is at his church retreat, and Kirk has been getting more minutes because of it. With 5:30 left in the third it's tied 30-30.

PCM ran a nice special against our zone defense (one we may have to steal). The ball started at the left wing, and our defense shifted accordingly. Our post players were trying to prevent an entry pass into their post by playing both in front of him and behind him. When the ball was cross-courted by a wing's skip pass to the opposite side wing, our bottom defender (this was a wing man who had dropped from his defensive wing position into the opposite side baseline area) had to run out to cover so he wouldn't give up an uncontested three-pointer. At that same time an offensive player away from the ball side in the baseline area was setting a screen on our post, who had come over to help double their ball-side post. The offensive post, who had started on the ball side, then curled around the screen and was wide open, because our man was being screened. It was an easy pass inside and a layup; pretty cool if it wouldn't have happened to us.

Lots and lots of ball movement by PHS ends up in a miss, but it also ends up in another offensive board for us by Kaleb, who puts it back in.

Kaleb's next offensive spin move (Magic) looks like a terrific move down the middle of the lane, but they called it a travel. Wow, that was pretty!

We thought we could run more match-up zone in the second half, so we reviewed whom we would be matching up with in different situations. We are running it when B-Mo makes a nice pick off of a lob pass. I think that pass occurred because PCM thought we were man-to-man, but since we weren't B-Mo was right there for an easy interception.

Craig's good hustle-play after a loose ball maintains possession of the ball for us. That one won't show up in the box score, but it was a really good play.

Colin makes the extra pass to Kaleb, and he slapped in a three. Kaleb is getting some space for his three because he has shown his ability to drive, and the defender is in a tough spot now, as he doesn't know if he should come out to guard the long shot or stay back to take away the drive.

The PCM gym is an older gym, but it is one that is fun to play in, as the fans sit close to the court on both sides. It is loud, and it is full for tonight's game.

Our next possession of match-up is just plain great, as it takes PCM forever to even attempt anything resembling an attack. Instead Kaleb ends up with a steal and two foul shots as he was fouled in his break away attempt. We are up 38-32.

These officials have done a good job in a tough environment.

This time we are in straight zone, and again I think PCM misreads the defense and attempts another lob, that again B-Mo makes the pick. Klarc comes down and penetrates off of the steal for about an eight-foot banker.

Kaleb pressures the PCM shot and creates a miss, and B-Mo has decided he is going to rebound this half, as he secures another defensive rebound for PHS.

Kaleb continues to create foul trouble for the Mustangs as he draws a blocking foul. B-Mo's on-ball screen helps get Klarc free, who draws defensive help away from Colin, and Colin bangs in another three.

Again they try to get the last shot of the quarter, and this time they draw a foul against us, and it's 43-41 at the end of three.

We tried Rover, but Colin fouled right away out of it the first time and then ended up late in his recovery from an out-of-bounds play, so it didn't work again, and now Colin has three fouls. That is the end of that defense for this game.

Kaleb, Klarc, and Colin, all with an extra pass, results in another three for B-Mo; Colin gets the only assist. It's too bad they all couldn't have gotten one on that play.

Our Open play results in a three from Kaleb in the corner with an assist from Klarc. PCM calls time—we have a six-point lead.

We come out and play match-up, and Craig makes a steal. Next defensive possession we are man, and Kirk ends up with a steal. Kirk also keeps the ball alive with a tip, and brother Kaleb finishes it off with a put-back basket and a free throw to boot. All of a sudden we are up nine, and they have some foul trouble.

Kaleb's next defensive board is probably about number four or five for him now. He also had a nice play on the offensive end. We've been running Partners offense, and Kaleb faked going high over a screen and instead cut baseline wide-open for an entry pass from Jesse for two more.

It's funny in a sad sort of way, because number 15 for PCM only drove the ball and never shot from out, and he always drove to his right, but regardless of that we just couldn't seem to get that stopped up. They made a run at us, really because of him or our lack of ability to control his play.

We've gotten better about our screen angles, and we are now starting to get the ball to the middle of the floor more.

Colin penetrates with the dribble and pitches the ball out to B-Mo, who tallies his fourth three of the night. Here we go again; now Colin (back-to-back good plays) gets a defensive board.

Kaleb's decision to throw the ball back out from the baseline turns out well for us, as it sets up Klarc's penetration to the hoop. He makes both throws.

We have played quite a bit of man-to-man in the fourth quarter, and Klarc is coming off of #23 looking to help against other PCM players. It seems to be working, as he has been in position a number of times to assist.

With 2:10 left we are up 59-48.

PCM must come out to press us now, and we respond well, as we actually have people flashing the middle, and our guards are getting them the ball there. We are also doing a great job of understanding clock (time and score). We are moving the ball, staying out of trap areas, and looking to attack the basket. We are not necessarily looking to score, but to draw and dish back out. They foul when we are up ten, and Clayton goes to the line and makes both. Next time Klarc gets fouled on his way to the basket and makes one of two. They do find #23 this time, and he notches a three to make it 62-54.

Kaleb's turn to get fouled, and he makes two.

The final score is 64-55. That's seven in a row! This was a good win over a good program against a team that had won four in a row.

By the way, I'm not sure how many free throws Kaleb shot, but it was a bunch, and he didn't miss any!

After the game the two older Korver boys, Klayton (from Drake), and Kyle (from the Philadelphia 76ers) are invited in to the locker room to help Kaleb celebrate a milestone for any player: his 1000th point in his high-school career.

I'm not sure I made 1000 points when I was in high school even if you counted all of my shots in the driveway with no one on me.

I talked with both Klayton, who I do see occasionally, and then Kyle, who I rarely see anymore since he doesn't get home much; it was nice to see them both.

I was just about ready to leave the gym when I found out the bus was in the ditch while all the players were standing around waiting for their ride back to Pella. I'm sure glad we drove ourselves over; Coach Core didn't look too happy.

No meeting and no practice tomorrow.

Thursday, February 19, Practice #52
Teachers, George, One-Four Offense, Washington, and the 20 Wrinkle

Today's practice will be short because we have parent-teacher's meetings today.

We did some shooting and ball handling and then warmed up with some one-on-one full-court play.

We then went right into our zone offensive plays. We are anticipating that Washington (our next opponent) will play both man and zone defenses. During this time we put in the zone play that PCM hurt us with. Like I said, most coaches will steal things from other coaches that work against their team. We weren't nearly as successful with this as PCM was. Kaleb immediately knew that this was the PCM play; that was nice to see that he recognized what had happened to him in the last game.

We will call this "George" in honor of the Georgetown play that we currently run with similar screens and cuts.

While I'm on the subject, I went to watch our girls play the other night, and they also run the One-four zone offense that we use against the zone. What I found was that they sure run it a lot better than we do. It just goes to show that it is the personnel that make your plays work, and different personnel have different abilities—therefore the same plays that had worked the year before or maybe even for decades may not work as well for your current team.

We believe that Washington's defense will try to intimidate by coming out really hard in a man-to-man defense for the first couple of passes—looking to pick off passes or pressure dribblers. And if our guys are shook by this early pressure the ball could well end up in a lay-up going the other way. But oftentimes these types of defenses will get much less formidable after three of four passes because they run out of gas both physically and mentally to play this hard. This was obvious as we had the white team members try to simulate the Washington defense. We did throw it away a few times, but if we just remained composed, we usually got something good.

Washington also runs a one-four offense, but they run it against a man defense. To give us our best chance to defend, the offense we will need to try to influence the point guard one direction or the other, so we will know which side is the weak side and where our help will come from. We will also play soft (not pressure) the passes to the wings so that they cannot backdoor cut us as Osky did the first time we played them. Washington has an outstanding athlete #22 (going to the University of Iowa to play football) who averages 16 points a game and is their leading rebounder. We will start with Klarc on him.

Number 22 starts on the wing in the one-four set. One of the ways that any defense can help contain a scorer is to limit his touches. The fewer times the scorer can catch it, the fewer times he has to shoot it. I agree with this theory. However in tomorrow's game #22 will be playing the wing, and if the ball goes away from him to the other wing, the man guarding #22 (Klarc) will need to sink down to the hoop to become the help defender, thus taking him off of #22. Just as a thought I suggested to Mark that maybe, because Klarc might get buried in screens trying to recover back to #22, we should force the ball towards #22. This would go away from the idea of limiting his touches, but it would put him in a position that would have our attention, as he would have the ball. This is just a thought to save for emergencies tomorrow night.

Since I've been at Pella High, Washington always seems to have outstanding athletes. This year seems to be no different. We have played four common opponents. Back in December Washington lost to Grinnell by eight and beat Knoxville by 16. Then in January Washington beat Mount Pleasant by 13 and lost to Pella Christian by six. Washington's record appears to be very similar to ours. It looks like we are in for a war. We have had good luck against them in the past, but got beat last year. We will need to play well on their home floor to win.

We added a wrinkle to our 20 out-of-bounds play—again it didn't seem to work really well. But honestly, this group seems to thrive on new things, so we will probably come back to it again and may even try it tomorrow.

Chapter 18—The End of the Regular Season

Tuesday, February 20, Game #20, Pella at Washington
Our Record: 13-6

The gym is one of those old-time gyms that reek of history. Old track records are up on the entrance walls; pictures of past athletes are up as well. The gym itself is one of those that you can hardly hear yourself talk when the crowd roars—the acoustics of that era weren't so good; a good-sized crowd is here to see the game. By the way, this is Adam Miller's old stomping ground, and his brother still plays for Washington.

The tip is a forerunner of things to come, as there is a scrum for the loose ball. They finally come up with the ball. With pressure on the shot by Klarc, they miss a close-in runner.

Washington opens in a two-three zone defense. This zone is not a packed-in zone but one that extends into the passing lanes. They are quick aggressive athletes.

With 5:48 left in the first quarter both teams are looking for their first points. Craig is off to a good start with a steal and a defensive board, and Klarc has drawn a foul on Washington's team. Craig now gets an offensive rebound and is fouled, making one of two throws to get a score on the board.

We opened man-to-man to make sure we were matched up and then went to our one-two-two zone defense.

Washington has always been a team of plays and offense. They seem to have dozens of them. I think our league in general spends more time on the defensive end while their league must work a little harder on the offensive end, because Mount Pleasant (another league member) executes offensively very well too.

Klarc finds Kirk for a baseline hoop and the first basket of the game. We are still pitching a shutout when Clayton makes a great hustle play, diving on the floor for a loose ball that turns into a pass to Kirk, who hits Craig under the hoop for a basket and a foul. So what looked like a sure basket for Washington turns into three points for us, thanks to Clayton.

Kaleb already has four defensive rebounds as we are heading down to the end of the first quarter. Washington's post player, who really isn't one of their scorers, has seen enough of our defense and has decided a couple of times to step out and launch—without any success by the way. Speaking of "D," I've seen a really nice hedge on a dribbler by Jesse, and Craig has closed out and pressured a shooter into a miss already.

B-Mo controls an offensive rebound on his own miss to keep us alive, this turns into an assist from Kaleb into Jesse right under the hoop for two more. We are up 8-0 with 1:30 left in the first quarter (Washington averages 60 a game).

Craig throws a good interior pass to Kaleb that results in a 10-0 lead after K makes both of his free throws. But they do score over Colin, who was in good position—the guy just made a tough shot, with about :30 left in the quarter.

Klarc banked in a three-pointer from deep at the buzzer to put us up 13-4 at the end of the first quarter; and we will get the ball back to start the second quarter.

B-Mo gets a jumper at the free-throw line with an assist from Kaleb. Our next hoop also came courtesy of an assist, this one from Colin to Kirk. Yet another assist from Klarc to Kaleb results in a three-pointer.

After they hit a three almost right back at us the lead shrinks to 20-9 with about five minutes left in the second quarter. Soon after this there is a very poor no-call by the official when Klarc drew a foul on a charge that wasn't called. The officials have done well, but that was a poor call. It happens.

Unfortunately, with about four minutes left, Klarc picks up his second foul, and that hurts because it means that Kaleb has to play point. This allows the defense to focus more on Kaleb, because he has the ball even as he comes up the floor.

Colin scores two free throws with two-and-a-half minutes left in the second to make it 22-14 as they have been on a bit of a run.

One of the things we asked Kaleb to improve upon is his ability to hit a pull-up jump shot, and he shows his improvement, as he pulls up from about six feet for two. In the past that probably would have been a charge.

The score is 24-16 at halftime. We have been careful with the ball in the first half, and they have also slowed their offense, trying to get some good looks. I would credit our defense for that rather than anything that they have intentionally done. Number 22 has really been a non-factor this half.

Washington started the half with the same play that got them a layup in the first half. It's really been about the only easy hoop they've gotten.

It's a simple play that we just didn't handle very well. Washington runs their one-four-high-set, and the point guard passes to the wing and cuts off of the post looking for a return pass from the wing. If that doesn't happen he gets a double down screen by the opposite post and wing and pops out looking for a pass and an open shot. In the meantime, the post that set the initial screen for the point guard, screens for the wing with the ball, and they run a pick and roll to the basket. Our defensive players guarding the guys setting the double down-screen men should have helped against the wing's drive but they were late, and Washington scored.

Washington's defense is really more a steal defense than a conservative positioning defense. I really don't think that Washington wants to play defense as long as we are playing offense, and B-Mo makes them pay as he hits two three-point bombs in a row.

Craig pressures a dribbler into a turnover and Pella has a 30-18 lead. Speaking of turnovers, either our sloppiness or their increased pressure seems to be causing us more turnovers this half.

We have defended their scorers well, but their point guard has hit a couple of shots to cut the lead to ten. Statistically, down the stretch I don't see this guy beating us; we are up by 10.

Craig (for some reason) isn't looking at the hoop much tonight, but he continues to make scrappy plays, picking up loose balls for us.

We just refuse to look inside to our post players, and the more we don't look inside, the more Washington's defense comes out to take away our outside game.

After attacking the basket with regularity against PCM's man defense we haven't seen Kaleb really go to the hoop in this game. Some of that is because they are playing zone, some may be because they are quicker, and it is more difficult to drive the ball. Anyway, this time he did, and he spun to create a foul and made both free throws.

The only thing that is keeping Washington in the game is their point guard, who gets really hot, and our ever-increasing turnovers.

So far Clayton has been fairly quiet except for his amazing early game hustle play, but now, in addition to another defensive board, he draws a foul with the dribble drive against the zone. Back-to-back fouls occur, as now it's Klarc turn to draw one. Klarc gets up off the floor after the foul shaking his already injured wrist. But he doesn't ask to come out; he is a tough kid. Another foul. This time it's Jesse creating a foul by hustling after an offensive rebound. For a small player he does like to board.

The Washington point is shooting out of his mind, as he hits two threes in a row, and probably three of their last four shots. The score has closed to 32-28 late in the third quarter; make it 34-28, hoop from Kaleb, assist Colin. It is once again our ball to start the fourth quarter.

B-Mo passed to Klarc, who penetrated and pitched to Kaleb, and he buries a three—we are back up 37-28 with 6:40 left.

There have been rebounds to be had off of our defensive board during this game so far, as Washington hasn't been able to solve our defense. Craig has added another one; Kaleb has gotten two more, B-Mo three more, and Klarc got one more as well. Craig also got us an offensive board to go along with an assist, while Klarc and Kaleb also got another assist.

Craig is doing so many good things, but he isn't looking for his shot. We are starting to play them four-on-five. Colin scores with a pull-up runner from about 12 feet.

Our offense hasn't been great, but we are composed, and we are also throwing the extra pass this game. That is why we are leading.

I asked Nate to chart the offensive boards very accurately for them because I was afraid of their ability to get to the boards, and now that they are down, and can't seem to solve our "D;" they are really going to the offensive boards.

Kaleb had a nice play—the ball rebounded long, and as it headed out of bounds, K came from about 30 feet away to chase it down and throw it back into the court area so that we retained possession. That is a play he wouldn't have made at the beginning of the year.

Craig and Kaleb draw back-to-back fouls against our opponents, and we are in the one and one; Kaleb makes both with about 3:30 left. They did us a favor on the next possession when they threw the ball away in an unforced error—we are up 41-34.

Washington's best three-point shooter did hit a three-pointer, and their defense is playing us for pass rather than shot, as we try to be smart with the ball and take only high-percentage shots.

It's 41-37 with 2:00, and Colin secures a defensive board for us. He is about gassed, but he is definitely fighting in there. B-Mo also got us a defensive board that results in a foul on them. Mr. Calm hit both.

Now Washington is sending everyone to the offensive boards, so when Kaleb pulled down the next defensive board he threw a three quarter-court length pass to Klarc for a layup; it's 45-39 with 1:19 left, and they press.

Washington can't get up a quick shot because of our defense, and when they do shoot Klarc gets the board.

Finally Colin gets another defensive board and gets fouled as well—he makes one of two. They get a put-back, but Kaleb hits one of two free throws to seal the deal, and we walk away with another win 47-41.

Defensively we did a super job in the first half of this game holding Washington to 13% shooting in the first quarter and 24% shooting in the first half; we gave up only four offensive boards in the first half. We weren't quite as good the second half. Their second shots hurt us, and they shot 48%. Offensively in the first half we shot 56% and in the second only about 40%, but we hit five threes and didn't turn it over too much, either. We also hit some big free throws down the stretch. It was a workman-like win.

The boys ate pizza on the way home.

Final Standings for the Little Hawkeye Conference

	Over All	Conference
1 Pella Christian	21-1	15-1
2 Oskaloosa (Osky)	17-4	12-4
3 Pella	14-6	10-6
4 Grinnell 1	4-7	10-6
5 Norwalk	13-8	10-6
6 Boone	7-13	6-9
7 Knoxville	7-14	4-12
8 Newton	3-17	2-14
9 South Tama	2-18	2-13

Pella High's Little Hawkeye All Conference Players

First Team

Kaleb Korver
Brandon Caldwell

Second Team

Klarc Korver

Honorable Mention

Colin Boswell
C.J. Newendorp

Chapter 19—The Start of the Tournament Trail

Wednesday, February 21, Practice #53

Clayton is out of practice with a sprained ankle; he did that in the last :30 seconds of the Washington game. Rob Blom is hopeful that he will back for Monday's game. Klarc hurt his groin and his wrists; he is also sitting out of practice. He thinks he will be back tomorrow. I'm not so sure.

This practice started with zone break-down drills. The teams that have been coming to scout us will surely at least consider running a zone against us, considering our lack of an inside game against Washington.

The break-down drills started with just a simple catch and face the basket at the free-throw line. It is truly amazing how often we will catch the ball and not look at the hoop. From there we added a dump-down pass into the low post.

We went then into dribble penetration against a zone. Initially we put three offensive players out against four defenders in a zone. Then Coach Core added another offensive player and then finally we went five-on-five. During the five-on-five segment the post players screened the zone. First it was on-ball screens and after that we worked on screens to destroy the defensive slides of the zone.

The white team, Tyler Linn, Zach, Nate, Justin, Brock, and Tyler T played on defense against the green team the entire practice; no offense, just defense. Tell me those guys aren't team players! I just wish we could get them more recognition somehow.

Practice was only an hour or so. Afterwards the boys sat down to listen to Coach Core's short scouting report on our first-round playoff opponent— Carlisle. The team match ups go like this—on our side of the bracket Chariton plays Knoxville, and we if beat Carlisle we would play the winner of the game between Chariton and K'ville.

The opposite side of the bracket has Clarke playing Saydel and Norwalk playing Winterset. If we get through our district we will have to play one of these four teams.

Coach Core's report went something like this. Carlisle is a scrappy team—very aggressive. He compared their game to something akin to last night's game. Their main defense was a quarter-court zone. They also ran some man-to-man defense, similar to our rover defense. They will shoot the ball from outside, up to the NBA three-point line. They have a six foot, five-inch, slim player that Mark compared to Kaleb. He can shoot the three, and he has the ability to attack the basket with the dribble. They have a small point guard (freshman) who looks to shoot the ball from deep. In the game that Mark saw he hit five three-point shots.

Coach Core then went on to talk about our team. He was really positive about the turn around that these guys have made from the beginning of the season to now. He said, "They used to be soft; there was a lot of pouting, temper tantrums, and there was a lot of making of faces. But now because of the players' willingness to be coached and to listen and to try they have become a tough, scrappy team, a tough, blue-collar team." Coach was especially appreciative of Tyler Linn, who before last night's game was laughing and talking and really seemed to be part of the team. He was also grateful for Colin's change in his approach to the game and to his teammates and his willingness to suppress some of his own game for the good of the team.

Practice is over—the boys had to get ready to dance!

Thursday, February 22, 2007, Practice #54

We warmed up and then went into break-down drills again, gearing up for the zone. The drill today was an extension of yesterday's drill, except after we flashed to the high post the post passer passed the ball back out to the wing for a shot rather than a dump-down pass to the post. The second drill was a dribble drive into the heart of the zone or at one single defender; this was followed by a shot or by a pass out to the wing.

Mark also went back to the footwork drill where the kids worked on stepping without traveling from a dribble-drive position; seems simple but we have done that drill a lot, and it has paid off.

We got them up and down the court today with the NC drill. The improvement we've made in that drill is unbelievable. In the past we have thrown it away unnecessarily and we have had poor defensive balance getting back. Today we really had a nice balance on both ends of the floor.

We re-worked screening the zone; screening on the ball to create dribble drives and posting and cutting against the zone as well.

We worked on press and press offense, did the old junior-high defensive mass-slide drill and also went one-on-one full-court.

We finished by putting in a couple of out-of-bounds plays.

Practice tomorrow at 10:15—no school!

Friday, February 23, 10:15 A.M., Practice #55

We've had shortened practices squeezed in between parent-teacher's conferences, and today is a day off of school so the boys are in for practice in the morning.

While I was taping up Klarc's wrists, Kirk came over and asked Coach if he wanted him to do some post-up work with Kyle. Wow, now that is really a good thing, the "Kirkster" is asking to get some extra post work in!

We warmed up with more shooting by the outside players and post-up shooting by the post players. Then we went right to our break-down drills in attacking the zone. We continued to work on catching and facing the hoop, posting up, and throwing passes from the high post to the low post. We also threw passes from the high post to the wing and worked on catching passes from guard to guard. We did dribble-drives, pull-up jump shots and catch-and-shoot jump shots.

After this we got up and down the court with the Michigan drill. The attitude and attention to detail looks good today.

I decided I would try to do more coaching of the white team today while Mark worked with the green team on their Partners offense. I should have been doing a lot more of this during the year. This is one way I can show my appreciation for the second-unit members, just simply pay more attention to them and coach them more during practice. The down side of doing this is that I can't watch the first team members at the same time. Anyway, the white team guys did a great job. Tyler Linn, Zach, Tyler T, Justin, Brock, and even Kyle were awesome. They really made it tough on the green team; in fact they probably outplayed them in most of the quarter-court stuff that we did.

Then we went up and down the court again in the one-break drill. The white team's ball handling is something that they don't do very well, and they weren't as good during this segment, but I also thought our green team woke up a little bit during this time.

Coach Core had the players do a new drill today called the change drill. When I first saw it listed on the practice schedule, I figured it was the hold-put-the-ball-down-on-the-ground-and-run-back-to-play-defense-while-guarding-a-new-man drill. It wasn't that drill. The guys stayed in the quarter-court after the ball was put down, and everyone on defense had to find a new man to guard before the white team could get a shot up; pretty effective drill in seeing, rotating, and communicating on the defensive end.

Our offensive players have a hard time recognizing the difference between a post player coming to screen on ball and breaking to receive a pass. We were throwing the ball to a man trying to set screens. Oops. We got better as we went on.

We made a change in the Spread offense. I like it a lot better. We've gone to a high-low post set with three outside players. The high post player is trying to set on-ball screens, and the low-post player is trying to destroy zone slides and seal defensive players. I like this a lot better than what we were doing. The light bulb is starting to shine with Kirk; he is starting to get this seal concept. He's not great yet, but he's coming.

Mark puts the guys in a zone and then puts six offensive players out to cover. It really makes them hustle, and hopefully communicate. They can't afford to have two guys cover the same man, especially when they are already outnumbered.

Finally we did talk a bit more about Carlisle and what they did offensively. The Carlisle set is a one-three-one set that has their best player, the six foot, five inch player, at the elbow position of the free-throw line. In one of their plays the point dribbles at him when he is at the free-throw line elbow, and the wing on the opposite side back cuts for a layup. It works because they put all of their players on one side of the floor, and the man that cuts is on the open side of the set. The correct defense for us to handle this would be for the man guarding their back cutter to play soft (not deny the wing pass) and for our man guarding their baseline man on the opposite side of the floor to help against the back-cutting wing player as well.

Carlisle really runs kind of a version of the same offense that Norwalk runs. I won't show it but if you want a more detailed description—look up Norwalk's offense (described earlier) to see how the offense continues its pattern.

Another offensive play that they run is one to get their best player in a position to make a decision with the ball and give him an opportunity to score.

It's a simple play. As the point dribbles the ball away from the best player at the free-throw elbow he pops up to the top of the key. The wings simply cross underneath the hoop looking to occupy their defenders so they don't help and to get them open as well. The low-post man steps into the lane as soon as "the star" makes the catch. He may now pass to any teammate or may try to go one-on-one from the top of the key area.

Saturday, February 24

No practice today—good thing, the weather is so bad that the kids would have had a tough time coming into the gym. Mark did call. He's got an idea to use our Blitz defense out of the zone; I'm in favor, I still think that the Blitz should work—it worked for George Mason during their run in the NCAA tournament.

The girls' third round tournament game has been moved from today, because of the weather, to Monday, the same day as our opening-round game against Carlisle.

Sunday, February 24, Practice #56

We never practice on Sundays, but since we play on Monday, we will today. Practice started today at 2:00, the day after a huge ice storm hit, which was followed by snow that I thought might keep a number of players away from practice. But instead, every single player was there.

Mark wanted to have a short, upbeat practice. We started with dribble tag, followed this with hot-spot shooting which is a shooting drill where players take shots from certain spots on the floor. The winners were Colin and Klarc. We then broke the players up into two teams that competed in a three-point shootout and then a game of knockout.

We got serious about practice when we went to the 11-man drill followed by shell drill #1, and then an on-the-ball screen shell drill.

Coach Core had the guys do a three-on-three drill. In essence it was a rebounding drill combined with a switching man-to-man drill.

We ran through all of our man-to-man offenses and the specials as well. Then we tried running the Blitz defense out of the zone. It didn't work, but I don't think it has anything to do with the defense as it does with our lack of anticipation; I think we will come back to it.

The one-break drill started getting the guys up and down the floor. We played only zone or match-up during this drill. We ran our new Spread offense against the match-up—I will repeat, I like this offense a lot better.

Then we went through all of our zone offensive plays. We anticipate a zone out of Carlisle.

Something that jumps out at me is Klarc's decision making. He is really making good and unselfish decisions with the ball. Another thing that jumps out at me is Kaleb. He really is starting to believe that he is a player now. At one time, for whatever reason, he didn't have quite the confidence that he is displaying both in practice and in games now. His outside shooting is going now; he has shown a pull-up jumper that he at one time didn't have, and he has really become adept at both the Magic and the Brunner move.

We added Valpo from the side today. It is the same offense that we run from the baseline when we need to go full-court, but today we did it from the sideline.

To end practice we had a relay race. The boys had to carry two marbles in a spoon around cones that were placed along the floor. I really think most coaches make their players too tight when tournaments come along; this was designed to loosen them up.

Pella vs. Carlisle, First Tournament Game
Our record: 14-6 Overall

About half the kids showed up with their hair shaved. I loved it. They seemed really excited by it themselves. It sounds like the other guys are going to do it too; they just ran out of time to get it done before the game started. I like this kind of thing, and since it was the players' idea, I took it to be a good omen.

Carlisle came into the game at 8-13.

Their opening possession was about 100 passes before they shot, and their next one may have been more! I might be exaggerating just a little, but they were protective of the ball and made a lot of ball swings before they shot. Our zone defense was ineffective against this type of offense because we couldn't get out into the passing lanes with it, and they handled our half-court trap like a team that had seen one before.

Additionally there wasn't a big or energetic crowd, as our girls were playing for a trip to state in another game at Osky. That did two things—it split the crowd between teams and took away some of our biggest supporters, as the girls have always cheered hard for the boys' team.

Thirdly, Carlisle came out in a zone defense, a two-three zone. This wasn't a surprise to us; this is what we had been preparing for, but we just flat out didn't play aggressively against it. Our shooters weren't looking to score, and some of the looks we got we just missed. Their zone was nothing special; it was more our lack of offense than their defense.

As I watched the game unfold it was obvious that they didn't have much ball handling, but they were well schooled in movement of the ball and of their men on the offensive end. When you combined that with our lack of intense play on the defensive end it was not a pretty first half.

The score at the end of the first quarter was 9-10 Carlisle. We shot 25% from the field with two offensive rebounds and they shot 38% from the field, but we also caused them to turn it over three times to keep us close.

The second quarter was really no better. We tried some more zone, although limited, and even some match-up, which was effective, but it was a time-consuming defense that allowed Carlisle to run their offense and make lots of passes. We would have liked to play more of an up-tempo game, and it was obvious that they wanted it slow and deliberate. They were 9 of 17 from the field at half.

We had taken 15 shots in the entire first half of play, while they hadn't shot much more. Kaleb shot the ball twice, and B-Mo shot the ball once in the first half; Kirk and Klarc each had two hoops, and we didn't make a single three in the opening half. In some ways I felt like Clayton, even though he didn't score, might have been our best offensive player, as he had at least two and maybe three assists in the half. Again we forced a few turnovers in the second quarter, and shot 63% to their 53% in that quarter. We just didn't get enough attempts; we didn't get enough shots up to the hoop. Carlisle's little (literally) freshman guard had 10 of their first 21 points, as they held a one-point lead on us at halftime. He wasn't a bad shooter, but we just lost him, he didn't have the ability to put the ball down on the ground to create his own shot. We just didn't always know where he was, and he ended up with open shots.

At halftime we talked about two things. One was to add pressure to the Carlisle ball handlers, guard them closer. They really only had one kid that could handle the ball, and even he wasn't great. We didn't think they could beat us off of the dribble, but we had become kind of a passive defensive team because of all of the zone we had been playing, and we were having a hard time making the mental adjustment we needed to create that kind of pressure. As a player you have to want to get in a stance and work to create pressure.

The second area was on offense. We wanted to get the ball into the paint. We felt like we were bigger and stronger in there. I whispered to B-Mo as we went out that he needed to seal inside, get the ball down low and then try to score. The kid that Carlisle had inside might get an occasional block on him (he was a little taller than B-Mo) but I really felt like that for every block he got we'd get a multitude of hoops and fouls in return. And that is the way it turned out in the third. B-Mo went to work and got us some good makes inside so we got a little offense going in the third. Someplace along this time Kaleb started to come on a little bit, too. We shot 60% in the third and raised our overall percentage to 48%.

Unfortunately our defense wasn't as good but we had decided that we just needed to play hard man-to-man. The kids were slowly inching up on the guys that they were guarding, trying to put some pressure on them. This was really pretty foreign to what we had been preaching—protect the paint, but Coach Core and I felt like we could do both if we just would.

In the third quarter we went from one down to four up, 33-29. We shot the ball in the third 12 times—only three less than in the entire first half, so we were starting to get some tempo as well. When I looked up at the scoreboard the little freshman had only 10—we had found him.

Finally in the fourth quarter we pulled away. We shot 53% during this quarter, as once we established a lead Carlisle had to come out and play us man, and they just couldn't handle us, especially Kaleb (finished with 25 points) and B-Mo, both on the initial move and on the offensive boards. We even got some other guys in the game late as Tyler T got a hoop to put the finishing touches on a 54-40 win.

Offensively by quarter we just kept getting better, as our point production by quarter went 9, to 12, to 12 more and finally to 17. We shot 25/40 shots for 62% shooting! For the game we made only one three-pointer out of nine tries.

Win and advance; lose and go home. We are going to South East Polk to play again. Our opponent—Knoxville. They had finished 7-14 and sixth in our conference with a two-point win over a 13-5 Chariton team that finished second in the South Central conference. I've felt for a number of years now that we have a really good conference. Of the nine teams in our conference at least six of them have been in the state tournament since I've been here.

Chapter 20—Round Two

Tuesday, February 27, Practice #57

We warmed up with dribbling and shooting and then went over some things we could have done better in last night's game, such as ball pressure on the man with the ball and denying the ball back to the middle of the floor. These were two things we got better at last night, but it took us a while to make the adjustments. Against a better team that could have been trouble.

We then turned our attention to Knoxville and the upcoming game. One of the first things we must do against Knoxville is rebound, and rebound with an intensity, a purpose, and a mission. We can't be ho-hum rebounders especially on the defensive end, or they will hurt us with offensive put-backs.

After reviewing our last game with Knoxville we are anticipating them using a two-two-one zone press for at least some of the game against us, as we didn't always do a great job against it in our last meeting.

We also reviewed the Panther's triangle inside offense. They form a triangle around the lane from block to block up to the free-throw line, and then set a multitude of screens within the triangle. The other two players are on each side of the lane, anticipating a catch-and-shoot option if there is help from our wing defenders down inside.

Knoxville runs an out-of-bounds play that requires a screen-the-screener move. So the man setting the first screen then receives a screen to get open. They run this both in front of the man who is taking the ball out and away from that man. It is really one play, but by taking it both on and away it results in two different plays. These plays are run out of a box set to make these options available either way.

Defensively Knoxville has shown a bit of everything including something new we didn't see last time, a one-three-one zone. We haven't seen this zone a lot, so we spent some time looking to attack that as well. To me, this type of zone is extremely open to diagonal passes, especially passes from the guard down to the opposite baseline.

Mark and I talked later as well, and we would be foolish not to anticipate some box or diamond-and-one as well against Kaleb. We really thought we'd see a lot of this type of defense this year, but Kaleb is really just now starting to show consistently that he deserves this kind of special attention from a defense.

Practice is short—one hour; the boys are off to dance.

Wednesday, February 28, Practice #58

Coach Core makes practices at this time of year go about as fast as they could possibly go and still have enough time to work on areas of concern. Today is no exception. Within minutes we shot free throws, jump shots, and done driving-line drills. We had also gone full-court into a two-on-one situation.

After we did those things we worked again on defending Knoxville's man offense. We added some passers to a three-on-three drill to put the green team at a disadvantage, but they handled it pretty well. What I'm finding out (in the last couple of days—I'm definitely a slow learner) is how much I can learn from our white team members after each drill if I will just take the time to speak with them. Tyler Linn and Zach have really been helpful. For example, after this drill I asked Tyler what it was like to be guarded by our guys and if he felt like we could have done better. Just a simple question, and Tyler and the rest of the white team has really had some good insight. I'm proud of them and their attitude; they are pulling together as a team.

We changed the drill into a five-on-five drill, and then went to a full-court situation that included working on our press and attacking what we expect to see out of Knoxville—a two-two-one zone press. In our press we would like to get early traps that occur away from the basket we are guarding, and when K'ville gets into the quarter-court we would like to just play solid defense. We also expect them to try to take away Klarc as our primary ball handler against their press, but Coach Core feels like Klarc's improvement, as a ball handler from last game to this game will negate that move.

When we are in our man-to-man defense we feel like we must guard #3 as a possible three-point shooter. He doesn't take or make a lot of threes, and that is not our number-one concern with him, but out of the rest of their players he is the most effective. In fact, I've spoken before about the fact that sometimes some of our guys don't look at the hoop enough, and it feels like we are playing four-on-five defenders when that happens. Well, in this case, we think that maybe we can do that to them. Some of their kids haven't shown much ability to shoot from out, so maybe we can help off of them into the lane to slow their post play, which is their strength.

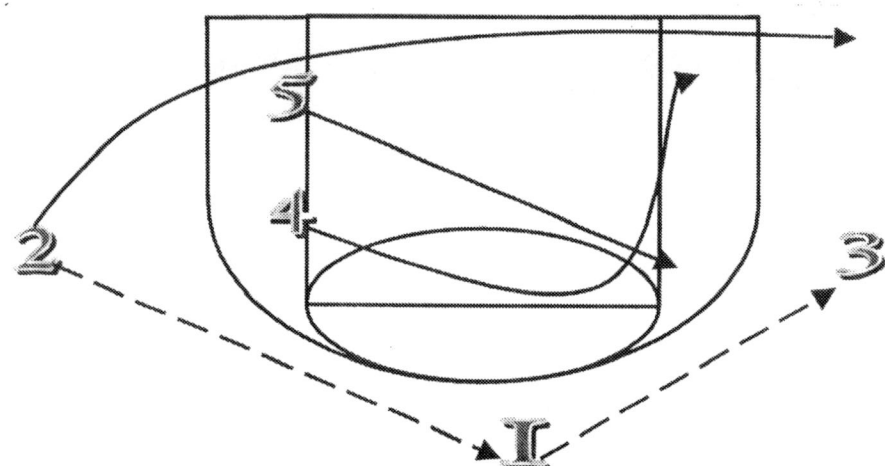

The Knoxville zone offense, while not complicated, is a good, sound way to attack a zone.

The previous diagram shows a possible zone move by Knoxville. They quickly swing the ball from one side of the floor to the other. Then the posts will switch from high to low and from low to high as they cross to the other side of the floor. Then finally they sneak a player along the baseline to create an overload. If nothing occurs from this move they would probably swing the ball again to the other side of the floor by #3 dribbling up to the point, #2 following him up out of the corner, and #1 sliding over to be the new wing where #2 once was. The next cut to create an over load could even come from the point man cutting down the middle of the zone into either corner, and the remaining two outside players reading and adjusting accordingly to create the overload.

Our practice continues with the one-break drill. The green team is switching between our regular zone and our match-up, while the white team tries to simulate the Knoxville zone offense. The white team has done this all year long. Within minutes they need to learn at least the basics of another team's offensive system and then perform it well enough that the green team gets an idea of the philosophy that they will be playing against.

We went through all of our man-to-man stuff, and then the white team ran all of the special or set plays that Knoxville runs. Brandon Esterbrook is usually the guy that simulates the opposing team's best shooter, and tonight is no exception. Brandon can shoot it, and tonight he is hitting almost everything he puts up; hope we do a better job tomorrow.

Thursday, March 1

School is called off because of the weather and the game is postponed until tomorrow. We had an extremely short meeting with the guys immediately after school and sent them on their way before the weather got any worse.

Practice #59, Friday, March 2

The weather remains bad today, so once again the game is postponed until tomorrow at 3:00.

We are in a delicate situation in that for the last two days we have been preparing like we have a game the following day. With that in mind a coach would be foolish to take the players legs out from under them by running too much, but at the same time the guys must work enough to stay sharp. I think Coach Core has done a nice job with his practice plans in balancing these two ideas.

We didn't do anything out of the usual practice wise other than put in a sideline out-of-bounds play that B-Mo and Kirk suggested—they saw it on TV and thought it might work for us. Even if it doesn't, the ownership of the boys in taking this one on is great; they are really starting to think of this as their team, the one thing that is a must if we are to get to the state tournament.

Another problem will be the fact that we would only have one day to prepare for our sub-state game should we beat Knoxville. I'd like to have to worry about that!

We have a shoot around tomorrow at 10 A.M., and then the bus leaves at 1:15.

March 3, 2007, Pella vs. Knoxville, District Finals at Southeast Polk
   Our Record: 15-6

We knew going into this game that it would probably be a war. Pella and Knoxville are only about 20 minutes apart, and the kids on both teams know each other by name.

We are thinking that most of the Knoxville scoring will come from their post players, #11 and #33, and most of that scoring will come from in close. But our main concern is the offensive board. That is what Knoxville does; they rebound the ball and put it back up.

By looking at the statistics on Knoxville it is obvious that their game is an inside-out oriented offense, and that while they have a guy that can shoot the three they really don't even attempt a lot of three-point shots. Their two leading scorers have attempted 378 shots combined, and only attempted 11 threes out of all of those shots (they are shooting 11%). The player on their team that has shot the most threes of anyone is only shooting 25% from that range, and he has only attempted 55 tries in 22 games. Contrast this to the number of twos that they have attempted and made, the number of free throws that they have shot, and it's obvious that we must guard them inside out.

Knoxville opened in a one-two-two zone, the same zone that we use. One would think that could give us some advantages, since we see it every day in practice, but it obviously wasn't a huge advantage to us because we were down 6-8 at the end of the first quarter. While the game wasn't an up-and-down game it wasn't an all-out stall game either; it was just a game that wasn't a big scoring affair exaggerated by the reality that both teams had four turnovers to go along with the poor shooting.

By the way, we opened with and played a lot of man-to-man defense in that opening quarter. Clearly our defense wasn't bad, but one of our huge goals (to keep Knoxville off the boards) wasn't going well, as they had four offensive rebounds in the first quarter.

It wasn't exactly an offensive game the second quarter either as we ended with 33% shooting for the half and Knoxville with 38% shooting. What got us the lead was our ability to turn them over, as they had five more than we had in the second quarter. The score was 19-14 at halftime.

We had done a nice job on the defensive end, but the offensive end we needed to be more productive. Defensively the only player they really had that did any scoring was #33, who had made what I thought were some tough shots from around the hoop. Conversely the only guy really scoring for us was Kaleb. He'd hit a couple sliding shots in the lane and a three-pointer as well. Clayton also contributed with kind of an unexpected three in the first half.

At halftime we felt like we should move the ball quicker rather than hold it so long and flash to the middle of the lane more often as well. I felt like we had lost our balance on the offensive end where we weren't really doing anything. We weren't looking inside, we weren't catching and shooting from outside, we weren't rebounding the ball; we were just catching and holding the ball and playing very tentatively.

Craig started us off in the second half with a nice duck into the lane for an inside shot and two points.

We had been effective with our new and improved Bulldogs play and got baskets from that each time. It's ironic; at halftime I told Kaleb, "They really seem to be playing you for your outside shot and your drive." So I asked him, "If you can't get the ball in the lane that way how else could you get it in there?"

He immediately replied, "Post up or flash."

I said, "Exactly," and walked away.

So what happens? Kaleb just starts to drive the ball like crazy in the second half. Hey, what do I know? I'm sure glad he did, because he not only got baskets but he got fouled as well and went to the line.

In the third quarter we shot a little better, and so did they, but neither team was exactly setting the world on fire. We tried to get B-Mo more involved, but he not only didn't make many shots, he really didn't even attempt many, I guess his confidence just wasn't there. Besides, the last game we played, B-Mo was dominant inside and maybe I should credit Knoxville with doing a good job of keeping him under control. Like us, I'm sure they scouted our game and maybe B-Mo was a point of emphasis for them on the defensive end.

We had maintained about a four-to-six point lead for most of the game, and in a low-scoring game such as this, that is a fairly substantial lead. We also were going to the foul line, thanks in no small part to Kaleb's ability to penetrate the zone with the dribble.

Knoxville played mostly zone, switching back and fourth between the one-two-two and a one-three-one. Some place in the middle of the quarter they went to a man-to-man, and they just couldn't handle us, but they were left with very little choice as our lead grew.

Coach Core had the guys switching defenses mainly between our Fist, straight man-to-man, and our one-three-one half-court trap defenses. This was effective for a couple of different reasons. One, they all look somewhat similar. Two, they were more aggressive than our zones, and in turn I think this made us more aggressive on both the defensive and offensive ends. And three, the switching defenses seemed to confuse the Knoxville players and made them more hesitant as to when they had or didn't have a good look at the basket; they were out of rhythm.

Klarc had been quiet in the first half, but in the second half got some steals that led to layups and also got to the line a couple of times. His scoring was timely. But Kaleb once again led us with 23 points on seven of 14 shooting, as we won this game going away 48-37.

We've got a quick turnaround now as we get ready for our next opponent, Norwalk, on Monday. We will practice tomorrow at 2:00 P.M. This practice will have to be more of a walk through, as the kids will have tired legs, and then they will have a game the following day.

At 6:00 P.M. I went over to Mark's house and watched a tape that we just got back from the Norwalk vs. Clarke game, which occurred that day as well. There were some things that we learned watching this tape, but now it will be up to the kids to implement the plan. I think we will have the best player on the floor in Kaleb. However, Norwalk has already gotten us twice, so part of our coaching will need to be a good selling job of how we will win this time.

By the way Mary Core, Mark's wife (he definitely married up) and Tricia were there and ordered pizza for us for supper; they gave us their basketball wisdom as well, thanks girls. . . for the pizza and especially for the wisdom.

Chapter 21—Sub-State

Sunday, March 4, Practice #60

Today Mark and I talked about match-ups on the defensive end and who would cover whom. Even though both of us feel that we need to play mostly zone defense, we do anticipate playing some man as well. In fact, I really think our best defense might be our match-up zone.

I thought originally that we would cover their best offensive player (#12) who plays post with B-Mo and have Kaleb help towards him off of his man. My thinking was that B-Mo's early defensive play with additional help and shot-blocking ability from Kaleb would be the way to go. Another thing that added to my thought process was that we sure couldn't afford to have K in foul trouble. However, I was out voted. Mark thought that helping off of #34 (who is a blue-collar player) opens him up to what he does best, the blue-collar stuff. Also when we asked B-Mo who he thought should guard #12, he said Kaleb, and when we asked Kaleb, he immediately said he wanted #12. By the way, I think they are right, and I'm wrong; probably won't be the last time that happens in my life either.

After visiting last night at Mark's house we both thought that we needed to do a better job of occupying Norwalk's point defender than we did in our last game. He was dropping down into the lane to the point that our guys were playing four-on-five because we didn't shoot it from the top of the key to make the defender pay for leaving. Mark came today with an idea of combining our Duke play with our Partners offense to try to get some extra movement and make it tougher on the Norwalk point defender.

We ran through not only our man offensive plays but also our zone offensive plays against the man-to-man as well. One of the things that we haven't done well this year is move without the ball. We've got, for the most part, a group of guys that stand unless they have the ball in their hands. That is one of the reasons we've run offensive plays more this year than before, just to give them some designated cuts that require movement away from the ball. Anyway, our zone stuff really worked almost equally well against the man too; this is an excellent idea on Mark's part.

Coach Core also came to practice with a new play. This is a play that Creighton ran for one of their best players in order to get him a shot. It's a simple play that gets Kaleb a shot, and I expect us to use it tomorrow night as well. I can't show you the entire thing because you may be a spy for one of our opponents, but at the core of the play is a down screen by B-Mo that gets Kaleb open, and then the "Beamer"(B-Mo) posts up after the screens.

The rest of the practice was spent going over Norwalk's stuff and what they do on their offensive end of the floor. They have been very creative offensively against our man-to-man, and the man "D" isn't our strength this year, so they have been especially effective with it. This time we've already talked with Klarc about our defensive set up for tomorrow's game. We want to start zone rather than man-to-man. We also want to use the match-up zone defense more. Our man-to-man will be our change-up defense, and the use of our trapping defenses is a real possibility because Norwalk loves to run their offensive stuff and doesn't really want to be pushed out of what they do. So that is what we would like to have happen: make them react rather than run their stuff, and this is what our traps (if we perform them correctly) should do.

Since we didn't play much zone against them last time we didn't see much of their offensive pattern during our game, but we did pick up some things off of the film.

Norwalk's basic zone offense runs something like this. They cut #22 from the top of the floor to the ball-side corner. They set #12 and #34 at the posts, and #40 and #30 are at the guard positions. The swing of the ball creates a cut by #22 to the opposite corner, and #12 and #34 cross to the opposite side of the floor.

They do run a couple of specials out of this as well. In the first one they use the momentum of the defense (who is used to switching from one side of the floor to the other as quickly as they can) against itself by bringing the ball back to the same side of the floor it originated on.

So this time as the ball goes back up from #22 (the corner man) to #40 (the closest guard to the corner) who then reverses it further to #30 (at the top of the key), #12 (a good shooter playing in the post) sneaks out behind two screens set by #22 and #40, set on collapsing defenders trying to get to the other side of the floor, giving #12 an open shot for a three.

One of the other specials they run is more of a high-low play. Their best ball handler is #22, and they use him to try to get the ball down low to their post. In this option #22 (who normally starts in the corner) does not go out to the corner but comes to the high post and looks to dump the ball down low. He is mostly looking to #12 at the block.

Norwalk shoots the three well. As a team they get around four or five makes a game from three. But their best offensive scorer is a post (#12) who is also a good three-point shooter. The guy that shoots the ball the second most for them is #22, who also leads them in assists (by far) but who really isn't a great shooter at 36%. Number 30 is a tough cover as well for us, because he can shoot the three, and in fact leads them in attempts from here, but can also post up and makes 81% of his free throws. Finally, #40, while not a big scorer, is someone that can make threes. We must cover him by flying out to him and encouraging him to put the ball on the ground rather than shoot. Although we don't really want to cover him like he is a big scorer, we must simply cover out quickly when he does get the ball.

After all this is said and done I also consider Norwalk to be a good defensive team, and a team that is tough to get an offensive board against. Our work is cut out for us. To get to the state tournament is going to be tough. To get to the state tournament should be tough!

Pella vs. Norwalk at Johnston in the Sub-State Final
Our Record: 16-6

There is a good crowd for both teams in this neutral setting near Des Moines. Our atmosphere in the locker room was very appropriate, loose but focused.

The opening minutes of this game are "The Craig Show," as he buries a couple of threes, gets an offensive board that he plugs back in, makes a two, gets a defensive rebound, is involved in a trap that creates a turnover for us, and all this is sandwiched around a bucket by Klarc. It's 7-0 with 5:51 left in the quarter and all then it's 10-0, and Norwalk calls timeout. By the time we get C.J. out, he is so gassed he has committed two fouls and is struggling to get some air into his lungs, but man did he get us going.

It's 12-2 with 3:30 left in the quarter, and #12 hasn't scored yet for Norwalk; in fact, their least offensive player has their only hoop so far.

Kaleb already has a dribble-drive two but then hits a really deep three, and we are on a roll. It's 15-4 with 2:30 left in the first.

Now it's Kirk's turn; he comes off the bench and buries a three. Then, the next possession, he does the same thing! We are up 21-3. Who would have thunk it? The next possession (this time after some passing), you guessed it—Kirk hits another three.

We end the first quarter with a 15-point lead, 24-9.

I'm not sure if it's us or them, (it's probably both) but this has been our best opening quarter of the year. Is it us shooting lights out or them being a young team (four sophomores and a senior start with a freshman coming off the bench)? I'm not sure, but so far this is a ball.

Now it's B-Mo's turn to connect with a three, his first shot of the game, and he knocks it down from deep. Kaleb also chips in with three, but it's the old-fashioned kind, a bucket and a foul.

Norwalk has played better and has cut the lead to 29-17.

Norwalk went empty a couple of times down, and I guess Colin wanted to get into the act, as he connects with a three, too.

With 49 seconds left in the quarter we decide to hold the ball for the last shot, and even with a busted play, Klarc hit a shot at the buzzer to end the half and make it 34-19 at halftime.

You never know how teams are going to come out at half; sometimes you just want to keep playing. A 15-point lead at half is more than we could have hoped for, but it is certainly not one that is insurmountable with the advent of the three-point line.

B-Mo helped to alleviate some fears of a slow start the second half as we ran the Open play, and he took the ball to the hoop for a lay-up.

After at least six empty possessions by Norwalk and four free throws between Colin and Kaleb, to go along with Kaleb's pair of two-pointers, this game is moving out. It's 52-27, and #12 is still not on the board for Norwalk!

B-Mo and Klarc didn't want to be left out of the fun, as B-Mo makes a steal and gets an assist to Klarc for a layup.

Again it's Craig's turn, as he makes a steal, and we've made back-to-back steals in our half-court trap.

The combination of B-Mo's two free throws and Kirk's put-back of an errant shot at the buzzer (again) makes the score 58-28 at the end of three. That was a 24-9 quarter to match our 24-9 first quarter; I guess I didn't need to worry about a let down.

Norwalk didn't give up. They came out in a press that forced us into a timeout, and later on we got caught in a trap that forced a timeout in the quarter-court. Their kids really came out to pressure our ball handlers as well; this is a compliment to their players and their coaches, in that it is a difficult thing to get players to do when they are down that far, but they kept trying.

With 7:00 in the fourth quarter #12 scored a three from the corner. Man, have we done a great job on a very good player.

After three more defensive possessions resulting in a steal and a defensive board by B-Mo and a defensive board by Kaleb, K now hits a man-sized deep three! After Kaleb knocks the ball off of a Norwalk player's foot, creating yet another turnover for Norwalk, we have a 63-33 lead!

But we aren't done, as Colin makes a steal, Craig gets an offensive board, Klarc has a defensive board, and B-Mo scores a hoop and a foul (an assist from Klarc).

One of the many highlights of the game for me was getting both Zach and Tyler Linn into the game with 2:45 left. Tyler and Zach are our two seniors who haven't played much this season. But they have been instrumental in turning our white team into a group that pushes our green team every night in practice. It's great to get them a chance to play some real game-time minutes.

Soon we have all of the starters out. Brock, Tyler T., and Brandon E. have entered the game. And finally Justin and Nate make an appearance as well. During this time our stats show Brock with a steal, Tyler T. with a free throw, Brandon with a defensive board, a steal, and a hoop, Zach with a steal, and with less than a minute, it's 71-35.

With little time left, but lots of action, Tyler T. has another free throw, Zach has a great play as he rebounds Tyler's miss, puts it back in, gets fouled, and then completes the three-pointer with a free throw. Brandon gets another steal. To top it off, Tyler Linn buries a three and smiles all the way back down the court. The final score is 78-36.

In the first quarter we made eight of 12 shots, and for the game we shot 52% with very few turnovers. We had three guys finish in double figures, while they shot less than 40%.

We are going! We were a four-five team after nine games, and now we are going to the state tournament with a record of 17-6 and a winning streak of 11 in a row!

There were lots of hugs after this game; we didn't leave the floor right away, as pictures were taken and parents, players, and students gathered out on the floor to celebrate a chance to play at least one more game in the state tournament; to top that off—no practice tomorrow.

Chapter 22—We Did It!

Tuesday, March 6, A Four-Five Team Becomes a 17-6, Going to the Big Dance

Due to weather postponements and rescheduling, the pairings for the state tournament didn't come out until this evening—we are playing Waverly Shell Rock; go Dutch! We play at noon on Wednesday, which isn't necessarily a great time to play, because if you win you play again the next day when all of the other teams will be resting the day before, but, hey, we will worry about that if we can win our first one. Oh, by the way, Waverly is 20-3.

Wednesday, March 7, Practice #61

Colin made the state in tennis, and he shared with Coach Core some thoughts about getting ready for state competition. One thing that he said was to practice taking every shot like it was a game in the state tournament, and that way when you get there it will be like you've done it before. Another thing that he said was that he knew he would face all different types of players in tennis with all different styles of play, and he needed to be ready for that. With that in mind Coach Core said that we (coaches) needed to be creative and put the kids into as many things in practice as we could so that they would be ready to go.

Waverly has a six foot, nine inch player that has blocked 63 shots in 21 games—we worked on head fakes to start practice. Then we worked on floaters, which make sense too. And finally we worked on our spinning and power layups. Other than the head fakes, almost everything that we did in preparation for attacking a six foot, nine inch player we've done often in practice before, so hopefully this will carry over for us.

We are in the preliminary stages of trying to piece together a scouting report on Waverly. The six foot, nine inch kid appears to be their do-everything guy. He is averaging 19 points and 12 rebounds a game. He shoots 54% from the field and even has some range to three as he shot 33% there as well. About the only thing he doesn't do really well is shoot free throws. He doesn't appear (on paper) to be a great passer either, because he only has 34 assists, but I'm sure that the hard part for him is getting the ball, so once he does he isn't about to pass it back out. Knowing all of this and working to prepare for it will be something we do in practice, but it is hard to simulate six feet nine inches. Kaleb and B-Mo have played with or against this kid in AAU ball, so both guys gave us a short scouting report. They indicated that he is a very good athlete who can dunk and plays much of the time, although not exclusively, on the outside. He is also strong and bulky, so not your standard, run-of-the-mill string-bean tall guy.

B-Mo and Kaleb had done a good job the game before making decisions about who should guard who in the post, and they had been totally right. Now B-Mo thinks maybe he should start on #34 (the six foot, nine incher) and Kaleb on #50. Funny, once again I would have thought the other way around, and this time Mark thought so as well. I'll bet we will revisit this subject again.

The boys also knew another player on the Waverly team, and gave us a short version of a report on him as well. They said that #50 is about six foot, six inches, strong and athletic, and a very good rebounder. Sensational: so far they are six foot nine and six foot six, both athletic and can rebound. With this kind of news I think we'd better stop talking; I hope it doesn't get any worse.

We did shell drills and the open-post drill. We also worked on most of our sets, both man-to-man and zone

Then we put in "Doc," so named for one of our teachers and the freshman coach here at PHS. It's yet another new defensive concept we hope to be able to use in our next game and from this point out. These guys have been really receptive to all of this new stuff. They seem to enjoy it; I think it has helped to revitalize the coaches as well. It was ugly, but hey, it's new; it seems to be working when we do this stuff. Let's not stop now.

Thursday, March 8, Practice #62

We did a little shooting and a little post work, as usual, to open up practice, and then Mark broke out the bats.

The bats are an attempt to simulate the height that we are about to encounter in the Waverly post player. Andrew Barber and Will are asked to stand near the hoop with the bats held up at arm's length, simulating six-feet-nine inches. Then against these guys (and their bats) the boys do all sorts of lay-ups, including Magic, Brunner, and floaters.

Next we did a one-on-one block drill. We paired the kids up and placed the one player with the ball near the basket and the other as a defender between the man with the ball and the hoop. The defender's job was to block the shot of the offensive player—that is all he could do. The offensive player was to fake or go up immediately or whatever he had to do to score.

Coach Core then had the boys work up from a one-on-one situation one step at a time to two-on-two to three-on-three until we eventually played at the five-on-five level.

After this we worked on our zone-defensive stuff; three-on-three match-up, and then our regular zone defense, and the slides that they would make against various positions that the ball might get to on the court.

Right now we are still kind of developing our game plan against Waverly and how we might both defend and score upon them. Defensively today we tried "jamming" with Justin acting as the big man for them. By jamming I mean we are trying to anticipate his moves without the ball and step in front of him before he can make his cut. We hope that this might destroy his timing and the timing of the offense; we also hope this might frustrate him a little bit as well and cause him a loss of concentration.

We had a good and again short practice, but it ended on a somewhat sour note when Craig went down with an ankle injury. I spoke with him for a while after practice as he iced in the training room, and he felt like he'd be okay with some rest. We will practice tomorrow and take the weekend off, since we don't play until Wednesday of next week, which should be good enough with the rest.

Friday, March 9, After Reviewing Tape

Some of Waverly's man sets:

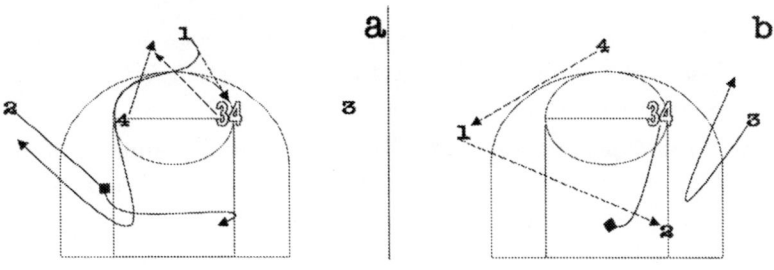

34 represents their six feet, nine inch Indiana State recruit. #1 passes to #34, who then passes to #4, who has back screened (and stepped out) for #1, who is cutting down the lane. #1 continues back out to the wing aided by a screen from #2, who continues across to the opposite side of the lane. In the second picture, #4 has reversed the ball back to #1 and #34, who will draw lots of attention, goes into the lane looking for a pass or a screen in for #2, who has stopped his cut and returned to the basket.

In a very similar play they just continue #2 on through and up around a screen down from both #34 and the wing man on the same side of the floor as #34. If they don't make the pass to #2, they will look for #34 down low. When the point guard taps his head, he is telling his teammates to run this play.

Waverly also runs a lob for #34. Using the **Diagram a** above—they clear #2 to the opposite side as #1 passes to #34. #34 flips the ball back to the point man and then receives a back screen from #5, who slips down to the baseline. #2 stays out because he is their best outside shooter, and his defensive man won't leave him, or if he does it will open up a three-pointer for the #2 man.

One thing that seems to be a reoccurring theme with Waverly is that they rarely start their offense on the side that they intend to attack the basket from. When I heard Bill Self (Kansas coach) talk at a clinic, he was an advocate of starting the ball on one side of the floor and swinging it back to the other side prior to attacking the hoop. That seems to be the case with Waverly. In theory it's a good idea; in reality if we know that the offense is going to do that, maybe we can take advantage of that knowledge and play more to the opposite side of the floor. The exception to this rule is that Waverly will enter the ball on the first side immediately if #34 is open to the Fist pass.

Friday, March 9, Practice #63

We initiated practice with head fakes against defenders under the hoop. Then we did layups against the bat, again simulating the Indiana State recruit.

We did the Michigan drill, and then three-on-two, and two-on-one, and then four-on-four working on dribble penetration. We are playing a game to 10 points in the shell drill, but the only way either team can score is by an offensive rebound. This is a pretty intense drill, but after about 15 minutes the score is something like 2-1. We've got to move on. Did we shoot well in this drill? Did we box out or did we just not get to the offensive boards? Yes, yes, and no; I think we did what we had to do.

We next went up and down the court in the NC drill. I spoke with Colin about his post passes in the previous practice. He has been lobbing the ball into the post so that it really doesn't do any good to get it in there, because by the time the ball is received the defensive help has had plenty of time to react to the pass and guard it. Today Colin got the ball in the drill and took a quick step and sent an equally quick bounce pass into the post, which may have been the best post pass that he has made all year.

We worked on our various zones match-ups, one-two-two and one-three-one. Coach Core thinks that Waverly does a really good job of running their man offense and feels that we will run more zone defenses than man. I don't necessarily disagree, but I know that sometimes what we want and what happens may not always be the same, and we must be prepared for both.

Once again we reviewed all of our sets on offense including some box-and-one work. We worked on using Kaleb as a seal man trying to screen other players in the box thus occupying the man guarding him and a member of the zone. Kaleb would then occupy two players, thus giving us a momentary four-on-three advantage. I much prefer using our man-to-man offense and movement against the zone; I think this will accomplish the same thing but will be more likely to also get Kaleb open. When Kaleb seals and slips, he rarely gets open. I think we can screen for him, and then slip, and hopefully we can get both open.

Craig got an electrical stimulation on his ankle, and he is already looking better than he did yesterday.

One of the things that we've learned over the years about the tournament is that the kids need to be fresh both mentally and physically, and with that in mind we stopped practice. We also gave the boys the weekend off because we don't play until Wednesday.

One of the interesting things about this time of year is the opportunity to speak with other coaches about a common opponent. Most coaches will not give out information about teams in their own conference but non-conference coaches are usually willing to give out information. We have contacted a number of coaches about Waverly. Sometimes what they say is pertinent and sometimes not so much so because of both the type of personnel they have compared to yours and the style of play they play compared to yours. What may work for them may be a poor thing to do for your team. What I'm really listening for when I speak with a coach are common themes; do they run, types of defenses etc. and if they do this consistently. Also and maybe at least as important is information on the Waverly individual players—one very common theme that comes out is that #34 is the real deal. To be successful, he must be guarded.

Monday March 12, 2007

Mark and I had a quick meeting this morning about Waverly and what we saw on film. Mark also came down later that day, and we discussed his scouting report on the Waverly-Harlan game from last year. In it he noted that Harlan played a defense much like our Freak defense, and it seemed to work pretty well last year; they also used what I would view as something akin to our triangle-and-two. Who knows what will work? It's just important to have some thoughts in mind prior to the competition itself in case the original plan doesn't pan out.

Monday, March 12, Practice #64

An advantage that we have on #34, should they play man-to-man, is that both of our posts can score from outside. After watching film it doesn't seem to me that he is really interested in coming out to guard the outside shot. but (like most big men) is more comfortable inside. Maybe we can take advantage of that as well; now if they play zone that advantage is much less.

I'm also more concerned about Waverly's press than Mark seems to be, but I tend to be a worry wart about this type of thing. What makes me most apprehensive is the fact that I think Waverly's press looks pretty quick on film, and it is almost always true that teams look faster in person than they do on tape. I am also anxious with what I perceive as Waverly's desire to stop ball reversal and keep the ball on one side of the floor. Should they be successful with that defense we will definitely be in trouble; we must get the ball from one side to the other.

We are in a delicate situation of trying to do some practicing and preparation for Waverly, but saving the legs of the players—hopefully to play three games. With that in mind we opened with dribble tag, played a round of (basketball) nine-hole golf, shot some free throws, did all sorts of layups over a bat, and then went to shell drill.

The kids worked on showing early help into the offensive post area. The idea is for the exterior players to get some extra help into the lane prior to the ball coming into the lane and then recover back out to their men. It is a difficult defense to run and takes a lot of extra steps and therefore effort on the part of the players but at this time of year, extra effort plays should be a part of the norm rather than the exception. As an additional drill design to help cover the post area Mark once again had the boys cover four-on-five with the open man being the guy in the post. That makes it everyone's responsibility to cover into the post area.

The next part of our practice was fairly discouraging, as our white team (trying to simulate what we expect out of Waverly) effectively disrupted our green team's ability to both attack the press and run their offense. The guys on the white team, Tyler T., Tyler L., Brock, Brandon E., Zach, Justin, and Jesse were awesome, they did a great job, but the guys on the green team didn't react very well to what the white team was doing to them. The saving factor may have been that in order to get the white team to play aggressively enough Coach Core allowed and even encouraged some fouling and holding to help alleviate some discrepancies between talent levels; also, it was Monday, and we rarely have great practices on Mondays. Tomorrow he will take off the fouling option for the white team to make sure that the green team doesn't lose confidence.

We then ran through some basics of Waverly's offense and reviewed our approach to them defensively.

The reality of this Waverly game is the simple fact that we will get a shot blocked. We will need to understand how to react to that. At the end of practice I tried to help them understand what a block really is—one play and not the end of the world. It also means that a shot blocker is more likely to leave his feet again in an attempt to block another shot, and when a player is off the ground he can move right or left and therefore has taken himself out of the play; there are some advantages to playing against a man that leaves his feet easily. Another attitude thing that I talked to the boys about was the whole Wells Fargo State Tournament attitude that I would like them to have. Personally I think that these kids have enough pressure without my adding to it, so I want them to think of this trip as icing on the cake. I want them to understand that they have really already accomplished the most important part of the journey, and that is simply making it into the tournament. Would it be great to win it? Absolutely! But if we don't—so what? We've made it, and from now on we're about to see what else we can do and how far we can go, but our goal is not to win, but to play hard, and if we do that winning will take care of itself.

The game plan is set; I know that and so do the boys. Now it's a matter of implementing what we hope to do.

This may have been my last practice with these boys, as I will be at the tournament tomorrow watching a potential opponent and Mark will have a light practice after school as usual. If we get beat on Wednesday our season ends, and there will be no more practices with this group, so I have a part of me that is sad as I drive away from school, but another part of me is excited about other possibilities and what could be; I choose to think of those instead.

Tuesday March 13

I left school today around 2:00 so that I could come up to the state tournament to scout teams that could be our upcoming opponents. I sat in the stands with my wife, who was filming the games for future reference, until about 8:30 when Mark (who came up later) took over the filming duties, and my wife and I headed home.

What I saw was size and athleticism that we would struggle with. Heelan and Harlan both had post players that were huge. Heelan's kid was six-feet-nine inches and 260 lbs., and Harlan's was six-feet-seven inches and 280 lbs. (going to Iowa on a football scholarship). In fact, Heelan's starting line up looks like a small college line up (6-4, 6-1, 6-3, 6-7, 6-9). Right now I actually feel "pretty good" about playing against an opponent that "only" has players six foot seven and six foot six inches tall.

I'm tired, heading home after a long day; I'm sure there is not much sleep in my immediate future either, watching tape and more game planning.

Chapter 23—At Wells Fargo Arena, the State Tournament

**Pella vs. Waverly at the State Tournament in the Sub-State Final
Our Record: 17-6**

For the only time this year I am riding the bus to the tournament; normally I drive myself to all of the games. I know what you're thinking: don't change now. It's working the other way, but this is standard procedure for me—I ride the bus during the tournament, and otherwise I drive myself, and we have won two state championships so I'm not tempting fate here.

The parents are there to see us off, and they give us some nice bags of goodies before our departure; they have all been good parents, and I can see why we've got such a nice group of boys.

Once we arrive in Des Moines the seniors are interviewed at the Iowa Hall of Pride while the rest of us tour the museum. We are there for only a little while as our next step on the journey is to get to the arena early to walk around and familiarize the kids with the setting.

The arena locker rooms are big and well kept (as a new building should be) and the men from the boy's athletic association are there to show us in and to make sure we are all accounted for.

Once we've dropped off our stuff, the boys head to the arena floor to see what it is really like. There are no other players or fans that are allowed in yet, and the building is ours to explore. Most of the kids walk some of the halls and then sit near the floor and just spread out, talk and relax. After we just kind of hang out for a while; we head to the locker room and get dressed. From there it is picture time, as the boys are herded to another part of the building, and they along with our cheerleaders and our water boys (three of the finest—-Jordan and Wade Pingle and Josh De Waard) are grouped into one picture which will come back to us in the form of a plaque awarded to all players and coaches who make the tourney.

In the locker room about 45 minutes prior to the ball game, both of our captains, Kaleb and Klarc, say a few things to their teammates. They thank the white team for their efforts and congratulate their teammates on a fine year and express a desire to continue with what we've got going. The Korver boys have been good captains and have brought us together as a team and as friends.

My pre-game talk is about four things. One is the team atmosphere that we have with this group that led to my other point, which was to talk with each other as much as they can now, during warm-ups and during the game, so that they don't feel like they are alone out on the floor. I also told them that I thought our conference in general was a defensive league born out by the fact that Grinnell (a league member) had the night before held a Carroll team well below their season's average in points scored and won their opening state game. Finally, I told them that regardless of the outcome, this is all icing on the cake from this point out, and that the real feat was making the tournament.

Mark's talk reinforced much of what the captains and I had said. He reviewed some things we had in our game plan, and I liked the atmosphere in the locker room prior to taking the floor, relaxed and yet confident in what we wanted to do. Then the boys were led out to the floor and given about 25 minutes to warm-up.

There was a large crowd there supporting both teams. It was 12:05 and game time!

I'm back now, and the game is over. We didn't play very well; they played even better than their statistics indicated they would, and it was over in a hurry. I wish I could tell why these things happen, but I can't. We were a much better team in the second half than the first, and we finished as a team that was competing hard enough to win the game, but we were just too far out before we finally got going and really had no chance to come back and win after the first half was over.

I can tell you that our main problem was our inability to shoot the ball. We actually took 24 more shots, attempted eight more threes, had three times the number of offensive rebounds, fouled less, and had half the turnovers and four more steals than they did! Those are some amazing statistics for a team that got beat by 22 points. Again it was shooting that did us in. They shot 54.6% from the field, and we shot 20.6% from the field; we also shot only 50% from the line.

After the game we had about four minutes, and then the media, both written and radio, want to interview coaches and players.

We stayed around for the 4A game that followed ours, and the same thing was happening to one of the teams that happened to us; they could just never get into the game.

Our game stats:

```
---------------------------------------------------------------------------
VISITORS: Pella 17-7
                          TOT-FG   3-PT            REBOUNDS
## Player Name            FG-FGA  FG-FGA  FT-FTA  OF DE TOT  PF  TP  A TO BLK S MIN
11 Boswell, Colin......  *  1-8    0-2     0-0     1  0   1   2   2  0  1   0 1  17
13 Korver, Kaleb.......  *  4-14   0-2     4-9     5  4   9   1  12  0  3   1 4  27
23 Caldwell, Brandon...  *  3-12   2-7     0-0     1  2   3   4   8  0  0   0 4  23
31 Newendorp, C.J......  *  1-5    0-2     1-2     2  2   4   2   3  0  1   0 0  17
33 Korver, Klarc.......  *  3-17   0-0     2-3     9  2  11   4   8  1  2   0 1  27
15 Linn, Tyler.........     0-2    0-1     0-0     1  1   2   0   0  0  0   0 0   4
21 Boeyink, Clayton....     1-2    0-0     0-0     3  2   5   3   2  0  2   0 0  17
25 Korver, Kirk........     1-5    0-2     0-0     0  0   0   0   2  0  0   1 0  10
35 Wineland, Jesse.....     0-0    0-0     1-2     0  1   1   1   1  1  1   0 1   7
41 Pothoven, Justin....     0-0    0-0     0-0     0  0   0   0   0  0  0   0 0   1
43 Estabrook, Brandon..     0-1    0-1     0-0     0  0   0   0   0  0  0   0 0   2
45 Morgan, Zach........     0-0    0-0     0-0     0  0   0   0   0  0  0   0 0   3
51 Pope, Brock.........     0-2    0-1     0-0     1  1   2   0   0  0  0   0 0   3
53 Ter Louw, Tyler.....     0-0    0-0     0-0     0  1   1   0   0  0  0   0 0   2
   TEAM...............                             2  1   3
   Totals.............     14-68   2-18    8-16   25 17  42  17  38  2 10   2 11 160

TOTAL FG% 1st Half:  4-33  12.1%    2nd Half: 10-35 28.6%    Game: 20.6%    DEADB
3-Pt. FG% 1st Half:  1-8   12.5%    2nd Half:  1-10 10.0%    Game: 11.1%    REBS
F Throw % 1st Half:  1-2   50.0%    2nd Half:  7-14 50.0%    Game: 50.0%      5
```

After that we all piled back on the bus and headed out to eat. It was 3:00 in the afternoon, and the guys were all given $15.00 by the association to defray the cost of their meals. The guys were fine when we stopped. While they were not yelling and overjoyed there were smiles and giggles as there should be.

And now it's done. This year's team will never play together again. They were quite the group; they pulled together when things looked worst. Back on January 12 our record was four wins and five losses, and it looked like things could go right down the tubes. At that time it was hard to even think about playing in the state tournament, but these guys never quit. They stayed strong and beat the odds (approximately a 12% chance) by getting to the state tournament, and there was about a two percent chance that they would win it.

The worst thing about the tournament is that regardless of winning or losing, it will be the last time that teammates will play with this exact group of kids; it will be the last time that Mark Core and I will get to coach them as well.

We've prided ourselves on a couple of things at Pella High that we think makes our program a pretty darn good one, and those things are attitude and effort. We think if we have those we will be a pretty darn good team and maybe better than our talent might really dictate. While this team was not perfect in either case, (as none before have been either) I feel as though they made great strides in both of these areas, and I hope they will continue to grow.

One of my favorite things about coaching is the opportunity to get to know the young guys that I coach better. I am so proud of all of these kids. And I feel like now I'm a small part of all of their lives; I hope I've made a minute difference and feel very blessed to have had the opportunity to be part of this. My son Luke captures it best when at his senior football banquet he said to the crowd and to his teammates (after they had lost to the eventual state champions in a late come-from-behind game), "I'd rather have played and lost with these guys than to have won a state championship with anyone else." It's my hope that these boys feel the same about each other as well.

—Coach "B"

Printed in the United States
200447BV00003B/95/A